D1614837

FRASERBURGH ACADEMY LIBRARY
M005390

THE HIGHLANDS AND ISLANDS

The Regions of Britain Series

THE HIGHLANDS AND ISLANDS by Francis Thompson

THE NORTH COUNTRY by G. Bernard Wood

THE WEST COUNTRY by S. H. Burton

The Regions of Britain

THE HIGHLANDS AND ISLANDS

FRANCIS THOMPSON

Photographs by Hamish Campbell

Robert Hale & Company, Publishers
London

First published in Great Britain 1974

ISBN 0 7091 4576 4

Robert Hale & Company
63 Old Brompton Road
London SW7

PRINTED IN GREAT BRITAIN BY
EBENEZER BAYLIS AND SON LIMITED
THE TRINITY PRESS, WORCESTER, AND LONDON

Contents

Illustrations

MAP

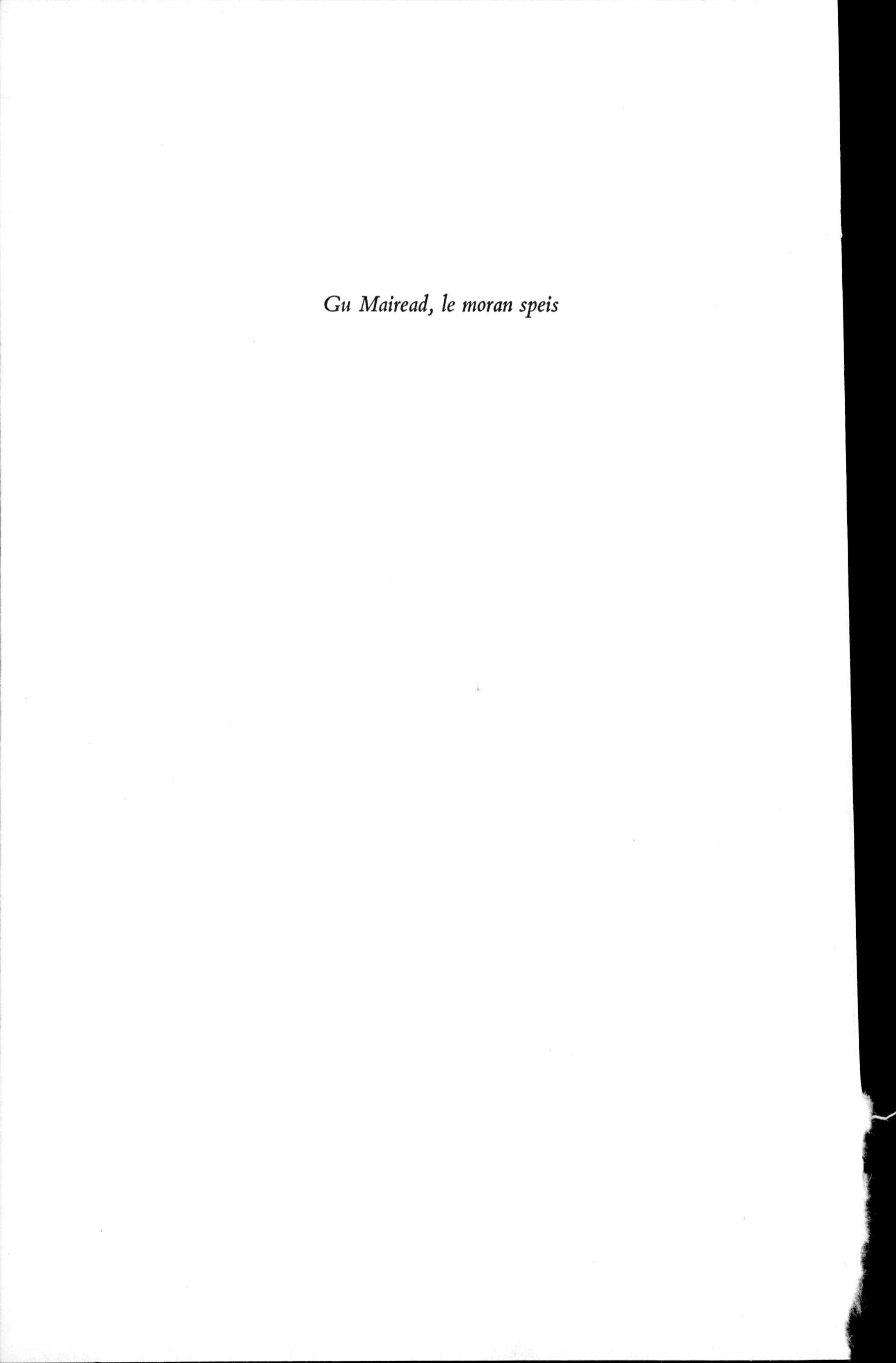

Gu Mairead, le moran speis

Author's Note

When one considers that the region known as the "Highlands and Islands of Scotland" constitutes one-sixth of the area of Britain; that the total population is much less than that of a suburb of London, Glasgow or Birmingham; that the region is second to none in its scenic variations; that it offers the individual the chance to experience a unique opportunity to refresh himself both mentally and physically; yet that it also offers the opportunity to probe deeply into a tiny part of it to reveal a wealth of socio-economic and cultural detail; the reader will perhaps bear with the author if this book is not quite what might be expected in a work with such an all-embracing title.

There have been few books written on the region as a whole which have done little other than to offer "cauld kail het again". Whether in print or out of print, these books are readily available to those who wish to be pleasantly 'guided' around the highways and byways of the region. The present work is therefore not a guide-book. Rather it tries to follow the handful of books written in the last two decades or so in which their authors have taken a dispassionate look at the region: back to its distinctive past; to its present, as it has been moulded by the events of the past; and to its future, as it is being shaped by the present phase of industrialization and its far-reaching consequences for the existing, and often vulnerable, socio-economic and cultural patterns.

The author has endeavoured to give each area within the region a fair deal. However, some burghs and districts may feel slighted by only a brief mention. This was not the result of bias, nor does it mean in any way that they are not significant elements in the whole regional scene. But to attempt to cover everything—in all aspects and in every detail—in such a vast region as the Highlands and Islands would be impossible in the space available.

At the risk of offending readers who like to be 'entertained', the author has concentrated largely on the objective, relying on facts to project themselves into the reader's mind so that, when the last page is turned, he has a picture of a region of the British Isles which displays the will to live to see its future years, yet which waits daily with some justified trepidation for its history to be written for it by the stranger's pen—his alien assessment of what he sees, hears and feels is the reason why the region ticks as it does, in a manner perhaps more attuned to his own familiar background and experience, rather than with the natural rhythm of the indigenous population.

In the writing of this book the author has drawn on much material already published and indicated in the Select Reading List. To include a really comprehensive bibliography for the region, even confining this to works which have appeared in the last half-century or so, would be to face the reader with a list of well over 600 titles. In any case, in 1971 the National Book League produced, for the Highlands and Islands Development Board, a catalogue of books on the region in print in that year; this is well worth its price of 40p.

The author has also drawn heavily on contemporary material, never before published, published on a limited scale for consumption by a small and specialist audience, or not readily accessible to the public. The writing of this book has been for the author something of an education in itself—to have had the experience of assessing the vast amount of contemporary material which has appeared in the Press and the publications of public and semi-public bodies in the region. The effect of the presence of the Highlands and Islands Development Board has been, in particular, to produce a steady flow of valuable socio-economic information. This information, being largely factual in content, would require the services and expertise of professional sociologists and economists to assess correctly and dispassionately and finally present as a base on which the region can be built anew, while still allowing for the preservation of all the distinctive and often unique aspects of character and values which exist at present. The lack of these professional qualifications has meant that the author has had to tread in areas which angels might well consider twice before stepping into. But in doing so, the author has drawn on his four decades of living as a native in the region and at least a decade of valuable experience gained while operating in a number of fields of specialist interest.

The author acknowledges with grateful thanks the help received from many people, in a private capacity or as officials of public and semi-public bodies and commercial interests. Their willing co-operation considerably eased the task of researching and writing this book, which it is sincerely hoped will serve as a suitable witness and reminder of their help. May it serve also as a stone of significance placed on the cairn of the Highland people, a cairn which has been built up over many years, not only by themselves, but by others who, although not natives of the region, have readily and sympathetically assimilated the identity and cultural ethos which the region still manages effectively to display—though the processes of erosion in the fringes are now acting on the centre to produce a change that may well, in the distant future, be sad to contemplate. *Togaih an obair an fhianuis.*

I

Introduction

FOR the sake of convenience the region dealt with in this book has been sub-divided into areas which are reasonably distinctive. All have, however, common aspects which are indicated in general and of necessity superficial terms in this introduction. The variations within these I have tried to bring out in the context of the areas themselves. Inevitably with such a large region, it has often not been possible to do more than pinpoint highlights of the many faces which it presents to the reader who is not, perhaps, familiar with the Highlands and Islands except as a place in 'north Britain': mountainous, difficult of access and traverse; one whose people rarely if ever appear in anything more serious than an article in a Sunday colour supplement or a "Look Stranger" report on BBC2. It will be a measure of the author's success if the reader is cleared of any false or hazy ideas he might have had of the region, and finds instead a place of intense interest which must be tasted at firsthand to savour the true essence of a part of the British Isles which is full of parti-coloured history, has a flamboyant geography and a characteristic people, many of whom speak one of the oldest of the indigenous languages of these European islands.

The region has been inhabited from the earliest of times, a period of perhaps some 10,000 years. The earliest evidence of Man's presence in the British Isles has been found in recent years in caves near Inchnadamph in Sutherland. The traces he left there, and in other places such

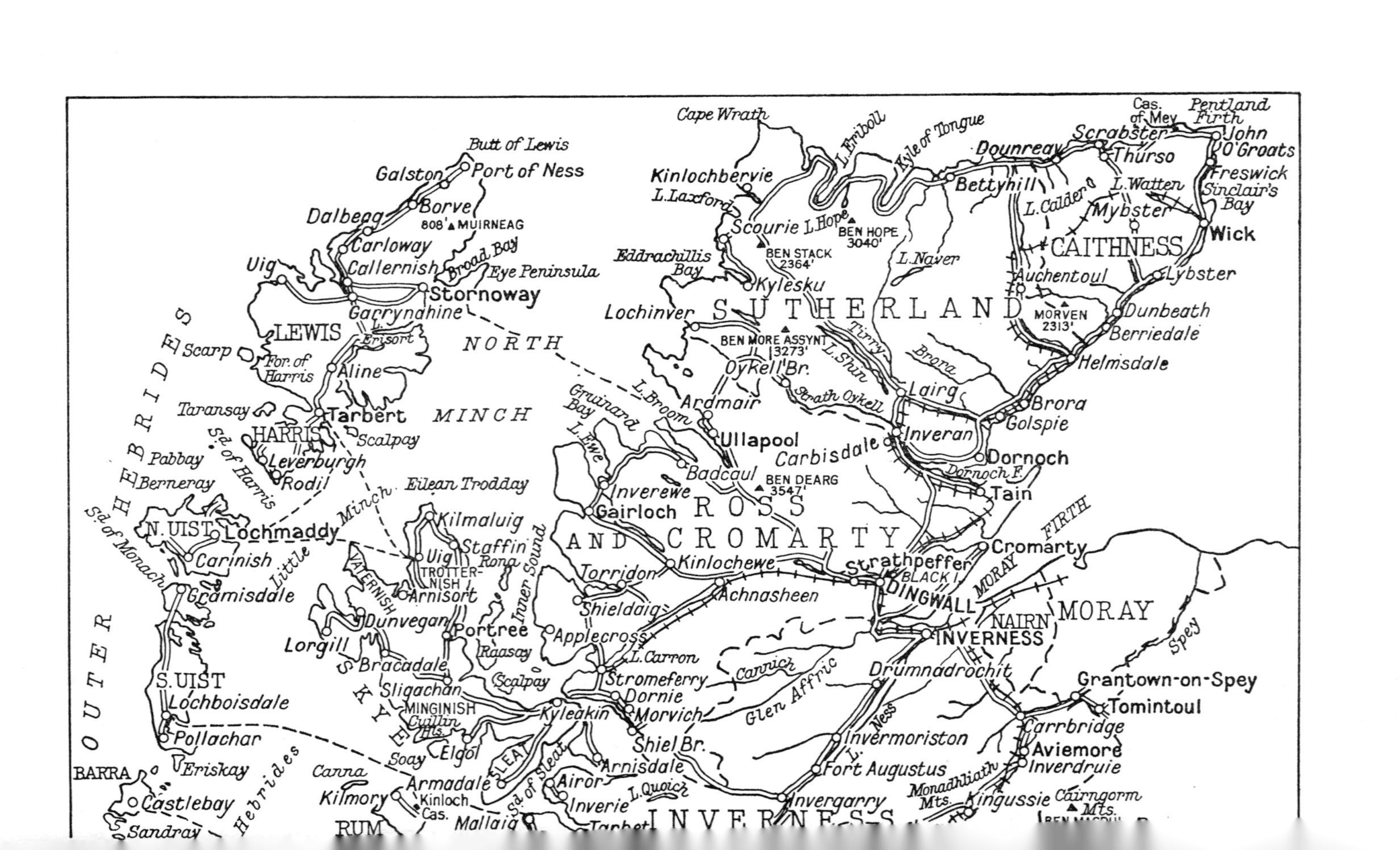

Cape Wrath
L. Eriboll
Kyle of Tongue
Cas. of Mey
Pentland Firth
Scrabster
Thurso
John O'Groats
Dounreay
Freswick
Sinclair's Bay
Bettyhill
L. Calder
L. Watten
Mybster
Wick
CAITHNESS
Auchentoul
Lybster
MORVEN 2313'
Dunbeath
Berriedale
Helmsdale
Butt of Lewis
Galston
Port of Ness
Borve
Dalbeag
808' MUIRNEAG
Carloway
Broad Bay
Callernish
Eye Peninsula
Uig
Stornoway
Garrynahine
L. Erisort
LEWIS
Scarp
For. of Harris
Aline
NORTH
MINCH
Taransay
Tarbert
HARRIS
Scalpay
Sd. of Harris
Pabbay
Leverburgh
Rodil
Berneray
Eilean Trodday
Little Minch
N. UIST
Lochmaddy
Sd. of Monach
Carinish
Gramisdale
OUTER HEBRIDES
S. UIST
Lochboisdale
Pollachar
BARRA
Eriskay
Castlebay
Sandray
Hebrides
Kinlochbervie
L. Laxford
Scourie
L. Hope
BEN HOPE 3040'
BEN STACK 2364'
L. Naver
Eddrachillis Bay
Kylesku
SUTHERLAND
Lochinver
BEN MORE ASSYNT 3273'
Tirry
L. Shin
Brora
Oykell Br.
Strath Oykell
Lairg
Brora
Golspie
Gruinard Bay
L. Broom
Ardmair
Ullapool
Inveran
Carbisdale
Dornoch
Dornoch F.
L. Ewe
Badcaul
BEN DEARG 3547'
Inverewe
Tain
Gairloch
ROSS AND CROMARTY
FIRTH
Cromarty
Kilmaluig
Staffin
Rona
Inner Sound
Uig
TROTTER-NISH
VATERNISH
Arnisort
Torridon
Kinlochewe
Strathpeffer
BLACK I.
MORAY
Shieldaig
Achnasheen
DINGWALL
NAIRN
MORAY
Dunvegan
Portree
Applecross
INVERNESS
Spey
Lorgill
Raasay
L. Carron
Cannich
SKYE
Bracadale
Scalpay
Stromeferry
Glen Affric
Drumnadrochit
Grantown-on-Spey
Sligachan
Dornie
Tomintoul
MINGINISH
Kyleakin
Morvich
L. Ness
Carrbridge
Cuillin Mts.
Elgol
Shiel Br.
Invermoriston
Aviemore
Soay
SLEAT
Arnisdale
Fort Augustus
Inverdruie
Canna
Armadale
Sd. of Sleat
Airor
L. Quoich
Monadhliath Mts.
Kilmory
Kinloch Cas.
Inverie
Invergarry
Kingussie
Cairngorm Mts.
RUM
Mallaig
INVERNESS

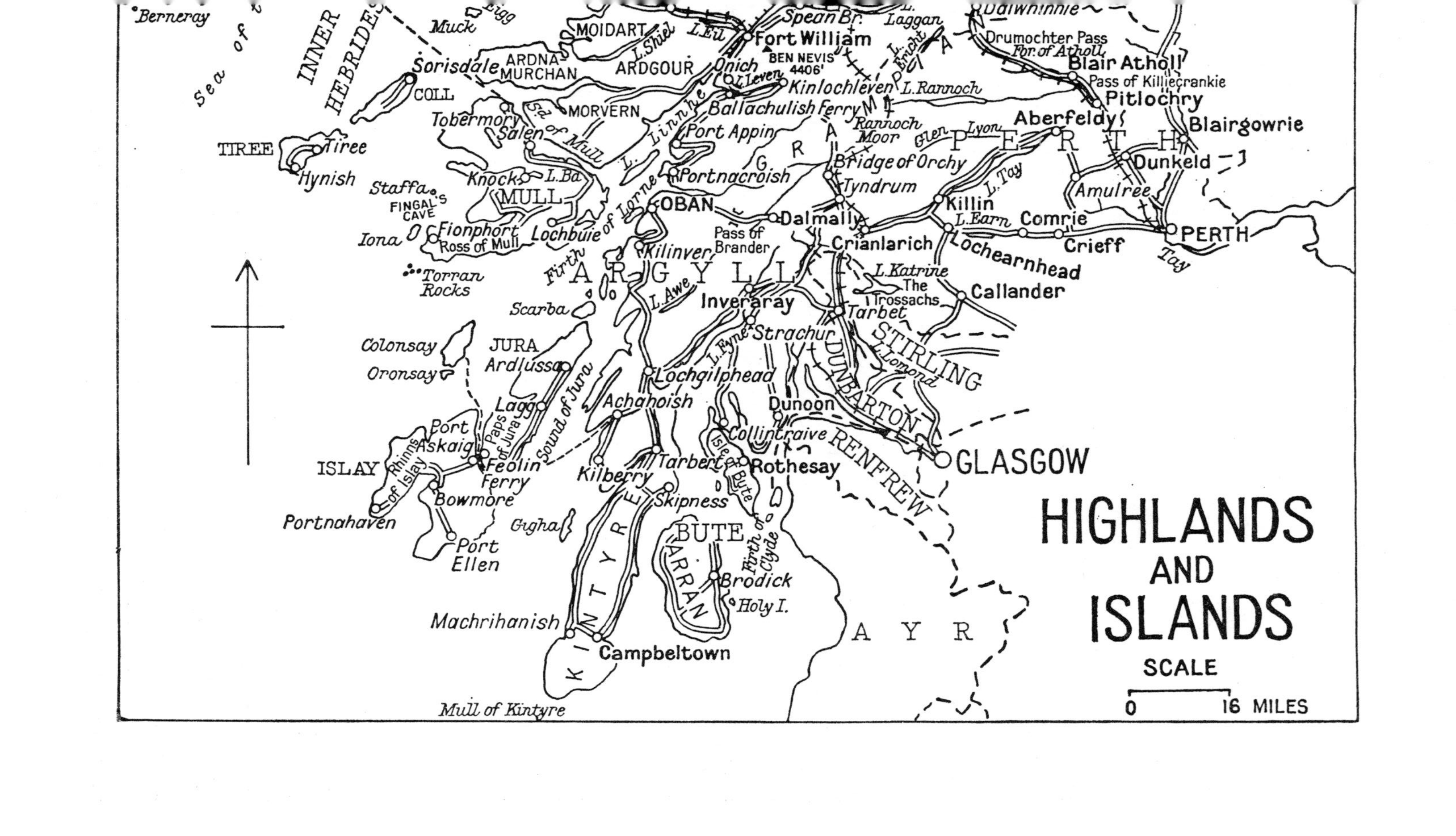
HIGHLANDS AND ISLANDS
SCALE
0
16 MILES
Berneray
Sea of
INNER HEBRIDES
Muck
MOIDART
L. Shiel
L. Eil
Spean Br.
Laggan
Fort William
BEN NEVIS 4406'
Drumochter Pass
For. of Atholl
Blair Atholl
Pass of Killiecrankie
Pitlochry
Blairgowrie
Sorisdale
ARDNAMURCHAN
ARDGOUR
Onich
L. Leven
Kinlochleven
L. Rannoch
COLL
Tobermory
MORVERN
Ballachulish Ferry
Rannoch Moor
Glen Lyon
Aberfeldy
Salen
Sd. of Mull
L. Linnhe
Port Appin
TIREE
Tiree
Hynish
Bridge of Orchy
Dunkeld
Knock
L. Ba
MULL
Portnacroish
Tyndrum
L. Tay
Amulree
Staffa
FINGAL'S CAVE
OBAN
Killin
Comrie
Dalmally
L. Earn
Iona
Fionphort
Ross of Mull
Lochbuie
Firth of Lorne
Pass of Brander
Crianlarich
Lochearnhead
Crieff
PERTH
Tay
Kilinver
ARGYLL
PERTH
Torran Rocks
L. Katrine
The Trossachs
Callander
L. Awe
Inveraray
Scarba
Tarbet
Colonsay
JURA
Strachur
L. Fyne
STIRLING
Oronsay
Ardlussa
Lochgilphead
DUNBARTON
L. Lomond
Lagg
Sound of Jura
Achahoish
Dunoon
Port Askaig
Paps of Jura
Collintraive
RENFREW
GLASGOW
ISLAY
Rhinns of Islay
Feolin Ferry
Kilberry
Tarbert
Rothesay
Bowmore
Skipness
Isle of Bute
Portnahaven
Gigha
BUTE
Port Ellen
KINTYRE
ARRAN
Firth of Clyde
Brodick
Holy I.
Machrihanish
AYR
Campbeltown
Mull of Kintyre

as Perth and Oban, bear witness to an era of inhabitation which goes back far beyond Christian times. Whether the occupation of the Highlands and Islands has been continuous or not it is extremely difficult to say; nor can one say with any certainty that the population was numerically significant. More likely it was small and found in distinct areas amenable to the prosecution of life and living; because of almost impenetrable woodland, safe and secure from nomadic marauders. Of these early inhabitants we know little except what can be deduced from the civil-engineering remains in the form of monoliths, multiliths, burial cairns, earth houses, crannogs or lake-dwellings, brochs and the like.

When Scotland first emerges from the misty past we are faced with notes and observations on the Picts made mainly by Roman writers. Whence these Picts came, what their language was and what structure their society had is not certain. But from its remnants, mainly in stone, their culture indicated a high order of appreciation of nature, society and religious belief, and one could perhaps ascribe to them a quasi-Celtic origin. They first appear in any substance towards the end of the third century A.D., when they clashed with the Roman advance and succeeded in halting the legions in the south of Scotland, to keep them there.

Some time before the Romans left Britain to bolster up their tottering imperial society, Scots from Ireland began to cross the sea to settle in that part of the country now called Argyll. These were a Gaelic-speaking Celtic people with ethnic and linguistic ties with the other branches of Celts found today in Man, Cornwall, Wales and Brittany. By the end of the sixth century they had populated Scotland in increasing numbers, bringing with them a Gaelic-based culture—which largely exists today in the Highlands and Islands—and Christianity in the form of the Celtic Church. The Christianization of the Picts began in earnest with St Columba after A.D. 563, and thereafter about 500 years of light shone in the region before the Celtic Church was absorbed by the Roman Church. For about two and a half centuries the Picts and the Scots were engaged in a number of confrontations until the Scots emerged victorious and an amalgamation, in which the Picts lost both their language and their identity, took place; some of their cultural aspirations, particularly as evidenced in the visual arts, were merged with the ascendant Scots equivalent. In 843 the two peoples were united as one political entity under Kenneth Mac Alpin, who became the first King of Scots. This title was significant in that it indicated it was held by consent of the people of the first united nation in Europe.

The nation held together—which was a remarkable achievement considering the state of flux in which much of the European subcontinent found itself at this time, particularly due to the incursions of the Norsemen who took advantage of their ascending star by raiding all the coastal areas of the British Isles. By fire and sword their influence was established, particularly on Scotland's western coast, then consolidated by marriage to form ruling families. The Norse hegemony held sway until the Battle of Clontarf in Ireland in 1064, when it fell into decline, to be broken completely, in a political sense, in 1263 when Haakon was beaten in battle at Largs. But the long occupation by the Norse of the western seaboard of the region and its islands left indelible marks. In particular, Norse-based surnames and place-names abound, and in some places Norse strains have modified the ethnic base of the former Celtic people.

The line of Scottish kings after Kenneth Mac Alpin sought to extend their range of influence to the south, and when Malcolm II won the Battle of Carham in 1018 Scotland included the Cheviots area, which encompassed a considerable English-speaking Teutonic element. The power of this section of the country was reinforced by the marriage of Malcolm III, Canmore or Ceann-mor, with the English princess Margaret, who set about introducing the English language, its customs and ideas into the Scots kingdom. So effective and influential was she in her activity that Gaelic, once the language of the royal court, the legal system and trade and commerce, became displaced and Celtic in the then Scottish ethos was diminished. This process of emasculation was further continued by the removal of the Scots capital from Perth to Edinburgh, which led to the court becoming more identified with the English-speaking south. To the north, however, the Celts held sway and kept faithfully to their own language, way of life and culture. This unfortunate cleavage was intensified under David I, who introduced feudalism to Scotland, something quite foreign to the Celtic idea of society, which was based on communalism, the family unit, as part of the clan, being the essential hub element. David I made grants of lands to his Norman friends, settling them on the territories of those Celtic chiefs who were actively opposed to the Anglicization of their country. The influence of English thus spread up the eastern coast of Scotland to Aberdeenshire and along the Moray Firth to create a line dividing what was now effectively a two-culture Scotland. This line coincided geographically with the beginning of the mountainous region of the country, a region in which the Celtic people lived and developed what was virtually a nation within a nation, prosecuting their own language and lifestyle under a different societal structure. The clan system differed from the feudal system in that it was based on kinship, the members being united to one another and to the chief through the bonds of blood relationship, fosterage (the chief acting as foster father to the children of his subordinates) and a common patronymic. The feudal system, on the other hand, was based on tenure of land and service to the Crown, and was an imposition on the freedom of the individual. The clan system operated reasonably well until 1745, when it was effectively broken to leave the fragmented patterns of a former mosaic in such disarray that it can never again be repaired.

Though to all intents and purposes separate, the region was not isolated from the main events in Scottish and English history. The War of Independence, fought under Bruce against the English; the struggles between the Scottish crown and the Scottish nobles, and the Reformation: all these affected the region in one way or another. The period of the Lordship of the Isles was a time of Celtic ascendancy which brought the region into the bright light of the European political arena as a Gaelic-based political entity which, had it lasted, would today have meant the Highlands and Islands being a distinct part of Scotland, perhaps as politically independent as is the Isle of Man today. Though effectively a separate region, significantly out of the reach of the Crown in Edinburgh, the region's history was not a peaceful one. Clan feuds, raids and reprisals all feature in a period of some three centuries; though in general the common folk sought primarily to establish some kind of resilient economic base on which their future, however uncertain, could be built. The feuds were in reality the life and living of the chiefs rather than that of the common folk who, inevitably, had to bear the brunt of massacre, rapine, looting and scorched-earth policies.

The Lordship of the Isles declined during the reign of James III to finally die out in the time of James IV, when the latter had some considerable success in joining the two parts of his kingdom. His influence was considerable: many clansmen, even Sinclairs from distant Caithness, fought and fell with him at Flodden in 1513. But his death was followed by renewed disorder, which lasted for a time. Then a period of more settled conditions prevailed until after the Reformation, an event which marked the watershed in Scotland's history as a nation and which created a distinct cleavage which has, to many minds, permanently damaged the possibility of Scotland ever becoming a nation in its own right, embodying something more than mere political and economic viability and standing as an independent country. The effect of the Reformation was indeed to vitiate any cultural development possible at the time and the results are with us today: a desert with a somewhat disconnected pattern of cultural areas tied by links which are fragile and easily broken, though there are signs that a move towards homogeneity is being made in an attempt to create a new Scottish cultural scene.

When the supremacy of the MacDonalds declined as the Lordship of the Isles faded, their place was taken by the MacKenzies in the north and the Campbells in the south. The latter family exercised a profound influence on the region, particularly after the Reformation. Whenever trouble broke out the Campbells sided themselves with the Protestant Lowlands against the Catholic Highlands. The general hatred for the Campbells was used by Montrose to unite many clans in the wars he waged in Scotland to keep the Stuarts on the throne. It was his military genius that recognized the qualities of the Highlander, a soldier whom he used on a national scale to prosecute a series of brilliant campaigns. Montrose's last campaign, however, was a sorry attempt to restore Charles II to the throne. In 1650 he landed in Orkney and, collecting a small force in Caithness, proceeded south. While waiting for a re-inforcement of MacKenzies at Carbisdale, he was surprised and routed. Fleeing west, he was captured at Ardvreck Castle and from thence taken to Edinburgh to be hanged. Montrose has now been recognized in historical perspective as one of the most noble of Scotsmen.

During the seventeenth and the first half of the eighteenth century the region enjoyed a period of reasonable stability and peace. Clan feuds became outmoded, the result of the sense of unity which the campaigns of Montrose and Claverhouse of Dundee had engendered. The building of roads by General Wade opened up the region to new possibilities of trade. The horizon was bright and promising and a period of real social and economic revolution was a probability. Then came the Forty-five....

This should have been an episode in history. Instead, as a result of a programme little short of genocide, the region became a virtual desert. The historians say that this was encouraged by the government in London to ensure that never more could there be a rising in favour of the Stuarts. The power of the clan chiefs was broken. A series of punitive Acts was passed, aimed at wounding the very heart of Gaelic-based culture. Even the playing of the bagpipes was a crime punished by transportation for life. All these measures, policed over a period of some thirty years, created a wilderness in which chiefs became less the leaders of their kinsmen and more the owners of land and property. An increasing population later created many social problems. Emigration became the normal practice, whether opted for voluntarily or forcibly induced. Between 1763 and 1775 no fewer than 20,000 took ship to settle in America alone, most of them from the north-west Highlands and Islands. Thousands of men were enlisted for the many Highland regiments that were founded about this time, and the fame they brought to the British army in ensuing years needs no mention here. The process of emigration and exploitation created a pattern that has continued to this day. Life has gradually ebbed away as alien influences increase, until today the consequent depopulation of the region presents its greatest problem. Bright comets, as transient as desert flowers, appeared: the boom in black cattle, the kelp industry, fishing and sheep. But all these made little or no contribution to the creation of a stable economic base and it was not until it was too late that the inherent political awareness of the Gael showed itself during the last half of the nineteenth century, to culminate in its crowning achievement: the Crofters Act of 1886. Perhaps one might be criticized for calling this an Act of fossilization, for though it provided the Highland crofters with a secure base, their scope for operation to better themselves by their own efforts was so restricted that it produced little else but stagnation. Further, the complete bureaucratization of the region took all power away from the people and vested it in the ubiquitous civil servants, of whom few in any position of real significance were natives of the region.

If the history of the region is here painted in sombre colours it is because the background is largely dark and unattractive. Yet, the fact that the Gael has managed to survive to some degree with a culture that is, even today, reasonably intact, is a measure of the instinct for survival which has stood him in good stead for many centuries now. The fact that the strength and vigour of his culture is largely inaccessible to outsiders is due to the policy of attrition. This seems to have been the dominant feature of all the centuries'-old influences which have done so much to force the Gael into a corner of his former land, with his back to the wall and his face to the future—hardly with bared teeth, but with a fatalism which has been not only a highlight of the Celtic psyche, but the instrument of its death as well.

If the effects of rural migration and national emigration have posed a problem for Scotland as a whole over the past two centuries or so, they have done so even more when one considers the Highland region. The region has experienced many phases of population redistribution and a continual drain because of emigration. The former has, in recent decades, been reasonably insignificant, though in 1973 it was reported that 250 men had left Lewis and Harris for work based on on-shore oil activities in Easter Ross, with a long-term implication which is serious to contemplate in the context of the small population of the Western Isles, particularly if families are also eventually drawn to that booming area. Emigration has been a continuous process, though latterly it has taken place under more humane, though no less insidious and invidious, circumstances. In 1755, according to Dr A. Webster's enumeration, the population of the crofting counties, including Orkney and Shetland, was just over 255,000 representing 20 per cent of Scotland's population. Fifty years later, though the population had risen to nearly 303,000, the percentage had dropped to 19. This trend continued: in 1851, 396,000 (14 per cent); 1901, 352,000 (8 per cent); 1951, 286,000 (6 per cent). There was a further slight decrease during the following decade to 278,000, which figure was held until the latest censual return.

The significance of this plateau has yet to be seen in historical perspective. The presence of the Highlands and Islands Development Board can be said to have had some effect on the halt in the population decline, but a closer inspection of the trends over the past decade or so indicates that part of the reason is the attraction of fringe populations to the burghs and those areas, particularly on the eastern side of the region, which have proved amenable to development and so have presented opportunities for work and living. In its first annual report the Highlands and Islands Development Board said: "No matter what success is achieved in the Eastern or Central Highlands . . . the Board will be judged by its ability to hold population in the true crofting areas." This was a courageous thing to do: to grasp at a nettle which had the ability to sting painfully if the board's failure to keep its promise were to be proved in its future years. When the results of the 1971 census were published it was shown that, in particular, the islands of the west had lost their population at the expense of an increase in the region's burghs and their hinterlands. The general burgh increase was more than significant: Inverness increased by 17 per cent, Fort William by 54 per cent (due to the pulp mill) and the other small burghs by some 40 per cent. The fall in the mainland population was about 1 per cent, mainly due to a drift from the islands. This figure may seem small, but it has to be viewed in its perspective against the total mainland population, particularly because when one is speaking about island populations one must consider hundreds or a few thousands. For an island like Barra to lose 360 people in a decade is more than serious; an extrapolation into the future would seemingly point to desertion of that island by the year 2000. The Highlands and Islands Development Board has thus not been able to stabilize the population in the rural mainland areas and in the islands. This may well be due to the board's 'growth centre' policy, which, while perhaps acceptable in other developing areas of the world amenable to textbook developmental tactics and techniques, has not had the desired result in the Highland region. Only restraint on the increasing role of a growth centre will hold back any influx into it by those residing in less favoured peripheral areas. The board's powers to direct incoming manufacturing industries to specific areas in dire need of an injection of economic activity have not been properly used. The board is of course concerned with this situation, but it has yet to produce evidence that it exists to create the right conditions for social and community development, whatever its economically-oriented statutory remit might conveniently say. This field is ripe for exploitation.

Another, perhaps more disturbing, aspect of the stable population figure of the region is that the state was achieved by a large flow of incoming workers and their families, attracted to such developments as the pulp mill at Fort William, the aluminium smelter at Invergordon and the on-shore developments in Easter Ross associated with North Sea oil. While this new population may well decide to integrate with the resident communities, there must surely be a period of change while values, social patterns and cultural and linguistic differences are levelled out. It has been the experience of some communities preferring a more traditional lifestyle to find themselves in a confrontation situation, which, due to the sheer weight and tactical experience of the incomer element, has resulted in a complete changeover from a previously accepted way of life and thrown older residents into a state of confusion. To highlight this situation is not to say that all those who comprise an incoming population are unsympathetic to what they find when they enter a Highland community, but to say that there is evidence that an imposition of different values and social requirements—and particularly regarding the provision of education in schools—has left an ugly scar in some communities. On the other hand, many incomers make a positive and often determined effort to become accepted and tend to act as catalysts in obtaining the right kind of changes necessary for the improvement of the established community, which have then been accepted by the aboriginal members after a period of careful tasting.

It is, of course, a huge task to ask a government agency such as the Highlands and Islands Development Board to strengthen its commitment to a programme of social regeneration while it is required to submit annually details of its cash requirements to a Treasury which is more interested in economic returns than the rather intangible benefits derived from community development. But certainly a shift of emphasis on the part of the board towards the social aspect of its work could be achieved without upsetting its London masters too much. One such shift could involve the setting up of a sociological study unit, not merely to act as an advisory facility but to have direct influence on developmental policies and techniques. This could win support, in that the board would be seen as having confidence in the natives of the region as people able to contribute to the moral fibre of the nation as a whole, and not as mere productive units in an industrial environment.

Apart from its topographical difference from the rest of Scotland, the Highland region also accommodates the residual Gaelic-based culture. This is now largely concentrated in the Western Isles and on the coastal fringe of Wester Ross, Sutherland, Inverness-shire and Argyll, with some of the islands of the Inner Hebrides. The decline in the number of Gaelic speakers in the region is a reflection of the region's long and tragic history of depopulation. The decline has largely taken place on the Scottish mainland, with the Outer Hebrides maintaining, but not improving, their position as the largest Gaelic-speaking community in Scotland. At the turn of this century the number of Gaelic speakers in Scotland was over 200,000, of whom 28,000 spoke only Gaelic. In 1931 these figures had fallen to 130,000 and 7,000 respectively, and further to 80,000 and 974. The history of Gaelic in Scotland has been one of recession and dispersion, with a retreat of its frontier from an area which hardly a century ago covered two-thirds of Scotland and encroached on places like Aberdeenshire and Fife.

This decline is seen by some supporters of the language as the result of a process of dilution of the cultural value of the language to Scotland. That monoglot Gaelic speakers are fast dying out is the most

(*top*) Lochinver, Sutherland. (*bottom*) The River Inver with Quinag in the background. (*overleaf*) Gruinard Bay, Ross-shire.

Stac Polly, Ross-shire

Loch Broom

serious circumstance which language fighters have to face, for it is this group which is regarded by many students of bilingualism as essential for the continued existence of a language. But no determined holding operation is being mounted, even though there exists a Treasury-financed organization, An Comunn Gaidhealach, commonly called The Highland Society. In addition, the value of Gaelic to the existing Gaelic-speaking communities has been debased as a result of compulsory English education; and the lack of opportunities for its local use has further weakened the language at its roots. There are immense forces at work against the language, ranging from the imposition of an English-language mass media, to the rocket range in the Uists and the cumulative impact of tourism. The experience of the Welsh has shown that decline in language is closely akin to the imperceptible process of Anglicization and developmental policies which take no account of social implications.

In a legal sense, nationality is conferred by birth or naturalization and has nothing to do with language. Yet, Gaelic has been at the heart and core of Scotland's identity for centuries. In Scotland the language has contributed significantly to the cultural pattern embracing tradition, history, religion, music, values, heritage and social institutions. Almost a century ago a non-Gaelic-speaking inspector of schools in the Highlands said:

> It is in and by the mother tongue of a people, along with its thousand memories of home and youth, play and friendship, nature and religion, and with its countless avenues to the deeper feelings, that the education of the heart and the higher nature, can be truly carried on: it is by it alone that sentiment, feeling, devotion and even the higher intellect can be really trained. And the mother tongue becomes a stronger instrument of culture when it contains a good and generous literature. . . . And such a literature exists in Gaelic, able to perform this higher function to the Highlander, abundant, varied, and powerful, full of fine sentiment, pleasant humour, lyrical beauty, deep feeling, practical wisdom and natural life.

This was said at a time when Gaelic-speaking children were under penalty of painful physical punishment if they were caught speaking their mother tongue in the schools. The majority of Gaelic-speaking children until the 1930s learned to read Gaelic in Sunday school, not in primary schools, and, contrary to good educational practice, the native language was not used as the medium of instruction. Consequently, Gaels became illiterate in their own tongue and in many cases were encouraged to abandon it. It was not until the late 1950s that education authorities in Ross-shire and Inverness-shire sponsored the teaching of children in primary schools through the medium of Gaelic. However, the secondary sector of education has yet to accept this policy. To some extent, the lack of achievement in Scotland and in the Highlands in recent years can be attributed to loss of culture and identity because the continuity of history cannot be broken without some psychological reaction. If it were allowed, the Gaelic language could still find a considerable part to play in the national and cultural development of Scotland. If only those who are in positions of influence would realize that the present process of cultural liquidation can only end with a charge of genocide against them.

Of all the social services provided by the State for a community, perhaps education has the farthest-reaching effects, influencing as it does the attitudes and opinions of children from their earliest years and inducing in them an outlook which bears to some degree on their future careers and lifestyles. It is generally accepted that if education is bad, it is society which is the loser in the long term. This is even more the case when the educational provisions in the Highlands and Islands are viewed in the context of a region which has a distinctive history and cultural and linguistic differences even from other parts of Scotland and of the United Kingdom, save the Celtic areas of Man, Wales and Cornwall. The predominance of an English education—and this is not meant in a purely linguistic way—has created in Highland children a sense of dissociation from their past history, the very background of themselves and their native community. The process of centralization has castrated many Highland communities which in the past were able to find the strength of meaning and purpose in their survival from the core of common action which had been built up and fostered over many previous decades. The uprooting of children for secondary education and their implantation in an urban environment has done serious damage to the social fibre of many communities in the region. The education process in itself has also failed the region in that it has supposed itself to be for the satisfaction of the requirements of industry and commerce instead of catering for the needs of communities in the region. The number of Highland children who enter university and then, after graduation, find that their new-found societal status and qualifications are incompatible with working in their home communities is enormous. In one ten-year period it was estimated that 1,200 young people had left the island of Lewis to qualify in higher education, and were largely unable to return to give their native island the benefit of their degrees. This export of brains is one of the reasons for the lack of vitality in many Highland communities and, indeed, is the reason why some communities have fought the decisions of their local authorities tooth and nail in order to retain enough of an educational provision in their locality to ensure that their children are educated for the needs of the community rather than for industry and commerce in alien conurbations in Scotland or England. Fatuous and facile statements made in 1972 by the Chairman of the Highlands and Islands Development Board in support of centralization in education revealed a sinister facet of the board of which many people in the region had not previously been aware, and reinforced the belief that its existence in the region was to perform as pure an economic function as it possibly could. The situation as it exists in the Highlands today is, however, only a reflection of what is happening in Scotland generally—where, for instance, Scottish history is regarded by the Scottish Education Department as "a parochial interest". (Readers may think this is a strong statement to make, but the author has a copy of a letter, written by that department to a friend, in which this statement is made.) To have control of the educative process is to control the future of any nation. And when that control is in the hands of theorists who have allowed themselves to become quite divorced from the social aspects of any educational provision, it would not be too far from the truth to recognize in the situation a process of genocide implemented and perpetrated by those who have had all sense of national and community identity washed out of them during their own education. The process is unfortunately cumulative and one only needs to discuss the problem with members of the communities who have suffered from centralized provisions to realize that the problem is urgent and serious—even more so in the Gaelic-based communities of the western seaboard of the region and the Outer Hebrides.

Contrary to the beliefs of many people who know the Highland region only as an area of scenic beauty, a Mecca for tourists, and a place where resources are exploited with no great economic benefit to the nation as a whole, the region in fact possesses many significant resources which have yet to be developed to provide the better economic and social conditions necessary for the regeneration of the region. Other resources have had a history of exploitation but are now abandoned; still others are not yet used to the full. It is reckoned, for instance, that if the diatomite deposits in Skye were worked again, the savings in British exports would exceed the loss of almost £300,000 which the Dingwall/Kyle of Lochalsh rail link is costing the British taxpayers, among whom can be counted those of the Highland region. A feasibility study carried out by the Highlands and Islands Development Board showed that there could be a good return on any capital invested in diatomite. There are many new, exciting and economically viable uses to which many of the minerals of the region can be put: limestone, dolomite, talc, serpentine, feldspar and so on. Only the traditions of architects and the construction industry hold back the introduction of these materials into the national building programme.

Land use in the region includes forestry, crofting, mixed and arable farming, hill-farming, deer forests, grouse moors and pleasure (the latter usually of the few to the exclusion of the many). The present patterns of land use in the region stem from a history which is varied and paradoxical, contains the elements of social tragedy and has in many respects created intense and emotional social feelings. The past has had an undoubted effect on the basic ecology of much of the region: it is thus important to recognize these changes when trying to assess its future potential.

Up to the seventeenth century, land was held in clan or individual peasant holdings; much of the area was covered with the Caledonian Forest, of birch, juniper, alder and scattered pine. Then, the red deer was a woodland animal which shared its habitat with natural predators, such as wolves, and the black cattle and goats of the smallholders. Economic shortfalls were a recurring event and were often made up by cattle-raiding.

During the seventeenth century royal gifts of large tracts of land were made to individuals. In particular, forests were cleared to provide fuel for iron smelting and an increasing population. Heather and bracken took over much of the cleared ground, and the red deer was forced to adapt to a new environment, open moorland, where it became a much smaller animal. The increasing population tended to exhaust the local natural resources.

By the end of the eighteenth century, much of the land was in the hands of a few powerful individuals. Smallholders found themselves being cleared out in enforced emigration schemes, partly because there was no future for them in a receding habitat and partly to provide for larger economic holdings devoted to the raising of sheep brought into the region from the Scottish borders. The black cattle, a former economic mainstay, disappeared, their place being taken by the sheep which rapidly caused formerly well-tended grazings to deteriorate. A coarser vegetation took over. To improve the situation, heavy burning operations were undertaken by graziers, but in certain types of soil this had an adverse effect: the destruction of basic soil nutrients. The overall result was affluence for a few; but inevitably a shortfall occurred as the grazings were increasingly unable to supply winter feed for the large flocks now spreading all over the mainland region.

By the nineteenth century, landowners tended to be very wealthy, many having made their fortunes from industry; their cash was poured into the maintenance of sheep, but the diminishing returns forced the introduction of the deer forest and deer-stalking as a sport. The vacuum left by the sheep was filled with deer, and the deer forest area increased by ten times in the following fifty years. Where the sheep were retained, the heavier Cheviot was replaced by the smaller Blackface.

During the twentieth century, many of the large estates were broken up by death duties and were made into small sporting estates. After the First World War, the State made its appearance as a landowner with state settlements of crofters and the acquisition of land by the Forestry Commission. Sheep continued to decline and the areas thus left vacant were afforested. Deer stocks rose considerably to create a conflict between the requirements of deer and trees. Crofters began to find themselves in need of a second source of income, failing which they emigrated with their families. The basic problem today has two sides. One is that the land has been impoverished by the spread of heather and bracken, with much of the soil being peaty podsols of very acid content; the other half of the problem is human. The older people tend to relive the history of their forebears, while the young are being introduced to the community-erosive influences of the mass media and different standards introduced through bad and incompatible education.

About one-ninth of all the land in the region is owned by the State; half of this area is under trees with the remainder in agricultural settlements. The rest of the land, about 84 per cent, is in private hands. The undesirable feature of this latter fact is that many estates are operated as sporting playgrounds for those who can pay high prices for shooting and fishing—which is a misuse of land and a disregard for the social responsibilities attendant on ownership of land. Land ownership should, ideally, be deemed a trust; and where the owner cannot see this, the State should be allowed to intervene. Because land is probably the only real major resource in the region, surprise has often been expressed that the Highlands and Islands Development Board has not made intensive efforts to exploit the available potential in terms of new settlements, regeneration of socially derelict areas, and new uses for the land, with programmes of refertilization.

When agriculture is mentioned in the Highland context, invariably crofting is meant. In fact, this emphasis is at variance with the situation as it exists at present. Other forms of farming exist, varying from the owner-occupied farms of some size on private estates; to smaller units worked by tenants on the better arable land in Easter Ross, the Black Isle and Inverness-shire; to many extensive rented hill farms. About 90 per cent of the Highland region classified as agricultural falls into the last category, which bears little relationship to crofting. Despite a steady decline in agricultural employment in recent years, hill and upland* farming and crofting still provide the equivalent of up to 7,000 jobs, or about 8 per cent of all occupations in the region. The average size of a hill farm is 4,600 acres, of which an average of 99 per cent is rough grazing. Upland farms extend to an average of 1,000 acres, with 84 per cent being rough grazing. The returns are better on hill farms: over 10 per cent compared with about 8 per cent on upland farms. Although a criticism of the Highlands and Islands Development Board has been made *vis-à-vis* agriculture, it does offer many incentives and forms of assistance to those who wish to improve their holdings, in the forms of loans and grants for farms, intensive rearing units, farm services and marketing schemes and processing units. As much as 70

* Hill-farming tends to be associated with sheep-raising while upland farms are on the lower slopes with opportunity for some arable farming.

per cent of the total cost of an improvement can be provided from public money through its agency.

Crofting activity in the region involves 1·4 million acres of common grazing, which includes some bog land. About 18,000 crofts exist today, of which over half are in units of less than 10 acres of in-bye land, that is land close to the farm centre, usually used for wintering. A programme of reclamation encouraged by the Crofters Commission has resulted in something like 35,000 acres, mostly now in-bye land, being made available for the better use of land. The Highland crofts produce about one-third of all stock in the region, and the tenacious crofting population has done much to prevent the area from becoming nothing more than a beautiful wilderness. Crofting produces no less than other forms of agriculture and, taking account of the quality of much of the land, more in some cases. The main problem of crofting as a form of land use with social overtones, is a lack of viability due to the small size involved. There is also the lack of capital. Even with 85 per cent improvement grants available, many crofters are unable to find the remaining 15 per cent required on any but the smallest scheme. Although the crofter in general depends primarily on external work for his income, he holds about 14 per cent of the Highlands in common grazings, a position which is carefully protected by legislation. In 1972 the Secretary of State announced that proposals made by the Crofters Commission would be accepted: a new deal in which crofters would become owner-occupiers. This, when implemented, would be a radical departure from the crofting custom. While these proposals are welcome in that the crofter will have the freedom to develop and use his initiative and all available resources to establish a more productive unit of his holding, fears have been expressed that what is being hailed as the crofters' 'Magna Carta' is in fact part of the continuous process of the Clearances. It is felt that more benefits would accrue to the region and its crofting communities if the proposals had been for the creation of owner-cultivators rather than owner-occupiers.

The presence of the Forestry Commission in the region has been a controversial one, particularly as the policy of planting has not been moderated sufficiently by social requirements of land. The commission is the largest landowner in the Highlands with its North Conservancy owning and managing 670,000 acres. It provides employment for 750 industrial workers and spends about £2 million each year. With the extensive planting programme being undertaken in the north of Scotland at present, the region constitutes the major share of the commission's British planting programme. The planting rate is about 16,000 acres per annum, about 24 per cent of the British programme. Timber production is also on the increase: at present about 150,000 tons, of which over half goes to the pulp mill at Fort William. Throughout the past fifty years the Forestry Commission has provided employment in many places where there was no other source, or only a very limited amount of employment. The commission claims that many Highland villages are viable today because of its presence and that one of the advantages of forestry is that it can provide more work in the rural areas of the region than any other form of land use. At present the forestry holdings give employment to about one person per 120 acres, i.e. a labour force growth of about 140 persons per annum, though some of this is lost as newer methods come into force, many of which tend to reduce the manpower needs of certain operations. If one compares this employment ratio to that of Highland agriculture, which is one man per 700 acres, a real difference between the two forms of land use is seen. Later in the life of the tree crop (at the time the first thinnings are removed and thereafter) the employment rate in forestry increases to about one man per 30 acres. This compares well with a sheep-farming unit of 3,000 acres which might employ six shepherds and ancillary workers. The adverse effects of forestry include the fact that land used for trees ties it up for not less than fifty years, with subsequent restoration of the land to agricultural use being costly; that there is alteration to the landscape and the creation of significant micro-climates; and that capital investment is tied up for a long period before a return is obtained.

The area used by red deer in the region is estimated to be about 30 per cent. A total of about 7 million acres supports a population of 200,000 animals, from which an annual cull of about 14 per cent is made, mainly for carcases to satisfy a significant Continental market for venison. Claims that red deer husbandry is a significant element in the region's economic structure are often contested. Certainly on the credit side, much of the land occupied by red deer at present could never be used for anything else apart from recreation of a raw nature. In themselves, the red deer make a very small income for those who have them on their land during the stalking season. Larger incomes seem to be more usual on the Continent, where smaller herds are managed for specific purposes. There are pockets of intensive rearing in the region, notably in Glen Feshie in Inverness-shire where the red deer play a dual role: sport and food. This bleak glen, where there is no land under 1,100 feet, has been carefully developed by the hand-feeding of animals, the regeneration of some level ground with lime and phosphate, selective cover planting, the regeneration of shrubs, re-seeding and control of grazing. The restoration of some reclaimed high pasture for the summering of cattle, once a common Highland practice, will lead eventually to an increase in the overall fertility of the soil.

Grouse moors in the region are a very poor form of land use and show pitiful returns. Extensive heather moorland was created by the clearance of original natural forest in the seventeenth and eighteenth centuries, together with the muirburn grazing policies introduced at that time. The shooting of grouse first became popular with the advent of the breech-loading gun, although most birds were still walked up over dogs. The modern practice of driving grouse arrived with the artificial pheasant rearing farther south, the number of birds in the day's bag being more important than the method of acquiring them. In terms of yield (3 ounces of blood and feathers per acre per annum or a gross income of from 30p. to 100p. per acre) the grouse moor is truly hopeless and only becomes economic when estates cater for very rich syndicates from America which can afford to pay upwards of £400 per week for the shooting.

The role of the fishing industry in the economic structure of the region has been significant for something approaching almost 300 years. Inevitably the pattern has changed since the first appearance of the Dutch herring busses off the western coastal areas, and only in a few places is the present industry a reasonable reflection of the former bustling times. It is in the fishing sector of its wide-ranging activities that the Highlands and Islands Development Board has proved itself to be of enormous importance to the region, and in particular to those communities which have made a concerted effort to complement the board's financial incentives. The announcement in 1973 of a further boost in the expansion of the Highland fishing fleet, to cost some £4 million, raised the possibility that the industry was already fully developed and needed only to streamline and consolidate what already existed, as well as to develop on-shore facilities. By 1973 it was said that the optimum catch had been reached in the waters immediately surrounding the region and that to expand catching capacity could well cause serious problems in terms of falling prices and incomes and lengthy periods of forced unemployment. The other black cloud was the possible effects of the implementation of the Common Fisheries Policy of the European Economic Commission, no detailed assessment of which had been made in the context of Highland fishings. The moving finger has, at the time of writing, already scrawled its message on the wall: the closure of the fish-processing plant at Thurso and the decision, early in 1973, of Campbeltown fishermen to sell their catches in far-off Aberdeen. In the seven years of the board's existence, assistance to purchase was given to more than 300 boats at a cost of under £3 million. Selecting and training crews for these boats introduced 1,500 jobs. The board's new proposals for the expansion of the Highland catching fleet were generally welcomed, though objections were made by the White Fish Authority, who were worried about the possible depletion of fish stocks. The board, however, were confident that the stocks were at a reasonably high level and would be able to sustain the addition of another 250 boats to the existing fleet.

Whisky has been for so long associated with Scotland in general

Dounreay Atomic Power Station, Caithness

Ullapool, Wester Ross

Beach at Sangobeg near Durness, Sutherland

it is little realized that the liquid is a truly Highland product. Yet, so much is the industry controlled from London, that the region benefits only marginally in terms of cash inflow and employment. A distillery with an annual output of 1 million gallons need only consider a work force of less than fifty people employed in various tasks. Even so, the fact that pockets of employment are offered by the distilleries makes the provision significant in social terms, in that communities can forecast their future years with some degree of confidence. Whisky is the world's premier spirit and is a major international commodity which continues to attract international finance, investment and ownership. Indeed, the latter aspect has caused concern in recent years, with the fear that the control of the industry could pass out of the British Isles; the dominant ownership of the industry has long ceased to be Scottish. There is still, however, a distinct Scottish element in the top management of the industry. One of the biggest whisky concerns is the Distillers Company Limited, the twentieth largest firm in Britain, which has its headquarters in Edinburgh. But, in these days of high finance, it is necessary for an increasing number of decisions to be taken in London and it may only be a matter of a few years before the industry is totally controlled from that city.

By the end of 1971 malt whisky production capacity totalled almost 70 million gallons. Stored in bond was a quantity approaching 870 million original proof gallons which could be represented in cash terms by a figure in the region of £2,000 million, a reserve of liquid gold which any country would be proud to have. The industry at present comprises 14 grain distilleries and 115 malt distilleries, blending, bottling and storage plants, giving, in all, employment to about 23,000 people, making it Scotland's fifth largest employer. For many years now the attitude of the Government to the industry has been merely to regard it as an important exporting facility and a handsome, albeit unwilling, contributor to the purse of the Chancellor of the Exchequer. At the time of writing a gallon of whisky at proof strength costs on average about £1 in bond, which is what the blenders pay for it. To take it out of bond, they have to pay the Chancellor nearly £18, so that every 5p. of whisky carries about 95p. of tax. This rate of imposition can be compared with paying about 45p. for a packet of cigarettes, almost £1 for a gallon of petrol and about £3,500 for the present-day £700 Mini car. Compared with other spirits, whisky is discriminated against—beer, imported sherry and imported table wines all get off more lightly. One can appreciate the feeling that other British alcoholic products are being subsidized, tax-wise, by whisky. Considering the industry's record, it is no wonder that complaints are made regarding the Government's unwillingness to ease off some of the restricting burdens it has to carry. For its size, it is capital intensive, decentralized, with no labour disputes, few pollution problems and a remarkable export record. It hits the headlines only when new records of production or an export achievement are announced, or when the tax is raised to a new high yet again.

The recent expansion activities which have taken place at many Highland distilleries, often financed by outside interests, will obviously place the industry in a better position to cope with its burdens. But, being a capital-intensive industry, the labour element has become less and less significant and, unlike times past when many jobs were offered (compare the Fort William distillery of Long John about eighty years ago) to generate good and worthwhile social conditions and stability in local communities, it may well be that the whisky industry, while still retaining its 'Scotch' identity, will be of little or no value to the region in any economic context. Being self-financing, it has escaped the attentions of bodies like the Highlands and Islands Development Board, who could have exercised some moderating influence in advising that the communities whose livelihoods are dependent on the local distillery are not decimated by the increase in production methods which require fewer men and have in a number of cases, as in Skye, already reduced the work force. Only a definite and declared social commitment on the part of the industry will remove the stigma it now has and bring whisky-distilling back again as a significant source of employment in the Highland region.

One of the most important events ever to have occurred in the socio-economic history of the region was the setting up of the North of Scotland Hydro-electric Board. The importance of this body lies in its statutory social remit, which has made it unique among all other similar energy undertakings in the whole of the British Isles. The story of the development of the region's massive water resources for the generating of cheap electricity goes back to efforts to set up the aluminium reduction works of the British Aluminium Company at Foyers, and subsequently at Kinlochleven and Fort William. The evidence produced by these schemes underlined the possibility of greater use of the available water power. In 1918 the President of the then Board of Trade appointed the Water Power Resources Committee "to examine and report upon the water power resources of the United Kingdom and the extent to which they can be made available for industrial purposes". Three years later the committee stated that, on the basis of an examination of twenty-eight schemes, a vast quantity of power could be obtained from the harnessing of the waters of the Highland region to produce something in the region of 78 per cent of all hydro-electric power in the country. The committee had only looked at the surface possibilities, for in the year it was established a paper was read before the Royal Society of Arts which indicated a total of 123 possible hydro-electric schemes capable of producing commercial quantities of electrical energy.

While the Government thereafter sat on the Power Committee's report, private and municipal enterprises were getting off the ground. A local supply of electric lighting and power for domestic purposes was provided by the development of Loch Luichart in Ross-shire. In 1926 a limited company was formed under local auspices, to take over a small company of prior origin, and proceeded with the hydro-electric development of Loch Luichart for the supply of power to Dingwall, Strathpeffer and adjoining districts. The undertaking later passed to the control of the Scottish Power Company Ltd which, before nationalization in 1948, had extended its supplies to an area of over 300 square miles extending from Beauly to Golspie. The scheme was partly financed by a loan of £20,000 at 5 per cent interest which was guaranteed by the Government under the Trade Facilities Act and which was repaid in a short time. The town council of Inverness profitably augmented the generated output of their steam station by developing water power harnessed from the River Ness. The Grampian Electricity Supply Co. also had a scheme at Rannoch, Tummel and Loch Luichart by 1943.

Development, however, was slow and aimed at providing large areas where consumer density was highest. Rural areas were left completely out of the picture. Then, in 1943, the Hydro-electric Development (Scotland) Act was passed by Parliament. This was engineered and guided through the House by the late Secretary of State for Scotland, Tom Johnston, a dedicated Socialist who considered the satisfaction of social and economic needs of Scotland of greater importance than the enhancement of the status of the political machine. That the Bill went through all its Parliamentary stages with an absence of conflict indicates the measure of Tom Johnston's worth and the regard in which he was held by Members of both sides of the House. The Act established the North of Scotland Hydro-electric Board and gave it the task of developing the water-power resources of the Highlands and Islands, and of supplying electricity to the ordinary consumer there, to industry and to existing supply undertakings. The board was also given a unique duty for an electricity authority: that of collaborating in measures for the social improvement and economic development of the north of Scotland. The Act which nationalized the electricity supply industry in the United Kingdom in 1948 recognized the difficult problems of the board's area and the special functions it had, and left it independent of the new set-up. In 1957 the report of the Select Committee on Nationalized Industries (Reports and Accounts) stated that "In the 14 years of its existence, the North of Scotland Hydro-electric Board has impressively justified the faith of its progenitors."

Evidence of the board's work is visible all over the region: dams, power stations (often underground) and overhead lines, which some people object to on amenity grounds—though in general the board is conscious of the need to preserve scenic amenity. The board has brought electricity to the remotest areas, which would have otherwise been deprived of some of the domestic amenities so taken for granted by more favoured areas of denser populations. A connection figure now approaching 100 per cent indicates the board's completion of the first phase of its statutory obligation to bring power to the glens. In the course of providing these supplies, many spin-off benefits have been created. Over 400 miles of roads have been constructed, about a quarter of the total being public roads. Some of these roads have opened up areas of outstanding beauty and have thus added to the development of the tourist amenity. The board's policy of providing housing for its staff has meant retaining craftsmen such as stonemasons, who use local stone for the houses and also for facing power station buildings and other structures. Over 400 houses built by the board have helped to stabilize existing communities or created new centres of population, to give a welcome stimulus to the social and economic life in places where there was a danger of decline. The 4,000 industrial consumers connected to the electricity mains have ensured employment for over 13,000 people, and many new industries have been established entirely by the board's efforts. The agricultural industry in particular has been developed and streamlined in operation as the result of electricity being readily available. In December 1948 the first small turbine station built in Morar by the board was put into operation by the widow of a local crofter. The ceremony was performed in Gaelic—"*Gun tigeadh solus agus neart dealan dhionnsuidh gach croit*" (Let electric light and power flow into each croft)—and was symbolic of what the board had to do for the people of the region. That it has performed its duties well, and that it is accepted as a particular and peculiar Highland product (even though its headquarters are in far-off Edinburgh), is a measure of the worth and esteem in which the board is held in the region. This kind of regard is unusual for any public organization and indicates, surely, the simple fact that if any body, public or semi-public, has written inalienably into its constitution or Act a statutory remit to consider the social problems of the region, to solve them with all its available powers, then the benefits are far greater than any which come from imposed direction and development.

Ever since the Highlands and Islands replaced the European Grand Tour as offering the final touch and polish to the catholic education of the rich, the region has been the destination for any who desired to add adventure to their tour. Not for them the well-worn roads to Rome. Rather, they sought the trackways of desolate areas in which there lived a people whose culture, language and very lifestyle was as strange as any to be found in other aboriginal parts of the world. What escaped many visitors, and this was largely because of the language barrier, was that the conditions in which they found the Highlanders living out their lives were no better nor worse than those which obtained in many parts of so-called civilized Europe, including rural and urban England. It was, however, the language difference which immediately enhanced the 'foreign' character of the region and gave a journey to the Highlands an African safari-like aspect which one might venture to say still exists for many people. It took a number of famous names to visit the region, to jot down their observations and comments, and to inspire other would-be travellers to go north; these included Robert Southey, the Wordsworths, Robert Burns and Queen Victoria—particularly the latter, who, with Sir Walter Scott before her, Balmoralized, tartanized and heatherized the region to a degree which was almost nauseating and which certainly did the region, and the remoter parts of it in particular, no good at all, transfixed as they became in a magic mist of romanticism, seen only through the dim glow of a Celtic twilight which was nothing if not contagious.

During the last decade or so the flood of tourists into the region has taken on alarming proportions, a situation to which the Highlands and Islands Development Board has contributed in its consistent and active support for the development of the Highland tourist industry. The industry has to be viewed from two sides. The first and most obvious viewpoint is that of the income which the industry generates in the region. But whether this income is of any real value to the communities involved in catering for the tourist is something which has never been subjected to any real in-depth investigation. In the case of the Aviemore holiday complex, much of the cash generated in the area is sucked to the south; little of it is left in the immediate area to circulate as re-invested funds and generate further benefits to the community. While it is accepted that a proportion of the income from tourism is significant in that it allows otherwise depressed communities to stay alive, the long-term prospect of becoming a region of hewers of wood and drawers of water for the itinerant tourist is neither a good nor a healthy one. Secondly, the rather inward-looking interest of the Highlands and Islands Development Board in tourism as a major economic prop in the region's economy has been criticized as producing an even greater distortion of the region's potential. An estimate of 75 per cent of the employment in the region being geared to cater for tourism is too high if it is anywhere near the mark.

The assistance which can be given by the board to tourism is wide-ranging. The projects which can be considered for financial assistance include new hotels, the extension or upgrading of existing hotels or guest houses, the provision of self-catering chalets, the extension of croft houses to provide more holiday accommodation for visitors to remote areas and the provision of recreational facilities for holiday visitors. The criteria set by the board for an eligible tourism project are: that it is or will become viable, that it provides fresh employment (or maintains employment), and that it will contribute to the economic or social development of the area. Viewed simply as a promoter of tourism, and of the region as a tourist asset, the board has done an excellent job. But whether the publicity has been effective enough to benefit the region is another question. In 1973 the Countryside Commission for Scotland reported that some parts of Argyll had become so popular that sheer numbers of visitors threatened to destroy the very qualities that made that area so attractive. It has recommended a regional coastal strategy so that the exploitation of coastal resources, in response to tourist and recreational demands, is in the best interests of the region and of the affected communities in particular. The report considered that the spectacular rise in the use of caravans and other types of mobile home had a profound effect on the coastline of mainland Argyll, an area which had the smallest number of beaches reasonably accessible to the tourist. The physical stability of many coastal areas was being disturbed by large numbers of people, particularly where the vegetation cover was fragile and based on sand dunes. The report came out against attempts to promote large-scale tourist and recreational developments. Along with other bodies such as the Nature Conservancy (which in 1973 issued its "Prospectus for the Moray Firth Area"), the Scottish Wildlife Trust and the National Trust for Scotland, the Countryside Commission expressed anxiety that land use for recreational purposes was not being considered in an overall plan or strategy which would include other requirements of land such as agriculture and settlement. Another question was raised in 1973: would the oil developments proposed for many areas of the Highland mainland oust the tourist? Already by that year it was impossible for the tourist to book into his favourite places on the eastern coast, particularly around the Easter Ross area, because accommodation had been taken up by incoming workers associated with the on-shore developments taking place there.

As readers will realize when they pick their way through the various chapters of this book, the region is no stranger to industrialization: not perhaps quite as the Industrial Revolution produced elsewhere in Scotland, Wales and England; the attempts in the Highlands during the last two centuries or so at establishing bona fide industrial complexes tended to be isolated, obnoxious at times, but served, at the very least, to give the region a background history of association with industrial processes and ventures. This history, of course, is not continuous. Even so, the present attempts by the Highlands and Islands Development Board and the North of Scotland Hydro-electric Board to attract industry to the region has some historical foundation, a factor in the publicity of these bodies which is often neglected; yet it is significant if only to indicate that the Highlander is adaptable—as he is now proving in the industrial environments at present existing at Thurso,

Invergordon, Easter Ross and Fort William, along with countless other smaller enterprises.

While attention given to the region in recent years has been strengthened by the existence of large capital-intensive industrial processes, less limelight than is really deserved has been thrown on the role of small industries. Throughout the whole of Scotland during 1972 some 2,000 small firms actually increased their overall employment facilities by some 6 per cent, in the face of increasing unemployment in much larger concerns, which was represented by a loss of 4 per cent of all available jobs. The report of the Small Industries Council for Rural Areas of Scotland of that year indicated that the small independent company had a firm base, an identity with its host community, and was well able to weather the effects of economic storms. Many of these small firms, of which a fair number are to be found in the region, employ only handfuls of people, yet, because of their size, they are able to offer a way of life which is thoroughly in tune with the environmentally conscious 1970s. As often as not, the small firm has a strong local allegiance; its management decisions have no element of remote control in them. The owner and the work force belong to the same community and the capital will often owe more than a little to the help of a friendly neighbourhood bank manager. There are, in addition, strong, built-in incentives for survival and growth, which, as has been proved, can endure through bad times as well as good. It was a past deputy chairman of the Highlands and Islands Development Board who said that if the £37 million spent on creating the 600 jobs at the Invergordon aluminium-reduction works had been spent on creating a close-knit network of small industries, a total employment force of some 22,000 could have been the end product. This is quite a thought; yet it is totally in line with the pattern in Britain and in other countries on the Continent, where one finds that the bulk of industry is made up of comparatively small firms. In Britain, these small firms are responsible for one-third of the total turnover; indeed, the output of many larger organizations is dependent on the components which the small firms supply. If Britain's 80,000 small firms were to close down tomorrow, 2½ million workers would lose their jobs, over £6,000 million of industrial output would vanish, and most of the larger firms would quickly grind to a halt. It is estimated that 97½ per cent of all U.K. manufacturing establishments have less than 500 workers. In the context of a 'rural industry', a firm is loosely eligible for this description if it employs less than ten persons. Some 50,000 firms in the U.K. employ less than twenty persons, a percentage of 70, which compares with over 90 per cent for France and Norway and over 80 per cent for Sweden.

Often called the 'Highland light brigade', the small firms in the region are more than just economically significant, for they perform an additional role as social sheet-anchors. These firms are found in all areas of the region. The presence of the Highlands and Islands Development Board has done much to strengthen the socio-economic role of the small firms; not all have met with success, but the greater majority of ventures started a few years ago are still consolidating or else are now entering a new phase of expansion. Many of the industries tend to be based on the processing of natural resources; but a significant proportion are creating new industrial facets to the overall picture in that they produce items from brought-in materials, which are subsequently exported from the region at an enhanced value.

Many of the region's small industries are craft-based, producing items from leather, paper, feathers, deerskin, clay, pewter, silver, wood, fur and stone. While originally started to cater for the tourist in the region, many firms have now reached the stage where they are satisfying a market located outside the region; some export overseas to cater for the demand from discriminating buyers of handmade and genuine personalized articles. The incentives made available to the incoming small industry, craft-based or whatever, by the Highlands and Islands Development Board are attractive and are particularly tailored to meet the needs of the miniscule enterprise which can show it is capable of enough growth to offer the adopted community or area a small local source of employment. The success of such utterly remote enterprises as Barra Perfumes prove that the will to survive and succeed exists only in the small venture, which has everything to lose—not in terms of cash, shares and public prestige, as is the case with the multi-million firm, but rather a basic job of work and the satisfaction of knowing that the existence of the industry is an integral part of the community and that failure of the venture would leave a gap in the area. Any increase in the number of small industries in the region will be seen as the most significant outcome of any redevelopment policies, in sharp contrast to the re-exploitation of the region which is now occurring with the massive, indiscriminate and rapacious growth to unknown final dimensions as is found in Easter Ross.

For almost a century now the region has been subjected to the attention of a vast number of government-sponsored agencies in attempts to promote its economic and social development. This process can be said to have started with the Crofters Commission in 1887, established to implement the Crofters Holdings (Scotland) Act of the previous year, and was followed by a long line of essentially bureaucratic devices which were seriously limited in what they could do simply because they were too closely tied in with the government of the day and policies which were often reflections of the party machine. Dr Frank Fraser Darling in 1955 pointed out the limits of these agencies: "... effective rehabilitation will call for an organization with effective authority, able to act in several fields and which will not neglect the scientific quality and interest of what is being done, not omit the humane studies which could be the lubrication of the whole intricate mechanism." Essentially Dr Darling suggested a body established on the lines of the Tennessee Valley Authority. This idea, however, was not new; it first appeared in the late 1920s when the Scottish Liberal Party adopted the idea of a Highland development authority as part of its policy. In 1938, the report of the Scottish Economic Committee recommended the appointment of a development commissioner for the region, a theme which was taken up in the following year by Sir Alexander MacEwen and Dr John Lorne Campbell (now of Canna) and defined at some length in a substantial publication which proposed a Highland Development Board. From 1951 the Scottish Trades Union Congress pushed for such an authority, until the Labour victory in the general election of 1964. During that campaign, Labour pledged itself to set up a Highland Development Authority, which it did in the following year by an Act of Parliament; this brought into existence the present Development Board, though not before some agitation was raised to get "and Islands" into the name of the proposed authority.

The Highlands and Islands Development (Scotland) Act of 1965 gives very wide powers to the board which was constituted "for the purpose of assisting the people of the Highlands and Islands to improve their economic and social conditions and of enabling the Highlands and Islands to play a more effective part in the economic and social development of the nation". The board has powers which no other agency engaged in regional development in Britain has ever been given. It can prepare, concert, promote, assist and undertake measures for the economic and social development of the crofting counties. It may acquire land, by compulsory purchase if necessary, and it may hold, manage and dispose of land. It may erect buildings, provide equipment and services and hold or dispose of these. It may establish businesses and also dispose of them. It may train people, produce publicity about the region and itself, and use a wide range of methods to bring jobs to the crofting counties. It can give grants or loans, on unspecified criteria, to anyone carrying on commercial business operations which would promote the economic and social development of the area. And it can also charge for its services, accept gifts, commission or undertake research, and borrow money.

In the years of its existence the board has had a number of successes, with about 10 per cent failure. Numbers, however, do not tell the whole story. The most outstanding record of success has been in the fishing sector of the region's economy. At the time of writing, about thirty new and fully-equipped trawlers have been floated, each equivalent to a £32,000 small industry. And it has secured for the Highland fleet a further eighty-five second-hand trawlers and seine-netters, along with forty or so shellfish boats. About 1,700 new jobs have been created, in many cases bringing stability and new purpose to some of the region's most remote communities. It has established twenty-four new fish-processing plants and eleven boat-building yards. In the light of the present landings of around £7 million per annum, the board's investment of just over £3 million in the industry is fully justified.

Since it started work, the board has established over 1,800 projects, with loans and grants amounting to over £10 million; a further £11 million have been invested by private enterprise. The jobs created by this activity now exceed 6,000. The board itself has also earned money, a sure sign that investments have been made in the right sectors and to the right people. Repayments on loans and interest from assisted projects have totalled nearly £2 million. The present rate of return is about 25 per cent of its total annual income of about £3 million. The board played a part in attracting the £37 million aluminium smelter to Invergordon. In the tourist sector the board has revitalized a flagging industry; though its enthusiasm to create this as a prop in the region's economy has attracted some justified criticism in that the tourist egg has hatched a rather horrifying cuckoo—which, in one respect, is seen in the large-scale purchase of holiday cottages by people outside the region who have quite seriously upset the equilibrium and social patterns of the communities now subjected to their annual and temporary attentions. The board's main handicap has been its assumption that it is a political instrument, reflected perhaps in the fact that its members are appointed by the Secretary of State for Scotland and not elected. It was in fact established as an experimental agency in regional regeneration and autonomy which could not, and would not, become enmeshed in traditional developmental machinery and techniques. Indeed, it was an experiment in fundamental socialism which was, perhaps, doomed to failure from the beginning in that the board and its potential were too dependent on capital directed and controlled by interests outside the region. Indeed, only wide-ranging statutory powers over all developments in the region can ensure that the long-term prospects in the region are not sacrificed to temporary gain and profits.

The board's committed welcome to oil has not been a good sign, mainly because the appearance of on-shore oil-based activity has been accompanied by serious social and environmental problems. It was stated by an ex-deputy chairman of the board in 1973 that the Brora Coal Mine, a social sheet-anchor of the highest order, was closed because there had been no effective control exercised by the board over oil-based developments. The board said in a statement on the Brora tragedy that it was "very sorry", words which must be seen against the ex-deputy chairman's comment: "Until February this year [1973] we were earning substantial profits. We got over the unexpected geological difficulties, but our death knoll was the start of a daily bus from Brora to the oil developments on the Cromarty Firth." If anything has put the Highlands and Islands Development Board into perspective for the people of the region it is the closure of the Brora mine, for had it exercised its full powers over oil development, the mine would have remained open; indeed, it only required the paltry sum of £10,000 to tide the mine over for a short period until a new arrangement could be put into effect.

The main impact of the board's presence has been seen in the intense interest taken in the region by agencies which otherwise would have ignored it because of its social and economic intransigence. The board has encouraged large complexes, concerned with the tourist industry in particular, to take over and become established. Where this has happened, it has not been followed by an increase in the number of local people employed. Indeed, the usual pattern has been an alien complex obtaining foothold, followed by the introduction of outsiders to take up the more senior employment opportunities thus created; profits then go outside the area and little is circulated throughout the local economy to produce a wider-based growth for the affected communities. In some cases, the special qualities of the Highland environment are exploited for the benefit of others, with local people playing the role of helpless bystanders. The present-day pattern of exploitation of the Highlands, rather than its regeneration and development, is a reflection of the old days in the region, when resources such as trees, herring and kelp were worked to the finish for the benefit of outsiders and not with a view to producing long-term economic growth within the region. Even as in the eighteenth and nineteenth centuries, when profits from the temporary economic booms were drained off by landlords and spent elsewhere, so today there occurs the same large-scale enterprise which reaps all the benefits and drains all the wealth.

The tendency of the board continually to resort to a self-imposed narrowing of its limits by increasingly stressing its economic role is seen as going against the basic intent of its constitution and the interests of the region. In 1971 the chairman of the board said that his organization was "a merchant bank with a social purpose", a description later to be challenged in the context of the board's study of the Strath of Kildonan in Sutherland. This study should have presented the board with the opportunity, for the first time in its career, to concentrate all its available socio-economic powers to transform a small area of the region into something which would be a model for social development elsewhere. Instead, the board's study was, in its own words: "... primarily economic rather than social in its orientation, in the sense that a positive return is expected on all the investment proposed". In the study it was seen that economic criteria were used to deny the feasibility of land settlement, and no weight was given to social and political factors in the redevelopment proposals. This narrowing of the board's activities is also seen in its refusal to obtain land for redevelopment. Yet, it has the powers to do this, for it can acquire and hold land, obtained if necessary by compulsory purchase, subject to the approval of the Secretary of State for Scotland. But, because the question of land-holding in the region is politically controversial, the board has made no attempt to affect in any way the present characteristics of land holding and land use. Where it has involved itself with the social facets of development (only one member of its senior staff is specifically charged with responsibility for social and community development), it has done so with a philosophy based on some curious and unexamined assumptions; one of its justifications for the development of the Moray Firth area was that immigration of managerial and professional people would enrich the social and cultural leadership of the area.

That the board is now regarded by the region as the latest in a long line of agencies intended to further bureaucratize the Highlands and Islands is seen in recent writings which have evaluated the board's performance since its formation and found it seriously wanting on the social side of its development policies and programmes. The effect of the re-organization of local government in Scotland, in which the various counties of the region will be effaced to become units in the new all-purpose Highland Regional Authority, has yet to be seen. It may be that the sense of identity produced as the result of the unification could well be the incentive needed to expand the thinking on Highland development to produce the necessary regenerative processes required to justify the region as a place concerned with its indigenous population and able to offer its people the *raison-d'être* for living. But the ghost of centralism, which has ever flitted over the pages of the region's history, will no doubt continue to influence the region, its history and the fate of its people.

2

The North-west

THE north-western tip of Scotland, and indeed that of the mainland of Britain, has an expressive atmosphere derived entirely from its contrasting scenery. At one moment one views tall rising massifs, set back across a flat expanse of moor and loch, and dominating the skyline with mysterious intention. At the next moment, one is wending one's way along a narrow road which twists and turns through miniature woodlands with rushing streams and rivers. The sea coast is high, inaccessible and awesome, and then relents to flat beaches, shining with sands that roll like a thin blade under the sea's skin into the depths of the North Minch, the Pentland Firth, and what is truly the North Sea. Vast, lonely wastelands, remote glens, glacier-strewn slopes, ravines, quiet loch-waters, multi-ringed by rising fish, jostle for the viewer's eye with the greenness of human occupation in places like Scourie. This is an area where the mind can expand in proportion to the scale of its vistas. It is, of course, sparsely populated. Even a glance at the population distribution map for the 1961 census will indicate the extremely low density of population per square mile, which is both one of the greatest attractions of the area, and also one of its tragedies. Though essentially a tourist Mecca, the area is significant both in the social and economic contexts, and particularly so on its western seaboard.

The north-west has for long been considered as a classic area by geologists, as there is no other part of the British Isles where the older rock formations can be so well studied. Archaean gneiss extends in great hummocky hillocks through Durness, Eddrachillis and Assynt and southwards into Coigach. It is the oldest rock formation in the world, an ancient foundation on which stratified rocks have been superimposed. The older groups (Torridon, Cambrian, Silurian and Old Red Sandstone) are disclosed in masses which appear in succession eastwards to the Pentland Firth. Through these rock formations, intrusive masses of igneous rock have penetrated in several places. In the region of Ben Loyal and Ben Stomino the intrusive rock is syenite, resembling granite but containing traces of the dark mineral called horneblende. A mass of grey granite extends between Loch Migdale and Loch Laggan, near Bonar Bridge, and goes farther eastwards and northwards into Caithness. The western archaean rock, which has been penetrated by numberless dykes of granite, syenite and other igneous rocks, rises to a height of nearly 1,500 feet in Glasbheinn and Ceannabeinne in Durness, and Ben Stroma in Eddrachillis.

Resting on the gneiss are great masses of Torridon sandstone, which rise into huge mountains of reddish-brown conglomerate in nearly horizontal beds of great thickness. Quinag, Canisp, Suilbheinn in Assynt, and Fashbeinn in Durness, are mainly composed of this ancient rock, while near Cape Wrath sea cliffs of the Torridon rise sheer from the waters' edge to a height of nearly 1,000 feet. Handa and Rhu Stoer are also Torridonian. Above the Torridon sandstone lie Cambrian formations of white quartzite, limestone and thin shales in which occur the fossil 'olenellus', the discovery of which first enabled scientists to fix the age of the Cambrian. These rocks form a band stretching from the west side of Loch Erriboll to Loch More and thence by the upper Oykell to Ullapool in the south-west. To this series belong the limestones of Durness and Assynt, which lie above the 'olenellus' beds and piped quartzites. The largest outcrop of limestone is at Stronechrubie in Assynt; considerable masses also occur at Durness and Eriboll. Great earth disturbances in the Cambrian period have tilted quartzite beds over the more recent pipe-rock formation apparent on Cranstackie, Foinnebheinn, Arcuil, Ben Uidhe and Ben More. Silurian metamorphic schists cover the whole of central Sutherland eastwards from the 'great thrust' to Strath Halladale and Strath Ullie. Along this 'thrust' rocks have been heaved up, overlapped and crushed together by the action of collossal natural forces. Its line can be followed from Whitenhead southward along the east side of Loch Eriboll until it crosses Loch More and Loch Gorm and, after following the east side of Loch Ailsh, sweeps westward to the Cromalt hills. This area is bare, tends to the monotonous and consists largely of boggy heather-clad moorland with occasional elevated masses such as Ben Hope, Ben Hee, Ben Clibreck and Beinn Armuinn. On the latter rise traces of the Old Red Sandstone, which was formed above the schists and stretches along the eastern side of the county of Sutherland from Meikle Ferry to Helmsdale. These metamorphic schists contain in irregular quantities gold, silver, iron and other minerals which occur in various localities.

From this brief description it can be appreciated why the north-west of Scotland has a particular fascination for all kinds of people. One need only enter Assynt to see the great sphinx-like mass of Suilven to sense the atmosphere of unreality, almost fantasy, which permeates even the character of the people who live here. Mountains such as Quinag, Ben Loyal, Ben Hope all have the power to impress; though perhaps Quinag, more than others, in its towering grimness, serves to emphasize that man himself is the alien element in this landscape.

Yet the area is not so inhospitable that Man cannot live here. Barren though the whole area seems to be at first sight, very generous allowances have been made by nature in the creation of environments where Man has established for himself appropriate life-styles. Instances of these occur in such places as Kinlochbervie, Lochinver, Scourie, Durness, all of which add an extra dimension of interest to the north-western tip of Scotland.

Possibly the most interesting area of the north-west, and that because it is isolated, is the Parph, derived from *hvarf*, an old Norse word meaning 'turning'. Access to the Parph is by means of a small ferry boat across the Kyle of Durness; then one must take a rough but ready road towards the lighthouse by minibus. Some 15,000 visitors make the trip each year, to sample the experience of real solitude. Just as inaccessible is Sandwood Bay, a few miles south of Cape Wrath. This is a beautiful sandy inlet with a romance all of its own, based particularly on the ghostly hauntings of a seaman, to which many people previously quite unaware of the spiritual associations of the place, have given credence by virtue of their own personal experiences. Others, while not being rewarded with some visible evidence of the hauntings, have been distinctly upset in the area around the bay. Only on the sunniest days does the atmosphere of being unwanted slip away with the ground mists, only to return later when the waters of the bay are given a red sheen by the setting sun.

The little port of Kinlochbervie is as remote as one could imagine, yet is the proving point for those who claim that many more 'remote' areas of the Highlands and Islands could support small but significant pockets of population, provided there is a sound and reliable economic base for the prosecution of activities based on natural resources.

There are two harbours here, which act as the *raisons-d'être* for the population of some 300 people, who also have an association with the crofting activity in the immediate hinterland. The fishing industry, however, has offered the stabilizing factor and a base for a further slow but steady increase in the population. The port, which has a fish-processing plant, is regarded by the Scottish fishing fleet as one of the new important centres on the Minch. Before the last war, however, this tiny port did not exist as a fishing centre. Its role began in 1947 when east-coast vessels started to call in to sell their catches. After the sales, the fish was taken away for processing, usually to Aberdeen. Since then the port facilities have been developed to include selling, transport and an ice-plant. Many projects, such as fish-filleting and fish-freezing, are off the ground, though a number of problems have yet to be solved to make these ventures viable, both for their promoters and for the community. The remoteness of Kinlochbervie seems to be a job advantage. When a leading firm in the port advertised for a factory manager, replies were received from many other parts of Scotland. Business at the port has increased since the harbour entrance was deepened in 1970. The turnover in cash terms is almost £500,000 a year. This growth is most impressive when considered over a period of twenty-five years. The main firm at Kinlochbervie, Pulford's Estates Ltd, estimate a growth rate of between 5 and 10 per cent per annum in the amount of fish landed. The port's two lochs, Loch Clash and Loch Inchard, provide good sheltering for the fishing fleet.

Most of the catch landed at Kinlochbervie is white fish, with shellfish coming a poor second with a value of under £12,000 per annum. About fifty men are employed at the port. Most of these are full-time workers, which makes the port more significant in socio-economic terms, and particularly when seen against the sparseness of the county of Sutherland as a whole—which supports a population of some 13,000, who live on average at 6·4 persons per square mile, making it the most sparsely populated county in Scotland.

However, the very fact that the port's community survives on one economic activity spells danger and one hopes that efforts by the Highlands and Islands Development Board to broaden the economic base of this small area will provide a future which could rise out of any recession in fishing. The whole area is, of course, a tourist attraction, particularly the seascape from Bealach-Tigh-Foingheal and the mountains of the Reay forest. The port has a good potential as a sailing centre. The hinterland supports many clachans and crofts. The latter are small, the harvest is often late, for the summers are invariably cold and the soil, being peaty, does not favour rapid growth.

At Ardmore is the Adventure Centre established by Captain John Ridgeway and Captain Rod Liddon. The centre offers courses in many fields where both the mind and body are stretched to reasonable limits, and offers students (young and old) the opportunity of merging with those aspects of nature which are less accessible to the visitor in his role as tourist. Sailing, climbing, camping, marine biology, outdoor survival techniques, self-reliance are among the subjects offered between May and September of each year. Ridgeway himself is perhaps better known for his single-handed sailing of a six-berth yacht, *English Rose IV*, direct

Scrabster, Caithness

Thurso, Caithness

John o'Groats, Caithness

Wick harbour, Caithness

from Eire to Brazil during the summer of 1968. The centre at Ardmore has a new dormitory building which contains good facilities. The students spend much of their time in the hills, where they are able to test themselves in situations which nature presents, often with little or no warning. The theme of the centre is to offer people from all walks of life an opportunity to throw off the artificial restraints, demands and worries which preoccupy them for most of their lives, and to give them the chance of measuring themselves against the sea, the sky and a landscape which, though beautiful, is primitive in its moods.

The township of Scourie, farther south, was once the centre for extensive loch fishings. It is one of the pleasant surprises to meet the eye after a surfeit of mountain ranges looming over one. A twisting road offers a fresh and tantalizing vista, with seascapes adding extra interest. Scourie is a compact crofting township with a hotel much favoured by anglers and ornithologists acting as a focal point. It lies in a wide but shallow seaside bowl. The crofts hereabouts produce mostly potatoes, hay and corn—all traditional crops. One of Scourie's major attractions is nearby Handa Island, which is a well-known bird sanctuary. It once supported a 'queen' and seven families living in glorious isolation. The island was evacuated after the potato famine in 1845. It stands on 400 feet-high sandstone cliffs and is as remarkable as the equally famous Stack of Handa. This rests on three pillars. Though it is separated from the parent island by a few yards, the drop between the two is 500 feet. The best time to visit Handa is in June or early July, for by the end of the latter month the bird population has begun to migrate. In 1962 the island was made a bird sanctuary under the Royal Society for the Protection of Birds, by agreement with the owner. During July and August part of Scourie school acts as a youth hostel, which is a great advantage to many, giving convenient access to the large areas between Scourie and Durness.

The car ferry at Kylesku is more than popular because, being operated and maintained by Sutherland County Council, it is free. The ferry crosses the meeting of three waters: Loch Cairnbawn, Loch Glendhu and Loch Glencoul. This is the area of the Reay Forest, once the hunting grounds of the chiefs of the Clan MacKay. In 1829 Lord Reay sold the land to George Leveson-Gower for £300,000. This man was to become the most hated person in the Highlands, for his responsibility for untold human suffering in the early years of the nineteenth century in the clearance of some 15,000 men, women and children to make way for sheep. This particular act was obviously ignored when, in 1833, the man was created Duke of Sutherland by King William IV. Thus were the captains and generals of industry rewarded in a society where the boot of the oppressor was respected and merited more attention than the cries of the oppressed. The process continues today in the Highlands, where leaders of industry and commerce hold almost feudal sway over their tenants.

South of Kylesku is the area known as Assynt, a name which occurs frequently in the clan history of the region, a history which rings more often than not with the clash of swords. North Assynt is dominated by the Quinag, a residue of Torridon sandstone resting on a firm base of gneiss. It has two main peaks—Sail Ghorm and Sail Garbh—with another five secondary rises, all of which are linked together by a ridge which offers an exciting and not too difficult walk.

The Assynt terrain is characterized by the poverty of both soils and vegetation. The greater part of the area is formed of Lewisian rocks, which include not only typical gneisses but also some schists; both are traversed from north-west to south-east by a multitude of igneous dykes which give grain to the country. The topography is extremely complex. The original dissection of a low plateau, sloping gently westwards, has been considerably modified by glaciation, so that there is now a fine confusion of hillocks rising to about 800 feet in the east, and declining to lower heights in the west. Loch Assynt is a major depression among the countless lochans carved out in the valleys. The feature of much of Assynt is that distance and accessibility is measured not in miles but in hours. The eastern part of the parish has its own special character. The oceanic influence is strong: high humidity, cloudiness and cool temperatures, which have contributed, in the past as at present, to the formation of peat on the slopes and blanket bog on the flat areas.

At one time the population of the area was considerable. John Home's eighteenth-century survey recorded 339 households with a total population of 1,718 persons. Of these, about 70 per cent lived in the coastal settlements, while the remainder resided inland, mainly in the great eastern valley. That there were many squatters who did not appear on the rent roll accounts for the much higher population figure given in the Old Statistical Account. This was to be exceeded, however, in 1861, when the census of that year returned a figure of 3,174. Such a pressure on the land contributed to the mass emigration and the development of the shieling system. This latter type of land use makes use of the out-pastures to be occupied by cattle and other stock during the summer months when pasture was available at this time of the year and at no other. It has been suggested recently that it is worthy of a close examination, particularly in Scotland, because rough pasturage constitutes a large proportion of the Scottish land area. If the time comes when we are required to win more food from our land, it would seem reasonable to suppose that those areas which once carried higher numbers of man and beast might be the first to do so again. Shielings occur wherever climate or topography cause a seasonal variation in the value or availability of pasture, so that man and his flocks and herds must move their base at least twice in the course of a year in order to win the maximum use from the land. The system occurs in Switzerland (where it is being developed and modernized), in the German-speaking Alps, in Norway and in North Africa.

The system was once used extensively in Assynt. The shielings can, even today, be recognized from a distance by the bright-green grassy splash they make against a background provided by the otherwise dun-coloured moorland. Often they are heavily infested with bracken. A recent survey in Assynt indicated no fewer than 246 shielings, echoing the many instances found in Assynt tradition of a land well used and able to support a significant population. At present, the crofts are too small to support a family at current standards. Those places which are sheep farms are sharing in the 'robber' economy which is slowly and steadily running down the vitality of the soils and vegetation in the Highlands. Far from attempting any improvement, most landlords' policies seem to be directed towards creating deer forests. This may be economical in terms of rent to the owner and rates to the county authority. But in terms of human occupation and national food and timber production, it can only be justified if we regard these as less important than deer-stalking. If Assynt were to be re-populated to the 2,000 mark, the farm of John Home's time would require to be single holdings worked on a co-operative basis, with rough pastures utilized to the full by every type of compatible stock, including red deer. And, to take some of the sting of isolation out of the lives of the families who would make up the small communities, it would be necessary to increase the incidence and range of social service amenities. This is just as economical as it is at present for local authorities to service communities with increasing numbers of 'summer-only' residents. What the land in Assynt was able to do some three centuries ago, it is able to do today.

On the western seaboard of north Assynt is Rhu Stoer and the Old Man of Stoer. This is a popular Mecca with tourists. The peninsula has sandy coves at Ardmelvish, Clashnessie and Clachtoll. Glencanisp, a walkers' paradise, is a hinterland of gneiss which has tracks which lead to either side of Suilven, by way of Glencanisp, and the River Kirkaig. Stoer Point is bleak. Cliffs rise to 300 feet on its eastern side, 200 feet to the west, and in the centre of a ring of foam stands the Old Man of Stoer. Two hundred feet high, it was for decades declared to be unclimbable; then Dr Tom Patey and Brian Robertson scaled the mass in 1966. At Culkein, a big open bay faces Oldany Islands, which offers bag-net salmon-fishing. Clashnessie Bay is favoured by lobster-fishermen, for the scores of small islands offer excellent breeding grounds. The principal village here is Drumbeg, which has a good fishing hotel surrounded by a dozen or so houses. It has a good potential for a sea-angling centre. Over fifty years ago the small coastal townships in north Assynt supported a substantial population. Stoer, for instance, had no less than ninety fishermen, mostly local, who were actively engaged in white- and shell-fishing.

The principal port of Assynt is Lochinver; it is the centre of an area of magnificent mountain scenery and a thriving fishing industry. The harbour is able to provide accommodation for large steamers, and indeed, the port was once a calling point for ships during the 'good old days' when vital communications for remote communities were regarded more as a social service than as an economic liability, as they are now—and particularly since the political economist has come into being to upset the delicate balancing acts which many communities had to maintain if they were to survive at all. At the turn of this century, the port was used for exporting cargoes of marble quarried at Drumbeg, but the venture did not last long before it was discontinued. Much tourist and freight traffic passed through Lochinver. Today, the port rivals Kinlochbervie farther north. But it is a friendly rivalry, for both are conscious of the fact that they are acting in concert as social sheet-anchors for the population which is growing around them.

Lochinver is built round the head of a sea loch which resembles a Norwegian fiord. The population of just under 400 has shared in the development of the port during a twenty-five-year period as a kind of 'entrepôt', offering landing and transportation facilities for fishing boats registered at east-coast ports. Involvement of the local fishermen and the stimulation of shore-based employment was modest before the establishment of the Highlands and Islands Development Board, and has remained so subsequently. Even so, the existence of the port is of vital social significance for the Assynt parish, which has witnessed a gradual decline in its population. Lochinver shared in this decline until after 1961, since when, with a slight dip in the middle of the decade 1961–71, there has been a steady increase. There are over 150 households in the port and its immediate environs, with four hotels. The number of local men engaged directly in the fishing trade is small, less than thirty men on nine local boats, with a further thirty or so engaged in fish-selling and the provision of ancillary services. The Lochinver fishing scene is dominated by 'stranger' boats, mainly from the east coast and the twenty or so boats from Stornoway which land catches regularly at Lochinver, favouring the mainland port for their own home-island facility. There tends to be a cosmopolitan community here, with a great deal of movement into and out of the area by persons who come to Lochinver for a job. The movements are to some extent accentuated by the central education system operated by the local authority, in which children of 12 years of age and over have to leave Lochinver to go to Golspie on the east coast of Sutherland to continue their education. There has been a new housing development of thirty-eight houses prepared by the local authority, but few of these have been taken up by men directly connected with fishing. There is little or no unemployment, since incomers arrive to take up a pre-arranged job vacancy, while local young men tend to move outside the area to look for work.

The tourist industry provides some employment, particularly for women. It is estimated that some 70 per cent of women aged between 15 and 64 are actively engaged in some tourist activity during the high season. Out of season, however, there exists a fair amount of slack which could be taken up by employment in such fields as fish-processing.

The rapidity with which Lochinver has developed is seen by comparing the 3,000 hundredweights landed in 1949, the 100,000 hundredweights in 1962, and, later, the 200,000 hundredweights landed in 1970. The fact that there is no fish-processing facility tends to reflect the already established link the port has, by through transport, with markets in the south and east. The Lochinver Fish Selling Company offers the basic 'husbanding' for boats of chandlery, ice, boxes and transport, all on an around-the-clock basis. As with Kinlochbervie, there have been attempts to offer facilities as an incentive to east-coast fishermen to reside in the area; there has been a small but significant success in this, in the leasing of some houses to young fishermen and their families originally from the east coast. The alternative to residence in Lochinver for these fishermen is a lifestyle which has been carried on for so long now that it has become second nature to the fishermen: putting to sea early on Monday mornings, making the last landing of the week on Thursday nights, and returning home to the east coast overland by minibus for the weekend. With the new and recently built pier extensions and a new services building, together with a net-repairing facility, there are prospects that Lochinver could stabilize its population to offer a permanent basis for real growth.

The landward area of Assynt is full of interest, not the least aspect being its archaeology. There are many flattened ruins of cairns hereabouts. Now but poor relics, they present little to the casual sightseer, but in fact have analogues in Spain and in Malta, sharing with these the same general plan: a round or polygonal chamber, sometimes preceded by an antechamber and entered by a definite passage. These cairns were burial chambers of an importance which can only now be assumed. Built by Neolithic colonists, these passage graves are the visible evidence of the prehistoric habitation of Assynt. Far less spectacular are the caves of Allt nan Uamh. These were excavated by the geologists Peach and Horne as long ago as 1917, but have since caught the imagination. Here were found the bones of the northern lynx, bear, arctic fox, reindeer, and two human skeletons attributed to the Azilian period, of around 6000 B.C. Though there are the inevitable arguments about the dates, the fact remains that Assynt proved to be of some attraction to human migrants and settlers many millennia ago. It does so today.

Loch Assynt is about 6 miles long. Each side of the loch presents a quite different vista. That to the west has a shore broken by wooded bays and capes, while the in-shore surface of the loch waters is interrupted by numerous tiny islands bearing old pines. The eastern side is bare and featureless, except for the gaunt ruins of Ardvreck Castle, which stands on a grassy point about a mile or so from Inchnadamph. The castle was built in 1597, to serve as the seat of MacLeod of Assynt. It was laid siege to by the MacKenzies, who reduced the structure to the state it appears in today. The guns used in the siege can still be seen. Assynt subsequently passed into the hands of MacKenzie of Seaforth until 1760 when it was bought by Lady Strathnaver who gave it as a present to her son, William, Earl of Sutherland. It was this grant of gift which caused the lands of Assynt to revert to the family of Sutherland who, centuries before, had given them to MacNicol of Ullapool from their authority as Thane of Sutherland. In 1913 the parish was bought by Major-General J. W. Stewart, a son of the parish who had made his fortune in Canada. The parish was again sold in 1937, when the main portion was bought by the present proprietor, Mr R. A. Vestey. The Sutherland family is not to be confused with the English family importation of Leveson-Gower, now styled as dukes of Sutherland, the first member of which was responsible for the Sutherland Clearances.

The limestone hill area at Inchnadamph, between Loch Assynt and Ben Mor Assynt, is, by agreement with the Assynt Estate, a National Nature Reserve of 3,200 acres. By strict control of burning and grazing, the herb-rich pastures and some unusual willow scrub are preserved. There is a great variety of wild flowers in the reserve, which is seen at its best during June. Changes in the vegetation are being watched in some fire-free enclosures, fenced off against sheep and deer. Permission is required to visit the reserve between July and October, and for parties of more than six persons at a time. The reserve includes the Traigill Burn, Allt nan Ugmh and the Stronchrubie cliffs.

The south of Assynt is known as the Inverpolly Reserve. Extending to nearly 27,000 acres, it is second only in size to the Cairngorms Reserve. The Nature Conservancy owns 36 acres; the remainder belongs to four estates whose managements co-operate in maintaining the present levels of wild life. The reserve includes the sandstone peaks of Cul Mor (2,786 feet), Cul Beag (2,523 feet), and Stac Polly (2,009 feet). Loch Sionascaig has an interesting group of birch-clad islets. The district of Coigach, in which the reserve is set, is the home of many wild animals, including wild cat, pine marten, fox, badger and otter, while an equally interesting range of birds is also to be seen. Many patches of relict natural woods are to be found. The main aim of the reserve management is to conserve the many different habitats represented and to acquire valuable knowledge by repeated surveys of the plants and animals of the reserve. The northern perimeter of the reserve touches Inverkirkaig, where, at the bridge of Kirkaig, one leaves Ross-shire to enter the county of Sutherland. The area here is a delightful tangle of small glens running in all directions between hollows, rocky outcrops, humpy hills, tarns and streams. The township of Inverkirkaig has a pleasant wooded bay and a beach. There is also an enterprising venture which combines handloom weaving and knitting with a craft shop where one meets probably the most comprehensive display of books for sale in the whole of the north of Scotland. The Falls of Kirkaig display a perpendicular fall of 60 feet.

Loch Broom is a long sea loch which reaches 21 miles into the heart of the Scottish mainland mass. It is the longest sea loch in the north-west Highlands and the parish which takes its name from it is the second largest in Scotland. Within its 400 square miles live about 1,200 people, about half of whom reside in and around Ullapool. The area offers three completely different kinds of scenery. There is low-lying ground towards the sea, a wild grey hillocky gneissian aspect at Gruinard and the north-west of Coigach. Overlooking this are the rises of red Torridon sandstone reaching a peak of 3,483 feet in An Teallach. Behind these, towards the eastern parts of Loch Broom, are more rounded peat-moor hills which spread themselves through the forests of Dundonnell, Inverlael and Rhidorroch. These are mountains of schist, called Moine Schist, after the Gaelic word meaning 'peat-moor'.

Gruinard lies on the southern shore of Little Loch Broom. It gives its name to the wide bay and its guardian island. The name is derived from the Norse *grunna fjord*, meaning a 'shallow ford'. This peculiar characteristic has made the bay a fertile area for fish and a feeding ground for great northern divers and long-tailed duck. Gruinard Island stands as a silent monument to man's spoliation of nature. Lying less than a mile off shore, it is contaminated and must not be approached by boat. The prohibition by the authorities on the use of the island's excellent pasture and fine beaches has been a bone of contention with local folk for about a quarter of a century. During the last war, the Microbiological Research Establishment of the Ministry of Defence used the island for experimentation in germ warfare. This use might well have been justified because the research was begun on the basis of a report that Germany was investigating the possibility of germicides as an offensive weapon. At Gruinard Island, anthrax was disseminated in aerosol form to determine whether it would cause infection of sheep and cattle. The answer was that it would indeed infect and a positive result was the development of an effective vaccination against anthrax for both man and beast. The experiments ended with the war, but the island remained infected and it is estimated that it will continue to be so for another century yet. Experts make an annual inspection of the island.

The western shore of Little Loch Broom is largely bare croftland, capable of sustaining several small crofting townships. A startling change, however, meets the eye at Strath Beg, which has a fine woodland with a great deal of natural growth of birch, rowan, hazel, oak and alder. This is one of the sharp contrasts between private estates and the areas of land owned by the Forestry Commission, whose planting activity tends to be dominated by the thought of profit. Trees such as beech, sycamore, chestnut and oak are hardly profitable, but they have many advantages in the cover they offer to wild life, plants, animals and birds, and tend to fertilize land in a way that fir trees cannot match. One has only to walk through a commission forest to realize the dead silence indicating a paucity of wild life on the ground, in the ground and in the trees.

The history of Ullapool was effectively established some 400 years ago when the Scottish Parliament of 1587 passed an Act which was intended to penalize the heavy fishing activities prosecuted by the Dutch in Loch Broom. Since then, the fertile waters have been more than attractive to exploiters, though the fishing industry as such was not able to develop until private enterprise had engaged experts to report on prospects. The result was the establishment of fishing stations at various suitable places on the west coast. Herring fishing in particular boomed towards the end of the eighteenth century and caused the erection of curing stations at Isle Martin (in Ardmair Bay) and Tanera (the foundations of these stations can still be seen). Success brought the attention of the commercial giants of the day who formed the British Fishery Society. In 1788 the society began to build their most expensive station at a cost of some £10,000, erecting public works such as a pier, an inn and storehouses, together with private dwellings, many of which are occupied today. Ullapool was a good choice for a station, for Loch Broom had established itself as a fertile herring ground. Local boats went far into the outer loch to lay their nets and reap rich harvests. The Statistical Account reads: "People are instantly afloat with every species of seaworthy craft . . . they press forward with utmost eagerness to the field of slaughter—sloops, schooners, wherries, boats of all sizes, are to be seen constantly flying on the wings of the wind from creek to creek, and from loch to loch, according as the varying reports of men, or the noisy flights of birds, or tumbling and spouting of whales and porpoises attract them." The herring boom on Loch Broom lasted half a century, during which time heavy catches of herring were obtained for export to Ireland and the West Indies. Needless to say, the rewards were immense. But the lack of any thought of conservation proved disastrous. By 1830 the shoals of herring were growing markedly less and by 1880 they had quite vanished from the waters round the Loch Broom–Gruinard coast. Ullapool fell on evil times and lapsed into a backwater, from which, happily, it has been revived to become once more a port of significance to the north-west communities, and the island of Lewis in particular.

The town today has a population of about 6,000. It is sited on a late Ice Age beach some 50 feet above sea level. It is well planned, with open streets and good-looking buildings which give it an air of well-being. The tourist industry is catered for by several good hotels, some forty boarding houses and a caravan site. These create a centre for the resident tourist who wishes to indulge in sea-fishing, pony-trekking and fresh-water fishing. Motor boats offer daily cruises to the Summer Isles or into Gruinard Bay. The herring, however, still offers Ullapool its principal *raison-d'être* and economic mainstay. The growth of motor transport since the Second World War has enabled the port to hold its own against the growth of other ports on the west coast. The herring fleet afloat is matched by the road fleet ashore, which takes the catch direct by road to the Aberdeenshire coast for canning and kippering.

The outcrops of limestone found just north of Ullapool have offered a welcome employment extra. In 1973 the port became the eastern terminus of the Stornoway–Ullapool Minch crossing, which will undoubtedly increase the importance of Ullapool to the Loch Broom area. Of particular interest is the development of sea-angling as a sport. Ullapool first hit the headlines in the angling press because of consistent reports of exceptional quality and quantity of fish landed at the port. These attracted keen anglers and within a few years Ullapool took on the aura of a piscatorial Mecca. Several international sea-angling festivals of importance have been held. Four kinds of fishing are obtainable: by rod from the shore rocks for cod, saithe and mackerel; by boat from Inner Loch Broom for bigger fish of the same variety, and for skate, haddock and whiting; by motor-launch in Outer Loch Broom for the plentiful and large fish to be caught off the Summer Isles, in Gruinard Bay and Little Loch Broom; and then there is the 'big-time' sport fishing for shark, conger eel, tope and huss.

The Summer Isles lie off Achiltibuie, a crofting township which takes all of 3 miles to spread itself along the coast, and does so in two distinct parts: the north portion, which locates the pier, church, hotel, and shops, with some large houses; and the southern portion which contains the crofts which run in a long line with their lands, strips of hay and corn, running seaward over flat ground. The biggest island in the Summer Isles group is Tanera, where a fishing station was established in the eighteenth century. The island extends to just over 80 acres. Old prints show a thriving population on it and many large sailing vessels lying at rest in the shelter of The Anchorage. The island always supported a large population; in 1901 it was seventy-one. The last resident left Tanera in 1946. Horse Island is interesting for the herd of island goats bred there over the past century. All other islands in the group support a rich variety of wild life. Twenty-nine breeding species of birds use Priest Island, the farthest outlier of the island group.

Lying in the eye of Ardmair Bay is Isle Martin, covering some 400 acres. Under the British Fishery Society an extensive curing station was constructed here, the ruins of which can be seen today. In 1901 the island supported a population of thirty-three persons. Before the last war a flour mill was started up but closed shortly after the end of the war, this event coinciding with the desertion of the island by its residual human population. The islands of Loch Broom supported many illicit stills until Customs officials found it too easy to locate the activities of the smugglers. The relics of these stills can be traced today after a century or so of disuse. Almost all the islands lying off this part of the western coast act as grazings for sheep, thus playing a small but important part in the overall economy of the parish and its inhabitants.

In the north, overlooking the Pentland Firth, Durness is essentially a crofting community which has a strong tourist appeal. It is the most north-westerly turning point and halting place for those who travel that circuit of the Scottish Highlands. There are rich limestone deposits in the area, first noted by Sir John Sinclair in his notes for the First Statistical Account for Scotland. To the west of the village lies the enchanting Kyle of Durness and Balnakiel Bay, overlooked by the House of Balnakiel, belonging to the Lords of Reay, and the ruins of the old church of Durness. The latter was erected in 1619 to take the place of an earlier structure. The site has connections which go back to the early times of the old Celtic Church. The old font in the ruins is one of the few genuine pre-Reformation relics in Sutherland. In the churchyard is the monument to the Gaelic bard, Rob Donn Calder or MacKay (1714–78) who, though unlettered, produced excellent poetry which is reckoned to be in the mainstream of the Gaelic literary tradition. Durness is becoming known for an unusual experiment initiated by the county council: the craft village. This was formerly an Air Ministry station extending to about 13 acres and including swenty buildings, each provided with water, drainage and electricity. Some twenty-nine artists and craftsmen have taken up the challenge to create a unique attraction for tourists—not only to see the creative processes in action but to purchase a wide range of items in pottery, weaving, knitwear, silk-screen printing, photography, wood-turning and painting. The venture is one of many to be found in the Highland region which proves that a combination of imagination, facilities of the right kind and encouragement will provide the base necessary for stabilizing population.

The Durness peninsula is bounded on the eastern side by Loch Eriboll, which has provided safe anchorages for convoys of war from the times of Haakon of Norway to those which assembled for safety in numbers against German U-boats before they ventured across the Atlantic. This loch extends deep into the northern coast of Sutherland and affords the only extensive safe anchorage hereabouts. It is a quiet loch, yet is surrounded by stern and forbidding scenery. Its claim to attention at the present time is based on the amount of research and investigation which its surrounding area has prompted, concerned with large deposits of minerals. If plans and ambitions come to fruition, the present tiny crofting township of Eriboll could be transformed into an industrial city with satellite towns located in connected straths in the Loch Eriboll hinterland.

The scheme for Kinloch-Eriboll was first drafted by John L. Kinloch, a Scots visionary who, as far back as 1903, was proposing hydro-electric schemes for the Highlands. Kinloch died in 1968 and his theories were taken up by another stalwart Scot whose fresh ideas, if planners and developers would only heed them, could transform many weak communities into strong growth points for social regeneration: Alex D. Craig. Craig's scheme is for creating in Loch Eriboll a deep-water facility for tankers of half a million tons, backed by the known mineral deposits and the availability of these for growth and expansion. This dream, if it can be called such, is more than one for yet another industrial estate. It is for "something new in planning in Britain . . . Kinloch-Eriboll would be the creation of an entirely new community and not mere overspill. It is not a distribution of industry alone that is required, it is also a distribution of population. We have to find work and room to live for 15 million people in the United Kingdom by the year 2000."

The whole scheme is of such a proportion that it would be unfair to dismiss it in a few words. Loch Eriboll is the very last deep-water site in the British Isles, and is on the sea route from the south Atlantic to northern and western Europe. It is thus an excellent trans-shipment point, if nothing else, at which crude oil, for instance, could be pumped from mammoth tankers to others small enough to negotiate the shallower depths, in much the same way as Gulf Oil are doing at Bantry Bay in Eire. The feasibility of an oil refinery stems from this harbouring proposal; although no oil refinery is viable in isolation, its profitability could be made to rise steeply if, as an industrial operation, it can be conveniently associated with others which make some use of the by-products. Grangemouth, on the Firth of Forth, is an object lesson here. From that refinery has grown a petro-chemical industry of amazing complexity. Loch Eriboll offers other possibilities, one of which is based on the existence of millions of tons of potash in the rocks extending from Ullapool to Eriboll. Other minerals include alumina, potassium, magnesium and silica. The potash is buried in the Adularia rocks in the Eriboll area. The potential of the whole area has not escaped the attention of exploiters. In 1971 an announcement was made concerning the setting up of a £500,000-plus mineral industry at Durness. The interest of this concern is in the feldspar deposits, reckoned to be the largest as yet undeveloped in Europe. At the time of writing, investigation is proceeding into obtaining the most economical methods of processing before setting up pilot and, subsequently, main production plants. The mineral will be processed at Durness and transported in bulk by ship from Loch Eriboll, making use of the loch's deep-water facilities. Initially, some forty key jobs will be created, with a number of secondary job opportunities as the project develops. Drillings have shown that the Durness reserves are well in excess of 2 million tons of recoverable feldspar of a quality acceptable to the glass and ceramics industries.

Of course, the question will be raised regarding the sociological effects. The Durness area is a truly Gaelic-speaking area and the rhythms and life-styles of the communities are on a profile which displays no peaks of sufficient height to indicate that they could ride out the impact on them of imposed conditions and new economic bases, together with alien, though not necessarily unsympathetic, cultures and values. Developments should thus take place gently, cognisant of the fact that to do otherwise would eventually justify the charge of cultural genocide against them.

The vast brooding waters of Lochs Loyal and Naver, and the imperious beauty of Ben Loyal, lead north to the majestic sweep of the Kyle of Tongue. Tongue differs from many other communities in the north and west in that it is green and well-wooded. Castle Varrich, an ancient peel of the MacKays, stands on a promontory west of the township. Excellent fishing, sea-bathing and boating have made the area an attraction for the insatiable tourist. The Kyle of Tongue, a long sea-finger stretching some miles inland, was breached in 1971 by a boon in the form of a combined bridge and causeway. The crossing, just over 2 miles long, replaces the original 11-feet-wide road, with passing places which detoured some 10 miles round the head of the Kyle. The new crossing is part of a long-term plan to improve the north coast road and will more than relieve the congestion which increases each year as more and more people find their way to the north of Scotland. As with most of the improved road facilities in the region in recent years, it is the tourists' requirements which receive primary consideration, with the long-standing needs of isolated communities taking a low priority. Thus, if for nothing else, the ubiquitous tourist is serving many remote communities by his desire to obtain solace and scenery. One of the difficulties which the Tongue causeway builders had to contend with was the tidal current, which was in excess of 6 knots at spring tides. The Kyle of Tongue crossing was constructed for Sutherland County Council under the Crofter Counties Road Scheme at a total cost of just over £500,000.

About a half-hour run on the road eastwards from Tongue brings one to the coast of Strath Naver, a name which even now opens up a floodgate of old Highland memories. The strath was the scene of some of the most atrocious exercises in the history of the Highland Clearances. The strath stretches some 20 miles southward along the sweeping River Naver to Loch Naver at Altnaharra. It is a gentle valley of no little charm, with a captivating atmosphere which must have made the clearance surgery more poignant and heart-breaking. Fertile fields border the river and snug crofts and farm buildings at present total only a fraction of what the strath was well able to sustain over a century ago. The strath was known to men as a pleasant place, providing most of the conditions necessary for satisfactory living over two millennia ago, for there are visible today the earthworks of prehistoric men and the ruins of Iron Age brochs. There is a megalithic tomb at Skail. Strathnaver has more Neolithic relics and Iron Age brochs than any other valley around the north coast.

The Clearances have been justly called the "rape of the Highlands". During the period beginning *c.* 1780 (though the process was in effect before this, and many would say that it continues today) many thousands of Highland folk were driven away from their homes to seek solace in death; families were split up, many never to have the opportunity to reunite again; murder and rapine were common, all carried out on instructions from agents of the Duke of Sutherland, formerly an Englishman with the name of George Leveson-Gower. It might be said that a number of Highland-born chiefs were also guilty of ill-treating their clansmen; but the Duke's minions seemed to have used perfected techniques of persuasion. The history of the Clearances has been written up many times, and one would recommend John Prebble's *The Highland Clearances* (Secker and Warburg, London, 1963) for an unusually full, dispassionate and wide-ranging assessment of the period. The Duke's main henchman was Patrick Sellar, given the title of 'factor' to add authority to his deeds. It took no great measure of intelligence to realize that Strathnaver in particular was ideally suited for sheep. This was a Celtic country; few of its inhabitants understood any language save Gaelic. Thus, they were fair game for the murderous bands of thugs whom Sellar used to empty the lands of Strathnaver and elsewhere on the Duke's estates. In 1818 Sellar went on trial, charged with culpable homicide, and with "wickedly and maliciously setting on fire and burning". Sellar had personally supervised many of the atrocities perpetuated by the clearing gangs. He was tried by a jury of fifteen men, eight of whom were landed proprietors, and it was a foregone conclusion, in a society which always protected its own—much as it does today—that Sellar would be acquitted, which he was. It has been argued many times that the Clearances were economically justified. But recent research has revealed that over a century of grazing by sheep has brought the general level of fertility in the Highlands to a dangerously low level from which it is unlikely ever to recover unless drastic action is taken. In common with other parts of the Highlands and Islands, Sutherland has a serious imbalance in the cattle/sheep ratio. In Sutherland there are just over 5,000 head of cattle, and the 1:20 cattle/sheep ratio presents a disturbing imbalance which is due more to the system of land tenure than to any other single factor. There are over 100,000 sheep constantly 'on the hoof' in the county. One needs only to read the old accounts of Highland exports to realize that the desire to make money (land was worth 2d. per acre before the Clearances with people on it, and then 24d. under sheep) has destroyed much of the foundation of a unique culture and ethnic grouping which was identified as being both Celtic and Gaelic—racial factors which made the victims of the Clearances objects of an intense hatred such as the gipsies and the Jews were to experience under the Nazis and other groups in the Western World. All ethnic groups which differ in outlook, lifestyles, culture and language have had to bear the 'colonizing' pressures of master races; and the Gaels were, and indeed are today, in no way different from the Red Indians, the Jews, the Eskimoes and the vanishing tribes of the Amazon River, all of whom face the prospect of extinction by processes of assimilation before another century is out. It is indicative of how effectively the process of oppression has instilled in the average Highlander of the present day a sense of inferiority and blind acceptance when one notes that in 1971 Lord Lovat, a Highland landowner, built a gate across a public road and locked it—all without a single protest of significance whatsoever.

In a speech delivered at Inverness on 18th September 1885, Mr Joseph Chamberlain, ten years before he became Colonial Secretary, said:

> The history of the Highland Clearances is a black page in the account with private ownership in land, and if it were to form a precedent, if there could be any precedent for wrong-doing, if the sins of the fathers ought to be visited upon the children, we should have an excuse for more drastic legislation than any which the wildest reformer has ever proposed. Thousands of hard-working, industrious, God-fearing people were driven from the lands which had belonged to their ancestors, and which for generations they had cultivated; their houses were unroofed and burnt down and they were turned out homeless and forlorn, exposed to the inclemency of the winter season, left to perish on the hillsides or to swell the full flood of misery and destitution in places overseas to which they were driven for refuge. They suffered unbearably; very many died. However, as time went on the descendants of those who did survive have contributed in no mean degree to the prosperity of the countries in which they finally settled. The Highland countryside was depopulated by those clearances. The general condition of the people left behind suffered and it has gone on deteriorating until it has become at last a matter of national concern. If I am correct in the statement in which I have endeavoured to summarise what I have read and learned upon this subject, I ask you whether it is not time that we should submit to careful examination and

review a system which places such vast powers for evil in the hands of irresponsible individuals and which makes the possession of land not a trust but a means of extortion and exaction?...

In the following year the Crofters Act was passed offering the crofter security of tenure, a closing of the stable door after the worst had been done to vitiate the whole of the Highland population, with its distinct culture. Driving through these deserted glens of memory, tourists rarely realize that the very solitude they enjoy, the chance to breathe in good wholesome fresh air, their pleasure at being able to lunch al fresco with little or no interruption, is due to a page in Highland history which is still being written as small unnoticed clearances take place today by a process of legislation which brings little publicity to the superiors of the lands, who exercise their feudal rights to keep land empty and therefore useless. In 1970 it was revealed that the Government, as represented by the civil service at St Andrew's House in Edinburgh, had produced a plan for the Highlands and Islands which was based on the principle that a modern-day version of the Clearances would be the economic answer to the Highland problem; remote areas in the region would be evacuated. The existence of the plan was vigorously denied, though the person who divulged the information himself took part in the discussions. It is quite a thought that those in authority are so free to produce plans for the electorate who remain in ignorance of them until the very last moment, when it is too late to make proper and effective objection.

Near the mouth of the River Naver lies the Invernaver Nature Reserve. The importance of this reserve lies in the fact that within a small compass it contains not only a wide variety of habitats, including those on the blown sand, but also a fine assemblage of northern plant communities in the north of Scotland. The mingling of species of montane and oceanic affinities is an added attraction. Tongue House, now a seat of the Duke of Sutherland, was built in 1678 by Lord Reay, head of the Clan MacKay. The township here is unusual in that it supports a first-class bakery and does not depend wholly on imported baked products as so many communities do. To the east of the Kyle of Tongue is the beautifully constructed, but little used, Scullomy harbour. Standing sentinel to the mouth of the Kyle is Eilean Ron, an island much visited by seals for breeding purposes. The island was evacuated of its human population only in recent years.

At the head of Strath Naver is Bettyhill, a township named after a countess of Sutherland. In common with many other coastal townships, Bettyhill owes its existence to the Clearances of the last century. In the churchyard at the west is the Farr Stone, standing about 7 feet high and representing one of the finest extant examples of Celtic art. The long shaft of the cross has the characteristic 'armpits' and is enclosed with a 'glory' or halo. The central boss displays a triple escaping spiral.

Similar spirals appear on the inner parts of the arms and crosshead, while the extremities bear panels of key pattern. The shaft is carved with interlaced work, as is the tumulus or arched base of the cross. Within the interlacing is carved a couple of birds with their necks intertwined, so that each seems to be pecking the other's back. The whole surface of the slab is highly ornamented, while the edges and back seem to be left plain. Dating from about the ninth century A.D., the cross stands witness to the existence of the old Celtic Church, serving the community in Strathnaver. The fact that the cross has weathered so well is due to it being carved not from freestone but in the hard and unyielding Highland schist.

The township of Lairg (population 318) has been described as the Rome of Sutherland. No fewer than six roads lead into it; it thus acts as a through-point of social and economic significance. Though small in extent, Lairg is the marketing centre for a quarter of a million sheep. The August Sales amount to a national agricultural event, attracting buyers from as far away as the north of England. The township lies at the end of the 21-mile long Loch Shin, now harnessed for hydro-electric power. Its importance as a centre in the county is reflected in the number of first-rate shops. Important to the economy of the area around Lairg is a transport firm which saw its foundations in the days of the horse-drawn cart, supplying transport facilities for estate afforestation programmes. Today, the firm has diversified into television, radio and camping equipment; but their main interest is still the large fleet of buses which plays such an essential role in maintaining contacts and communications between communities in the county. The buses carry the Royal Mails under contract. As with other townships in the north-west, there is an enthusiastic progress in development for tourists. The tourist trade is in fact the county of Sutherland's biggest single revenue-earner. It is estimated that a figure approaching £4 million represents the amount spent by visitors to the county each year. This figure reflects the obvious attraction which the area has for the tourist: unsurpassed scenery, and wide open spaces, coupled with the possibility of obtaining a stretch of coastal sand which one rarely needs to share with others seeking similar goals. Many of the locals offer bed and breakfast, or have converted their homes into guest-houses for more permanent residents. Caravan sites have been developed at a fast rate, there being more than ten in operation at present, most of which provide facilities ranging from basic essentials to showers, laundrettes, restaurants and television rooms. The tourist development has, however, created something of a problem for landowners, some of whom own vast acreages of moor and hill. In much the same way as the original proprietors of Sutherland cleared the area of people to populate it with sheep, so now the industrial population of Britain is swarming over these same estates. The landowners have been forced

(*top*) Dunnet Bay, Caithness. (*bottom*) Berriedale, Caithness

Caithness flagstones

Lybster, Caithness

into accepting that ownership of land does not imply the right to completely exclude those who wish to enjoy what raw nature offers. Most estates have now accepted the inevitable: the need for easier access to the countryside, while advocating regulation and supervision.

At the head of Loch Shin, in the Shiness valley, the Duke of Sutherland, in 1870, tried the experiment of steam ploughing on a grand scale. This attempt to encourage arable farming ended with the agricultural depression of 1878, but it was an interesting start. Already the realization had dawned that not so many sheep as before could be run on the same land. As one writer noted in 1877: "Considerable portions of the grazings are becoming foggy and rough and of little value as sheep pasture. We could point to one or two hirsels which carried stocks of from 1,000 to 1,100 over winters some twenty years ago and which will now scarcely winter 800. The cause of this, we believe, is the covering of the land for so long a period exclusively by sheep, without any cattle being allowed on it...."

Not so well known, perhaps, is the suggestion promoted in 1798: "The greatest improvement of which this part of the kingdom is capable (and indeed it is a national concern) is that of making an inland navigation through this parish from the E. to the W. sea. It is but five computed miles (or about 7½ English) from the end of Loch Shin to a navigable arm of the Western Ocean.... It would soon be the means of establishing fisheries, manufactures, commerce and industry all over the neighbourhood. Perhaps it might also prevent the dangerous and circuitous navigation through the Pentland Firth."

South of Lairg lies Strath Oykell, along the southern bank of the River Oykell which forms a boundary between Ross-shire and Sutherland. Just over 100 people live here, many on the southern side of the river along a dead-end road, for the main east–west route from Invershin to Assynt takes traffic over a good road on the northern side of the river. The cul-de-sac situation has resulted in a decade of agitation for a bridge to link both sides of the river to enable the three main communities in the strath to participate in the sidestream of the tourist traffic which virtually passes by their door on the other side. The idea of a bridge, however, has met with some local opposition based on the fact that a new road would be required to replace the old Arday–Doune road, and that the tourist is in any case a doubtful factor in the economy of any community.

3

The Eastern Highlands

FOR the most part, the eastern Highlands of Scotland—taken for the purposes of this book as ranging from Caithness south to Inverness and the western shores of the Moray Firth—comprise an area which is as different as chalk is from cheese from much of the 'highlands' as described in other chapters. Apart from an intrusion of hard rock into the North Sea coastline, all the area lies in a sea-washed strip of Old Red Sandstone. The real meaning of this occurrence of sandstone outcrops is evidenced in the fertility of the area, which is in total and sharp contrast with, for instance, the western coastal areas of the Highlands. The contrast is also seen in the straight smooth cliff and sand-dune coast facing the North Sea and Moray Firth, compared with the deeply-indented mountainous west with its numerous sea lochs and a sea filled with something in excess of 5,000 islands, varying from pin-points of rock to habitable areas. The geology of Caithness is rendered somewhat simple by the fact that the surface of the county is largely made up of two rock formations: the upland parts, which consist of stratified schists common over much of the Highlands and Cambrian quartzites; and the low-land country composed of Old Red Sandstone. Overlying the metamorphic schists is sandy glacial drift, covered with peat and moorland supporting heather, sedge and coarse grass. Overlying these primeval strata are a series of conglomerates, flagstones and sandstones. Fossil remains, chiefly freshwater fishes, show that the Old Red was formed by deposits in a freshwater lake. The thickness of the Old Red deposits in Caithness has been estimated at more than 18,000 feet. The flagstones of Thurso represent a middle-aged stone. The soil derived from the erosion of the flagstones and sandstones became the subsoil of lowland Caithness. The fish beds in both these stones yield an abundant and characteristic fauna, which is an attraction of particular interest to those who, armed with simple tools and a good guide-book, can literally pick out from the rock the mementoes of a very ancient past.

Perhaps one might be forgiven for highlighting yet another contrast between this area of the Highlands and the west: that is the significant socio-economic development activity which has occurred in recent years, chiefly because the eastern area has been particularly amenable to development of a kind which could offer quick results and so increase the credibility of the whole of the Highlands region in the eyes of potential industrial and commercial entrepreneurs. The present intense activity in Easter Ross underlines this feature, which, while acceptable from the point of view of population stability and a shifting to a more northerly location the centre of Scottish industrial gravity, raises questions of a possible imbalance between east and west, with all systems going for the area which yields maximum development results from a minimum investment, and that at the expense of the more difficult area. The accessibility factor of the eastern coastal areas and their towns has, in the context of the discovery of fields of oil and gas in the North Sea, thrown the area into a blinding light in which decisions have had to be made all too quickly to accommodate the rapacious demands of the oil exploiters who bring spoliation in their wake and who have 'conservation' marked down as a dirty word.

Caithness has a total area of nearly 700 square miles and supports a population of some 28,000 people, more than half of whom live in the county's two main towns, Thurso and Wick. The 1971 census returns for the period 1961–71 showed a rise in the total population of 1·5 per cent, with a fall of over 7 per cent in the total population of the landward areas, indicating a slow but inevitable migration of people to these growing urban centres, and also a drain to places outside the county. Thurso is the larger of the two burghs, with a population of almost 10,000 compared with Wick's 8,000. Both maintain a healthy respect for their past and have not allowed their planning facilities to rip the hearts out of the towns, as has happened elsewhere.

About a quarter of the Caithness land area is under cultivation, mostly around the coastal strip. The scene is comparatively treeless, a condition resulting from its exposure to the winds blowing across the flat terrain from both the Atlantic and the North Sea. The Forestry Commission has taken an interest in a limited part of the county, but climatic conditions are on the whole unfavourable to wide-scale exploitation of the possibilities of growing commercial timber. Communications include a good main arterial road south to Inverness. Internal roads tend to be narrow but well surfaced. Air travel is considered commonplace; there is daily contact to the main Scottish centres and par time to London is three and a half hours. The rail link, while it is of great importance, is at the same time a disadvantage when one considers that the route by road to Inverness is 127 miles, compared with 161 by rail and 73 by air. The county's main traditional industries are agriculture and fishing. These are now beginning to find their own levels after a long period of setbacks, and are now relevant to what the area can support. Tourism is still wide open to expansion but will eventually assume a role of significance in the economic structure. The highlight in the industrial picture is Dounreay, a one-off injection which has undoubtedly added to the general well-being of the county and nearby Thurso in particular, which before Dounreay had a population of under 4,000. There is an increasing industrial diversification in Caithness, which augurs well for the future should some of the mainstays, such as Dounreay, be withdrawn eventually on the grounds that they have fulfilled their original functions.

In early times Thurso was an important seaport and, indeed, was the chief such in the north of Scotland, linking for many centuries Norway, Denmark and the Low Countries. When the Continental trade declined, Thurso developed an export trade in grain and other local products, to the south of Scotland and to the Hebrides. In 1633 it had been made a Burgh of Barony by Sinclair of Ulbster. For nearly two centuries thereafter it was to all intents and purposes the county town, although Wick had been created a Royal Burgh in 1589 and had been made head burgh of Caithness in 1641. Thurso has ever been a market town and as such attracted an air of prosperity. From about 1881, however, the population began to decline steadily until the arrival of Dounreay, on which the town's present and future now depend. Dounreay is a research establishment of the Atomic Energy Research Authority; its arrival in the Thurso environs in 1954 was more than significant and made Thurso something of a phenomenon.

The burgh has, however, attracted attention, both on account of its strategic position for trade and as a growth point for development. The new note struck by Sir John Sinclair of Ulbster, the indefatigable genius who was the M.P. for Caithness from 1780 to 1811, has been maintained ever since. Sir John's finely planned new town of the eighteenth and nineteenth centuries is seen today in the broad, evenly-spaced streets and pleasant squares, carefully matched by subsequent developers. The commercial history of Thurso covers some few centuries, including the original grain trade aimed at Scandinavia and the Baltic countries. It was the importance of this trade which drew the attention of David II of Scotland, who marked it by making the

Caithness 'pound' weight the standard for all Scotland. In the seventeenth and eighteenth centuries it enjoyed a considerable export trade, mainly in meal, beef, hides and fish. The town's Rotterdam Street is a reminder of the thriving traffic of former times. In 1824 the flagstone industry was established by James Traill of Rattar and Castlehill, and as the venture flourished cutting and polishing yards sprang up on both banks at the mouth of the River Thurso. During the subsequent century or so cargoes of paving stones left Thurso regularly for ports throughout Britain and the Continent, and some went as far as Melbourne, Australia. The industry then fell into decline and today the last of the paving is disappearing even from Thurso's streets. The sheltering flagstone fences which are such a pleasant and unusual feature of the Caithness fields, are also going at such a rate that a Flagstone Preservation Society was formed in 1972 to preserve what remains are left of the functional uses of flagstones in the county, stones which are in fact a unique product of the locality.

The presence of Dounreay gave Thurso many advantages. Its population mushroomed; social facilities developed and employment opportunities appeared on the local scene almost overnight. There was a boom period of high wages being freely spent by the construction force employed in building the research laboratories and the power station, and the new housing facilities. More than half the employment at Dounreay is made up from natives of Caithness; the Atomic Energy Authority is, in fact, the biggest and best-paying employer in the area. Inevitably the presence of Dounreay changed many aspects of Thurso. From being a market town of some significance, which to some extent it still is, Thurso became the residential facility of the atomic establishment. The investment of some £40 million produced a 'boom-town' character which is nowadays on a low key. The fact that the station required technically-qualified personnel (about 250) introduced a whole new stratum of population never experienced before into a corner of the north-east Highlands. Some 2,000 new houses have been built in the past two decades of Dounreay's existence, half by the local authority and the remainder by the U.K.A.E.A. Almost certainly as a result of Dounreay, Thurso found its previously 'comprehensive' educational facilities stratified into distinct, primary and secondary education layers, with the building of Thurso Technical College adding a tertiary education facility where there was none before. The roll of the college is at present about 1,100 students receiving education and instruction at levels from craft-oriented courses to Higher National and Diploma Certificates. About half a dozen students each year are 'exported' to universities in Scotland.

The influx of an 'alien' population into the Thurso area raised many misgivings at first, but the ensuing years have indicated that instead of ghetto aspects appearing in the societal structure of the area, the 'atomics' have interested themselves in the affairs of the community and are today found serving on local authority committees, to have taken up part-time crofting and established interesting craft and other small industrial activities. The new fast-breeder reactor, built at a cost of some £30 million, has recently given a fresh lease of life to the community, adding a note of confidence, particularly after a scare report in the national newspapers in 1972 that Dounreay was to be closed by 1975. The report brought an out-and-out denial from the Minister for Industry and an assurance that Dounreay would continue in existence "for many years". One of the bases of the 'false' report was founded in the fact that Dounreay and its reactor is a sodium-cooled type which is susceptible to radio-activity over a period and this raises doubts as to its degree of safety. It was suggested that the reactor was sited in Caithness in the first place because of its being potentially dangerous and that it was better to site such a doubtful facility in a thinly-populated area than close to densely-populated areas. The other 'spectre' which is raised in the Dounreay context is the problem of handling radio-active waste from the fast-reactor power station. At present, as indicated in an H.M.S.O. report issued in 1972, strontium-90 is stored as a liquid in stainless-steel tanks at Windscale in Cumberland. These have to be continually cooled with water, since the heat given off by the radiation would otherwise raise the temperature to above boiling point. These tanks will have to undergo a process of continuous cooling for many years, even if no more nuclear reactors are built. The contemporary switch to fast-breeder reactors will aggravate the present situation even further, for they produce large quantities of radio-active substances which remain dangerous for many thousands of years.

Recognizing that all one's egg production is not safe if placed in one basket, there has been an attempt to diversify the economic structure of the Thurso locality. This now includes industries designed to meet the needs of the farming interests in the environs, and to a lesser extent the fishing community. There have been ups and downs. A fish-processing plant was set up in September 1971 and was closed early in 1973. When the factory was opened there was a glut of fish and some catches were being dumped at sea because they could not be sold. Since then, landings in nearby Scrabster and other ports have diminished, and by 1973 the factory was unable to obtain sufficient quantities of fish at an economic price for processing. There was a loss of fifty well-paid jobs, mainly for women. During the summer of 1972 the factory workers downed tools and walked a mile to the harbour to lobby fishermen and buyers in an effort to win support for the continuance of the factory. The closure was put down to the lack of co-operation from the majority of the fishermen. To stay in production, the factory needed an average of 35 stones of fish from each boat in the local fleet, a small proportion of the total catch. A glove-making enterprise in

Thurso produces 10,000 pairs of gloves each week; and other activities, such as an egg-grading station, a foundry and a precast-concrete works, provide variety in the industrial scene.

Typical of the small enterprises which exist in Thurso is Caithness Books, started by John Humphries, an 'atomic', who has, over a period of a decade or so, created a publishing entity which, originally producing books on Caithness, now ranges over a wide spectrum of Scottish literary interest and has helped to justify the existence and role of the 'small press' in Scotland. His example, watched closely by others for a number of years, has undoubtedly been the incentive for the other small presses and publishing interests which have appeared in Scotland in the last three years or so. Mr Humphries' perseverance and determination to contribute something significant to his adopted community has given hope to those who object to the importation into the Highlands from other parts of the British Isles of population with different values and life-styles.

Close by Thurso and nestling in the west corner of Thurso Bay is Scrabster, a sheltered port which has a long and interesting history of sea communications, linking in particular the northern isles of Orkney. In both the major wars of this century the port had a strategic importance, based on its geographical position serving both eastern and western approaches. In 1957 a large oil depot was built on the site of the old Jubilee Dock, at a cost of £250,000 and with a storage capacity of more than a million and a half gallons, to serve the needs of Dounreay and the surrounding area.

Scotland's first-ever ferro-concrete fishing boat was built at Scrabster and launched early in 1973. Though the use of ferro-concrete instead of timber for fishing craft is novel, the small industrial concern, sparked off by an expert in ferro-concrete work and supported by a staff of six, has bright hopes for the future. One of the strong selling points of the product is the long life of the hull with low maintenance costs because it is virtually immune from rot and there is no corrosion. After a term of fifteen years in the water, when most wooden hulls are badly in need of repair and attention, the ferro-concrete version is claimed to look much the same as when it was built. The Highlands and Islands Development Board have encouraged this venture, mainly because it has export potential and because the method of manufacture makes use of semi-skilled labour, which is not the case with the building of traditional timber hulls. Staff can be trained in a few months compared with the traditional five-year period required to produce skilled joiners and shipwrights.

Mail steamers sail regularly from Orkney to Scrabster and are names in a long line of ships which have used the little port over the centuries. It was from Scrabster Lord Kitchener sailed in the ill-fated *Hampshire* in June 1916. There is an efficient seine-net fleet based on the port. The proposals for a roll-on/roll-off car ferry have brought a renewed interest to the locality and the new Scrabster–Stromness (Orkney) route will no doubt be of vital importance in the development of the tourist industry in particular, offering as it does an extension to the main road system of Scotland and the prospect of 'pastures new' to discover.

Some miles to the west of Thurso, along the coast, is Dunnet Bay. This is 2 miles of smooth firm sand fringed by crystal-clear sea and backed by a wide circling sweep of green hills. Here the popular sport of sand-yachting has developed, to become an undoubted tourist attraction. Whether this character of Dunnet Bay will remain is a matter for concern. In 1972 a proposal was announced for the establishment of a construction yard for North Sea oil production platforms, a venture which required about 100 acres of Dunnet Bay. Those in favour (a petition was signed by nearly 6,000 people who wanted this project) looked at the new employment facilities to be offered by the yard, amounting to a proposed 600 jobs, which were seen against a county unemployment rate of 10 per cent. Those who objected to the proposal saw the loss of an area of coast which had a high scenic and amenity value and considered that despoliation should not be allowed in favour of short-term industrial benefit with no guarantee that the area would be allowed to revert to its original character once the production of oil-rigs ceased to satisfy a dwindling market. The objectors also pointed out the hypocrisy of the county council in the matter, for in 1967 the council sought and gained at a public enquiry the powers to maintain and preserve the foreshore and sand dunes at Dunnet and by their support in 1973 for the proposed development they were going directly against their original commitment. It was observed that if, as in the case of Dunnet Bay, environmental 'quality' is established and put into a county development plan, its 'quality' cannot be changed. The flexibility of such a plan can extend to changes in the principles of environmental quality and any rehabilitation clause would be of little value as there was no possibility of recreating the sand dunes. Other objectors pointed to the possible dangers of the development, which would expose large areas of sand to the action of north-westerly gales, with the attendant risk of blowing sand obliterating the rare plant communities on Dunnet links. About a million cubic yards of sand would have to be disposed of to accommodate the yard. Its life expectancy was suggested to be ten years, but this period was questioned in the light of possible developments in oil technology which could make a construction yard obsolete within a period of less than four years. It was also not realized by those who favoured the scheme that the rigs which would appear on Dunnet beach would have bases of 500 by 500 feet, and be 500 feet high; the nearest equivalent was the Eiffel Tower.

Farther to the east, towards Duncansby Head, lies John o' Groats.

Here the influence of the ubiquitous tourist has converted a once-pleasant and interesting stretch of coastline into a rather vulgar growth, with brash and alien items offered for sale. The occasional genuine and locally-made souvenir can be bought, but there is really little here for the discerning visitor. The original house of the de Groots, a Dutch family who settled here in the reign of James IV is now gone. The family once operated the Orkney ferry. The beach hereabouts is well known for the Groatie Buckies, a small cowrie shell which is now being made the basis of an unusual form of new jewellery which has, in fact, an origin in the prehistoric ornaments found in the area. The shells are difficult to find and most people prefer to take the easy way out and buy a few locally.

The seaward view from the coast in this area takes the eye on to Stroma, lying off-shore in the stream of the Pentland Firth and, behind that island, the Orkney isles of Hoy and South Ronaldsay. In all weathers, when the sun quietens the land and the sea is sleek and when storm and precipice batter each other, there is ever a feeling of exhilaration at many spots on the coast: Dunnet Head; Duncansby Head, with its stacks, square-blocked and rising taller than the nearby cliffs; and Holborn Head, which has an inspiring rocky splendour, with the Clett, a massive isolated pillar 200 feet high and the home of innumerable seabirds, and the Deil's Brig, a natural bridge over a deep chasm a similar height above the water. That rather rare flower, *primula Scotia*, grows on Holborn Head in some small profusion.

The plastic safety-clothes factory in the village of Halkirk represents one of the few examples of industrial spin-offs from the presence of Dounreay. This factory, an outpost of a Midlands organization, employs about twenty people; it not only supplies Dounreay with all the required safety clothing, but is on contract to supply similar clothing to all the atomic-energy research establishments in this country. This venture is typical of the Caithness industrial scene: small, yet socially significant, with a potential for expansion and acting as a working example of what can be achieved at a distance from the recognized normal industrialized areas of Britain. The range of industrial activity in the county includes timber-based industry, engineering, electrical engineering, textiles, knitwear and leather, food-processing, distilling, glass and the extractive industries. The emphases on craft production have yielded many interesting activities and it is from these that the visitor, seeking a genuine and native-made memento of Caithness, should make his purchase.

To the south-west of Halkirk one enters the peatland of Caithness. Altnabreac bog spreads its 21,000 acres across the centre of the county and contains some 13 million tons of peat solids. Today the bog displays the sad remains of an experiment designed to put peat to use as a fuel for the generation of electricity. The idea was not new, for Eire had peat-fired power stations which at the time were producing nearly 40 per cent of that country's power requirements. As a spin-off from this activity there was a thriving briquette industry, selling blocks of peat as a clean and amenable domestic fuel, and a flourishing export in horticultural peat. In 1948 the North of Scotland Hydro-electric Board and the Scottish Home Department produced a pilot scheme for a peat-burning station. In 1954 a ninety-nine-year lease was taken on Braehour Farm and the site prepared for the peat-winning machines. By 1957 these machines were each year skimming over 6,000 tons of peat from the drained bog. They churned off only 8 millimetres at a time and left the peat-milling streams strewn behind them. Since peat in its natural state is 80 per cent water, this allowed air drying and partially solved the problem of removing the water economically. The £500,000 plant designed to form the mechanical side of the scheme ran into difficulties. The plant took longer than planned to reach the running and commissioning stages. Eventually, in August 1959, the plant was on site and ready to run. The two-week test period was not a happy one. Two attempts were made to run for 168 hours, but on each occasion the turbine air-heater became choked with fluffy brown ash and had to be shut down. Other problems ensued and were said to be too costly to justify further investment to make the plant economic. Finally, in 1962, the main plant at Altnabreac was dismantled and sold. The gutted buildings today stand as a reminder of the failure of the Scots to do with their peat what the Irish had proved and are still proving: to produce a number of significant economic and social advantages as anyone who knows of the Irish Bord na Mona activities appreciates. The element of unseemly haste in closing the Altnabreac experiment, at a time when the Government was spending money rashly and to no effect in other fields, is one which is still debated and, like an unexorcised ghost, hovers over the reputation and record of the Hydro-electric Board.

The landward area of Caithness is criss-crossed with an excellent road system linking up farms and townships, and allows the visitor to see the excellent use made of the better lands of the county. Only some 200 years ago the larger part of Caithness was peat moss, which was eventually reclaimed and made to blossom. Sir John Sinclair, 'Agricultural Sir John', and James Traill of Castletown are the two great names associated with the transformation, which was backed by the sturdy farming families who had the vision to follow the lead given by these two men. Expansion and development is still taking place. In 1938 Caithness farms produced under 300,000 gallons of milk. Ten years later the figure was just over a million gallons and it is growing well beyond that today. By that same year, 1948, the milk cattle had increased by over 60 per cent, with a significant increase in the herds. The road from Wick to Castletown passes over the Bog of Killimster, which displays its high peat banks to demonstrate what Caithness once was. Watten Loch, the largest area of fresh water in the county, is a famous anglers' paradise. Georgemas Junction is named after one of the many old Caithness fairs which survived until after 1850: Petermas, Candlemas, the 'foul-tained' Fergusmas, Roodmas and Marymas, which latter survived at Dunnet until the last war killed it off. While the emphasis is on farming in the county, some 40 per cent of the agricultural holdings in Caithness are less than 20 acres and are operated as crofts.

The history of roads in Caithness begins in 1790 when the first road of any significance was constructed, by means of statute labour, between Thurso and Latheron. Prior to that date inland communication was maintained by horse tracks. Communication with the south of Scotland was conducted almost entirely by sea. Under the provision of the Highland Roads Act (1803), the 'Parliamentary' road from Inverness to Thurso was extended from the Ord to Wick and thence to Thurso; this was completed in 1811. One half of the cost of this project was provided locally, chiefly by proprietors and farmers, with small tenants paying their quota, as statute labour had been commuted to a money payment in 1793. During the first half of the nineteenth century further roads were constructed, and today there are over 300 miles of excellent roads. The railway from Helmsdale, in Sutherland, by Forsinard to Wick (with a branch from Georgemas Junction to Thurso) was completed in 1874, which brought Caithness into daily communication with the rest of the country. The Lybster Light Railway, constructed in 1885, proved to be of invaluable service to the villages on the east coast, though the benefit would have been greater still had it been possible to carry this line direct from Helsmdale. The detour by rail from Helmsdale to Lybster illustrates the dependence of communications upon the contour of the land. Even now, the large section of the county lying to the west of a line from Latheron to Reay tends to be almost destitute of roads on account of natural obstacles.

Forestry activity in Caithness has taken place mainly on private lands which were planted last century and now display fine woods. It was not until 1949 that the Forestry Commission started to plant Rumster Forest. This lies some 3 miles north-east of Lybster. At present almost all the suitable land of some 900 acres has been afforested, mainly with Sitka spruce and other natives of the Pacific coast of North America. Four small-holdings within this forest are tenanted by forestry workers.

Almost it seems as a result of the influence of Dounreay, Caithness has produced evidence of deposits of uranium, some of which are of sufficiently high grade at the surface to merit further investigation. A programme of assessment, sponsored by the U.K.A.E.A., is being undertaken to find out what the problems are and what the economic prospects might be if full-scale exploitation is undertaken. The deposit is in the Loch Calder area, some 10 miles south of Dounreay. Since uranium is considered to be the most valuable mineral in the earth's crust, any substantial find in the north of Scotland (there is another deposit near Kildonan in Sutherland) could mean the eventual setting up of mining operations in areas which have long been depressed by lack of job opportunities.

The Royal Burgh of Wick is the county town of Caithness and tends to be the centre of much of the economic activity in the county. The site of the burgh is of long standing, dating at least from Norse saga times. Rising gently on each side of the River Wick, it was for a long time merely a settlement with a small collection of houses; and it remained so until the rise of the fisheries of Scotland towards the end of the eighteenth century. In 1786 the British Fisheries Society set up an organization which founded the twin burgh of Pultneytown. The society commissioned the famous engineer, Thomas Telford, to lay out the town; its fine wide streets and attractive wooded squares are an excellent example of his care and attention to amenity. In 1902 Wick and Pultneytown combined under the single name of Wick, so that one finds on the north side of the river the original fishing port and on the south side the planned development of the more recent town. The improvement in Wick's harbour facilities have continued intermittently since 1810. Ever an important fishing port, it continues to base its economy largely on fishing. The middle years of the last century saw the 'boom' days; in 1862 over 1,100 boats were fishing from Wick and the town saw as much activity as would a Gold Rush town of the American west. Then, in Wick as elsewhere, the industry declined and the town now concentrates on white fish rather than herring. The present fleet of about twenty-six boats is capable of coping with the conditions imposed on it by the fishing grounds—which, fortunately, are not far away from the home port. There are hopes that the Highlands and Islands Development Board will change matters and clear away the relatively aged fleet of middle-sized vessels which can offer only fishing which is limited in range, time and intensity of effort, and which does not offer bright career prospects for new entrants.

Perhaps the most interesting of the industrial activities in Wick—among a kaleidoscope of activities which include hosiery, engineering, distilling and wool—is that of glass-making. This latter is the concern of Caithness Glass. The firm is an outstanding example of how steadfastness and faith win out in the end to become finally established as part of a flourishing enterprise. The venture was begun in 1960 with the object of producing hand-blown glassware of high quality and good design, at the expensive end of the middle range. To start with there was no local glass-blowing skill, no local usable sand and the site was quite remote from the markets. Key workers were recruited from the

Continent and design work began, alongside the training of local people. By 1963 the losses totalled more than the firm's nominal capital of £50,000. Later that year fresh capital was injected by an assortment of backers, and management consultants brought in. But by 1966 the company had run through its second dose of capital and the end looked as though it was only a matter of time. Then a rescue operation was mounted, led by George Mackie, a former Liberal M.P. for Caithness. He recognized that, through all the trouble, two vital facts had emerged: one was that the firm had built up a valuable reputation for high-quality glass; the other was that there had been created a source of local skill. Further financial operations pushed the firm's capital more in line with its assets and, with careful planning of work and sales and the build-up of outlets for the product, the year 1967 saw a trading profit for the first time. Turnover now exceeds £300,000 per annum. The firm is at present organized in five divisions: Caithness Glass, Caithness Engraving (the biggest engraving undertaking of its kind in Britain), Caithness Paperweights, Caithness Jewellery and Oban Glass. The Wick factory employs about eighty, and is the largest source of employment in the town.

Another Wick enterprise which has established an overseas market for its produce is Caithness Cheese. This operation was started by local men and now, though still of small scale, employs about twenty people as cheesemakers and packers. Much of the light industrial activity takes place at Wick Airport, where the county authority, with the aid of the Highlands and Islands Development Board, established an industrial estate to accommodate the requirements of the many new industries which have been attracted to this part of the Highlands. Some firms have had startling successes. In 1971 an enterprise was begun by the only British-owned firm manufacturing microfilm and microfiche information storage and reading machines. The product caught on rapidly, to the extent that early in 1973 the firm announced orders worth £250,000 and plans for expanding their work unit which at present employs some fifty people.

Any visitor to Wick would be well advised to taste a drop of the wine of the country, 'Old Pulteney.' This is a product of a distillery which has come back into production after a twenty-five-year period of shut-down. Neil M. Gunn, the late Highland novelist, once said of Old Pulteney: "It has to be come upon as one comes upon a friend, and treated with proper respect." The whisky is eight years old and sold at 85 proof, strong enough to keep winter's ailments well away. At one time during the eighteenth century, Caithness whisky was regularly exported to the Hebrides. The distillery at Wick was established in 1826 after the owner's small still, located farther inland, had generated for itself such a reputation for quality that he was forced to set up the larger works to produce his Highland malt of excellent vintage, with a rare peaty flavour which put it in great demand. At the turn of this century the output was in the region of 80,000 gallons per annum.

The road south out of Wick hugs the coastline, teetering on high cliff tops and plunging dramatically into glens to make an exhausting climb back up on the other side, affording all the time a seascape with a full-frontal vista of fishing villages, castles, magnificent houses and, if one cares to look, surprises. One of the latter can be seen at Whaligoe. This hamlet was once used as a supplementary harbour facility when the Wick harbour was chock-full with herring drifters. Its 365 hand-hewn steps (of which there are now only about 300 in good condition) were used by fisherwomen, who hauled up the catches in creels on their backs and then walked the 6 miles to the Wick market. Lybster, one of the biggest villages in Caithness, has attractive harbour facilities which are still used by a small fleet. Latheron and Dunbeath are former fishing villages. Berriedale is a spot with fine scenic features, one of which is the drop which the main road takes of 540 feet in 1 mile on the north brae, to rise 500 feet over the same distance on the south brae. The gardens of the large mansion houses are generally open to the public at various times. To the south of Berriedale and the Ord of Caithness one crosses into the eastern coastal area of Sutherland.

Running almost parallel to the marches between Caithness and Sutherland are Strath Halladale and Strath Ullie. The former runs from Melvich on the northern Caithness coast; the latter takes a turn towards the east to end in Helmsdale. Melvich is a scattered community forming part of a combined village with Portskerra and supports a population of under 300. At one time these were prosperous fishing villages. Strath Halladale carries a road south through a thoroughly depopulated landscape, save for a few crofting townships which are mere reminders of the larger communities which once existed in the area. Kinbrace station lies at the southern end, its existence being due to the geography which the planners of the north railway line had to contend with in routing the line. The River Helmsdale follows Strath Ullie, through brown hills with the tell-tale green which is always evidence of former land cultivation. There is everywhere further evidence of a continuing population from the Stone, Bronze and Iron Ages down to the period of the evictions which were completed in 1820. The meagre population is dependent on sheep and salmon-fishing for a living. Northern offshoots of Strath Ullie include the straths of Kildonan and Suisgill, in which gold was found in some small quantity last century, occasioning the 'Kildonan Gold Rush'.

Deposits of alluvial gold occur in Sutherland, the earliest recorded going back to 1245, referring to the north-west of the county. The fields which are known at present are in south-east Sutherland and are associated with streams flowing from the north to join the Helmsdale river, and also with two streams farther south flowing into the head of Loch Brora. The whole goldfield area is moorland with extensive tracts of marshy ground. Published records of the Kildonan goldfield date back to 1868, to a period lasting about two years, during which it is said that at least £12,000-worth of gold was extracted by 400 freelance miners before mining permission was withdrawn. Since then numerous official and unofficial attempts have been made to work the gold on both commercial and private bases, but without much success. A report of 1911 said that the recovery of the gold in the area could not be undertaken economically. In 1964 an investigation by the Geological Survey indicated an irregular distribution of gold in sediments from the stream draining the north-east flanks of Strath Kildonan, and a small amount of gold was obtained from samples of decomposed granite. The subsequent report said that "at least as much gold exists in Strath Kildonan as was won by the 400 or more gold diggers operating during the year 1868 and 1869". This deposit is the richest of its kind in Great Britain. Silver is also found in the area. It has been suggested that the area be declared a tourist asset and facilities afforded for walking tourists to 'pan for gold'. The suggestion also included the setting up of a local museum and centre of information about the history of the area, the 'gold rush' and the Clearances.

Land in the strath tends to be under-used and has much potential for forestry plantation. The highlight, however, is Achentoul Estate, of which a recent report said: "This development shows what can be achieved when the capital resources are available for investment and there is a will on the part of the landowner to undertake the work. The deterioration of the land, which past land use had caused, has been reversed. The Estate has exercised the widest possible choice in demonstrating a range of land uses best suited to the area." The development includes almost 200 acres of land reclaimed for arable purposes, 260 acres re-seeded, and nearly 400 acres in shelterbelts wide enough to make them productive. On the old scheme the estate originally supported forty cows. The present herd is nearly 200 head with followers. A 400-acre low-ground farm was incorporated recently to make for more flexible management, to hold lambs and calves until the usual autumn gluts are past.

The village of Helmsdale (population 705) has one of the best harbours on the Highland east coast. While the settlement has a certain attraction, it tends to be disfigured by a number of derelict and semi-derelict buildings which exude an atmosphere of decay. Yet the potential for a facelift to push the village into a tourist-attractive category is there to be exploited and turned into an incentive to attract much-needed light industries into the area. As the only port that lies between Lybster, in Caithness, and the Black Isle, and that has resident fishing boats of over 40 feet in length, with piers in good condition with a good breakwater, Helmsdale offers some considerable scope for development. The fishing activity (demersal and shellfish) tends to be stable and prosecuted by family interests, each boat being very much a family concern with family ties between individual boats in the small fleet. At one time sloops and schooners traded between Helmsdale and Leith and Newcastle, dealing with (as imports) timber and slates, with fish as exports (mainly herrings).

Both road and railway run south from Helmsdale, hugging together as they skirt the coastline, past Loth (where the last wolf in Scotland was killed) to Brora, a small but vitally important centre of industry which acts as a stabilising element for a population which could otherwise be discouraged by the lack of employment prospects offered by agriculture, fishing and tourism.

The industrial spectrum of Brora includes woollen mills, a coal mine, brickworks and a distillery. The casual visitor to Brora might think that the term 'industrial village' is something of a boast, because these activities tend not to be so obvious as one expects in the more industrialized south, where industry pushes a brass neck forward to intrude its ugliness into the common core of life. One might be forgiven if the coal mine is placed in a prominent position, if only for the fact that its occurrence in the Highland is so unusual and unexpected. In many ways it is something of a phenomenon among Highland communities, resembling as it does a micro-transplant from the Scottish lowland industrial belt, but without the scars and horrors associated with the mining communities of, say, Lanarkshire.

Coal has been won in Brora since 1529. Indeed, so important was the discovery of coal in the area that by 1601 King James VI made the village a "free burgh of Barony and regality to be called the Burgh of Inverbroray". At that time the coal was worked on a narrow strip of level ground above the beach. Salt production was also started at Brora round about the same time, but this lapsed eventually. A couple of stagnating centuries passed by, though not without the occasional peak of interest. In 1614 the 'coal heughs' were repaired after some damage. In 1634 five new pits were sunk, in one of which fifteen men lost their lives by the collapse of a roof. In 1746 a certain John Williams took the Brora mines in hand, but his five-year venture was most unlucky for him. The coal which he mined was really too good. If exposed to air and moisture when lying about in heaps it was apt to go on fire by spontaneous combustion. The last straw for Williams came when a cargo of coal shipped from Brora to Portsoy, in Banffshire, caught fire in this way, due, it is said, to the ship springing a leak. This mishap caused so much alarm and despondency that afterwards no one would buy such 'dangerous' fuel, and Williams had to give up his lease of the mines. In 1814 the present mine was sunk to a depth of 250 feet, where the coal seam was about 40 inches thick. The mine

Mervyn Tower, Auckengill

Helmsdale, Sutherland

Dunrobin Castle, Golspie

Dornoch Cathedral and Castle, Sutherland

was powered by a water-wheel operating in a dam on the River Brora. Much of the coal produced was used to obtain salt from salt water, and for a time Brora supplied all the salt requirements of the fishing villages along the shores of the Moray Firth. When the salt tax was abolished in 1823 the mine continued for a further five years, exporting coal until it was closed in 1828. In 1872 the colliery was re-opened by the Duke of Sutherland, who also started a large engineering works, in which it was planned to make everything from nuts and bolts to large locomotives. This work was initially associated with the Duke's railway, built between Golspie and Helmsdale to link the district more closely with the south, and contained a railway repair shop. It seems that only one locomotive was ever built at Brora. By 1890 the works were converted to a wool mill. The colliery, however, continued on a varied career from 1872.

In 1914 the lease of the mine was taken over by Brora's native entrepreneur, T. M. Hunter, who ran the mine until 1949, at which time the National Coal Board expressed little interest in such a small venture and the mine was proposed for closure. However, a rescue operation was mounted and the mine was leased by Sir David Robertson, M.P. A briquetting plant was installed, the new product finding a ready market over all the north of Scotland. Disaster came, however, in the form of a fire in 1960 and again in 1961, when the colliery was again closed down. But the miners had by then formed themselves into a strong lobby; with the help of finance from the Highland Fund, the mine was re-opened in that same year as a workers' co-operative venture and has been open ever since. The miners are shareholders in their own mine. A cloud loomed over the colliery in 1969 when it was announced that the workings were then only fit for a further five years. When the news of the impending closure was released, efforts were mounted to investigate the real extent of the coalfield. The Highlands and Islands Development Board supported the cost of making trial bores to prove the deposit beyond the Clynelish fault which bounds the present workings. This survey indicated that there were some millions of tons of coal available for working from a new development. A new mine was sunk about a half-mile up the Brora river from the old pit and modern screening and bagging plant erected. The mine in 1973 offered employment to about thirty miners and thus provided an essential element for population stability. It is now closed (see p, 42).

Closely associated with the colliery is the Brora Brickworks. This was started in 1818 when the Duke of Sutherland decided that his plans required a steady supply of bricks and was closed with the mine ten years later. The works' history has much the same chequered pattern as the coal pit and indeed was threatened with closure along with the mine in 1961. But the intervention of two local interests gave the works a new lease of life and today the products, which include bricks and drainage tiles, find a ready market all over the north of Scotland. The employment here is for about thirty.

When the Duke of Sutherland's railway line was merged with the Highland railway, the engineering works became redundant, but were taken over to become a spinning mill. This venture had a fitful existence until 1900. In the following year the premises were re-opened by T. M. Hunter, a local businessman, who installed carding and spinning plant so that all processes could be carried out on the spot, from raw wool to finished articles. Under his own personal leadership and initiative, and later that of his family, the mill thrived and there is now a very modern mill producing tweeds, blankets, travelling rugs and knitting wools. The total employment is in the region of 100 jobs. Much of the raw wool comes from Highland sources, although the mill serves a much wider area than this. For instance, yarn is spun for handloom weavers in all parts of Britain, and much of their production comes back to Brora for the finishing processes. Demand for Brora woollen products is on the increase and a good export market is being built up at the present time. Mr T. M. Hunter was also responsible for the creation of the Brora Electric Supply Company, founded in 1913 to supply electricity to shops, houses and streets in the village, the generators for the supply being driven by steam from the mill boilers. In this way, Brora enjoyed electric power some decades before many other Highland towns.

The Clynelish Distillery was established in 1819, having been preceded by a brewery which did not last long. The distillery was built to absorb the considerable increases in grain yield from newly cultivated land. The distillery quickly won for itself a reputation and made a business out of supplying private customers with duty-paid malt whisky. The demand grew to such an extent that the distillery was obliged, at the turn of the century, to refuse trade orders. The present-day product is a fine, full and mellow whisky. Its purchase requires a careful search, for it is not a widespread product, though it often features in 'top ten' selections.

The population of Brora has been fairly stable with no overall decline for about a century now. In 1851 the peak was reached in 1,933 persons. A decade later it had fallen to 1,886 and by 1871 a further drop to 1,733 was recorded. The present population is 1,884 persons, indicating the worth of Brora's industrial activities with their attendant employment facilities and potential for a population in a county which has suffered much in the past from excessive migration, and is still looking nervously at the prospect of further migration to the job market represented by the on-shore industrial support activity connected with North Sea oil in Easter Ross. The sense of community in the town is intense and is reflected in the excellent uses made of the facilities available in the Brora High School and the community centre which is linked to the school. Plans for the improvement of the town's amenities and the industrial estate, to attract further industry, will undoubtedly add to the role which Brora plays in the county of Sutherland, being a social sheet-anchor and foundation on which a confident future can be built.

The village of Golspie (population just over 800) is a seaside resort situated in a rich agricultural district. It acts as a distributive centre for the coastal farmlands to the south and for the crofting hinterland of Rogart. The influence of the Dukedom of Sutherland has been felt here as elsewhere in the county, some of it applied for the benefit of the community. In 1862 a gas-works was built by the third Duke and was in continuous operation until, in 1964, the Scottish Gas Board, faced with an increasing deficit and an increase in the use of electricity as an alternative domestic fuel, proposed to close the works. But in view of its role as an employment facility, there was a reprieve. Its proximity to Dunrobin, the Sutherland 'seat', has made Golspie a kind of county town which attracted those who wanted to use the ducal connection to some commercial profit. The local authority has its main offices in the village. Golspie houses the county weekly newspaper, which is owned by the Countess of Sutherland. A recently established printing works, associated with the paper, produces a range of specialist periodicals mainly for the army.

An earlier countess was responsible for a significant innovation in education in 1903: the Sutherland Technical School, founded as a residential school and provided for the benefit of the sons of crofters from the northern counties. It was then an entirely new departure in education and became a model for others, notably Keil School in Dumbarton. The cost of the school was met by the fourth Duke and Andrew Carnegie of Skibo Castle. The school was run by a board of governors until taken over in 1923 by Sutherland County Council. In 1948 the council bought the farm of Drummuie (about 100 acres) for educational purposes connected with the school. It is run as a mixed farm. The school itself offers intensive courses in commerce, agriculture, building and motor engineering.

Another educational venture by the Sutherland family was the conversion of Dunrobin Castle, a magnificent building standing on the coast a mile east of Golspie, into a boarding school for boys, run on the same lines as Gordonstoun. The school catered for boys from 13 years to university standard. When it opened in 1965 there were forty-six boys, with high hopes for expansion to eventually provide facilities and accommodation for 200. In 1969 the Highlands and Islands Development Board turned down an application for a grant to help with the development of the school. At the time the rejection was thought to be inconsistent, when viewed against the board's previous history of grants to schools already receiving grant-aid, direct or otherwise. By 1969 there were 115 boys at the school and it was beginning to develop into a useful economic facility at the very least, offering, as it did, much-needed work for local tradesmen—even the food bill approached well over £200 per week. In fact, the school was something of an economic growth-point. The free education offered in excellent modern high-standard amenity surroundings by Golspie High School (roll over 500 pupils) makes Dunrobin something of a massive and unwieldy paradox.

South of Golspie one approaches the Mound, at the head of Loch Fleet. This loch is an inlet of the sea, at the mouth of the River Fleet and was made a nature reserve in 1970. The area forms part of the Sutherland estates and approaches closely the Mound Alderwoods National Nature Reserve which lies astride the river upstream of the Mound. The reserve has a number of particularly interesting physiographical features, which include low-lying shingle and sand, planted pine woodlands, ground flora rich in species characteristic of pine and birch woodland sites, a salt marsh and a loch basin which is a popular feeding ground for wintering ducks. In the woodlands there are roe deer, and wild cats have been seen on occasion. The reserve is something of a Mecca for ornithologists at the time of the bird migrations.

When the Mound was constructed as a causeway over Loch Fleet by the Duke of Sutherland in 1812, this dry-land crossing cut the Little Ferry traffic business. Until that date sea transport was the vital factor in communications; the sea was the only access route between Sutherland and the rest of Scotland. To landward, the county was reached by the Little Ferry (sometimes called the Meikle Ferry), Bonar Ferry and Portinlick. At these ferries droves of cattle for the Trysts at Falkirk and other southern markets swam the Kyle of Sutherland on the journey south. It was believed among the people in these old days that if an ox readily took to the water and crossed the ferry without turning back, it would be sure to fetch a good price at the market. When the first roads, and then the railway, were built, Little Ferry harbour declined somewhat, though there was still trade maintained between it and Leith and Newcastle. During the First World War the jetty was extended to cope with the traffic in timber, and in 1950 the first steamer for ten years loaded a cargo of wood for Shetland. But the jetty was in a ruinous state and it collapsed in March 1966, being finally reduced to rubble by explosives the following month.

Dornoch, situated on the north side of the Dornoch Firth, is the county town of Sutherland. With a population of just over 900 it has been developed into a seaside holiday resort. Once the seat of the bishops of Caithness, it still retains the character of a cathedral town. The Bishop's Palace is now a hotel, something of a dramatic change in function. It was in Dornoch that the burning of Janet Horne, 'the last witch in Scotland', took place in 1722. In a garden near the golf course a simple slab of rough whinstone bears this date and is said to mark the spot where the old woman breathed her smoky last.

Dornoch Cathedral, while it has neither the size nor beauty of many of the greater cathedrals, has a simple charm and dignity of its own. First erected in 1222, on the lines of Elgin Cathedral, the structure was destroyed by fire in 1570 in a clan feud between the Murrays of Dornoch and the Mackays of Strathnaver. Although subjected to a programme of restoration over a long period of time, it was not until 1835–7 that the final stage in the restoration took place. In 1924, to commemmorate the seven-hundredth anniversary of the foundation, the whole of the lath and plaster, with the exception of the fine vaulted ceiling, was removed, to reveal the building's natural masonry work, which, apart from the nave, is original.

Kitchen middens at Earl's Cross indicate a history of continuous habitation in Dornoch going back some 3,000 years. During the summer months the town's population is quadrupled by tourists attracted by the town's fine beaches and seaside facilities. The caravan site was created in an exercise of community help. A group of enthusiasts drew £25 from the town's Common Good Fund and, doing the labouring work themselves, established a site which recorded just under 1,000 bed-nights in 1956. The current figure is approaching 40,000, a marked degree of success which is reflected in a recent investment of £10,000 for the further development of this important facility. Dornoch is far-famed for its golf links, which were first mentioned in records dated 1616 and are now attracting competition-standard players to strengthen the town's growing reputation as a holiday resort.

The sleepy village of Spinningdale was in 1973 hit by something like an investment bombshell when it learned of the plans of a German multi-millionaire to turn the place into a major international spa and holiday centre. A first-stage investment of £12 million was proposed to create bungalows, terraced holiday houses, a luxury hotel and major facilities including indoor swimming pools and a yachting marina. Bonar Bridge, a straggling village with a population of about 350, marks the gateway northwards into Sutherland. One main attraction is the salmon-fishing industry which injects a useful element into the local economy.

The eastern approaches of Ross and Cromarty County include two important peninsulae which together promise to become the socio-economic centre of the whole of the Highland region—and this despite the dominating presence of the Fort William capital-intensive industrial activity in the Lochaber district. Part of this trend in Easter Ross in particular is already under way, with Invergordon acting as the industrial hub. Each peninsula pushes out into the Moray Firth; both are based on Old Red Sandstone, which affords land with a high degree of fertility. The area has a varied relief rising to 838 feet in Mount Eagle.

The firths of Dornoch, Cromarty and Inverness are the drowned successors of superimposed rivers which became incised, in the case of the Cromarty Firth, in the gneissic rocks on the east coast. Glaciation produced a further deepening to leave boulder-clay and fluvio-glacial deposits. The raised beaches are very prominent; excellent examples are found along the margins of the Cromarty Firth. The 15-foot and 25-foot beaches cover about 8 square miles in the vicinity of the Bay of Nigg and these are backed by 50-foot and 100-foot remnants. The Dornoch Firth, the most northerly, is shallow and encumbered by sandbanks which caused the decline of Tain as a seaport. The Cromarty Firth, on the other hand, offers the finest deep-water harbour facilities on the east coast of Scotland north of the Tay; this fact led to the establishment of Invergordon as a naval base in the past, and the present use of the area as an on-shore base for a wide spectrum of industrial activity largely connected with North Sea oil. The general economy of the area is based on agriculture, this activity taking advantage of the good loams and light arable soils which, favoured by a warm climate and low rainfall (about 25 inches per annum on the coast), offer excellent conditions for good and efficient land use.

Tain was once an important port on the Dornoch Firth, but progressive silting has reduced its role in this context. At one time the capital of Ross, it now acts as a business centre for the hinterland. Its population has tended to increase (1,551 in 1921 to almost 2,000 in 1973), the more recent increase being the result of its popularity as a residential centre for the new executive classes associated with the industry which has grown up in and around Invergordon. An attempt is being made to broaden its economic base by setting up an industrial site which already has a number of service-industry activities on it. The site is serviced by the railway station in the town. Tain serves the many small dairy farms in the area and is developing its facilities as a holiday resort. Tain has recently been presented with a development plan in which it is expected to experience a population increase to 7,000.

Local interest is particularly homing in on the potential Tain might have as a centre for small industries. The rich mussel beds of the Dornoch Firth, owned by the burgh as common property, have a future as Scottish sea-foods increase in popularity. A lease of ten years has been taken by an Oban sea-food firm. Another firm operating from Tain with a similar product exports deep-frozen and packaged scampi and baby lobster tails to Canada and the United States. A small boat agency is finding it profitable to operate from Tain, as does another firm making parts for electronic devices. A particular Tain product is a new type of rough-country transport capable of moving goods and personnel over difficult terrain. Perhaps in the more traditional vein is the firm which specializes in Highland cheeses based on old Highland recipes; a range of products catering for a growing British and continental market. Other industries in the town include a large sawmill, a large contracting business and a distillery producing the much-demanded Glenmorangie malt whisky.

Eastwards beyond Tain lies the Tarbat peninsula, reckoned to be one of the driest areas in all Scotland. Small and picturesque villages are scattered about the area, joined by a criss-crossing of quiet roads. The isolation of Tarbat has attracted a rich vein of bird-life, notably eider duck and, in winter, common and velvet scoters. Loch Eye is an interesting patch of isolated water in the peninsula which acts as a focal meeting point for the birds. The main blot in this area is the gunnery range at Morrich Mor, facing the Dornoch Firth. While one accepts that this country must have its military testing areas, one asks why these must, with all the logistical facilities at the disposal of the Ministry of Defence, be located by civil servants in areas which are accessible to the general public and close to small urban communities. The answer may be somewhere in the deepest and darkest recesses of the civil service mind. Small wonder that there are frequent protests at the mounting of aerial battles over the Morrich Mor involving huge bombers and fighter planes.

In rather sharp contrast to the quiet and relaxing environment of Tain, the developments around the shores of Nigg Bay seem almost like a nightmare. Good farming land has been raped by industrial requirements, many of them short-term, and former pleasing contours are being reshaped by giant earth-moving equipment. The rhythmic social patterns of former communities have had an alien syncopated beat introduced to create a bewilderment which is in keeping with the dwarfing of the human element by the huge, almost gargantuan size of the new buildings and structures. Virtual small cities have and are being created, to the detriment of wild life and the natural and essential amenities which are so characteristic of the Highlands. Of course, it is accepted that people cannot eat scenery, but the seeming lack of control at both local and national levels of the rate and character of the development which has taken place already in this small area seems to underline the sense that here, if anywhere at all in the Highlands, there is a fast buck being made with no regard for the basic essentials which provide for 'quality of life' as an element in the need to work for a living.

Invergordon first came into its own as a sheltered port with a safe anchorage to which easy access could be gained at all times; and its use by the Royal Navy as a base in two world wars tended to define its one and only function. Though this function has now gone, it is playing a similar role as a fuelling depot for deep-water ships. Perhaps the first main industrial development was Invergordon Distillery which, started in 1961, is now the largest single distillation unit in Europe, with an annual production of about 10 million gallons of grain whisky per annum.

The second development of major significance for Invergordon in the sixties decade was the setting up of the smelter of the British Aluminium Company. In 1967 the first hints of the Government's interest in making a significant increase in the production of aluminium in this country were made public. The company expressed a keen interest in Invergordon and, after much debate, the site was cleared for operations in 1968. The smelter went into its first phase of production in May 1971. Though the smelter is designed to produce 100,000 tons of aluminium metal annually, it came into use at a time of diminished world demand. Thus it started off at half-cock and, considering that the works represented an investment of £37 million, was something of a damp squib. Late in 1972, however, production was increased to 75,000 tons per annum with the hopes of getting into full production within a further year or so. The presence of the smelter was important in the context of providing jobs for local people. The company has always made a point of recruiting locally and the smelter work force is in fact 75 per cent local-based. Three-quarters of a million pounds each year is paid out in salaries and wages—which, with the multiplying function which this amount of cash represents, has raised the general level of incomes in the area to a significant platform.

The problem of possible pollution in the area as a result of the smelter is one which looms large in Invergordon. In 1972 a 'Doomwatch' maintained by the Forestry Commission on its 42,000 trees around the smelter site revealed that lichens on trees in the vicinity of the plant had died and concern was expressed that air pollution from the smelter, while satisfying the statutory clean-air requirements, might be affecting tree and plant growth. An extended time-scale is required to assess the cumulative effects of atmospheric effluents containing fluorine and gaseous fluoride, and the full import of the commission's report is yet to be confirmed. A further, and greater, hazard in the area will be the sulphur and oil-bearing effluents from petro-chemical operations based on the on-shore oil services now being constructed in the area.

Across the Bay of Nigg, once-neglected communities have been rudely awakened to face the fact that their village greens and narrow streets are vibrating with the noise and traffic of the activity resulting from North Sea oil. The destruction of social patterns in the parish of Nigg, extending over flat, fertile farming country, points to a serious lack of foresight on the part of the planners, whose influence seems to be ubiquitous but who are rarely seen in public to explain their thoughts, ideas and actions. One main result of the industrialization of Nigg has been the number of residents who have sold up and left the area.

Down at the ferry at Balnapaling, on the very doorsteps of the narrow-built, sharp-roofed little houses, with their gables turned towards the sea, yawns a modern graving-dock and fabrication yard,

Dornoch Firth looking towards Ardgay

Salmon leaping at Mound Loch Fleet near Golspie

Spinningdale, between Bonar Bridge and Dornoch

Kyle of Tongue and Ben Loyal, Sutherland

Shin Falls, Sutherland

(*top*) Loch Shin and Lairg. (*bottom*) Salmon fishing, Kyle of Sutherland

incorporating what has been called "the biggest man-made hole in Europe". The visitor to the area has his eye caught, not by a natural skyline, but the bulk of huge buildings and the skeletal arms of massive lifting and lighting towers. By night, a continuous pool of brilliant light bathes the small villages of the neighbourhood with a permanent midnight sun, which can be seen in the night sky from Inverness many miles away. Local roads, which a handful of years ago bore the light weight of private and small commercial traffic, are now literally bending under the weight of massive loads. It is a common sight to see a road surface actually sink and rise again after the passing of one of these loads on its way to the construction yards. Paradoxes abound. Almost overnight a power cable was strung up within yards of crofts whose inhabitants have for years been patiently waiting for a connection to the public power supply. The effect on these communities of wages averaging £90 per week has yet to be assessed in the long term. In the short-term view, it has released previous pressures on prices, and a plate of convenience foods at the time of writing costs almost £2, with a plate of coolish and rather indifferent consommé setting one back 20p. There is no tendency to save money or invest surplus cash against an eventual return to square one when the developers have sucked up their last crumb of profit and leave to despoil newer pastures.

Down the road from Invergordon, Alness has had the weight of industrial development placed heavily on its small community. From a village in an attractive green and wooded setting, Alness is now billed as a 'showpiece settlement', with an eventual population of 16,000 being projected by planners. Alness has an established history of being a dormitory facility, having had the experience of catering for the requirements of Services personnel in two wars. Now the emphasis is on creating large areas of block housing for workers associated with the smelter and oil-based developments. Industry, not content with the despoliation of one area and leaving it at that, has been catered for by three sites in Alness, totalling nearly 50 acres. While this is acceptable in terms of providing a good employment stratification in the town, so that it does not assume a ghost and matriarchial character during the daytime, there are indications that the scrabble and scramble for light industry are signs of no confidence in the supposedly long-term provisions represented by the multi-million investments based on metal production and oil. A more traditional and stable industry in Alness is Dalmore Distillery. Established in 1839 it came into its own as a producer of pure Highland malt pot-still whisky in 1868. The distillery is a family affair and offers employment to about forty locals. The product is a heavy whisky, peatier than some and full-bodied, and is an excellent after-dinner drink. One benefit of the new developments in the area was the re-opening in 1973 of Alness Station, closed to passenger traffic in 1960. The station is an unstaffed halt.

It is inevitable that the flush of development around the shores of the Cromarty Firth would raise many questions, particularly about the changes in the social patterns of communities which have now been almost literally blasted open to receive injections of new blood, people, ideas and values. It was said of Alness at one time that one could fire a cannon along High Street without fear of hitting a soul. Now car-parking is one of the most serious problems the local council has to deal with. The American impact is seen in the growing range of new and strange-sounding convenience foods in new shops and super-markets. Strange accents are heard, and those factors which make for significant social change are already operating from school level upwards through the community structure. The inability and in-experience of local authorities to handle, or even grasp, the meaning and implications of the vast amount of investment funds pouring into the area has been seen in the haste with which the welcome mat was put out for the foreign industrialists. While the demand for labour has undoubtedly eliminated the unemployment problem, which was in the region of 12 per cent, the rate of growth has tended to underline the lack of expertise available to local authorities to help them make the right decisions and to slow down the demand for housing, schools, leisure facilities and the like. Problems of a particular nature assume serious long-term proportions. Local labour trained by American firms as welders to perform special functions are not trained in the context of a nationally-recognized craft certificate course; this means that when the oil-rig firms move on to the next boom site, their Highland ex-employees will be able to get a skilled, highly-paid job in the oil industry anywhere in the world, but will be ill-equipped to transfer to another industry in their home area—should there be one to go to. Training for long-term community requirements seems at present to be of secondary importance to the training of new workers to fulfil immediate and rather narrow industrial needs; this is only one of many aspects of the boom which seem to ignore long-term and second generation requirements. Even to consider the possible leisure requirements of the new fast-growing population (live professional theatre, international-standard swimming pools, floodlit stadia for sports and even dog tracks) one's mind boggles at the load placed on local authorities to arrange for these while attending to other equally important items such as schools and housing, medical facilities and communications. The total effect on the existing community with its indigenous population of the demand of the new-found population for sophisticated facilities already enjoyed in the more densely-populated areas of the south is not entirely unassessable if the experience of other boom-time growth centres, catering for short-term industrial demands, are looked at.

The problem of a looming 'leisure crisis' was foreseen by the Easter

Ross Council of Social Service, and its forecast of an increase in the incidence of petty crime is now seen to be correct, though by the beginning of 1973 the dimensions were not significant. The council urged the Highlands and Islands Development Board to launch, as a matter of urgency, a full-scale study of the recreational needs of an area which, it was estimated, would experience a population explosion from the present 25,000 to about 140,000 by the end of the present century. But nothing was done. Another feature of the problem was that industrial and land speculators had bought up virtually all available land in the area, leaving next to nothing for recreational purposes. The labour camps used as accommodation for much of the work force in and around the Cromarty Firth were a particular evil and were sources of trouble in the area, as these facilities have always been in other parts of the world.

The Burgh of Dingwall is the present administrative centre for the county of Ross and Cromarty, with a royal charter dating from 1226. Occupying as it does a strategic position, Dingwall has been a place of note from very early times. It was here that the Norsemen held their thing, or court of justice, during the era of their occupation. Its function as a gateway to the Highlands has added to the importance of the town through the centuries. The economy of the present population of some 4,000 includes a hand-weaving mill, and the market facilities it offers to farmers. Two busy livestock marts and a large abbatoir serve a fertile hinterland. The town's role as an administrative centre has tended to attract professional classes of people into the area. An industrial estate has been created to attract light industry in an effort to counteract the effects of the creation of Inverness as the administrative centre for all of the new Highland region, which will undoubtedly detract from the many unusual features which Dingwall presents to the incomer at present.

The Black Isle peninsula enjoys a temperate climate and a high degree of fertility which is extremely productive. The agricultural uses are interspersed with young forests. Large farms (between 200 and 300 acres) produce rotation grass, oats and turnips, in addition to barley for distilling. Wheat is grown in selected favourable and sheltered areas below 100 feet, and seed potatoes are grown on the sandier soils. The area, with other parts of Easter Ross, leads Scotland in the production of virus-free seed potatoes, grown from stem-cuttings provided by the Department of Agriculture. Large herds of Aberdeen-Angus-Shorthorn cross-breed cattle are raised, the animals being marketed at Tain or Dingwall when about 2 years old. The main town hereabouts is Cromarty, which, situated as it is on the tip of the southern entrance to the Cromarty Firth, has found itself in an isolated position but may gain some benefit from the developments taking place to the north of the firth. Located in a varied and scenically beautiful hinterland, the town has many old buildings of some character, particularly the court house built in 1782. The cottage of Hugh Miller, the geologist, which dates from about 1650, holds an interesting geological collection. Miller was also a naturalist, theologian and writer. The son of a master of a sailing ship, he became a journeyman stonemason and, through his unique and natural powers of observation and deduction, rose to eminence in the science of geology. His books include *Old Red Sandstone*, about the rock which is the heart-core of his birthplace. The remarkable variety of his achievements is illustrated at the cottage.

In Cromarty there has developed a group of craft artists which produces items of excellent quality, including hand-thrown pottery, ceramic costume jewellery, handmade knitwear and an art gallery. These activities are housed in three old cottages, reflecting Cromarty's past role as a fishing village, all brought into a modern setting while still preserving their original air. The town has relied for many years on the tourist industry, but the recent appearance of speculative builders interested in the construction of houses for the new industrial influx may well change Cromarty's former image. Whether the prospect of becoming a combined tourist and dormitory centre is a good prospect is something which the 600 people in Cromarty will have to decide for themselves. The news that 100 council houses were to be built in a short period of time was something of a bombshell where the previous record of local authority building was in the form of two or three houses erected in gap sites about the town.

Near Cromarty is the South Soutar, one of a pair of high, bold and strident headlands which guard both sides of the mile-wide entrance to the Cromarty Firth. But nothing is inviolable. In 1971 permission was given to a commercial interest to begin quarrying operations on the North Soutar. Immediately there was a public reaction, mainly because the operations were to be carried out on a site which directly faced Cromarty. A further site was chosen, but this too was the subject of objections and in the end an undertaking had to be given by the landowner that the outline of the North Soutar, as seen from Cromarty, would be protected. All land to the west of the North Soutar, at Nigg, is under zoning for industrial development and therefore any land recommended for conservation is under great pressure. The cliffs are said to be the only auk-nesting site in Ross-shire, apart from their being unique coastal landmarks.

The other towns in the Black Isle include Fortrose, a royal burgh of some considerable antiquity, formerly the ecclesiastical centre of Ross and the seat of the bishop. It is situated on a terrace overlooking the Moray Firth. Rosemarkie, nearby, was the earliest seat of Christianity; its former importance has now been eclipsed by Fortrose. Avoch is a small fishing village of long standing and still manages to thrive; its harbour facilities are a particular attraction to yachting enthusiasts, who find the Inverness Firth an excellent sheltered area of water on which to pursue their sport. Munlochy is a village situated at the head of a very attractive small bay.

The burgh of Inverness was sited at an early fording point on the Ness River, on morainic ridges and fragments of the raised beaches which are common in the area. Recorded history shows the burgh to have a long standing as a port, dating back at least eight centuries to when skins, hides and wool were exported to the Baltic and the Mediterranean. Even as late as the eighteenth century, trade with the ports of the Low Countries was very brisk, with some not insignificant emphasis on the smuggling of wines, silks, spices and other valuables into the Inverness area. The present-day port is no more significant than port facilities offered in places much smaller than Inverness. However, if the town's status as a Highland port has declined, its importance as an administrative centre for the Highland region has grown considerably over the years, together with its role as a market and tourist centre. Industrial activities in Inverness, though on a low profile, are growing and at present include a narrow range of specialist activities such as woollens, whisky, and, in particular, automatic electric-welding machines for use in the automobile, ship-building and steel industries. Other light industries have arrived in the burgh since the advent of the Highlands and Islands Development Board in 1965, but these have yet to make their true mark on the economy, though some are now long enough established to make some significant contribution to the overall picture of an industrial town. The remoteness of Inverness from the main markets has detracted from its ability to attract large industry, even though road, rail and air facilities are good. Of late, however, interesting pockets of industry have arrived in the area, and, if their parent offices in the south are not hit by the 'English disease', they should offer long-term employment and opportunities for expansion to the stage where they become entities in their own right.

For a long time Inverness has stated its claim for the title 'Capital of the Highlands'; this, however, is a mere phrase conjured up to impress tourists. While it is certainly the administrative hub of the region, it is by no means the capital of a region which has such distinctive characteristics, few of which are displayed in Inverness, even with a 15 per cent Gaelic-speaking population. There have, in fact, been emphatic denials by the burgh fathers that there exists any cultural and historical link with, for instance, the western Highlands which are so Gaelic-based. Indeed, one has to look at Inverness under the microscope to find the rather delicate links which the 'capital' has with the region as a whole. One would rather say that Inverness tends to be a far-flung branch of the English-speaking Union, with rather interesting though peculiar mutations.

Having said that about Inverness, it must also be declared that the town has ever been, and will always be, more than a leader in the region. It is, in the first place, the largest town north of Perth and west of Aberdeen, and its sphere of influence extends as far west as the Hebrides, as far north as the outer isles of Shetland and eastwards into the joint counties of Moray and Nairn. It is the headquarters of a large number of public and semi-public bodies, including the Highlands and Islands Development Board and the Crofters Commission. All of the bodies concerned with agriculture, forestry, and hospitals have important regional offices located in the burgh. The number of branch offices maintained by nationally-known business enterprises increases each year. As befits a large town serving an extensive hinterland, the burgh has its own twice-weekly newspaper of long standing. Three national daily newspapers and one weekly paper have offices here, in addition to a base for a group of weekly papers serving various parts of the region in special issues.

For some reason or other Inverness has never developed a sense of good planning. Nevertheless, there were a number of buildings of character and some architectural interest by the early 1960s. But by the beginning of that decade the planners decided that Inverness had gone on long enough as a planning backwater and thereupon began to tear the heart out of the town. Little was regarded as sacrosanct. Physical changes in the last handful of years have wrought havoc with the old Inverness. The previous character and beauty of the place was raped and concrete structures appeared in conflicting juxtaposition with buildings of an older generation, only serving to impress the visitor with the fact that whatever shortcomings Inverness had before the planners' era, it was much better aesthetically than some of the multi-storey jungles which are rising high above the old skyline to dominate completely the Inverness scene. Yet . . . with the River Ness and its small, mid-stream islets, there is often a comparison with the Seine and Paris. From a number of vantage points which exclude the modern buildings, Inverness displays enough of a scenic amenity to place it high on the list of contenders for the title 'Paris of the North'. Much of the burgh has been razed to give the ubiquitous and often iniquitous motor car some parking space. In a town built for the more leisurely dray, cart and coach, the streets are jam-packed with tourist vehicles during the summer months, creating queues some two or three miles long on the town's outskirts. The projected bridge to be built over the Inverness Firth to join up with the Black Isle will remove the town's image as a bottleneck rather than its self-projection to the tourist as a gateway to the northern Highlands. But this project will take some time to complete, and the residents will have to continue to suffer the same kind of traffic density which only giant conurbations like London and Manchester experience daily and with some degree of long-suffering.

The estuarine land around Inverness has recently been the subject of an investigation with a view to possible reclamation. Planners' estimates for the increase in the population of Inverness from the present 35,000 to a figure of 60,000 in the next two decades or so have raised many fears about the pressure for land for housing, agriculture and industrial users. The present emphases on agriculture in the area have produced new demands from farmers for increased economic operations which can only come about by expansion of livestock and crop enterprises. Many possibilities exist for reclamation and the Highlands and Islands Development Board have expressed serious interest in better use of the available land than obtains at present.

The introduction to the area of the oil industry, represented by on-shore activities, may well mean the sacrifice of reclaimed land to the demands of this new phenomenon to the detriment of the needs of the farming community around the Firth of Moray. In particular, the small village of Ardersier, close by Fort George, found itself early in 1972 proposed as the next-door neighbour of a gigantic oil-production platform construction yard with an ultimate employment figure of 7,000. Its population of about 1,000 have high hopes of the employment potential which the yard will bring, but at the same time fears are expressed that this boom will leave the village a ghost town once the requirements for oil-platforms decline. At present Ardersier acts as a dormitory of Inverness and Nairn, to which towns most of the working population disappears for a day, leaving the village inhabited by children and a few adults. One cannot but agree with those who say that even a short-time and short-term feast is better than a long-term famine. Only those who cannot see compromise of any kind between the demands of industry and those who advocate an enhancement of the quality of life at a smaller cost, with more accessible goals, might quarrel with the unwilling unemployed in the area. But one hopes that where industry steps in, local authorities will be one step in front to demand that social patterns, life-styles and long-standing values are not destroyed or changed beyond recognition. Only in this way will the best of the past be brought forward to encourage the present, which in its turn will make for a better future in which the ordinary human being has a definite and recognizable place and a role to play in the new kind of society now emerging in the Highlands.

4

The Western Seaboard

THE western seaboard of the Highland region is, for the purposes of this chapter, taken as extending from Loch Broom in the north to Arisaig in the south. The area has particular importance because it contains virtually all the land–sea links which connect much of the mainland of Scotland with the Western Isles and Skye. In itself, it is an area chock-full of scenic beauty: seascape and landscape mingle under a never-ending display of moving skies. One might venture to say that there are few other areas in the British Isles which have such a variety in beauty and interest. The area, if one excludes the parishes described in Chapter 2, is the only coastal part of the true (i.e. Gaelic-speaking) Highlands. The western seaboard is deeply indented by the sea which, in millennia long past, flooded into long, westward-running glens to produce a serrated coastline. Here fiords push anything up to 40 miles into the mountains. Much of the area is difficult of access, making a factor which enhances the 'mystery' element in the Highland region as a whole. The climate is mild; mean temperatures in midwinter are several degrees higher than those of Scotland's east coast. This warmth, however, tends to be confined to low ground, for as the land rises so does the temperature fall quite rapidly to produce genuine Alpine conditions. It is the mildness of the climate which allows such exotic plant life as palms and fig trees to grow in wild profusion—yet they will not, outside of the south-west corner of England, grow anywhere else in Britain. As a whole, less snow falls in the area than on the English Pennines.

While the sea-lochs have been called 'fiordlike', they are in fact peculiar to Scotland; their scale is not Norwegian and they display their own native characteristics. Loch Hourn, for instance, twists and turns between high walls and craggy flanks. A casual glance at the map will reveal that, but for a few miles or so of hard unrelenting rock, many of the present sea-lochs would be channels connecting up with inland, land-locked lochs (Lochs Awe, Shiel, Quoich and Garry), to create more than a dozen new off-shore islands to be added to the already full firmament of Scottish islands.

The southernmost part of the seaboard area is Arisaig, perhaps best known for its association with Glenfinnan and the Forty-five Rising. At the head of Loch Shiel stands a tall monument to the Rising, surmounted by a stone Highlander who represents, not Prince Charles as is commonly supposed, but the clansmen who rallied round the Prince for reasons of their own and of their chiefs and kinsmen. One of the Prince's supporters, among the few to survive the event and die in peace in his native land, was Alexander MacDonald, the seventh Chieftain of Glenaladale, at whose house the Prince spent the night before Glenfinnan. MacDonald suffered much for his adherence; he was among the small band of faithful friends who helped and guided the Prince in the latter's wanderings among the hills and glens until he left Scotland for France. Glenaladale afterwards lived the life of a hunted fugitive until the Act of Amnesty enabled him to set about rebuilding his house and reconstructing his life. He died, aged only 48, in 1761, to be succeeded by his son, who in his turn found that life as a Catholic under the Penal Laws was not to his liking. In 1722 he sold his lands to his cousin, MacDonald of Borrodale, who then began a new line of Chieftains of Glenaladale. By 1815 a descendant, Alexander, decided that enough time had passed since the Forty-five, and that it was only right and just to erect some kind of memorial for those who had ungrudgingly given their lives and goods, and who saw their families suffer for the cause, yet who were left unsung except in a substantial corpus of Gaelic poetry. The monument was thus erected in 1815, built of coarse stone rubble and standing 65 feet high. It is dominated by the dramatic statue of a kilted figure carved by the sculptor John Shields of Carluke in Lanarkshire. The statue was added in 1834. In 1845 there was held in the vicinity of the monument a centenary celebration, repeated in 1945 three days after the official ending of the Second World War, and attended by nearly 3,000 people, among whom were descendants of Highland emigrants and families whose predecessors had taken an active part in the rising. One of the latter was the Duke of Atholl, who wore a faded white cockade in his bonnet—the very cockade which his ancestor, Lord George

Murray, the Jacobite general, had worn throughout the campaign. Each year, on the Saturday in August nearest to the anniversary date, clansmen meet to take part in the Glenfinnan Gathering and Games. Situated at the head of Loch Shiel there could be no finer setting for such an occasion, so redolent with emotive history and atmosphere. The monument has been in the care of the National Trust for Scotland since 1928. In 1959, in order to ensure preservation of the unspoiled character of the site, Mr Archibald MacKellaig of Glenfinnan entered into a restrictive agreement with the Trust for 28 acres of his land, which surrounds the monument.

The road going westwards from Glenfinnan passes through Kinlochailort, at the head of Lochailort, a 5-mile-long, twisting sea-loch. It then makes its way to Arisaig, passing Loch nan Uamh, yet another place with a historical association: it was here that the Prince disembarked from the *Du Teillay* to set foot on Arisaig. After Arisaig, the road turns north into South Morar and North Morar. These two areas are separated by Loch Morar, now reasonably credited with 'Morag', the equivalent or maybe cousin of Nessie, the Loch Ness monster. This loch is barely a quarter of a mile inland from the sea and is one of Scotland's geological freaks. It is 12 miles long and is over 1,000 feet deep. Yet it lies close to shallow seas and in fact there is no equivalent depth reached in ocean waters until the dip of the continental shelf 170 miles north-west, between St Kilda and Rockall. The loch is the deepest water in Britain. The answer to the question of how it was gouged out of the basic rock is still a problem for geologists. Glacial gouging is the solution most readily to hand, but some further questions do remain. The road to Mallaig borders the shore of the Atlantic and is fringed with white sands which act as magnets to countless tourists. Some areas are particularly beautiful, such as the little inlet where the River Morar flows into the sea. The sands are formed out of fragments of a coral-type algae pounded into tiny particles by the action of the sea. From the small village of Morar both road and railway stick close together in a companionable journey to Mallaig. To the east of these routes is a beautiful desolation, quite unpopulated, which may yet, like other parts of the Highlands, have one of the world's most valuable assets: remoteness.

Mallaig is primarily a railhead and a fishing port. It is by no means beautiful, yet it displays a liveliness which befits a doorway to Skye and the Inner and Outer Hebrides. The harbour is always chock-full with fishing vessels, puffers, freight craft and the usual accompaniment of small boats. The population is around 1,000, a figure which is easily doubled in the summer months. As a specialized fishing port all other activities in Mallaig tend to fall into insignificance. The total value of the catches landed here in 1972 was well over £2 million. Some fifty herring boats use the harbour, and the lobster fleet based on Mallaig fishes along some 200 miles of coastline—which makes the port the most important not only on the Highland western seaboard but on that of Britain. As much as 10,000 pounds of lobster can be seen auctioned on the piers on Saturday mornings. Prawns are packed in wooden tea-chests, with alternate layers of ice and fish, before being sent to Whitby and other marketing centres.

In the early 1900s Mallaig was a tiny community in which fewer than 100 people wrested a livelihood from this inhospitable corner of the rocky coast. By 1973 it was being hailed as the leading herring port in Europe. Its importance was enhanced when a Norwegian TV unit made the town the subject of a television programme which was screened throughout Norway on Christmas Day 1972.

The present prosperity marks a fitting end to a decade of growth. In the early 1960s Mallaig was merely a humble west-coast port of low-ranking status, and often a port of call or convenience. In 1962 the total catch landed was some 12,000 tons of fish worth £450,000. Largely through the endeavour of local entrepreneurs and initiators, the port has grown under its own impetus, and it is unusual that it has not been deemed eligible for the same kind of crash-aid programme and financial assistance by the Highlands and Islands Development Board as needed by other ports such as Stornoway on Lewis. It was by dint of hard work and the endeavours of its business fraternity that this bustling Inverness-shire port is now accepted as a prime example of what can be achieved through foresight and determination to win through to an accessible goal. The present herring landings are worth something in the region of £1·9 million, representing some 261,000 crans of herring (the catch was 32,000 crans in 1957). White-fish landings, which stood at 9,000 hundredweights in 1957, were, in 1971, well over 25,000 hundredweights, worth £120,000. Shellfish landings valued at just over £40,000 sixteen years ago were, in 1971, worth ten times that figure. Altogether something like £2·75 million changed hands at the port during 1972.

There is still a great deal to do at the port in order to consolidate the present growth and prepare for further expansion. Plans are now being made for the development of the port's facilities. At present fewer than twenty berths are available for an average of thirty boats per day landing herring during the season. At peak times there have been as many as fifty boats queueing for berths. However, this does not detract too much from the port as by nine o'clock each morning the pier has generally been cleared of fish, the result of port workers handling catches with high speed and efficiency. The problems of the port are mainly physical, due to restrictions of land, space for operations (and piers) and an unsatisfactory road exit from the town. These conditions exist at the present time despite a £700,000 reconstruction of the inner harbour and the rebuilding of the fish pier, completed in 1972. A new order, outlining further improvements, estimated to cost £870,000, was laid before Parliament in 1973. Future improvements include the construction of a breakwater by extending the existing steamer pier and a facility for the use of roll-on/roll-off car ferries. The landward facilities are also under a close scrutiny for improvement and re-development. For these improvements the Highlands and Islands Development Board are to contribute a 35 per cent grant, the remainder being left to Mallaig to find by itself.

The growth of Mallaig has proved to be a lure to large commercial interests. Associated Fisheries have acquired a cold store at the port and have plans for development which has the prospect of offering extra jobs. A food-processing firm has also taken a place in the town's economic picture with a good jobs prospect. Upwards of 65 per cent of the male population in the district earn their living through the fishing industry, either directly or indirectly. The 1973 figure of boats working from the east coast and the Clyde with Mallaig as a base was sixty. In addition, about eighteen local boats (mainly in the 50- to 60-foot range and fairly new) form a useful home-based nucleus for further expansion. The total working population is 500. In addition to this figure are fish salesmen, fish buyers and their staffs, and a variety of pier workers and lorry drivers.

In such an environment of prosperity it is one of the many paradoxes to be found in the Highlands that this situation does not exist without a certain Gilbertian element in the picture. This latter is the road out of Mallaig. It is a tortuous 47-mile road. Much of the road is single-track, which is not only a hazard for private users but also for the fleets of lorries taking fish away from Mallaig. Although the town is connected to Fort William by rail, all the fish traffic goes out by road in 32-ton lorries. The road is used regularly by a couple of German refrigerated vehicles, each 70 feet long. During the height of the summer season, when the road is crowded with tourists who use Mallaig as a stepping-off point for Skye and the Outer Hebrides, the road is commandeered by an average of sixty articulated lorries, 32-ton laden, every day for six days a week. On some stretches of this road there are corkscrews and twists and a startling variation in road width which almost point to criminal negligence on the part of the local authority's roads committee. At Glenfinnan there is an additional problem of a bridge which has a clearance of under 12 feet. Part of the road on Locheilside is also used by lorries carrying timber for the pulp mill at Corpach; these add excitement if not danger to road users in private vehicles. As if this were not enough, road blocks are frequently caused by heavy lorries which fail to take a hill, or else veer too close to the road verge. A slight sprinkling of snow is all that is required to cut Mallaig off from the outside world for a day or so. In 1972 a fire-engine was delayed for almost an hour because of fish lorries, and its journey from Fort

William to Arisaig was rendered rather pointless. Another road danger is lorries driving nose-to-tail. At one time, fish lorries were 'flagged out' of Mallaig at intervals of fifteen minutes, a device which allowed private road users to overtake in safety. Plans are now being made to improve the road, and it is expected that by 1975 some 31 miles of the 47-mile stretch will have a good 18-foot carriageway. This, however, is still not good enough to serve a port which stands head and shoulders above others and, if the matter is left to the slow process of government action, future years could well see Mallaig suffering from its inability to make the most of the considerable attention given to it.

In many ways Mallaig shows the signs of a boom town, with transients, such as the 150 lorry drivers who crew the fleet of trucks, mixing with the fishermen who jam the town at weekends for some kind of relaxation. Inevitably, the town's resources for entertainment are stretched to bulging. Public houses are small gold mines. The emphases are not, however, all on the refreshment aspect. There is an excellent community centre, built at a cost of £25,000, two-thirds of which sum was raised by the community. It houses dances, concerts and badminton among a variety of entertainments for all sections of the resident and transient community. There is also a good nine-hole golf course complete with clubhouse, again built by the Mallaig folk. The local secondary school provides educational facilities of a high standard to third-year level, but then falls short in the way of adequate accommodation. The proposal for a new school is now being given high priority. A swimming pool is mooted for a community from which so many will eventually earn their living at sea. A Seamen's Mission building has been erected to provide much-needed facilities for itinerant workers whose problems have been the subject of a special study carried out by the Mallaig Harbour Authority, established in 1968. The developments proposed in total will create for both men and women many more jobs which cannot be filled from the existing labour pool. It is envisaged that an influx of population will be needed to maintain the present growth and produce a 50 per cent increase in Mallaig's population in the next decade or so.

The northern coast of the Morar peninsula edges on Loch Nevis. This loch is quite open, uncrowded by lowering masses. It contains a large bight called Inverie Bay, a wide and spacious opening guarded by both hill and headland. Growth around here is luxurious. The hill-slopes around Inverie village on the Knoydart side of the loch were well wooded until recently and now look like the result of bad cropping. At one time the land supported a thousand people who lived on cultivated produce, vegetables, corn and cattle—which, with fishing, offered a good and satisfactory life. Now there are in the whole of the Knoydart peninsula but seven small settlements, whose members are occupied in crofting, forestry, sheep-farming and deer-stalking. Indeed,

Knoydart, with its rough bounds, is about the only large peninsula of the west Highlands to retain to the present day the isolation of many centuries. The roads here are purely functional and aimed at providing links between the communities. The motoring tourist has never been considered here as he has in so many other parts of the region. The walking enthusiast, however, can have the pleasure of many miles of unsullied shorelands and five mountain glens and passes.

Knoydart's once-large population, compared with today's handful, were resident until just after the Forty-five, when there was a long period of emigration to Canada. By 1846 there were about 600 people, who suffered from the first of a series of disasters. First, potato blight created famine conditions. Then the expected shoals of herring in Loch Nevis failed to appear in their former numbers. Further emigration followed. In 1852 Aeneas MacDonell of Glengarry died and his widow, in an attempt to create a sheep farm of Knoydart, cleared by force no fewer than 400 people from Airor, Doune, Sandaig and Inverie. Their holdings were destroyed and the folk driven like cattle aboard a waiting transport supplied by the British government. It is quite a thought that the Mother of Parliaments could so willingly and unfeelingly lend a hand, just over a century ago, to the atrocious efforts of landowners to clear people from land which their ancestors had occupied for centuries. Perhaps the greater shame rests on the Highland chiefs and their families who perpetrated such services on their kinsfolk. Knoydart today is a living memory and monument to all the long-departed communities that once thrived in the Highlands.

The parish of Glenelg, situated as yet another peninsula between Loch Hourn in the south and Loch Duich in the north, is an area of sharp contrast. The central part is mountainous, with the Saddle rising to 3,317 feet. To the north, east and south, the ground falls away to flat green land. To travel into Glenelg from the north is to cross over a mountain range by way of the Mam Ratagan Pass. The climb is one-in-six, with many hairpin bends. But the road surface is good and, with a reliable vehicle, and undaunted by approaching bulky timber lorries, one obtains one of the really magnificent views in the whole of the British Isles. From a vantage point one can look towards the Five Sisters of Kintail, a range of peaks extending 6 miles down Glen Shiell and in fact the western peaks of a continuous range of mountains which run some 20 miles from Glen Moriston to the east. Once over the ridge, one drops down through Ratagan Forest, planted by the Forestry Commission, into Glen More, and thence to the western shore of Glenelg which borders on the Sound of Sleat. The shoreland is flat and ends in a stony beach from which one looks over to Skye and Kylerhea. A ferry service operates between Glenelg and Kylerhea across the sound.

Near Glenelg, on the road to the ferry, stand the ruins of the old

Bernera Barracks, in which the Hanoverian troops were quartered for a period of seventy years from 1722. The ruins are most impressive but in a bad state of repair as the result of their being used as a general rubbish dump. Perhaps their neglect is the just consequence of their former association. Even so, they do form a visible part of the past and often unhappy history of the Highlands, and as such deserve better treatment and care, if only to display to good effect their interesting constructional and architectural details. During the course of their Highland jaunt, Boswell and Johnson had hoped to spend a night at the barracks for, as Boswell observed, "soldiers have always everything in the best order". But, when they arrived they found only a sergeant and a few men in the place and had to seek quarters in an inn where "a lass showed us upstairs into a room raw and dirty; bare walls, a variety of bad smells, a coarse black fir greasy table, forms of the same kind, and from a wretched bed started a fellow from his sleep like Edgar in King Lear: 'Poor Tom's a-cold!' "

Glenelg has always been a gateway to Skye. In the days before motor transport and before the opening of the railway to Kyle of Lochalsh in 1898, the Kylerhea crossing was the main route between Skye and the Scottish mainland. By it Johnson and Boswell approached Skye in 1773. By crossing the strait of Kylerhea, enormous droves of cattle were 'exported' from Skye *en route* for the Crieff and Falkirk Trysts. A writer in 1813 describes the cattle crossing from Kylerhea to Glenelg:

> All the cattle reared in the Isle of Skye which are sent to the southern markets pass from the Island to the mainland by the ferry of Caol Rea. Their numbers are very considerable, by some supposed to be 5,000 but by others 8,000 annually, and the method of ferrying them is not in boats as is done from the Long Island where the passage is broad, but they are forced to swim over Caol Rea. For this purpose the drovers purchase ropes which are cut at the length of 3 feet, having a noose at one end. This noose is put round the underjaw of every cow, taking care to have the tongue free. The reason given for leaving the tongue loose is that the animal may be able to keep salt water from going down its throat in such a quantity as to fill all the cavities in the body, which would prevent the action of the lungs: for every beast is found dead and said to be drowned at the landing place to which this mark of attention has not been paid. Whenever the noose is put under the jaw, all the beasts destined to be ferried together are led by the ferryman into the water until they are afloat, which puts an end to their resistance. Then every cow is tied to the tail of the cow before until a string of 6 to 8 be joined. A man in the stern of the boat holds the rope of the foremost cow. The rowers then ply their oars immediately. During the time of high water or soon before or after full tide is the most favourable passage because the current is then least violent. The ferrymen are so dextrous that very few beasts are lost.

The last crossing of cattle in this way took place in 1906.

It is on record that as many as 2,000 animals at one time were made to cross the strait by swimming, with a very low percentage loss. It was the existence of this great cattle trade which led, in the end, to the complete reconstruction of the roads to Glenelg from the Great Glen. The route was surveyed by Provost Brown of Elgin in 1792. The original road was proposed in 1746 to make a military route from Fort Augustus to the Bernera Barracks. The bridges were first erected by contractors who had the choice of those crossings over the waters where materials could be had at the cheapest rates. By this means, roads were unnecessarily lengthened and carried over steep and high precipices. In July 1804, Lord MacDonald and other Inverness-shire proprietors signed a memorial pleading for a Glenshiel–Glenelg and Glenshiel–Lochalsh road "as the only practicable line for driving cattle to market" from the isles of Skye, Uist and Harris and the extensive grazing estates of Glenelg and Lochalsh. The commissioners heeded the prayer and by 1824 the road to Glenelg was built with others which opened up much of the west Highlands.

In common with other Highland districts, Glenelg suffered from the clearing acts of proprietors. By the end of the eighteenth century hundreds had been forced to emigrate from the district; a figure of 324 is given in the Old Statistical Account, and in the New Statistical Account, of half a century later, the Rev. Beith lamented: "The large farm system has come more freely into operation. . . . By it the country has been bereaved of her worthiest children, and in the exaltation of a few individuals thousands are doomed to poverty. The ease to the landowner in securing the returns of his property can be no compensation for this evil." Between 1831 and 1901 the total population of the parish fell from 2,874 to 1,503. In 1951 it was 1,406 and in 1971 the figure was estimated at around 1,000.

There are three important glens in the parish. Glen More is heavily forested in its upper part and is a farmed strath in its lower reaches. Two miles south and running parallel to Glen More is Glen Beag, which gives access by a path to the north face of Ben Sgriol, to Arnisdale on Loch Hourn, and to Kinlochourn. The third glen is Arnisdale. The first two glens are particularly fertile and it may well be this factor which led to their being inhabited for at least 2,000 years. In Glen Beag the fields display luxurious growths of grass and the road winds through woods of hazel and alder. In the glen are two brochs, Dun Telve and Dun Trodden, now under the care of the Department of the Environment. The date given for Dun Telve is 'Iron Age', which in Scotland began around 100 B.C. It is regarded as being second only to the Broch of Mousa in Shetland in its state of preservation. The ruins, which are considerable, are a delight to the eye with their excellent shape and symmetry, careful construction and general appearance; one can readily appreciate the workmanship which went into their building. The height of the Dun Telve tower is about

Loch Hope and Ben Hope, Sutherland

Inverness Castle

Glen Shiel, Ross-shire

(*top*) Glenelg ferry to Kylerhea in Skye. (*bottom*) Yachts moored on Caledonian Canal at Inverness

33 feet, which applies only to about a third of the circumference. The walls are double, with galleries spiralling up within their thickness, narrowing as the walls taper to the top to become a single wall. The inner courtyard is about 30 feet in diameter and is overlooked by two windows in the inner wall. Built for shelter and protection against raiders, they are excellent models of their kind. Dun Trodden, a little farther up the glen, is smaller but no less interesting and, like its neighbour, is incomplete.

When Dr Johnson described the scenery of the west Highlands as "awful", he was using the older and more correct sense of that word, implying that it was 'full of awe'. He also observed that it was a place "where the imagination was amused", referring not to diversion but to intellectual stimulus. The Kintail area falls into this category of description, with some of the oldest mountains in the world towering into the sky to make the human element in the area, with its equally diminutive communities, almost insignificant in their own magnificent context. The main feature of this area on the north shore of Loch Duich is the Five Sisters of Kintail, peaks which, along with Beinn Fada (3,383 feet) and the Falls of Glomach, now belong to the National Trust for Scotland. The Trust property covers some 15,000 acres. The Five Sisters lie between two narrow glens that lead into the head of Loch Duich, Glen Lichd and Glen Shiel. The peaks rise abruptly from the lochside to present the steepest grass-sloped mountains in Scotland. The money for their purchase was presented to the Trust by the late Mr P. J. Unna, at one time president of the Scottish Mountaineering Club and a climber of great experience. At Morvish, the Trust has established an adventure centre which in 1970 was let to Outward Bound, Morayshire, for a five-year period. The centre is a base for the well-known Outward Bound courses, which aim at the development of character by using the outdoors as a physical and mental challenge. The building was constructed for the Trust by the army under the scheme O.P.M.A.C. (Operation Military Aid to the Community). The Falls of Glomach, difficult of access but well worth the effort, are among the highest in the British Isles and are on the comparatively short mountain burn that runs into the River Elchaig from the high watershed of Beinn Fada and its neighbours to the north.

The small village of Dornie is at the meeting place of the waters of three lochs: Duich, Long and Alsh. It is better known for its nearby castle of Eilean Donan, which sits comfortably on a small rocky promontory jutting out into Loch Duich. It is probably the most photographed structure in Scotland, if not in the British Isles, for its setting is magnificent—though the original castle site was chosen more for its strategic value, the scenery being an incidental bonus. Excavation has revealed evidence of a Pictish fort on the site. In 1230 a fortified stronghold was built on the rock and for the next five centuries it figured in many famous raids and sieges until 1719, when it was shelled and destroyed by English frigates. The ruins remained to gather moss and grass for another two centuries until it was rebuilt between 1912 and 1932 at a cost of over £250,000. Every detail of the restored structure is faithful to the original as confirmed by old plans of the castle preserved in Edinburgh.

To the west of Dornie, once a thriving fishing village, lie Balmacara and Lochalsh, comprising a promontory lying between Loch Alsh and Loch Carron, the nose of which faces out into the Inner Sound of Raasay. This area was opened up only comparatively recently. The railway first penetrated as far as Strome Ferry, half-way along the southern shore of Loch Carron, and was then extended, along embankments and twisting through deep cuttings, to Kyle of Lochalsh in the 1890s. Until the year 1941 there was no through road from the south to Kyle, the approach was cut by the waters of Loch Long where they flow into the confluence of Loch Alsh and Loch Duich at Dornie. Then Loch Long was bridged in 1940 (by a toll bridge; the tolls were abolished in 1946 after local pressure was brought to bear) and the promontory became more accessible. Further improvements in the late 1960s and early 1970s cut out many of the difficulties which daunted even local travellers and now, perhaps predictably, the area swarms with tourists during the summer months.

The Balmacara Estate was bequeathed to the National Trust for Scotland in 1946 by Lady Hamilton. It comprises some 8,000 acres and consists of almost the whole of the western part of the Loch Alsh promontory, with the exception of the Plock of Kyle which Lady Hamilton bequeathed to the community there. The lairds of Balmacara kept their estates well wooded and planted with some attempt at discrimination. The mixed woods at Balmacara House are well tended, though Coille Mhor, felled between the wars, has not been restored.

Balmacara House is a rather plain white building dating from the eighteenth century. It was purchased from the Trust by Ross-shire Education Committee to be run as a boys' school, specializing in agriculture, horticulture and carpentry. The school was designed to offer further education to boys aged just over 14 years. Entry to the school was available primarily to boys from the county of Ross-shire, but also to boys from neighbouring counties in the Highlands. The school provided a sound initial practical and theoretical training for students who eventually sought the National Certificate in Agriculture. The school farm was the focal point of activities. Run on a commercial basis, it was developed to cover a wide range of farm enterprises and facilities for practical instruction. Dairy and beef cattle were raised, with produce being sold locally. This enterprise came to an end in 1973, closed by the high running costs of Balmacara School combined with low recruitment figures. The loss will be a significant gap in the technical education provisions in the Highlands and Islands generally, and one trusts that the closure and its effects was subjected to a full socio-economic investigation before the final decision was taken.

On the northern shore of the Kyle promontory lies Plockton, probably one of the most attractive Highland villages in a beautiful setting which combines both seascape and landscape into a unique whole. Before the railway was built to Kyle, through Strathcarron from Inverness, this haven was a busy port for schooners trading from the Baltic. It was also used by Hebridean fishermen who made the sea journey from Stornoway by rowing across the Minch in heavy boats. Its importance as a port has now disappeared, though it serves as a popular watering place for yachts. Until the advent of the Kyle railway, Plockton was the main centre of population in the parish. A description of 1846 runs:

> Plockton is the principal seat of population in the *Quo ad civilia** parish of Lochalsh. . . . The census of 1841 gave this village a population of 537. The houses, of which several are two storeys high and slated, are erected behind a craggy promontory that runs into the loch, answering all the purposes of a breakwater pier, and forming a fine natural harbour, in which the small fishing vessels of the population ride in perfect security from storms. In addition to the ordinary fishing boats, fitted only for loch fishing, there are several small sloops capable of trading with the Clyde. By means of these smacks they are enabled to carry their herrings to Greenock and Glasgow, where they can also supply themselves with salt and other materials at prime cost.

Today Plockton is something of a backwater, despite its excellent secondary school, until recently run under the direct guidance of Europe's foremost Gaelic poet, Somhairle MacLean, now retired. Many of the houses in the village are holiday homes for townsmen. The population is about 240. In 1966, on rough ground next to the village, the army's Royal Engineers made an air strip which is now being used to give the district an air ambulance service.

Close by Plockton is Duncraig Castle, set in woods and overlooking Loch Carron. The castle was built about a century ago; in the 1930s it was converted into a residential school for girls to learn domestic arts. The original school was run by the owners, Sir Daniel and Lady Hamilton, on lines which they had found successful in India where they were involved in rural training. The experiment at Duncraig, however, was not too successful and other functions for the school were considered. The Second World War intervened, during which the building was converted into a hospital. At the termination of hostilities, the

* A civil parish as distinct from a parish the boundaries of which are defined by former ecclesiastical courts.

school was taken over by the County Education Committee to give residential accommodation to about sixty girls. When the school was opened it was intended for 14- to 15-year-olds, to bridge the gap between formal education and the outside world. This has been acknowledged by its recognition as a college of further education since 1960. The courses often have a strongly vocational value. There are at present about eighty-five places for girls who come from many parts of the Highlands and Islands to take the first steps on their chosen careers.

Before the arrival of the railway in 1898, the village of Kyle of Lochalsh comprised an inn and four houses. Although Kyle had been from early times used as a crossing to Skye, it was the Kylerhea ferry which was more favoured, mainly because the roads in the area tended to go through Glenelg rather than across the peninsular route offered by Lochalsh parish. But the coming of the railway changed things for the village. As the new railhead, it assumed considerable importance and the building of substantial piers enhanced its position as a port. Expansion took place rapidly and the small town mushroomed along the barren rocks and hillocks in the vicinity. The fishing trade helped Kyle to prosper, especially during the war period. But since the end of the Second World War, and in spite of the building of a new pier, Kyle has experienced a diminishing fishing trade in favour of Mallaig and Ullapool. At present the village is dependent on passing tourists for much of its livelihood. The existence of the railway is important from an economic viewpoint and the threatened closure (at the time of writing) has caused the local people to look hard at their means of existence and investigate alternative means of support. An industrial site exists in the village and is expected to attract small industrial enterprises which would offer new kinds of employment to the 600 folk in Kyle and the 3,000 people who live in its catchment area. During the last war, Kyle was made a restricted area and the village itself was the centre for naval operations.

When the Kyle railway was threatened with closure in the mid-1960s, it was revealed that the railway was the largest single source of employment in the area (fifty-seven workers), with the post office coming second (with twenty-seven). The fight to save the rail link between Kyle and Dingwall was won—for a short season. When the line again came under the scrutiny of British Rail's hatchet-men, well-trained by the infamous Dr Beeching, another fight was engaged, this time to win a reprieve of two years. After the announcement that the reprieve had been granted by the Minister for Transport, a massive attempt was launched to prove the line's viability by the re-organization of the services and the publicizing of the line to attract its increased use by tourists. In 1972 the British Rail headquarters in London estimated, with their familiar bad arithmetic which often produces figures distorted by multipliers of two or three, that the costs of the line were £318,000. Earnings from fares were estimated at £51,000, to leave a deficit of some £267,000. The financial workings of British Rail are too well known all over the British Isles to warrant a discussion here, but they have time and time again been proved to be so distorted that they always act against any attempt by objectors to closures to prove a line's viability in economic terms. The greater problem seems to be to have the remits of the Transport Users' Consultative Committees changed to allow the admission of evidence based on community hardship and not merely, as at present, hardship sustained by individuals as the result of a line closure. The social benefits resulting from maintaining a line are of great importance in areas where the rail link is the one and only reliable means of communication while roads are blocked with snow during the winter months. Small wonder it is that Highlanders look askance at the vast sums of money spent on road improvements, underground railways in the London area, and Channel tunnels, which they (in theory at least if not in practice) subsidise, while their own vital link is threatened with closure for a small sum of £250,000, a fraction of the money spent by the Government on such doubtful projects as Concorde. Mr Tom Weir, a great outdoorsman in Scotland, wrote of the Kyle line: "Everyone agrees that main line railways are civilized conveniences worth having even if they run at a loss. . . ."

During 1972 attempts were made by an independent group to take over the Kyle line. The group, Steam Enterprises, with a subsidiary, Wester Ross Railway Company, already owns four steam locomotives and have access to four others, as well as various rolling stock. The aim of the group was to provide an all-year-round service with both diesel and steam engines, after leasing the line from British Rail. In addition, the group intended to establish a railway museum on the line, and workshops to support both the Kyle line and other of the group's activities, overhauling and repairing locomotives for industry, museums and private owners. The group was faced with a totally unrealistic demand from British Rail of £750,000 for the track, station and other facilities and were told that a lease was out of the question. The very refusal of British Rail to consider the lease indicated the deeply entrenched attitude of officials to the real problem of reliable communication links in the west Highlands. The group, with other experts in railway finance, not all employed directly by British Rail, suggested that a figure of £450,000 was more realistic and, if accepted by British Rail, would indicate a desire on the part of a public body to see justice done to satisfy a community's needs. The line is still due for closure by the end of 1973 at the time of writing, and it remains to be seen what in fact will be the disastrous long-term results of this deed; though it may well confirm what has been forecast by those who have studied the implications for the area, and who have shown a far greater concern for the community than have the various government bodies, including the Highlands and Islands Development Board, who function on behalf of the Great British Public.

Perhaps one of the more ominous developments around Kyle is the increasing interest in the area being taken by the Ministry of Defence and its agency the Royal Navy. The area, with its well-protected sea waters, has always been of interest as testing and manœuvring grounds. In 1970 the Ministry of Defence notified the Scottish Development Department of its wish to establish in the Inner Sound of Raasay an underwater acoustic tracking range, including hydrophones to be placed on the sea bed and linked by cable to a shore-based station. Following on this intimation, a variety of consultations then began, culminating in a letter in March 1971 to two county councils (Inverness-shire and Ross and Cromarty) and the Highlands and Islands Development Board, setting out the Ministry's requirements. A meeting was held in Kyle in April 1971 and a number of interests were represented, notably the fishermen of the area who stood to be deprived of good fishing grounds for the purposes of testing the navy's torpedo. Further meetings were held and then, in June 1971, the Scottish Office Press Department issued for publication a notice describing the navy's requirements; this was followed by a statement by the Scottish Development Department, acting for the Secretary of State for Scotland, that, from the standpoint of public interest and from the planning point of view, the Ministry of Defence was free to proceed with its proposals. Just like that!

In all the consultations and meetings, it was obvious that the fishing interests of the Kyle area were regarded as being of secondary importance to the opinions of paid officials such as the county planners, 'alien' (i.e. non-native) county councillors, such as landowners and others (there are many retired brigadiers, generals and high-ranking officers in the area), who stood to gain financially from the increased commercial activity resulting from the project (which was said to offer employment to 150 people, of whom fifty would be drawn from local resources) or who acted in favour of the project because they were ex-Service themselves. At one meeting it was strange to observe that the only local supporter for the navy project was a councillor (a Minister of the Free Church) who said that defence was important to the country, and people (though why the Kyle folk?) had to make sacrifices. *Hansard* reported: ". . . the record of consultation demonstrates the continuing concern of the Ministry of Defence to ensure that local interests are fully consulted, in order to minimize the effect on them of our proposals. During the course of these consultations, the likelihood that some 80 to 90 permanent jobs would be created for local people was pointed out."

What *Hansard* and the official spokesmen for the Ministry of Defence failed to indicate was that the jobs offered would of necessity be of an inferior grade. At one public meeting, the skipper of a local fishing vessel asked whether, should he have to dispose of his craft as the result of the Sound of Raasay being closed for testing purposes, he would be offered a job with the navy, for example as a skipper of a launch or some craft similar in dimension to his own. He was told he would be able to get a job as a deck-hand. The fifty or so jobs originally quoted as coming from the project were in fact semi-skilled jobs. Also brought out at a confrontation meeting between the navy and the local fishing interests was the abysmal lack of appreciation and knowledge of the real problem which would be created for fishermen in the area if the navy were allowed to take over some of the best fishing grounds on the west coast. In the end the Secretary of State refused to acknowledge that a public enquiry was necessary.

The total and long-term effect on the Kyle community of the presence of the Royal Navy is quite unknown. As with other government 'developments', no initial or preliminary sociological survey was carried out and it is significant that the Ministry had decided exactly what it wanted and where it wanted it long before the local community, or even the county authorities involved, knew about the requirements. Indeed, the county authority was sufficiently moved at one stage of the proceedings—or perhaps only peeved—to make a statement that insufficient time had been left to it to arrange possible objections to the scheme when it was first publicly announced. This trend, to impose 'development' on otherwise powerless communities is most disturbing; the remoter they are the more vulnerable they become. Any injection of economic activity into an otherwise potentially depressed area is no guarantee for the future if it is based on government expenditure. Those who raised objections to the Sound of Raasay proposals had, on the one hand, to consider that the prospects of jobs, new or alternative employment, was important to the area; and, on the other hand, to consider the stultifying and vitiating effect, as is evidenced on South Uist, of a military presence, as being erosive and corrosive in the context of societal stability. The very fact that the Sound of Raasay was to be closed, not only to fishing vessels (thirty-seven boats involved in all), but to trade and coastal shipping for 143 days in each year indicated that the enforced clearance of the Hebridean waters by the navy would create a desert which could never be filled again if the navy chose to leave as a result of a possible change in the Government's defence policy. The fact, too, that the navy were unable to offer skilled work to any native who found himself jobless as the result of the sea clearance was totally unacceptable to some objectors. The possibility of an escalation of use by the navy of the Sound of Raasay was not ruled out completely by the Ministry of Defence, despite some skilful, but unconvincing exercises in assuaging fears on this point. If it seems that this particular matter has been written about at undue length, with the possible effect of boring readers, I should point out that it has been done to indicate the kind of pressures which are being placed on small and defenceless communities in many parts of the Highlands today; and while commercial and industrial interests can be fought on reasonably fair terms, a battle with a government department is lost before the battle has commenced.

The long sea-loch on the northern side of the Lochalsh promontory is Loch Carron, which narrows at the ferry crossing of Strome, a constriction which tends to protect the inner length of the loch from sea storms. Strome became a place of importance when the railway reached there in 1870. A large station and pier were constructed and passenger and mail steamers sailed out from Strome to the Hebrides. Cattle, sheep and large quantities of fish were entrained at Strome for southern markets. Strome lost its importance as a railhead when the Highland Railway extended its tracks to Kyle, and now acts as a bottleneck for cars waiting to cross Loch Carron by ferry and pass into the Applecross peninsula.

Strome has at least two niches in history, both rather entertaining episodes. Between 1880 and 1881, the S.S. *Ferret*, a ship belonging to the Highland Railway and stationed at Strome, made world news after she was 'hired' by James Henderson, alias Smith, who took her to South America, Africa and Australia. Her disappearance caused her erstwhile owners no end of concern; despite cables to agents in ports all over the country, nothing was seen or heard of her. Then in June 1881 news was received in London and Glasgow by Reuters telegram that the steamer, really a coaster of 346 tons, had been located in Melbourne, as far away from her home port as could be conceived. "The reputed owner, the captain, and the purser of the steamer *India*, alias *Ferret*, have been arrested on a charge of forging the ship's register, and have been remanded. The discovery of a telegraphic code on board the vessel leads to the belief that there were accomplices in England concerned in the fraud." The ship was recognized by a native of the area who was struck by the astonishingly similar details of the *India* and the *Ferret*, which he had known intimately. The culprits were ultimately sentenced. The ship was sold to an Australian company and was wrecked in a storm in 1920.

The other incident which threw Strome into the gaze of the public eye occurred in June 1873 when the village became the centre of what the august *Times* called the 'Sabbatarian Riots'. The cause of the Strome affair was the arrival at Strome pier of two cargoes of fish on the steamers *Lochiel* and *Talisman* at about 1 a.m. on a Sunday morning. Fifty local folk appeared on the scene and took possession of the pier. The man in charge of the off-loading crane was seized and dragged from his work and a complete stoppage of pier activity followed. The

Thatched cottage by Loch Alsh

Eilean Donan Castle, Dornie

Schooner off Plockton

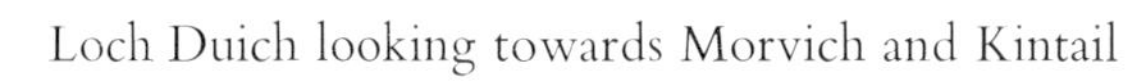

Loch Duich looking towards Morvich and Kintail

nearest policeman, at Plockton, was called up but he was not available. The following day, the Chief Constable and six men arrived from Dingwall, but found they were unable to cope with the situation. Eventually drafts of policemen from Perth, Lanark, Inverness, Nairn and Elgin, a total of 160 men, were called in. A confrontation was expected on the following Sunday, when 2,000 people were due to concentrate on a mass rally, but the matter was settled when the local Free Church ministers intervened and saved what might have become a sore and bloody disaster.

In 1972 a large industrial concern expressed an interest in Loch Carron as the site of a yard for the construction of giant concrete oil-production platforms. The company, in association with the Highlands and Islands Development Board, said that the presence of a railway and sheltered deep water were two important factors which had led the company to place Loch Carron on a short list of possible sites. Immediately the tourist interests in the area, and particularly Plockton, protested at the detrimental effect a 500-feet-high oil rig would have on the scenery. Others, however, welcomed the proposal in its context as a jobs producer. Another company also expressed its interest in the area close by the village of Drumbuie. Opposition to the development proposals was expressed by the crofters on the affected land, which is part of the Balmacara Estate and held for the nation by the National Trust for Scotland. This body backed its tenants' objections and publicized the fact that it cannot be divested of its ownership of the land without a parliamentary order. It remains to be seen to what extent these oil-construction interests can influence parliamentary procedure and persuade the government departments involved with North Sea oil that the sites required for the benefit of the nation are not necessarily for the benefit of the crofting communities who stand to be completely swamped and dispossessed for the sake of short-term profits which would certainly not be even fractionally applied to the enhancement of the area in which the sums will be generated.

Lochcarron village lies on the north shore of the loch. This area was once an important fishing community with a population of over 2,000 people: "In a calm evening, when hundreds of boats are seen shooting their nets, and scores of vessels lying at anchor, Loch Carron exhibits a scene of rural felicity and of rural beauty that seldom is to be witnessed." The herring shoals, however, eventually vanished and with their disappearance, along with the decline of salmon and sea trout, the population was decimated. Today the number in the area is about a quarter of the maximum population sustained last century.

North of Loch Carron lies hard country. The rock here is Torridon sandstone, Archaean gneiss and Cambrian quartzite, material which refuses to break down and weather into good soil. Great tracts are wild, windswept and empty save for tokens of wild life; the human factor is insignificant except in those pin-points of land where the soil yields up a chance for survival. To the north lies Coulin Forest, a deer tract; to the west lies the Applecross peninsula with a vast dam-like rise of mountains which almost defy their crossing. There are two National Nature Reserves in the area: Rassal Ashwood and the Allt nan Carnan Gorge. The former lies about a mile north of the head of Loch Kishorn; it consists of over 200 acres of grassland and an ashwood with characteristic plant associations. A policy of fencing in 5 acres of ashwood has yielded good results, with some spectacular growth of ferns, herbs and young trees, all of which would otherwise have succumbed to the attention of farm stock, rabbits and deer. The Allt nan Carnan Gorge varies from 30 feet to 80 feet in depth and is interesting for its collection of oak, birch, hazel, Scots pine, wych elm, bird cherry, goat willow and other tree species growing in the area.

Kishorn village lies in quite lush countryside, with large hayfields which contrast sharply with the brown heath of the hinterland. Kishorn is not so well known today. But during the middle of the last century, the place was well enough known on account of its unusual ambassadors: the Kishorn dwarfs. These were reputed to be the last family of dwarfs born in Scotland of parents who were of normal stature. In 1846 a certain William MacKenzie took the dwarfs on tour with a travelling company and caused no end of excitement. The Highland dwarfs were then engaged to go to London. They consisted of two brothers and a sister. The eldest was 22 years old and 45 inches high, the second 20 years old and 45 inches, the girl 18 years and 43 inches. They each had double elbow and knee joints. They were dressed in MacKenzie tartan and could chant Gaelic melodies, a particular attraction with audiences. In 1847 the dwarfs appeared before the Queen at Buckingham Palace: "Their trip to the South has greatly improved them, not only in personal appearance, but in smartness and in intelligence. They have also acquired the English Language, of which they were formerly ignorant. Their performance was considered superior to that of Tom Thumb exhibited by Barnum." The memorial stone to this remarkable family still stands in the old churchyard of Lochcarron. The last surviving member died in 1912.

Much of the greater part of the Applecross peninsula is deer forest; human settlements appear as welcome surprises on the coastal fringe facing the Inner Sound, looking across to Raasay, and on the northern part. To get to Applecross village one must cross the Bealach na Ba (the Pass of the Cattle). Flanked by soaring cliffs, this narrow glen bites deeply into the ancient sandstone mountains which ascend in giant steps to a barren plateau 2,000 feet high, where the bedrock often thrusts through a threadbare turf and clouds race past one's head seemingly, and often literally, a few feet above. The road through the pass, the highest in Britain, virtually cajoles permission to make its tortuous way through to the main part of the peninsula. In winter time, the pass is often blocked with heavy falls of snow, and Applecross has often been described more as an insular community than one recognized as 'remote mainland'. The community has learned not to depend too much on this link, the only one it has with the rest of Scotland, built by a former landowner merely to satisfy his love of the chase and not for the convenience of his tenants. The road is truly Alpine in character, and as one's car negotiates the zig-zags one expects at every turn to see high, sharp-pointed mountainous and snow-clad peaks. Though the area is a rock desert, it is not without its characteristic wild life (red deer, wild cat and golden eagle). The unrelenting scenery gives way to some relief and contrast as the road descends to Applecross village, through some woodlands. At the village, the road turns south to serve four communities before ending at Toscaig pier. These communities are in a truly wonderful patchwork of vegetation with wild flowers growing by the roadside and tiny patches of fields, yielding potato crops or hay. The scent of the lush summer growth mingles with the salt air from the sea and excites the nostrils. On this route, at Camusterach, there is an excellent bay, superior to that at Applecross, which is a natural harbour in which fishing boats can lie protected by Eilean nan Naomh, the Holy Isle, on which the old saint Maelrubha is said to have landed when he first visited the district in A.D. 673. The pier at Toscaig is in sea contact with a boat from Kyle of Lochalsh.

Considering the secondary and unreliable nature of the land link, the sea link is vital in the life of the Applecross community. Yet in 1970 closure of the ferry was proposed and it was only after a vigorous campaign of protest that the link was maintained when Ross and Cromarty County Council took over the running of the ferry from the Scottish Transport Group which, with a typical unconcern for the result of its actions, had announced without warning in July 1970 that "as from the 21st July the Toscaig mail boat will cease to operate". This ferry carries most of what the Applecross community needs for its basic existence: bread, groceries, plastic guttering, cement, fish-hooks, general building hardware, newspapers and mails. Though the ferry service was undoubtedly uneconomic, it was an essential social provision and one which had the withdrawal taken place, would almost certainly have meant desertion, to add yet another small pin-point of tragedy to the Highland clearance process which has been a continuous operation and drain on the region for more than a century now. The insular, rather than peninsular, character of the south Applecross community is a dominating one and therefore the sea link is truly vital. As if to underline the Gilbertian character of official administration, almost coincident with the announcement of the Toscaig closure, building contractors were invited to inspect the Toscaig pier with a view to submitting tenders for a new pier! This was an unnecessary amenity, for the old pier was in excellent shape and perfectly capable of functioning as a ferry terminal. The money for this new pier was to have come from an allocation made for this purpose some years previously by St Andrew's House in Edinburgh, the seat of the Civil Service in Scotland. And, having fixed the use to which the allocation was to be put, the administration could not find it in their hearts, minds, books or files to re-allocate the money to, say, put a much-needed tarmacadam surface on the road through Bealach na Ba. The existence of the 200 people on the Applecross peninsula is still under a cloud of uncertainty, a fact which must introduce an element of instability into the whole community and can hardly be an incentive to perform the basic, but seldom acknowledged, function of all remote communities: to keep land open for future generations.

The coastal communities of north Applecross are better served. A good road east of the peak range goes through Glen Shieldaig to Shieldaig village where rather too many of the houses are being converted into holiday homes owned by a new affluent breed, popularly called 'white settlers', which has in recent years made its appearance in the Highlands. To the west of Shieldaig are five small crofting communities, linked together by footpaths. The handfuls of people in these townships often pose the thought of how long they can continue in existence. Certainly proposals of evacuation have been raised from time to time, but considerations and factors, probably incomprehensible to modern urban-dwellers, have overridden any advantages which might accrue as a result of evacuation and desertion. The social problems remain, of course, and perhaps only the injection of new, young and sympathetic blood can overcome them.

Gairloch is the name of the land which lies between Loch Torridon in the south and Gruinard Bay in the north, a southern inlet at the mouth of Loch Broom. Within its confines lie some of the best which the Highlands can offer in the way of scenery. Vistas open up, unfolding on each other, as one proceeds both north and west. The southern marches of Gairloch begin with the Torridon area. In 1967 the Torridon Forest was given to the National Trust for Scotland, an area of some 14,000 acres which extends westwards from Sail Mhor (the peak at the west end of Beinn Eighe) to Inver Alligin on Loch Torridon. The eastern boundary marches with that of the Nature Conservancy's reserve on einn Eighe. Perhaps the most impressive sight in Torridon is that of Liathach. As viewed from Glen Torridon the mountain mass rises from a broad base to remind one of some ancient Stone Age knife-edge. The name of this massif of red sandstone is 'The Grey One', and it reaches 3,456 feet. It has seven tops, four of which are quartzite, stretching along a ridge 5 miles long. The Beinn Eighe (the File) Reserve extends to just over 10,000 acres and is an area of high biological interest and classical geology, displaying clearly all the main rocks of the north-west Highlands: gneiss, schist, Torridonian sandstone and quartzite. The reserve is part of the old Kinlochewe deer forest, and contains one of the few surviving fragments of the western type of Scots pine forest. Within the reserve are red deer, roe deer, pine marten, wildcat, ptarmigan and golden eagle. There are rich communities of Arctic-Alpine plants on the mountain tops. Since the establishment of the reserve in 1951, the first in Britain, the Nature Conservancy has been managing the woodlands and the deer, using the area as an open-air laboratory and an educational facility, in a kind of outdoor class-room. New forest is being created from the old, in fenced-in plots which keep out animal marauders. The red deer are managed to produce a sustained yield of venison; about thirty carcases are sold annually to the local market. Beinn Eighe itself is another multi-peaked mass, with seven peaks running along a 7-mile ridge; the bulk of the mountain is red sandstone with four peaks entirely of Cambrian quartzite.

Perhaps the main outstanding single feature of the area is Loch Maree, interesting for a number of associations with the Highland past. The loch is 12 miles long and is enhanced in its beauty by the Slioch, a peak which rises on its north side. "Utterly savage and terrific" was a description given to Loch Maree in 1811. Another writer, in a letter to Sir Walter Scott, was constrained to set down his impressions: "The first day of Creation was not more beautiful. July was in its full glory, a few thin silvery clouds rested on the clear blue sky, and the sun shed a flood of light on the bright surface of Loch Maree which reflected every rock and every tree that hung over its glassy surface. No one can know the full value of summer who has not known it in a land of mountains. No one can feel who has not felt it among such hills, the joy with which the sun can fill the mind." Queen Victoria also paid the royal visit to grace the shores with her presence and she, in her journal also waxed eloquent.

Loch Maree was the site of iron-smelting activities some centuries ago. It is just over three centuries now since the Loch Maree Ironworks were closed for good. Loch Maree was of course only one of a number of places in the Highland region where iron was worked. There are, in the north, some eleven known sites in Sutherland, and some thirteen sites have been identified in Ross-shire; Inverness-shire boasted of fourteen. Early inhabitants of the Highlands knew how to get iron for weapons, and for domestic and agricultural purposes. The older of the works are usually found built high up on hillsides, or in valleys with little water, so that the prevailing winds gave good blasts to the furnaces. Much of the ore came from adjacent bogs, though eventually ore was imported from other parts of Britain. There were three main ironworks in the Loch Maree district: Fasagh, Letterewe and Red Smiddy. The Fasagh works were very large and covered acres of ground on the south bank of Amhuinn an Fasaigh, which flows from Loch Fada to Loch Maree. The works were situated close to the shore of the loch. At Loch Fada there are traces of a sluice and a dam, the purpose of which seems to have been an attempt to retain water at certain seasons. The whole site is surrounded by heaps of iron slag. There is a tradition in the district that some of the workers were English, or at least English-speaking. A spot of ground nearby is known as Cladh nan Sasunnach, the burying-ground of the English. This Fasagh works was one of the last at which bog iron ore was smelted direct with peat charcoal, which latter material was made in the area up until the middle of last century, mainly for local blacksmiths. The local people used to make it in their kitchens and take it to the smithies when they wanted their horses shod.

The furnace at Letterewe was the earliest historic ironworks in the country. It was situated on the north bank of the Furnace Burn, which flows into Loch Maree about a mile south of Letterewe House. The first mention of these works is dated 1610, when Sir George Hay obtained the woods of Letterewe for use in his ironworks. This Sir George probably gained his knowledge of the manufacture of iron in Perthshire for, in 1598, he obtained from James VI the Carthusian Priory of Perth and the ecclesiastical lands of Errol, a country well known for iron making. The works at Letterewe were going well in 1608. In fact, so rapidly was the countryside denuded of wood that in January 1609 an Act was passed "commanding, charging and inhibiting all and sundry of His Majesty's lieges and subjects that none of them presume nor take upon hand to work or make any iron with wood or timber under pain of confiscation of the whole iron". But Sir George was an influential man and managed to have this Act repealed. In addition, he obtained in 1610 the privilege of making glass and iron within the whole Kingdom of Scotland. In 1621 he got the right of selling his iron in any royal burgh. Sir George grew rich on the proceeds and died Earl of Kinnoul in 1634. The iron from the Loch Maree works was put to many uses, some good and some bad. The metal was, of course, as might be expected in those times, in great demand for swords, hilts, armour and the like. It was indeed a sellers' market in the seventeenth century. More peaceful uses of the metal included plough socks, pots, fire bars and grates, and nails. In the end it was the supply of iron for military purposes that brought the ironworks to a close. For the product was used for casting cannon to be used subsequently in rebellions against the London government. The politicians, as always, had the final say and the works were brought to an abrupt end, to close an interesting chapter of Highland industrial history when Loch Maree was a rather unusual 'Black Country'.

The bulk of the population and settlements of Gairloch border on the sea coasts, from Redpoint round by Loch Gairloch to Melvaig, and round the bight of Loch Ewe to Gruinard Bay and Little Loch Broom. The scattered village of Gairloch serves as a focal point for communities such as Badachro, Shieldaig and Opinan, and Strath to Melvaig. The main township contains about 300 people, with a further 1,500 or so in the hinterland served by the village. The Minch fishing fleet uses a pier here to land catches, which has resulted in Gairloch being placed sixth in the fishing-port league on the Highland coast. The catch comprises mainly white fish and shellfish with a total value around £300,000. The small port is, however, used in the main by 'stranger' vessels, a situation which does not encourage any developments on shore. Even so, the fishing interest provides an element of economic viability which the area in general would feel if it were to find itself relying on the tourist trade only for its *raison-d'être*.

Next to Loch Maree, Poolewe is perhaps one of the best-known names on the west coast, for the nearby Inverewe Gardens draw more than 100,000 visitors each year from all parts of the world. Inverewe Gardens cover about 50 acres and are operated by the National Trust for Scotland. The origins and history of the gardens are well documented. In 1862 Am Ploc Ard (the High Lump) was a bleak, peat-covered mass of Torridonian sandstone, its only vegetation being heather, crowberry and two small, wind-swept dwarf willow trees. Its new owner, Osgood MacKenzie, had a love of nature, however, and sought to make something of this wilderness. Knowing that the district has a mild winter climate, due to the influence of the Gulf Stream which sends warm water round the west Highland shores, he decided that by a process of sheltering and creating good soil, he could grow many unusual and tender plants. He fenced off the small peninsula and planted a belt of Corsican and Scots pines as a windbreak: this was followed by thick hedges of *Rhododendron ponticum* and by hardwoods—birch, oak, beech and rowan. "For four or five years my poor peninsula looked miserable, but at last we could see some bright specks appearing above the heather." These were the pine trees which required another twenty years of growing before they were able to offer the necessary shelter for the exotic plants MacKenzie started to grow in his garden. The enterprise was developed for another sixty years until his death in 1922, after which his work was carried on by his daughter. In 1952 the gardens were handed over to the National Trust for Scotland. Inverewe is primarily a spring garden and is best visited in late May or early June when the magnificent rhododendrons are at their peak. But there are rare sights to be seen at other times of the year. The charm of the gardens lie in their informal layouts and seen against the barren hinterland are as sharp a contrast as can be expected. Lest it be thought that the gardens were in the nature of a 'folly', it should be mentioned that the work created by the gardens over a period of many years was important for the local community. There were no Clearances in Gairloch last century. On the contrary, the MacKenzie family subsidized the fishing industry in the area by buying wood for local boats and guaranteeing sale-money for catches. The immense amount of work required in transforming Inverewe into a garden needed the employment of a small army. Sour peaty ground had to be drained and rocks dug out. Soil was carried up to the promontory in creels on mens' backs to fill troughs between rocks to create deep earth-beds. The growth of the garden was a continuous development which offered employment to a steady number of people, a fact for which MacKenzie, were he to be remembered for nothing else, would, one expects, have been quite satisfied.

On the north shore of Loch Ewe is Aultbea. It is at present an Admiralty depot, an echo of the busy base which served through two world wars. A boom across Loch Ewe can still be operated if the need arises. In the last war the place was used as a merchant harbour, in which ships would assemble to await a naval escort. Many convoys for Russia left here to run the gauntlet thrown down by German U-boats. Recent extensions include piers and quays; these and other work in progress offer much unskilled and semi-skilled employment to local crofters who find their crofts unable to offer them subsistence livings. The injection of ready cash into this district has produced a prosperous air which is reflected in the well-kept houses.

5

The Great Glen

GLEN MORE, or the Great Glen, generally regarded as being one of the world's best examples of a topographical schism, is now occupied by a series of long, narrow and deep lochs, stretching over 50 miles from Inverness to Fort William in a north-east to south-west direction. Included within this area of the Highlands are the very ancient Lewisian gneiss, Torridonian sandstone, mica-altered Moine schists, Old Red Sandstone and tertiary basalts. To savour this gift of nature at its best one must, by some means, travel by water from Fort William to Inverness; it is possible to hitch-hike this route. Otherwise, it is a second best to take the road route and, instead of completing the journey in under three hours, a whole day would be devoted to sampling the many fascinating vistas, both panoramic and in small local detail, which this Highland rift offers. The area includes the Caledonian Canal, which threads its way across the floor of the glen and which nowhere rises more than 115 feet between the North Sea and the Atlantic Ocean. The Great Glen fault is regarded as a wrench fault. Strontian (Argyll) granite has been identified with Foyers (on Loch Ness) granite to support this theory which, if correct, gives an estimated horizontal displacement of some 65 miles. The frequent recurrence of minor earthquakes indicates that adjustments are still taking place along its course. Further proof of the Great Glen dislocation is shown by the fact that over a distance of 40 miles between Fort

William and Foyers, there is a broad crush-belt along the south-eastern flank of the glen, with a characteristic geology showing in the stretch between Loch Lochy and Loch Oich.

The area of the Great Glen covers some of the highest ground in Scotland and a great deal of interior country where the mild oceanic climate of the west coast is lost. Much of it is excessively wet: Glen Quoich, for instance, registers the highest rainfall in the British Isles at 225 inches per annum. Many of the glens in the area—Affric, Cannich, Cluanie, Lyon, Quoich and Kingie—once sustained large and magnificent forests. Remnants of the original afforestation exist at the eastern ends of Affric, Cannich and Strathfarrar. Their destruction is a permanent loss to Scotland. The northern mountainous part of the glen area once represented the best of Scotland's deer forests. Now, though the deer remain, they are, by and large, the only animals which can occupy much of this part all the year round on a basis which introduces them as a viable economic factor. The glen, with its drift-covered hillsides sheltered from the wind, forms an important element in the work of the Forestry Commission in the Highlands. The glen is lined with plantations of various species of conifers, in many places on both sides. One of the blots on the commission's record hereabouts was its lack of interest, when it began work in the early years of its existence, in preventing the wasteful clear-felling of good oak timber in the feeder glens which run east and west of the Great Glen. The dominant ecological factor which made the Great Glen important in the past was its forests. They continue to represent the main asset of the area; and undoubtedly have been the cause of the halt in the decline in population around 1921, referable also to the existence of the industrial activity in Fort William.

Perhaps the most famous aspect, indeed, prominent aspect of the Great Glen is Loch Ness. Much of its fame is due to the possible existence of a number of creatures in the loch waters who combine to make sporadic appearances as 'Nessie'. The argument as to whether a creature, or a family of creatures, exists in the loch will go on until the time when it is eventually proved beyond all shadow of doubt that life does exist in Loch Ness. The stage of investigation has now been reached where one leaves the area of outright scepticism and enters the field of probability. Too many witnesses have seen convincing phenomena in the loch and on the surface of its waters; and to throw their evidence out of court as inadmissible would be indefensible. Many of the sceptics are under the impression that 'Nessie' is a creation of a fertile imagination during the early years of this century and so is of recent origin. But the fact is that references to the loch creature are found in the mists of tradition, and in particular in the life of St Columba, written by Adamnan, an abbot of Iona, about a century after Columba died. Columba's encounter with the creature took place in Loch Ness. The deepest part of the loch is located opposite the Falls of Foyers and is some 774 feet in depth. Many old accounts of the loch have stressed that its waters never ice up, even in the hardest of winters. The loch is about 24 miles long and is nowhere more than 2 miles wide. As such it forms about half the route of the Caledonian Canal. The sides of the loch are steep and support much birchwood. The roads on each side afford some of the most exhilarating scenic views in the whole of the Highland region. And if an opportunity is taken to go up on to the higher ground, for instance on to the high road on the eastern side or on the road which rises ambitiously to Abriachan, the views afforded are enhanced to such a degree that even bad, unclear weather takes little away from a scenic beauty that must surely influence the most phlegmatic of tourists.

The Loch Ness landward area contains much of interest, both historically and socially. To the east lies Strathnairn, through which the River Nairn makes an interesting way from its source on Beinn Bhuidhe. The northern part of Strathnairn includes the parishes of Daviot and Dunlichity. These lie along the axis of the valley of the Nairn for a stretch of wild and beautiful country extending for over 20 miles up the strath. This area has had a turbulent history. At least three stone circles stand as witness to human interest, if not habitation, going back as far as the Bronze Age. In more modern times, the carnage which took place on Drumossie Moor, at Culloden, speaks of a continued sadness which seems at times to fill the area..

Daviot village lies in the midst of a hummocky landscape caused by the series of sandhills which are a feature of this stretch of the valley of the River Nairn. The derivation of Daviot, a name which first appeared in records about 1210 as 'Daveth', is thought to be similar to the Welsh 'Dyfed', and refers to the tribe Demetae, from the Pictish word for sure or strong. Other opinions favour the derivation from Dava, a 'davoch', a land measure equivalent to four plough-gates. The parishes of Daviot and Dunlichity were linked in 1618. Much before that time there existed the considerable castle structure of Daviot. Both the Old and New Statistical Accounts of Scotland give details of the destruction of this building, of which little now remains except part of one of the angle-towers overlooking the define of the Nairn, a little to the north of where Daviot House stands at present. It was a place of great strength, with a dry ditch and drawbridge which separated it and secured it from approach by the level ground on the west, and a strong wall on the other sides, where the height and natural declivity of the sandhill on which it stood added much to its security. It was a square building, enclosing an area of some 360 square yards. It had four circular towers, one at each corner, and contained three storeys, all vaulted; there were secret passages in the middle of the wall communicating with the large vaulted rooms for the main guard at the principal entry. Except for a small breach at the main gate, the whole structure was standing around 1757. In 1784 a wadset was obtained from the Laird of Mackintosh of the lands of Daviot, on which the castle stood. Within a few short years, the building material used in the castle was removed to build a modern farmhouse and offices. The final destruction of the castle was seen in 1794 when its last vestiges were used to enclose, of all humiliating things, a farm dunghill.

To the south of Daviot House stands Taum Muodh, or Council Hill, where the chiefs of olden times tried wrong-doers. The kirkyard at Dunlichity is one of those places redolent with atmosphere. It is a fascinating area with the present church building built on the site of a chapel of St Finan (A.D. 575). The kirk was reconstructed in 1768 and again in 1826. In the vestry is an old communion bell dated 1704.

To the south of Strathnairn lies Stratherrick, with Foyers as its focal point for many reasons, perhaps the most dominant being that it is the site of the new pumped-storage, hydro-electric scheme of the North of Scotland Hydro-electric Board. This public body, the only one of its kind in the British Isles with a social remit written into its statutory constitution, has more than proved its worth to the Highlands and Islands of Scotland, even though, rather strangely, it maintains its head office in Edinburgh, a place quite outside its own generation area. In the more immediate past Foyers laid claim to being the exception to the rule that, along with Fort William and Kinlochleven, it was not possible to establish in post industrial-revolution times, a major primary processing industry in the Highlands. Yet, in 1896, the Foyers factory of the newly-formed British Aluminium Company, which had Lord Kelvin as a director, went into production for the processing of bauxite into aluminium, using electricity generated by machines which, when they finally ceased to run in 1967, were still in excellent condition.

The famous Falls of Foyers were harnessed to provide the abundant quantities of electrical energy needed to make the processes and the final product both economic and viable. The whole scheme was the first example in Britain of the use of water-power on such a large scale. At that time there was no village at Foyers. All supplies for the factory had to be brought in by water from the canal, because the road from Inverness was little more than a track. Labour also had to be imported. Old Foyers House, then a ruin, was restored to become a temporary hostel for workers while more permanent houses were being built. By 1898 an early booklet produced by the company declared: "At Foyers the Company has built a village which now counts a population of some 600 souls, all of whom are dependent on the new industry for their daily bread. The impoverished crofters and fisherfolk of the Western Highlands acclaim with gladness the advent of this industry into their midst, offering as it does a thrice-welcome addition to their scanty opportunities of wage earning. It inspires them with a genuine hope that the devastating tide of emigration may be stayed, and that their beautiful but desolate glens may ere long witness a prosperity hitherto unknown." By 1967, when the Foyers Works was closed down, second and third generations of workers were there, direct descendants of those who had built the scheme and then stayed on as factory workers. For many years the Caledonian Canal played its part by offering a direct-to-sea route for the ingots of aluminium produced at Foyers. Later the production of aluminium metal was developed at Kinlochleven and Fort William. In 1954 the Foyers Works was converted to the production of super-purity aluminium employing about seventy employees. The decision to close Foyers in 1967 was no little shock, but had to be taken because the product was subject to wildly fluctuating demands and a number of price variables which rendered the product commercially unstable. In the same year the North of Scotland Hydro-electric Board announced a plan for a 300 MW (Megawatt) pumped-storage scheme which would make use of the natural waters offered by the area. The original Foyers scheme used the fall of 360 feet from the top of the Falls of Foyers to Loch Ness. The flow of part of the catchment area of the River Foyers was regulated by a reservoir created at Loch Mhor by the construction of two dams. Under the new scheme, the flow from 98 square miles of catchment area is used through the full head of 589 feet between Loch Mhor and Loch Ness to produce about 110 million units of electricity per annum. The amount of storage provided by Loch Mhor is not in itself sufficient to ensure that water is always available for generation; this deficiency is overcome by using reversible pump-turbines to pump water up from Loch Ness to Loch Mhor during those times in each twenty-four-hour period when the electrical load is light. The Foyers power station is located underground about a half mile inland from the shore of Loch Ness.

In 1969 Foyers village, with the former British Aluminium Company houses, was sold to a property company which intends to develop the area into a focal point for a new community based on holiday and tourist activities. There is, too, the possibility that Foyers could become one of the important growth points in the Inverness hinterland.

The history of Foyers is inextricably woven in with that of its parish, Boleskine, which, according to the New Statistical Account, means "the summit of the furious cascade". Although the first church of the Celtic faith in the district was founded by St Moluag near Inverfarrigaig towards the end of the sixth century, the parish of Boleskine was formed, like most parishes in Scotland, about the middle of the twelfth century. Its first church stood in the middle of the ancient kirkyard of Boleskine. The first manse was on the site now occupied by the present-day Boleskine House; this is occupied by a pop singer, but was once the home of the famous Aleister Crowley. The kirkyard in the vicinity was a special last resting-place associated with Clan Fraser.

At the south end of Loch Ness lies Fort Augustus, from which a track road wends its way on an eastward route to the Corrieairack Pass. This route, the only west–east connection by land between Inverness and Spean Bridge, a distance of some 50 miles, has figured large in Highland military and commercial history. The pass is full of interest. Many of General Wade's little bridges, quite redolent with the atmosphere of their past, cross burns in summer and miniature rivers in spate during the rainy months of the year. Of the hill of Mealgarbha, Thomas Pennant, Highland tourist, records that "people often perish on the summit of this hill, which is frequently visited during winter with dreadful storms of snow". About seventy years later, Anderson, another redoubtable traveller, says: "The whole stage being one continued hill, the traveller is obliged to dwell for hours on the dreariness of this forlorn region, and patiently to endure the cutting blasts, which he is sure to encounter towards the middle of his journey, when he gains the summit of the ridge, where snow posts, lining the road for miles, denote the horrors of a passage in winter, and make him thankful if he does not stand in need of their guidance."

The pass was used as a west–east route for cattle and sheep as late as 1896 and 1899. A century and a half earlier, in 1745, the pass featured in the historical events of the Forty-five Rising, when Sir John Cope was faced with a decision: either to take his men through the pass to Fort William—if he could for it was held by 2,500 Jacobites—or strike northwards for Inverness. In the report of the inquiry into Cope's conduct of the campaign, a long passage describes the formidable nature of the pass. Cope made for Inverness, and so allowed the Jacobite troops to descend on the Lowlands and to take Edinburgh.

The western side of Loch Ness includes Glen Urquhart and Glen Moriston, in an area which contains some surprisingly good land. Drumnadrochit, at the head of a small delta, has probably the best conditions for agriculture, because it is at this place that the remnant of Old Red Sandstone yields better soils than in those areas where it occurs with metamorphic rocks. The altitude is low and the situation, being on the sunnier side of the glen, has its obvious advantages. More to the west the alluvium of Strath Glass provides good flat land which is fairly well used, particularly where flood-control techniques are efficient. The occurrence of galena (lead sulphide) is predominant in an area of Strath Glass just to the south-west of the village of Struy. Small-scale working for galena took place at three localities here during the first half of the nineteenth century, from veins which also contained baryte and a little sphalerite. Some samples of galena were found to be markedly argentiferous when they were assayed.

Several small farms in Glenmoriston carry sheep stocks on easy moors and the whole activity is placed on a reasonable and acceptable economic basis. In the glen there are some native pinewoods, now carefully preserved. Depopulation, however, is still a serious problem in the area. But, with its high rainfall, steep slopes, and inter-connecting valley systems, the hydro-electric potential has been developed to the full to offer some kind of economic base for the residual population. The activities of the Forestry Commission, though perhaps these are not always quite successful in social and land-use terms, also point to the possibility of a better use of the area's potential, with a view to an increase in employment opportunities. The Abriachan district is of particular interest. Its small but rather significant local museum and preserved old croft house (fully furnished) is an example of how a community can look back at its roots, preserve the best of what the present has inherited and show some kind of visible base on which the future years of the community can be built. Viewed in this light, the museum has a valuable social function. In time past, this district was well known for its activity in illicit whisky distilling. This was due to the inaccessible nature of much of the land, the roughness of the terrain and the purity of the water. These Abriachan smugglers, the quality of whose product was only just inferior to that produced in the Strathglass district, were most cunning at avoiding detection, and were well noted for the infinite variety of their tricks used to escape when attempts to arrest them were made. They used fires of burnt heather and juniper, which raised very little smoke, and thus were able to carry out much of their work during daylight hours. In 1750, Lachlan MacLachlan, appointed to the local school, described Abriachan as a "nest of incorrigible smugglers". At a later date and up until 1875, young people commencing the school were taught entirely in Gaelic, a system that was not always encouraged or even tolerated in most Highland schools. The school at Abriachan was in this respect quite unique.

Past Drumnadrochit and its satellite Lewiston, is the Strone which carries a medieval stronghold of some importance. This is Castle Urquhart, now in the care and keeping of the Department of the Environment. It occupies a commanding position on the promontory which juts out into Loch Ness. The castle stands on the former site of a vitrified fort. The structure began as a motte with a double bailey, the defences of which were fashioned in stone during the thirteenth and fourteenth centuries. Most of the existing buildings date from the sixteenth century. The castle has played an important part in Scottish history, from the time of the invasions of Edward I to the Jacobite Rising of 1689, after which event it was blown up. In Glen Urquhart, 8 miles west of Drumnadrochit, is the Corrimony Cairn, a megalithic chambered cairn, probably Neolithic, surrounded by a peristalith of stone slabs, on the outside of which is a circle of eleven standing stones.

The south end of Loch Ness meets Fort Augustus, a fine-looking spacious town with the abbey affording a focal point of interest. It was built in the eighteenth century as a fort, one of a number constructed to control the Highlands. Fort Augustus was formerly the terminus of the railway from Spean Bridge at the pier on Loch Ness. The rail service then connected with a Loch Ness steamer service to Inverness. The Great Glen figured a number of times during the nineteenth century in proposals for a railway to reach Inverness; the amount of traffic, however, would never have justified its construction. Even so, many Highland lines have been uneconomic since they were built many years ago, but their significance in social terms has been incalculable. Underground lines are now in operation in London which are designed to lose large amounts of money per annum (running into millions), so the £1 million which is the present total estimated loss of all the Highland railway lines must always be kept in a proper and fair perspective. Originally named Cill Chumein, after the saintly Cummein, who was one of the early abbots of Iona, the village was re-named Fort Augustus in commemoration of Butcher Cumberland. Boswell and Johnson stayed a night in the fort where the Governor treated them kindly, so we are told. The garrison was supplied with provisions from Inverness by a sloop which sailed regularly on Loch Ness. The fort at Fort Augustus is now incorporated in the Benedictine abbey, completed in 1878. The room in which Lord Lovat of the Forty-five was confined as a prisoner is still known; and a tree planted in memory of the Battle of Culloden still survives. The cricket ground of the abbey was the scene of the shooting of a number of Jacobite prisoners of war in 1746. The abbey is a highly-rated school for boys of the Roman Catholic faith.

The southern end of Loch Ness is joined to the head of Loch Oich by the Caledonian Canal. A few miles south lies Invergarry, which conjoins old and new in the power station and the ruins of Invergarry Castle which overlooks Loch Oich. The eastern approach to Invergarry is through Glen Garry, with Loch Garry now double its original length. The area here has excellent woodland and river scenery which attracts many tourists. The road on the north shore of the loch has been widened recently to allow for an easier passage, though one wonders whether the tourist, now able to motor along at faster speeds, is really able to see, absorb and appreciate fully, the vista which was forced on to former tourists who had to make their slower way along the older road. Farther east lies Loch Quoich, also enlarged by the demands of hydro-electric power. The Loch Quoich dam is over 1,000 feet long and 122 feet high and presents a scenic element in itself. The catchment area of the loch has one of the highest rainfalls in the Highlands (over 200 inches). This fact, combined with steep gradients and convenient cross-valleys, has made the area ideal for the harnessing of natural water resources, a blessing which, though the tourist might question the

Kyle of Lochalsh fishermen with the Cuillins of Skye behind them

Applecross, Ross-shire

despoliation of the countryside, has produced far greater benefits in the continuous employment it provides both directly and indirectly for Highland people.

Loch Oich is joined to Loch Lochy by the Laggan Locks. The loch is some 8 miles long and deep enough to accommodate ocean-going liners. The River Arkaig flows into the loch from the east. This is a short river, little more than a mile in length, which has its source in Loch Arkaig, one of the last haunts in Britain of the osprey. This bird has now returned to the Highlands of Scotland but has expressed a decided preference for the Cairngorms for its new nesting sites. Loch Arkaig presents some beautiful scenery. To the west there is a forest of old Scots pines, and to the east there are oak woods. It is on record that the loch supports some kind of 'monster' which has a head resembling that of a horse. Another association is the French gold and treasure that was said to be concealed in the neighbourhood of the loch during 1745. The country around the loch rises little above 3,000 feet, and then at a few points only. The slopes here tend to be gentler and the glens much lower, so that sheep stock is found in the deer forest. The big valley of Loch Arkaig lies west of the Great Glen and its feeder glens of Dessary and Pean reach west to the watershed only a handful of miles from the western sea-lochs. Even there, the glen floors are below 500 feet and so provide good wintering. Each of the feeder glens has a footpath, a degeneration in each case from a one-time fairly good track. The path in Glen Dessary is well marked, however, as it has been in constant use for centuries. The Glen Pean route to the west was that taken by Prince Charles Edward just after the Culloden defeat in 1746.

To the east of Loch Lochy lie two glens: Gloy and Roy, the latter well known for its 'parallel roads' of nature's making. Farther east, Glen Spean leads on to Laggan Loch. The lower half of Glen Roy is of a 'lowland' character; rather than presenting a rough, high and steep-sided glen, there is a wide and green expanse with low hills which are covered with sparse woods. The parallel roads of Glen Roy are best viewed from the highest point of the Glen road, which, rather conveniently, is beside a commodious car park. The origin of these parallel terraces goes back to the end of the last Ice Age, when a huge glacier, flowing northwards off the massif of the Ben, dammed up the outlets from the glens. Mountain waters, flowing in from behind, formed deep lochs for which the parallel roads formed the beaches. As the ice retreated, or was more likely breached, the water-level sank and new beaches were formed at successively lower levels. Both Glen Spean and Glen Gloy display these 'roads' phenomena, though Glen Roy is the area which springs immediately to mind at their mention, because they can be seen more clearly. The roads stand out because of their different colouring—from coarse grass or bent which is in contrast to the surrounding heather and bracken. Glen Spean is an off-shoot of the Great

Glen, branching eastwards from Spean Bridge for some 13 miles. It is traversed by road, railway and river, the latter now having much less water than in former days, before 1934, when the large Loch Laggan which lies east of the glen, was lengthened by 4 miles and stopped by a dam. The Spean River waters were diverted by an underground passage to Loch Treig, and then by tunnel through the heart of Ben Nevis to supply water power for the aluminium works at Fort William. Recent geological surveys along either side of the Great Glen have extended the known reserves of sand and gravel in a district where bulk material transport via the Caledonian Canal might be considered feasible. These deposits are generally products of erosion and waste accumulation that took place during the various Ice Ages. The Spean valley in particular has an outstandingly large resource of material.

Of course, the dominating feature of the Great Glen is the Caledonian Canal, though it is rather modest in looks, for only a third of the canal's total length of 60 miles consists of canal cuttings. Its direction is almost exactly north-east to south-west and joins Lochs Dochfour, Ness, Oich and Lochy. The canal summit occurs at Loch Oich (106 feet above sea level). There are twenty-nine locks with a total of forty-two pairs of gates, each leaf of which weighs about 25 tons. There are ten swing bridges over the canal. The entrances to the canal are by sea-locks, both of which are tidal. The history of the canal has recently been written up in a full-length book by Inverness author Sandy Cameron, produced in time to mark the hundred and fiftieth anniversary of the opening of the canal. Even so an abridged version of the canal's history would be appropriate to round off the present chapter. It as yet remains with the social historian to assess the effects and influences which the canal has produced in the time of its existence in the economic context of the Highlands.

About the middle of the seventeenth century, some 150 years before the canal was built, Coinneach Odhar, the Brahan Seer, prophesied: "Strange as it may seem to you this day, the time will come, and it is not far off, when full-rigged ships will be seen sailing eastwards and westwards by the back of Tomnahurich, near Inverness." It is said that the man recording the seer's prophesies thought that this particular one was so absurd that he threw the manuscript of what he had written into the fire. Witnesses, however, remembered the prophesy and we in the twentieth century know that the seer was absolutely correct in his vision of the future. It could, however, be said by the sceptic of the gift of second sight that any man of penetration and great natural shrewdness might, from the appearance of the country, and of the Great Glen in particular, with its long chain of inland lochs, be able to say that the latter could be joined to form an inland waterway. In the event, prophesy or not, were it not for a fault of nature, one of the world's best-known canals would not have come into existence.

One of the first of many to suggest a canal to link north and south Scotland was Captain Edward Burt in 1726. But after due consideration he rejected his idea because he thought the channelling of the wind between the mountains would make navigation too precarious. Later, in 1773, the Commissioners of Forfeited Highland Estates became anxious to assist the Scottish fishing industry and asked James Watt to survey Burt's original route. Watt published his report in 1774: a plan for a 10-foot navigable waterway from Fort William to Inverness through Lochs Lochy, Oich, Ness and Dochfour. Provided with thirty-two locks, Watt estimated that the cost would be in the region of £164,000. Watt pointed out that the proposed waterway would cut out the dangerous sea route round the Pentland Firth in the north of Scotland. But, after all Watt's effort, the Government of the day took no action. Eleven years later, in 1785, John Knox tried to revive the plan once more. He was followed, in 1793, by William Fraser, who said that nature "not only favoured such an undertaking but had finished more than half of it already".

For another decade, pro-canal writers pressed hard for the Government to take some action to make the canal a reality. Finally, in 1801, Thomas Telford was asked to investigate the causes for the high level of emigration from the Highlands at that time. Telford did his work thoroughly, and underlined the fact that the provision of suitable public works schemes, such as the canal, would help to stem emigration by offering employment to those who otherwise had no future in the region. The final incentive for the construction of the canal came with the hope of safeguarding British shipping from attacks by French privateers. At last, in July 1803, an Act was passed which granted the sum of £20,000 towards the cost of the project. A board of commissioners was set up to supervise the work and Thomas Telford was appointed principal engineer at three guineas per day plus travelling expenses.

The canal was to run from a harbour near Inverness, "a little way to the east of the Ferry Pier", to another harbour some distance west of Fort William at the mouth of the River Lochy. The commissioners were given the responsibility of determining the route of the canal and they were also given the powers of compulsory purchase if disputes about lands threatened to hold up the work. Work on the canal began in 1804, starting with the terminal basins, each of which was to be 400 yards long and more than 70 yards wide. Turf houses were built for the canal workmen and workshops were erected for blacksmiths, carpenters and other tradesmen. Wood for the project, principally fir and birch, was bought locally. Food for the labourers was stored at Corpach. Initially, 150 men, including some Highlanders who had worked on other canal projects in the south of Scotland, were employed at the rate of 1s. 6d. per day. Any man who demanded more was summarily dismissed. In June 1804 a further Act was passed authorizing the sum of £50,000 towards the cost of the canal and making provision for private subscriptions of sums not less than £50.

Even at this early date in the canal work, labour problems were looming. In 1805 it was decided to establish a small brewery at Corpach in order "to induce the workmen to relinquish the pernicious habit of drinking whisky"; there were also plans for one at Clachnaharry, near Inverness, though this was deemed less urgent. A herd of cows was established to give the canal workmen a fresh supply of milk daily. In a very short time the number of labourers employed on the canal works had risen to over 900. Most of these were natives of Inverness-shire and Argyll, with the result that their attendance at the work marked out for them daily was more than intermittent: the claims of potato harvesting and herring fishing, each in their season, was important enough to them and to their families to desert their jobs. The problem was serious, however, and in an effort to establish a regular non-local workforce, the canal engineers recruited labourers from the shores of the Moray Firth, Skye, Morar and a number of crofters who had been evicted by Cameron of Lochiel from their lands at Loch Arkaig.

In 1804 James Hogg, the Border poet and novelist, visited Corpach and commented on the progress of the canal works: "While observing how carelessly the labourers were dabbing with their picks and spades, and how apt they were to look around them at everything which was to be seen, while others were winding slowly out with each a little gravel in a wheelbarrow—while contemplating the exertions of these men, and wishing to anticipate in my mind the important era when they should join Lochiel to the Moray Firth, I could not help viewing it as a hopeless job: my head grew somewhat dizzy, and I felt the same sort of quandry as I used to do formerly when thinking of eternity."

Despite many difficulties, work proceeded, almost imperceptibly at times. Parts of the project began to take shape. Three of the eight locks known today as 'Neptune's Staircase' were completed in 1809, with the remainder expected to be ready by the following year; it was to be 1811, however, before they were completed. At Clachnaharry the workmen experienced more than a little trouble. The excavation of the lock-pit was accompanied by a continual encroaching and flooding by sea-water. Hand pumps were replaced by a large chain-pump worked by six horses, and when the strain began to tell on the animals one of the canal's 6-horsepower steam engines had to be brought into operation before work could proceed normally.

By 1812 less than half the canal had been finished and the expenditure had amounted to nearly £343,000. Telford was cautioned against using too many workmen; though not this but rather the unforeseen difficulties which incurred, were the major cause of the increased costs. The Corpach basin, for instance, had to be excavated from solid rock, and indeed presented so many problems that the dimensions had to be altered to save work and expense. Legal problems arose when a labourer accused one of the canal engineers of fraud in the mismeasuring of the volume of earth dug and said that an agent had "bestowed 200 yards on me and upwards for my treating him with a few bottles of porter". The charges were later dismissed by a court of enquiry.

Many times Telford was hard put to it to justify the high rate of expenditure. But investigation showed that, just as in modern times, costs had risen almost beyond control. Labourers' wages had increased from the equivalent of 7½p. to 12½p. per day. A good horse cost upwards of £25. Baltic timber had trebled its cost. And the price of oatmeal to feed the workmen had doubled in a decade. By burning a great deal of midnight oil Telford at last managed to calculate that only another £234,743 would be needed to complete the work, and he forecast that the canal "might be opened for all purposes of commerce at the end of 1817". Sir Walter Scott, who visited Loch Linnhe in August 1814, was much less optimistic: "Had the canal been of more moderate depths, and the burdens imposed upon passing vessels less expensive, there can be no doubt that the coasters, sloops and barks would have carried on a great trade by means of it. But the expense and plague of locks, etc may prevent these humble vessels from taking this abridged voyage, while ships above 20 or 30 tons will hesitate to engage themselves in the intricacies of a long-lake navigation, exposed without room for manœuvring to all the sudden squalls of the mountainous country."

Trouble was not always provided by nature. Some of it was man-made. This was particularly so when Colonel Alexander MacDonnell of Clanronald and Glengarry decided that he was going to oppose actively the progress of the canal construction. He had originally opposed the canal project on the grounds that it was a threat to his privacy and to his house, which stood near the ruins of Invergarry Castle on Loch Oich. He was assured by Telford that the route of the canal would follow the southern shore of Loch Oich and be separated from the loch by an embankment. As Glengarry owned a stretch of 10 miles along the Great Glen, a sum of £10,000 compensation was fixed by a jury—a very large sum for those days when an income of £50 per annum was reckoned to provide for a life of reasonable comfort. This sum was accepted by Glengarry. But early on the morning of 3rd September 1816, "Glengarry came to the east end of Loch Oich accompanied by about thirty persons variously armed as if for deer-hunting, who drove away the workmen and having seized a boat belonging to the [canal] Commissioners sent it to Loch Garry." The boat was later recovered and Glengarry was not prosecuted for the "outrage".

In September 1819 the author Robert Southey visited the works at

Fort Augustus: "Such an extent of masonry, upon such a scale, I had never before beheld, each of these locks being 180ft in length. It was a most impressive rememberable scene. Men, horses and machines at work, digging, walling, and puddling going on, men with wheel-barrows, horses drawing stones along the railways. The great steam-engine was at rest, having done its work; but the dredging-machine was in action, revolving round and round, and bringing up at every turn matter which had never before been brought to air and light. Iron for a pair of lock-gates was lying on the ground, having just arrived from Derbyshire." As the year 1822 approached there were many public and private controversies on the usefulness of the canal. Telford had to defend the canal every inch of its way. In one article he described the project as "one of the most magnificent and splendid of our national structures" and commented on "the change which had been produced even in the last ten or twelve years upon the intelligence and the manners of the inhabitants".

The Loch Ness and eastern district of the canal was opened for navigation in May 1818; coasting vessels, importing tar, oatmeal and coal, and exporting wool, staves and timber, made 150 voyages in the first summer. By September 1819 the practicality of the voyage from Inverness to Fort Augustus had been proved "even by some square-rigged vessels of 140 tons", the latter perhaps echoing the vision of Coinneach Odhar some 150 years previously. In November 1820 Henry Bell established a steamboat service on this part of the navigation: the *Stirling Castle* (68 feet long, 23 feet wide and with an 18-horse-power engine), which left the Muirtown Locks at Inverness at 08.00 hours and arrived at Fort Augustus at 14.00 hours. The locks at the Corpach basin were in operation from 1819 and received an increasing number of vessels of 100 tons burden. By 1822 criticisms of the canal as a feasible economic venture had reached a peak. The project was being attacked from all sides, including opposers in the Houses of Parliament, and, in an effort to take some heat out of the controversy, it was decided officially to open the canal in October 1822. The *Inverness Courier* reported:

> Amid the hearty cheers of a crowd of spectators and a salute from all the guns that could be mustered, the voyagers departed from the Muirtown locks at 11 o'clock, with fine weather and in high spirits. In their progress through this beautiful navigation they were joined from time to time by the proprietors on both sides of the lakes; and, as the neighbouring hamlets poured forth their inhabitants, at every inlet and promontory, tributary groups from the glens and braes were stationed to behold the welcome pageant, and add their lively cheers to the thunder of the guns and the music of the Inverness-shire militia band, which accompanied the expedition. . . . The reverberation of the firing, repeated and prolonged by a thousand echoes from the surrounding hills, glens and rocks, the

martial music, the shouts of the Highlanders and the answering cheers of the party on board produced an effect which will not soon be forgotten by those present.

After a night spent at Fort Augustus the two boats with their celebrating company entered Loch Oich early on 24th October: "On approaching the mansion of Glengarry, the band struck up 'My Name it is Donald MacDonald', and a salute was fired in honour of the chief, which was returned from the old castle, the now tenantless residence of Glengarry's ancestors. The ladies of the family stood in front of the modern mansion waving their handkerchiefs." The two boats were now joined by Glengarry himself, resplendent in Highland outfit, and the steamboat *Comet II*, and the little flotilla proceeded through the Laggan cut and down Neptune's Staircase to Fort William. "The termination of the voyage was marked by a grand salute from the Fort, whilst the inhabitants demonstrated their joy by kindling a large bonfire. A plentiful supply of whisky, given by the gentlemen of Fort William, did not in the least tend to damp the ardour of the populace."

Criticism tended to die away after the official opening, and the canal was left to prove itself a useful route between the northern and south-western waters of Scotland. Traffic did in fact increase. A total of 844 vessels used the canal in the twelve months between May 1823 and May 1824, of which number 278 ships passed from sea to sea. By the summer of 1824, one of the lock-houses at Banavie had been converted into an inn for the benefit of the steamboat passengers. The average time for the canal passage was three to four days—and there were no complaints at all about detention by unfavourable winds. Three steamboats were put into operation between Glasgow and Inverness; they did the return journey in six days. Two sailing boats also began to ply between Liverpool and the Moray Firth. But all was not quite rosy. The Highland fly in the ointment, Glengarry, was still persisting in his claim for further compensation on the grounds that Loch Oich had been opened to navigation. The Gairlochy regulating lock was found to be in a dangerous state, a condition which Telford said was due to the fact that it had been made with inferior stone. When part of the side-wall of the lock finally collapsed it had to be repaired at a cost of over £3,000, a sum which was as much as was in the bank earmarked for current expenses only and not meant to cater for premature repair work. By 1829 other serious defects were showing themselves. Faults at Banavie and in other locks caused the canal to be closed to shipping for a fortnight in April of the same year. But the canal entered the decade of the 1830s with a reasonably hopeful future; in fact, the project, being on such a large scale, was proving to be a great tourist attraction. A guide-book of the period writes: "A spectacle more gratifying to every patriotic feeling can hardly occur, than to see stately ships which the day before had been surmounting the billows of the ocean, and loaded with the produce of foreign climates, sailing on the placid lochs of Caledonia, under the brow of her lofty mountains, or gliding along the lake, whose banks are covered with corn and cattle, while the seamen are cheered with the rustic lay of the shepherds, or the sounds of rural industry within her peaceful valleys."

But however much the smell of success pervaded the operation of the canal, the shadows of problems were always in the vicinity. During the 1830s more defects in the canal's construction appeared, particularly in the middle sections. The termini at Clachnaharry, the Muirtown basin and locks, and the sea-lock at Corpach were sound, however. Seemingly, inferior stone and timber had been used in the defective sections and Telford's acceptance of the work was brought into question. It was later discovered that the contractors had concealed their shoddy work so well that Telford had passed it in all innocence.

During the ensuing years the history of the canal is full of accounts of motions to have the canal closed altogether; of suggestions to lease it rent-free to a joint-stock company (there were no takers); of pleas to the Government for grants to effect repairs; and of a general increase in the frequency of reported faults, hazards and work which required urgent repair attention. Eventually, in 1842, the Government made a grant of £50,000 for the repair and final completion of the canal. A survey was made which revealed that three years' work were required to bring the canal up to full navigational operation and estimated the cost to be in the region of £136,000. Work was started immediately and gave employment to up to 1,500 men, at work in both stone quarries and on the canal. As the work proceeded, further estimates pushed the expense up, and by the time the canal was re-opened for traffic in May 1847 the government grants for the reconstruction work and for the purchase of tugs to be based on Lochs Linnhe, Lochy, Ness and the Inverness Firth totalled £228,000.

Problems were still never so far away. The inhabitants of Inverness complained that an outbreak of cholera in the town had been caused by water from the canal. The Ness Woollen Manufactuary claimed £5,000 for damages as the result of seepage of canal water into the works. And repeated floods at Dochgarroch caused no end of damage to the canal. As if these were not sufficient to contend with, in 1850 the moderator of the Free Church Presbytery of Abertarff asked the canal commissioners to put a stop to all "unnecessary labour" on Sundays and protested against the regulation that allowed tugs on special business to pass through the locks at all times. Revenues from canal dues and the like fluctuated and many times fell far below the overall sum needed to maintain the canal efficiently and also pay just wages. Matters became so bad at one period that when a lock-keeper with forty years' service

(*top*) Carbisdale Castle, Easter Ross. (*bottom*) Road to Applecross with Loch Kishorn in background

(*opposite*) Gair Loch, Ross-shire. (*above top*) Beinn Eun, Ross-shire. (*above bottom*) Castle Urquhart, Loch Ness

Laggan Locks, Caledonian Canal

Loch Lochy, Inverness-shire

behind him was drowned in a lock, the commissioners decided because of the "very precarious state" of the finances not to assume a "permanent burden" for his widow and child, but to give them a "gratuity of £10" when they left their house.

By 1858 revenue was suffering from the fact that the sea route round the Pentland Firth in the north of Scotland had been made less perilous by the preparation of new charts and the erection of numerous lighthouses, beacons and buoys. The American Civil War, however, created a welcome but slight increase in the flax and linseed trade from the Baltic. But while the merchant shipping was lacking, the passenger traffic increased to very satisfactory proportions. In the summer of 1863, a total of 15,560 people travelled through the canal in "fast and slow" steamers. Three years later the popular *Gondolier*, which Queen Victoria was to use on her passage through the canal in 1873, came into operation on the Inverness–Banavie service. The number of passages by sail and steam vessels rose accordingly.

Until the end of the nineteenth century passenger traffic remained a very important element in the revenue of the canal, despite potential opposition in the form of a rail link between Inverness and the south. There was continual fierce competition between the many shipping interests which used the canal. This was exaggerated at one time by the myth that one company had cut the Glasgow–Inverness fare down to 6d. and another had immediately responded by making it "nothing and a bottle of porter thrown in". In due course, the rival companies using the canal for the Glasgow–Inverness traffic were gradually taken over by David MacBrayne, whose company had virtual monopoly over the west coast of Scotland sea routes. By 1893 this company was operating "commodious" steamers between Inverness and Oban. An Inverness guide-book of the time made a point of advising tourists to catch the 7 a.m. boat from Muirtown to Fort Augustus, spend just over three hours enjoying the "beautiful surroundings of the village", and then join the north-bound boat at 2.15 p.m. for the return journey. The opening of the West Highland Railway Company's Banavie branch line in 1895 helped to increase the canal traffic.

The dawning of the twentieth century was accompanied by a submission made to the Royal Commission of 1906–9 that the canal was "antiquated" and "practically useless", even for ordinary coasters. As if to underline the statement, one of the Laggan locks collapsed in January 1910, and serious defects were reported in the original masonry at Corpach, Banavie and Fort Augustus, all requiring urgent attention. The canal was still dogged by bad luck and, not the least, the bad work carried out over eight decades previously. During the First World War, American bases were set up at Muirtown, Inverness, and on the Cromarty Firth to help in the laying of a minefield from Orkney to Norway, the purpose of which was to exclude German submarines from the waters of the Atlantic. Some 48,000 tons of mines and naval stores were shipped to these bases through the canal. During the war years there was no revenue, due to the fact that most of the vessels—fishing-boats and cargo steamers—had been brought officially under Admiralty control. A Treasury loan of £20,000 made during 1916–19 partly made up the canal losses.

An Act of 1919 transferred control of the canal to the newly-established Ministry of Transport. In the following year the canal commissioners made their final report and attributed the canal's failure to regain its pre-war goods and passenger traffic to unfair competition from the well-established railways. In 1926 the canal was closed for nine weeks so that a general repair of masonry could be carried out and the eight locks at Banavie were thoroughly restored.

The anniversary of the opening of the canal in 1922 caused the *Glasgow Herald* to observe that it was "questionable whether the canal had ever justified the expense it entailed"; and the Ministry of Transport refused to consider plans submitted for the reconstruction of the canal.

In 1927 the Member of Parliament for Inverness drew attention to the fact that the canal's bridges were too weak to bear the weight of fully-loaded buses. In 1929 a herring drifter burst through two lock-gates at Banavie, causing flood damage to the value of £4,000 and the closure of the canal for three months. The years up until the Second World War saw a fitful existence for the canal. The residual passenger service between Inverness and Fort Augustus was withdrawn by 1930, though the pleasure trips on the canal remained until 1939. During the years of the Second World War the canal was again used for the transport of military goods and personnel.

In 1948, the year of nationalization in Britain, the British Transport Commission acquired the Caledonian Canal. Seven years later, in 1955, the commission issued a report in which was expressed the hope that the traffic on the canal might be stimulated by afforestation, the development of hydro-electric power and the establishment of an atomic station at Dounreay in Caithness. In the following year the Forestry Commission declared that it could not use the canal because the destinations to which their timber was sent were not directly accessible by boat. It was found that the light industries which were expected to follow the hydro-electric and atomic schemes tended to prefer road transport rather than canal. By this time the canal was being used mainly by fishing boats (65 per cent of the total) and by small cargo boats. Though users of the canal found that they did save on fuel costs, the slowness of the hand-operated locks and the lack of illumination at night made a journey through the canal as time-consuming as one round the north of Scotland and through the Pentland Firth. Obviously plans were needed to give the canal an undoubted navigational and economic advantage to the ships using it.

In 1960 the British Transport Commission initiated a scheme for the mechanization of all the locks on the canal so that vessels could pass through them more quickly. In 1962 the British Waterways Board assumed responsibility for the canal, and the following year saw the inauguration of the newly-mechanized flight of four locks at Muirtown, Inverness. In 1964 the board signed an agreement to last thirty years with Wiggins, Teape and Company for the enlargement of the basin at Corpach to accommodate up to 100,000 tons a year of raw material for the pulp mill at Annat Point, Fort William.

The present traffic on the canal includes pleasure cruisers, fishing boats and cargo shipping (including foreign vessels) with such commodities as grain, salt, oil, chemicals, fertilizers and building materials. The mechanization of all the canal locks was completed in 1969, at a total cost of some £200,000. The new system means that the passage of a boat through the canal's 60 miles is cut by some two hours. Traffic has doubled in the past few years and many more people are taking advantage of the canal as a real road through the Highlands and on to the islands of the west. A great tourist potential is only now beginning to be developed; when this reaches its peak it may well wipe out the canal's present annual deficit of some £60,000.

Though an inland waterway, far removed from the hazards associated with the deep seas, the Caledonian Canal has a shipping history which is as interesting as any of the shipping lanes across the Atlantic. Two years before the canal was officially opened in 1822, the *Stirling Castle* was operating from Inverness to Fort Augustus and back. This ship was one of Henry Bell's steamboats. Bell, who died in 1830, was the Scottish steamship pioneer who designed the *Comet*, a 40-foot steamship launched on the Clyde in 1812. The *Comet* began her career on the Firth of Clyde and was later out on the service to Fort William via the Crinan Canal, becoming the first west Highland steamer. She was wrecked in 1820 at the Dorus Mor, near Craignish. Her place was taken by the *Stirling Castle* which was later taken off the Inverness–Fort Augustus run, to provide a Glasgow–Inverness service by way of the canal. In January 1828 she went aground at Inverscadail, near Ardgour, and a butler to the Chief of Glengarry was drowned; while the chief himself, in landing, sustained such injuries as to eventually cause his death.

The *Comet II* made her debut on the Fort William station in July 1821. After the canal was fully opened she plied as far north as Inverness. In 1825 *Comet II*, on her home run, was rammed by another ship off Gourock and she sank with considerable loss of life. She was afterwards raised and sailed in other waters as the schooner *Ann* until 1876. The paddle steamship *Highlander* also plied on the canal waters for a short time. Other craft which made an appearance during the 1830s were the *Inverness* and *Rob Roy*. Both of these craft were small steamers which operated a service between Oban and Inverness; their sailings were later extended to serve Cromarty and Invergordon. In the middle of last century a number of rival shipping operators used the canal. The *Edinburgh Castle*, for instance, was a paddle steamer operated by the Steam Packet Company to oppose Messrs Ainslie's (of Fort William) *Glencoe* on the canal. In a guide-book published in 1886 the *Edinburgh Castle* is advertised as working the Inverness–Banavie service in conjunction with the new *Gondolier*, the two ships between them giving a daily service in each direction. In 1875 the *Edinburgh Castle* re-appeared on the canal waters, this time named as the *Glengarry*, and became a well-known sight in both lock and loch. The ship was extensively refitted in 1919–20 and appeared again on the Loch Ness mail run. Her end came in December 1927 when, 83 years old, and generally acclaimed to be the oldest steamer in the world, she was broken up at the Rose Street Foundry, Inverness, in the port which had been her home for so many years.

The *Gondolier* was one of three steamers built for the Hutcheson fleet in 1866 by J. and G. Thomson at Clydebank. She was specially designed for service on the Caledonian Canal and was a very attractive little paddler. There was comfortable accommodation for no less than 622 passengers and a crew of thirteen. The *Gondolier* was a happy ship, and perhaps of all the ships that sailed on the canal she was the best known to the travelling public. She used to set off from Inverness at 11.00 hours to reach Fort Augustus at 15.30 hours. It took the *Gondolier* over half an hour to negotiate the five locks at Fort Augustus necessary to bring the canal down 40 feet to the level of Loch Ness. During this time the passengers were allowed ashore. The deck hands operated the locks manually, with assistance from anyone willing to lend a hand in pushing round the capstans. The *Gondolier* also made calls at pier termini on Loch Ness-side such as Temple Pier and Foyers. On her return journey she arrived back at Inverness at 18.30 hours. The *Gondolier* had a very long life and left the canal service only in 1939, when she was taken over by the Admiralty to be virtually stripped and gutted and then towed to Scapa Flow for scuttling to block a passage after the sinking of the *Royal Oak*. Thus ended the career of an inland-water ship—in the swell of the deep Atlantic among the northern isles of Orkney.

Yet another familiar sight on the canal was the paddle steamer *Gairlochy*. Built in 1861, she served on other runs before she entered canal service in 1894. She provided the summer runs between Inverness and Banavie. The ship met a sad fate, however. She was working the Inverness–Fort Augustus mail service when, on 24th December 1919, she caught fire at Fort Augustus and sank. Her keel is still visible from Fort Augustus pier when the level of Loch Ness is low.

The passenger and cruise traffic on the present-day canal is much less than it used to be. In former years there were no less than four regular steamers, two of them running all the year round. Now there is the *Scott II*, well known for her trips on the deep unfathomed waters of Loch Ness, with passengers keeping eyes peeled for a tantalizing glimpse of anything that might suggest the Loch Ness monster; she is a small screw vessel owned by the British Waterways Board. Accommodation is available for sixty-five persons. She was built at Leith for duties as a tug and ice-breaker, and performed these services until May 1961, when she was re-fitted as a passenger steamer and converted to diesel propulsion. Her new career has met with the unqualified approval of thousands of tourists who take advantage of her two-and-a-half or three-and-a-half-hour mini-cruises on the waters of what is probably the most famous loch in the world.

The Caledonian Canal presents a unique asset with an immense tourist potential as yet quite undeveloped. The Highlands and Islands Development Board has initiated a feasibility study for boating development on the navigation, including the 40 miles of natural lochs. Any development towards the commercial exploitation of the Great Glen will have to be carefully controlled if the natural beauty and charm of the area is to be preserved intact and unscathed. Unobtrusive development, such as the self-drive charter boats (increased from three in 1970 to over twelve at the time of writing), is an obvious choice. This enterprise expects to have some sixty boats operating on the navigation by 1980. There are plans for the provision of shore-side facilities such as chalet villages, camp sites, car parks and marinas. One views these with natural suspicion, and expresses the hope that the area will never become so congested, and ultimately useless as a recreational facility, as the quite spoiled Norfolk Broads are at present.

6

Lochaber and Morvern

THE area known as Lochaber is geologically complex, with its Dalradian rocks and the results of volcanic disturbances which further complicate the geology. The area includes Ben Nevis, the highest mountain in the British Isles, and is furrowed with magnificent glens, rivers and sea-lochs. The landscape hereabouts is on the grand, almost flamboyant, scale. Glen Nevis is only one of many outstanding topographical features. Its south flank, which contains the Mamore mountain range, stretches some 7 miles and includes sixteen peaks whose tops are distinctly pointed on account of the cappings of quartzite which protect the mica-schist beneath. Three peaks, including Ben Nevis, exceed 4,000 feet, and a fourth just fails by a foot or so to make the first division. These peaks link up with the Grey Corries whose seventeen peaks run east to Loch Treig. Amid this magnificence the River Nevis runs for a 14-mile course to Loch Linnhe. At Steall there occurs one of the three tallest waterfalls in Scotland (350 feet). The river first falls through a gorge to lower Glen Nevis, and then flows through green fields and the woods planted by the Forestry Commission on the slopes of Mamore; on the other side a denuded mountain wall rises dramatically into the huge back of Ben Nevis. The Ben itself is almost an isolated massif and is a major attraction to climbers; other, more casual, tourists make the three-and-a-half-hour journey to the summit to sample the view from the roof of Scotland. All enthusiasts, however, are advised to carry plenty of warm clothing and wear good boots. In the last decade or so over forty people have met their deaths on the mountain on account of its micro-climate, which can produce a dangerous situation very quickly. Snow can fall on the mountain on any day or month of the year. The reason is the atmospheric condensation which tends to cover the summit even when the rest of the sky is clear. There is an average of only two hours of bright sunshine per day and an annual rainfall of 157 inches. The mean monthly temperature is just under freezing point, which results in the permanent winter on the mountain from October onwards. In hollows under the cliffs, snow accumulates in beds of more than 100 feet deep.

South of the area of the Mamore Forest lies Glen Coe and Glen Etive. This area is redolent with atmosphere, is gaunt and uncompromising; yet, particularly on the lower parts, and where the glen merges with Loch Leven, there is a lighter tone to detect. There are mountain forms, gullies, walls, ridges, corries, buttresses and peaks to delight the eye. Much of this wild scenery can be seen from road level and enjoyed without the need for muscular exertion. Glen Coe and Dalness were the first stretches of mountainous country to be bought by the National Trust for Scotland, and were purchased between 1935 and 1937 with help from generous contributions from members of the Scottish Mountaineering Club, the Pilgrim Trust and from the general public. The properties comprise 12,000 acres forming a rough triangle with sides of about 6 miles in length between the River Etive, above Dalness, and the River Coe, above Clachaig, together with the Aonach Eagach ridge on the north side of Glen Coe. Within this area are found Bidean nam Bian, the highest summit in Argyll, Aonach Eagach, Buachaille Etive Beag and Mor; the rocky north-eastern peak, Stob Dearg, towers high above the wide expanse of the Moor of Rannoch to the east. The road which runs through Glen Coe was reconstructed in 1932; parts of the old road, now disused, still survive alongside in the upper parts of the glen. With an average rainfall of some 90 inches, Glen Coe is shrouded in mist and rain on many days throughout the year; it is this aspect which lends a gloom to the atmosphere and causes visitors to think about the Massacre of Glencoe, which took place in February 1692.

The population today is a tiny fraction of what it was, even soon after the massacre. Later, in the more peaceful years which followed the Forty-five, the glen carried a fair number of people and, despite the employment opportunities offered by the opening of the slate quarry at Ballachulish in 1760, there were suggestions that the area was over-populated by the end of that century. Sheep farms, were, however, being introduced about this time and their advent was accompanied by the absorption of many small-holdings into a few larger enterprises. The crofts at Carnoch, on the southern shore of Loch Leven, were originally formed to provide for the displaced tenants. When the Wordsworths visited the glen in 1803, Dorothy noted the signs of former cultivation where then there was only pasturage. She was told that "formerly the glen had had many inhabitants, and that there, as elsewhere in the Highlands, there had been a great deal of corn where now the lands were left waste". Another writer some fifteen years later observed: "The sheep-farming system has done the work of extirpation more effectually than the Secretary's massacre; and but slight traces now remain of the warlike tribe of this little valley."

The village of Carnoch, commonly called Glencoe village, spreads south across flats to the new main road and enjoys an excellent view down Loch Leven to the hills of Ardgour. A small museum was opened in 1971 to contain, among other things, items of interest connected with the Glencoe Massacre. It is a main attraction to something like several thousands of visitors each year. The museum is housed in two formerly derelict cottages which have had their traditional 'cruck' design restored. There is a fine selection of seventeenth- and eighteenth-century weapons, including rampart guns and muskets. Of particular interest are the period dresses on display. At the old Bridge of Coe, a side road runs upriver a short way to a hillock on which stands a tall, slender Celtic cross, a memorial to MacIan, Chief of Glencoe "who fell with his people in the massacre of Glencoe".

As the tourists slowly opened up the Highlands, Glen Coe became a 'must' in their itinerary. In 1841, Dickens wrote: "Glen Coe itself is perfectly terrible. The pass is an awful place. There are scores of glens high up, which form such haunts as you might imagine yourself wandering in in the very height and madness of a fever. They will live in my dreams for years . . . the very recollection of them makes me shudder." By and by the Victorian painter rejoiced in oils and in the scenic grandeur of the place. In 1839 an inn at Clachaig became a stage for coaches running between Glasgow and Fort William. In 1873 Queen Victoria picnicked in the glen, where her faithful John Brown was hard put to it to save his royal charge from the attentions of a persistent newspaper reporter.

Today, the area attracts many thousands of visitors; and facilities have been developed as a consequence of their interest. The White Corries in Glen Coe were the first mountain slopes in Scotland to be developed for ski-ing, and still provide some of the finest ski slopes. The company which has built a chair-lift and the accompanying ski-ing tows claims that the White Corries have no equal for natural quality of slopes, extent, reliability and certainty of main access. Development has in fact brought to the White Corries a carefully designed and sited service of chair-lift and ski-tows to make the most of the snow fields, to be effective in all weathers, and especially to handle peak traffic conditions. Ski instruction is available. The Glencoe Mountaineering

School was founded by the late Ian Clough, offering courses which have been running for many years now. The aim of the school is to give pupils the best value for money, combining an enjoyable holiday with five days of good rock climbing. Adventure week holidays are also being developed and involve camping holidays on the west coast and on some of the Hebridean islands.

At the beginning of 1973 proposals were announced for a winter sports centre to be developed on the 3,999-feet-high Aonach Mor. The area was previously the subject of a three-year study commissioned by the Scottish Tourist Board. The report indicated that on the basis of access to the snowfields being gained by tram rail or even overhead aerobus from Fort William, instead of by road and then uplift to the summit by cable-drawn mountain railway, the project would be both feasible and environmentally acceptable. A disused narrow-gauge railway to the area, extending from the British Aluminium Company Works at Fort William, was thought to offer possibilities. The project would, if it were realized, relieve Ben Nevis and Glen Nevis of the damage now being done by hordes of summer visitors, in that these would be more willing to take the opportunity of visiting areas at present difficult of access. The scheme would also enhance the role of Fort William as a tourist centre and offer hotel and other accommodation interests the chance of an extended, if not an all-year-round season.

Near the junction of Loch Leven and Loch Linnhe is Ballachulish, where a vehicle ferry plies across the narrows of Loch Leven. The ferry cuts out a circuitous 2-mile detour round the head of the loch, by Kinlochleven. This crossing has been made the subject of a feasibility study which eventually produced a decision to build a bridge. The plan involves a high-level structure and approach roads to take the Glasgow–Inverness road across the narrows at Ballachulish. The bridge is to be a steel structure 980 feet long. Its main span, 600 feet long, will clear the narrows about 60 feet above water level, to allow passage for yachts and commercial vessels. It will carry a 24-feet-wide single carriageway flanked by two 5-foot footpaths. Over a mile of approach roads will be built to link with the existing road system. The economics of the project are favourable and when completed will bring two main west-Highland centres, Oban and Fort William, that much closer together and create stronger links which could, in time, offer incentives to those of the area's existing population who wish to enhance their lifestyles by being in better contact with the facilities offered by the two Highland burghs.

Ballachulish is famous for its slates. These grey or black shiny rocks were originally mud; they are now mica-schists or slates. The cleavage which allows the Ballachulish slates to be used as roofing material is a metamorphic character due to compaction by pressure. It is easy to see in the slate quarries that this cleavage often cuts across the original layering or bedding of the slate, now much contorted. The slates have been a local industry since 1697 when the Ballachulish West quarry was opened, using workmen who had gained skill and experience at Easdale on Seil Island. The slates from Ballachulish are superior to many other Scottish varieties in their hardness and toughness, and they can therefore be cleaved thinner. There have been proposals for the re-use of the slate 'waste' of which there are unsightly mounds in the village. There are two possibilities. The first is using the coarser material to make a lightweight aggregate of the type now being used increasingly by the building industry where load is a critical factor. The other possibility is crushing the waste to produce a powder for use as a filler for many purposes in industry. The quarries at Ballachulish are now silent, having been closed down only in recent years.

The employment at the quarries about a century ago was, men and boys, in the region of 400, with an annual production of some 15 million slates. The population of Ballachulish was then 2,000, compared with the present 700, indicating the important role the industry had to play as a social sheet-anchor. The men who worked in the quarry were grouped into crews of five, six or seven men. Each crew chose a certain part of the rock face on one of the levels and made a bargain with the employer to work that particular spot for a year, receiving an agreed sum of money for every thousand slates made by them, so that their wages depended on the diligence with which they worked as well as on the quality of the rock they selected. A visitor in the 1860s noted that "education is deficient, on account of the boys being sent early to work in the quarry". Schools were attached to three of the religious denominations then in the area, but these were in general poorly attended. The quarry owner tried to make amends by starting up a Mechanics' Institute which attracted a number of 'students'; most of the workforce were members and received a rudimentary education, not only in basics but also in the techniques of their trade.

The aluminium industry is one of the youngest and fastest-growing industries in the British Isles, and the Highlands of Scotland were favoured with the first attempt to establish a truly industrial base for the Scottish economy. An essential element in the manufacture of aluminium was, and still is, cheap electric power. With its considerable resources of water, the region was the natural home for the new industry. The first industrial hydro-electric scheme was at Foyers. By the turn of the present century, four years or so after the first aluminium metal was produced at Foyers in 1896, world demand began to rise and it became obvious that the small designed output from Foyers was insufficient to capture any significant proportion of the new market. The directors of the British Aluminium Company had their eyes on the future, however. In 1901, at a time when world production was actually in excess of demand, a period of expansion was planned based on parliamentary powers obtained in that year. The Foyers plant was put on a full production programme of more than 1,000 tons per annum and the company began to exercise the water rights it had obtained when the Foyers estate was acquired, and which were included in an area extending almost as far as Kinlochleven on the boundary between Argyll and Inverness-shire. The Bill presented to Parliament in 1901 was designed to permit the development of water power and so the necessary machinery was on order when, in 1904, a further Act was passed, and a statutory company, the Loch Leven Water and Electric Power Company, was set up to carry through the new undertaking being planned for Kinlochleven. This statutory company was, in 1910, ultimately merged with the present-day British Aluminium Company, but not before it had carried through the most dramatic industrial development which had taken place in the Highlands up to that time and added to the production of aluminium a factory with an output seven times that of Foyers.

The work carried out at Kinlochleven consisted in the construction of the Blackwater dam, which until some time ago had the largest cubic content of any dam in the British Isles, a conduit of reinforced concrete almost 4 miles long, a pipe-track of six lines over a mile in length leading to a power house, an aluminium reduction works, a miniature township to house workers, and a deep-water harbour for handling incoming supplies. The building of the complex created something of a Gold Rush situation in the Highlands. A whole district, previously sparsely populated, was opened up; a new community came into existence and a new source of national wealth and local employment was created. The small village at the head of Loch Leven narrowly escaped being called 'Aluminiumville', a name seriously proposed at the time. The transformation was startling; originally, there was nothing in the district but a shooting lodge and a small croft. Then between 3,000 and 4,000 men appeared from 1904 to 1909 to form the work force necessary for the project. Conditions were rough; the hours were long and the work was heavy and of a kind that today would be done by machinery. There was an inevitable high turnover of personnel, as men drifted into the area for work, and then left after a few weeks, with a few pounds in their pockets, to have their place taken by others. Many men came from the Outer Hebrides; they spoke Gaelic only and it was necessary to meet this unique situation by employing foremen who were proficient in both Gaelic and English.

By the year 1907 Kinlochleven was producing aluminium metal for the world market. The hydro-electric scheme on which the works are based is the Blackwater dam, a storage reservoir with a capacity of almost 4,000 million cubic feet. The catchment area of the reservoir extends to about 60 square miles of hilly country, with an average rainfall of more than 80 inches per annum. The Kinlochleven Works employ about 300 men, most of whom are housed in Kinlochleven. The houses were built partly by the British Aluminium Company and partly by the Kinlochleven Village Improvement Society, constituted under the Friendly Societies' Act, with the aid of government grants and insurance society loans, the latter guaranteed by the main company. A self-contained community was thus created with many social amenities. Single men and short-term employees live in a modern company hostel built near the factory. The population of Kinlochleven is at present about 900. This 'new town' of the early twentieth century has suffered from its reputation of being a sunless town, due to its being overshadowed by the mountains which tower over it. Building at Kinlochleven was originally on the Argyll side of the village, at the foot of Beinn Barabhein. And each winter, from late October to early February, the valley was in shadow as the sun moved south. Since then house building has spread towards the sunlight, and by the mid-'20s houses were being built on the Inverness-shire side of the River Leven, which loses sun later and has it back earlier. After the last war, a new housing scheme at the foot of the Mamore mountains was constructed and the most recent houses are in the sun practically all the year round. Despite its being a popular spot with tourists, Kinlochleven has been described as the ugliest place in the Highlands, shrinking to 'wart-like' dimension under the towering mountains. This is perhaps too unkind, and the observer might well have paid his visit in really inclement weather, for the village, when the sun is shining, is a busy and pleasant place. One could call ugly many of the areas in our overcrowded cities and, depending on one's appreciation of them, many newly-built architects' bad dreams well merit the description. At least Kinlochleven hardly dominates its setting as do so many urbanizations today.

At first sight Fort William seems to consist only of a high street, narrow and stretching for 1 mile, and pressed in between the steep slopes of Cow Hill on the one hand and the shore of Loch Linnhe on the other. In fact, the burgh is a sprawling place, chock-full with new housing, both private and local authority. Although the town lacks a good situation, it does not lack character, the atmosphere here being west Highland with a touch of industrial prosperity. This is the chief town of Lochaber and is the most important centre of the western seaboard. The burgh is a close rival to Oban as a tourist and shopping centre, although inadequate accommodation is a serious drawback to the development of the tourist industry. Even so, the town's 3,000 inhabitants display a certain justified pride when 'The Fort' comes into general conversation. The original fort, built in 1645 by General Monk, is no longer extant. The site of Fort William is at a natural crossroads, and though it is rightly called 'inland', being 20 miles or so from the open coast at the Sound of Arisaig, it is a seaport in every sense of the word, with a canal which stretches right through Scotland to the east coast by way of the Great Glen. By land, the routes are road, coming from all the cardinal points; and the West Highland Railway, opened in 1894, runs its lonely way from Crianlarich, across the Moor of Rannoch to Fort William, and thence to Mallaig in North Morar. The railway was given an enhanced economic base when the pulp and paper mill was built at Corpach, and carries well over 1,000 tons of timber to Fort William each week.

The burgh acts as the centre for a hinterland containing a population of about 15,000. It has a senior secondary school and a modern hospital which has facilities for major and emergency surgery. Sites are being developed for small industries to broaden the economic base of the area. This is essential because the main industries can offer only limited opportunities to young people coming on to the jobs market; and if these cannot be absorbed, fresh unemployment problems will be created with renewed migration activity and depopulation. The arrival of the pulp mill revitalized Fort William and its environs, bringing with it many young families. Experts have foreseen problems, however. In 1966 the Scottish Council (Development and Industry) carried out a study of the Lochaber area and, in particular, looked ahead to the employment situation extrapolated to 1981. The report found that the pulp mill had created a 20 per cent increase in population; that the local schools—of which a number more had to be built to cope with extra pupils—would feel the 'bulge' in the coming years; and that the employment gap between those available for work and the actual jobs on hand would rise to a theoretical 1,300 by 1981. The report urged haste in the provision of 500 new jobs in a first crash-programme stage, and a further 500 in a second stage. Some way towards meeting the requirements of the present and the near future has already been made in the successful attraction of the new small industries which have been set up. Progress received a slight setback when the Glenlochy distillery was closed down in 1968. The present distillery is in production with a staff of over twenty.

The Ben Nevis distillery was built in 1825 by Mr John MacDonald, who was later to become known as 'Long John', as famous as his whisky. It was the first legal distillery to be erected in the district. At first the production was small. By about the 1840s it was producing some 200 gallons each week. The advent of the 1880s saw the whisky manufactured by Long John with a famous name and production exceeding 3,000 gallons per week. The distillery had its own pier built on the shores of Loch Linnhe for MacDonald's own fleet of steamers. In 1878 the proprietors built another distillery to meet the growing demand for 'Long John's Dew of Ben Nevis'. More than 200 were employed in a wide spectrum of tasks, not only connected with distilling: for instance, carts and lorries were made in the distillery's wheelwrights' shops. Some twenty horses and carts were engaged in a continuous procession between the distillery and the harbour. Within six years of the erection of the new distillery the production was just over 260,000 gallons per annum.

Typical of the small industries in Fort William is a hosiery factory; service industries thrive in the area. Employment in the distribution and civil services sector of the economy has risen by over 50 per cent in recent years. Of particular interest is a printing works with a staff of over twenty persons involved in colour printing of high quality; it attracts orders for print from all over Britain and is able to compete in the open market for print orders running up to 3 million leaflets at a time. The industrial scene, however, is dominated by aluminium and paper production; the story of their presence in Fort William has a saga element.

While the Kinlochleven project confirmed the early faith of the British Aluminium Company in the future expansion of the industry, the world market was in no stagnant mood. By 1911 the company's output had risen to 8,000 tons per annum, representing about 20 per cent of the total world production. The First World War, in particular, had a dramatic effect on both aluminium production and consumption. In the six years between 1914 and 1919 world output soared from 70,000 tons to 130,000 tons per annum, and it is a striking testimony to the adaptability of the metal that, after the enormous expansion occasioned by the war, the ground gained was held. Once the change-over to civilian production had been carried through, the increased capacity was taken up in a short time to supply the normal demands of industry. In this climate, the British Aluminium Company took a further step to increase its production and also its share in the rising market. The final result, which took some twenty years to complete, was the Lochaber Works at Fort William and a hydro-electric scheme which was the largest ever undertaken in Britain.

Originally, a scheme had been devised to bring the water of the Lochaber area of Inverness-shire, potentially the greatest source of water power in the country, to enlarge the Kinlochleven factory by driving a tunnel through the mountains from Loch Treig. In 1918 the British Aluminium Company promoted a Bill in Parliament for this purpose, but it was withdrawn in the face of opposition, the nature of which was that the scheme involved transferring water from one watershed to another and "taking water from Inverness-shire for the benefit of Argyllshire". The scheme as first envisaged had thus to be modified to utilise the water in the same county by placing the new power station and reduction works at Fort William; the Bill, in its new form, received royal assent in 1921. The Lochaber Power Company and, later, the North British Aluminium Company, were duly formed and, by 1924, with the help of a government guarantee covering the issue of £2,500,000 of debentures, work was started. Welfare buildings for a work force of 2,000 men were constructed; a temporary power station was set up for the operation of contractors' equipment; and 20 miles of surface railway were laid. These were the preliminaries to the main undertaking of drilling a 15-foot-diameter pressure tunnel a distance of 15 miles from Loch Treig to Fort William—through the heart of the Ben Nevis range. After four years of intensive work labour in the tunnel was terminated some 20 feet away from the waters of Loch Treig, the rock to be blasted away in a formal ceremony; thus the longest tunnel of its kind in the world was commissioned in 1929. The scheme uses the water from a catchment area of 303 square miles of mountainous country with an annual rainfall varying from 41 inches near Laggan Bridge on the River Spey, to 161 inches on the summit of Ben Nevis. This first stage had an output of 10,000 tons per annum of aluminium metal. The second stage in the development was undertaken in 1931, when the level of Loch Laggan was raised to provide storage capacity of some 40 million tons of water. This was completed in 1938 to raise production by another 10,000 tons per annum. The third stage of the Lochaber development was the impounding of the head waters of the River Spey, an operation which was completed in 1943 with the help of Canadian troops. When completed, the total production from Fort William was some 30,000 tons per annum.

The effect at the time of introducing some 600 new employees into the small burgh of Fort William was considerable, though the problem was eased by the British Aluminium Company building new houses as a first essential with other amenities for the community. Inverlochy village, near Fort William, comprising more than 300 houses, with post office, shops, children's playground and village hall, was erected by the Inverlochy Village Society Limited, constituted on much the same lines as the Kinlochleven Society. In the development of its hydro-electric schemes, the company had found on occasions that it was more economical to purchase estates, or portions of estates, rather than pay compensation to the owners. Thus, the company today finds itself listed as a considerable landowner in the Highlands, operating two sheep farms and some 150,000 acres of arable, marginal and hill land; afforestation is part of the company's operations. On one occasion the company had to purchase 38,000 acres of hill land in order to obtain a mere 75 acres of level ground suitable for village expansion. The present employment strength in the Lochaber Works is about 700.

For some two decades it looked as though Fort William was to be the industrial 'one-off' example to prove that only rather special types of industry could be sited in the region. Then, in 1966, the largest single building in the Highlands was opened: the Scottish Pulp and Paper Mill at Annat, close by Fort William. The impact on the overall picture of the declining Highland economy was both considerable and profound. The impact on the Lochaber area, centred on Fort William, was dramatic. The area before the aluminium era had always been something of a slack backwater, affected seriously by the Clearances of the eighteenth and nineteenth century. In more recent decades there was a constant emigration of young people, an activity accepted as a fact of life and only interrupted by the setting up of the aluminium-production facilities at Kinlochleven and Fort William. The building of the West Highland Railway was a turning point, but the total effect was hardly measured in significant socio-economic terms. In the early 1920s forestry began to create an increasing number of jobs and could be said to be the forerunner of the eventual decision to build a paper mill in Lochaber.

In 1963 a site on the banks of Loch Eil, under the glowering shadow of Ben Nevis, was surveyed and pronounced suitable for the projected mill. Long before this, however, in 1954, an Act of Parliament was passed which enabled the Government to lend up to £10 million on a paper-making project, the concept of which was on a large scale. Not only had the mill complex to be constructed, but a water pipeline had to be built, housing for mill workers erected (amounting to 450 new houses), three new schools built and the size of the existing school doubled (to cope with an influx of workers' children numbering 640); in addition, the Caledonian Canal was to receive the first major improvement since its opening in 1822—the construction of a new quay and mechanical lock to receive shiploads of softwood and hardwood brought by native and foreign ships. A 'bonus' in the scheme was the retention of the West Highland Railway, which was due for closure but saved at the eleventh hour because of its economic importance to the mill; the line was pressed into service to convey a daily load of logs from a railhead at Crianlarich to the mill, some 63 miles away. Highland hauliers were commissioned to convey logs from forests in Inverness-shire, Perthshire, Argyllshire, Ross and Cromarty, the upper Spey valley and the Western Isles. About 10,000 trees were expected to be felled daily. Two artificial concrete-and-steel islands were to be erected in Loch Eil to enable 16,000-ton ships to unload cargoes of wood chips from Canada. Originally the mill was conceived as a pulp-maker only, but an investigation of its economics proved that Scottish forests would not bear sufficient wood for almost twenty years. Thus, an integrated pulp and paper mill was mooted; in relation to the estimated yield of Scottish forests, the bigger scheme was deemed viable. Though the present complex seems huge to the uninitiated, the pulp mill at Corpach is the smallest possible economic unit. However, as an integrated pulp and paper-making facility, the mill has no rival for size in Europe and has strengthened the growing image of the Highlands as a suitable region for industrialization.

While the employment opportunities offered by the mill were welcomed, there were misgivings about pollution of the environment and the effect of mill effluent on marine life in Loch Eil. Investigations were carried out before and during construction of the mill, and scientists pronounced that there would be no ill effects. However, in 1972 the mill had to spend the sum of £100,000 for a new large fan to replace a smaller unit which had proved itself unable to cope with a noxious product resulting from the burning of waste liquors, and about which the community lodged strong complaints. The problem about the biological changes in Loch Eil remain unresolved.

One qualified school of thought has maintained that the build-up of waste from the pulp mill is cause for concern, and will tend to affect marine life in upper Loch Linnhe and in Loch Eil. Because of its treatment before the effluent leaves the mill, toxic waste is negligible. But, the build-up of non-toxic waste, namely wood pulp, on the bed of the sea loch between Corran Narrows and the head of Loch Eil was the main problem for the future. During the first four years of production, the deposit was coped with by the natural biological processes of oxidation. Surveys carried out in 1970 showed that as the build-up increased, the mass of deposited pulp became too much for breakdown by oxidation, and the biologically-vital seabed underneath was gradually becoming sterile and incapable of supporting life. An opposing, and equally qualified, school of thought challenged the 1970 survey findings and maintained that other surveys did not reveal any potential danger; indeed, there was, in some water areas, a considerable increase in the numbers of certain animals, which was probably due to the organic material from the pulp mill effluent providing an additional source of food. Continuous surveys, it was maintained, were necessary to provide useful information on the natural ecology of the loch systems and also foresee the build-up of danger so that remedial steps could be taken. The pulp-mill authorities have in fact been most anxious to keep aware of the possibilities of a problem assuming significant dimensions and have, to date, made considerable and successful efforts to reduce the amount of particulate organic material in the mill's effluent stream. To the layman, unversed in the lifestyles of marine life, these problems might seem unimportant against the economic advantage of employment offered by the mill. But, as has been proved elsewhere, long-term effects of short-term gains must be assessed to prove the feasibility of any project as expressed in ultimate human terms.

While the life in the lochs was left to make out for itself with the help of a few human protagonists, the members of the Fort William community have been left in no doubt as to the benefits derived from the mill's presence among them. During the construction of the plant, some 1,600 workers descended on the area to concentrate on the main installation and associated projects. Within weeks, Fort William found itself in the headlines of the national Press, which went wild in its descriptions of the Highland boom town with over £30,000 per week going into the pockets of local tradesmen. In time, this prosperity spread its ripples into the Fort William hinterland. About 8,000 applications were received for 700 full-time jobs at the new mill. The company's policy was to take on Scots living in the Highlands, Scots from the industrial belt with family connections in the north, and Scots from the development areas. A small proportion of the workers are of English origin. The recruitment programme was carefully planned and executed in an attempt not merely to build up a work force, but to create an employment facility which could operate harmoniously both in and out of the mill situation. It was surprising, therefore, that the mill management refused a team of social workers the facilities necessary to carry out a study of the impact the mill had made on the community.

The social multiplier represented by the mill was seen operating in the years after 1966: increased and better services, better schools, more teachers, nurses, doctors, shopkeepers, and opportunities for local service industries. The mill employs about 930 people. Allowing for an employment multiplier of two jobs outside in the forests to each one in the mill, approximately 2,000 people are indirectly employed in forestry, harvesting and transporting wood. It is in the forestry context that the mill fulfils its role as a 'Highland regenerator'. First of all, forests have to be planted on prepared land; the trees have to be thinned out at regular intervals; the trees have then to be felled and transported to the mill. The new dimension of employment brought by the mill into the Highlands will be seen after a few years of operation. The mill is at present geared to produce 80,000 tons of pulp and 52,000 tons of paper annually from its annual intake of 400,000 tons of Scottish softwoods. The paper output is concentrated on the commercial printing market. The types of finished products include paperbacks, text-books, guide-books, road maps and educational notebooks.

The viability of the whole exercise as centred on the mill was further enhanced in 1974 with the opening of Scotland's largest sawmill in Annat Farm, adjoining the mill site. This new mill, extending to some 20 acres, was first mooted in 1970 when the owners of the pulp mill, Wiggins Teape, and a firm of timber merchants based on Rothiemay in Aberdeenshire, A. G. and W. J. Riddoch, decided on a partnership to create a sawmill facility to handle the vast quantities of timber at present maturing in and around the Great Glen. The need for such a facility was also recognized by the Forestry Commission, who came in on the project to offer a large sustained contract of timber from their plantations along the Great Glen and as far north as Strome and Rattigan in Wester Ross. The supply of timber is in the region of 50,000 tons annually. Private woodland owners also supply timber to the mill, which will in turn supply the pulp mill with residues.

The discovery in recent years of North Sea oil and gas led in 1972 to the setting up of Britain's first sea-water proving ground for underwater systems, with Loch Linnhe as the focal point. The weather conditions encountered by oilmen in the North Sea have subjected their equipment to the most severe tests and it is essential to have an adequate testing facility to prove all types of underwater and oceanographic equipment, ranging from instruments to large off-shore structures. Loch Linnhe was chosen because it satisfied a number of basic requirements: it is a sea loch, there is in existence a suitable pier installation (formerly used by the British Aluminium Company), and the waters are sheltered. Above all, the loch is deep, down to more than 500 feet, with depths of about 1,000 feet nearby. The new company, U.E.G. Trials Ltd, was backed by a group representing more than seventy member firms and by the Highlands and Islands Development Board. The venture represented an investment approaching £200,000. The final employment prospects are for fifty persons, mainly men.

The area to the west of Loch Linnhe includes Morvern, Ardgour, Sunart, Moidart and Ardnamurchan. Part of the county of Argyll, these districts are the most remote and westerly; Ardgour is the most mountainous. Rising steeply from Loch Linnhe, its high hills extend 11 miles to Loch Shiel. Ardgour is roadless in its interior, which is deer-forest country in the hands of sporting proprietors. It is the most sparsely populated parish of Argyll with employment for the resident population largely stemming from several farms, a score or so of crofts, and sheep and cattle raising. The population density is less than two persons per square mile.

Strontian is a small crofting community near the head of Loch Sunart, with a population of about 150. Its present communications link with the 'outside' world is a twice-weekly bus, a fact which contributes to the creation of a lifestyle commonly found elsewhere in the Highlands and Islands. The main claim to fame is that it gave its name to the element strontium, first discovered in the area in 1764, when it was known as strontianite. Later, in 1787, Cruickshank discovered the element in the mineral and subsequently, in 1808, the yellow metal was isolated by Humphrey Davy. It is hard, yet ductile, and is used in the manufacture of fireworks, since it burns with a brilliant crimson flame. Strontian is also well known for its lead mines, a main lode being worked in the area since early in the eighteenth century. The workings have been idle since 1904, mainly through lack of financial support. In the past two decades, however, the economic potential of the Strontian deposits have been subjected to successive surveys, particularly with regard to the feasibility of deep drilling. Although so far these surveys have not been followed up by any development, commercial interest has not been abandoned; at least one company has recently appeared with a view to continuing exploration at depth when sufficient financing has been raised.

The history of the Strontian lead mines is full of interest and gives the lie to the frequent statement that the Highlands have never until recently seen any kind of industrial exploitation or development. In the British Museum is a plan of Loch Sunart, dedicated by its maker, Alexander Bruce, to General Wade. It contains a description of the mines which "ranked among ye richest of their kind in Europe". The mines were worked by a company which included as principals the Duke of Norfolk and General Wade, with a thirty-year lease of the workings from the owner of the barony of Ardnamurchan and Sunart. The company erected such buildings at Strontian as a smelting mill with four hearths, bridges, housing for the manager and staff, and other buildings to house workers and stores. "As they were ye first planters they met with ye greatest difficulties." The company did not, however, meet with any great success. During the first four years or so only 244 tons of ore were smelted and the receipts from sales did not meet the expenditure. In 1665 the York Buildings Company became the new owners, but over the many years which followed, it, too, failed to obtain the riches which were supposed to be lodged in the mines. The workings were abandoned in 1740 and the workmen dismissed. After that, the mines were worked continuously on a less ambitious scale until 1815 when, during the Napoleonic Wars, they became a source of considerable income for the proprietor. In 1846 sections of the mines were let to the Strontian Mining Company, which carried out development of the workings, though the results were disappointing. One of the principal operations carried out was the sinking of a shaft in the Belsgrove mine some 200 feet below ground level. There were five main mines: Belsgrove, Whitesmith, Middleshop, Corintee and Fee Donald. The most extensively worked was Belsgrove. Whitesmith was said to be the richest in ore of the group but was not worked extensively owing to difficulty of access. A company called the Fee Donald Mining Company leased in 1852 the Fee Donald mine and carried on operations until 1871. The last work at the mines was carried out from 1901 until 1904, when the Belsgrove mine was let to a Mr Robertson. At the height of operations, in 1733, no less than 500 men were employed in the area.

Small though it is, Strontian has two other claims to fame. The first is recent. In 1968 the Minister of State for Scotland announced that the first of a series of redevelopment experiments to bring new life to small villages would begin at Strontian. The first phase has now been completed: the erection of a central building containing a shop, tearoom, information kiosk and other facilities, designed to form the nucleus of a new village. This will, in time, be followed by new village housing, a school, an old people's home, a football park and showfield, and a caravan park. When the scheme was first announced, Strontian had fallen into decay, with a fall in population of 16 per cent experienced in the decade 1958–68. The present scheme is designed to help the renovation of some 2,000 villages in Scotland which are falling into disuse and which merit reconstruction, in economic as well as in social terms. Typically, when the scheme was announced, a protest telegram was sent to the Minister by the villagers, who claimed to have been left in the dark over the plan. But the plan was accepted with the whole-hearted support of the people affected once the intention of the planners had been explained in full.

It was at Strontian, as a result of the Disruption in 1843 which split the Scottish Church wide apart, that the famous Floating Kirk was situated. At that time virtually all the inhabitants of the area seceded from the then established Church and, on being refused permission by the landlord to build a new church, carried on their worship in the open air until someone hit on the idea that a floating church, moored off-shore, was feasible and could be located outside the landowner's jurisdiction. The landowner, an Episcopalian, had refused even a request to erect a tent for the congregation of some 500. In 1845 the Glen Shipyard, Port Glasgow, was asked to quote for a floating church, complete with vestry, pulpit and pews for 700 persons. The vessel was, perhaps appropriately, Ark-shaped; being unpropelled, the task of towing it round the Mull of Kintyre and past Ardnamurchan Point was not an easy one. In 1846 the £1,400 church was moored in Loch Sunart. An account of the time reads: "It was a singular spectacle on each Sunday morning as the time of worship drew near to see the boats coasting along from north and south, each with its contingent of hearers, while numerous groups could be descried far inland wending their way down from the hills. Ropes and cables were run out from the church and the boats were rapidly passed backwards and forwards conveying the worshippers aboard . . . the church sank one inch for every 100 people in the congregation." One preacher wrote: "Here I preached thrice on the Sabbath, twice in Gaelic, once in English. I was thanked by the office-bearers and told that their church had never been so deep down in the water before (6 inches)." The church was eventually driven ashore in a storm and was used regularly until permission was given for a stone building to be constructed; this was consecrated in 1873.

Of particular interest is the Ariundle Oakwood Forest Reserve. In completely afforested land, this reserve would pass unnoticed. But in a country whose natural tree cover has been reduced in extent from about 60 to 6 per cent in much less than two millennia, it has the rarity of a fine gem. Even some centuries ago there was extensive natural woodland, mainly of sessile oaks (the species generally found in western Scotland, Wales and Lakeland, in contrast to the pendunculate oak of England's heavy loams and clays). These trees clothed the valleys and loch shores of Sunart, Morvern, Moidart and other parts of Argyll.

Much of it was cleared for agriculture and large areas were devastated to satisfy the iron-smelters' insatiable appetite for charcoal. In more recent times much has been cleared to make room for Sitka spruce. Because of its relative remoteness in the glen which leads to the old lead mines above Strontian, the Ariundle wood has fared better than most. It covers some 400 acres and since 1961 it has been managed by the Nature Conservancy in collaboration with the landowner, the Department of Agriculture and Fisheries for Scotland. Typical plots on the reserve comprise mainly closed-canopy oaks well over 100 years old, with a relatively bare floor beneath them, carpeted with dead brown leaves and glittering with wild flowers such as tormentil and cow-wheat. Scots pine, Norway spruce and beech trees also over a century old grow here, though the spruces have not done well. The whole valley has a parkland appearance against a background of rising blue mountain masses. Oak seedlings are springing up on their own and, if left alone, will undoubtedly make for something like a living tree archaeology museum. With the sheep now banished from the area there is the promise of a new lease of life and growth, and Ariundle could well become a worthy reminder of the pristine glory which once covered much of Scotland not so many centuries ago.

The district of Moidart is low and hilly in its south part and rises to the north in some fine high peaks. The area has figured much in Highland history and no less in the Forty-five Rising. The Prince stayed at Kinlochmoidart House, attended by a bodyguard of fifty men of Clanranald, while he laid plans for the campaign. The population of Moidart today is less than a quarter of its maximum of 2,556 which occurred in 1841. Employment opportunities are few and far between in the district, but at Kinlochailort a fish farm, started in 1966, breeds sea-trout and salmon. Only a pilot scheme as yet, it employs but a handful of men; but there are good hopes that the venture will be successful and that big development, financed by Unilever Ltd, will give a much-needed employment boost to the district and help to stabilize population in an area that has much to offer the spiritual self but little to offer those who seek some small touches of the material benefits available in other more prosperous areas.

Loch Shiel stretches a full 17 miles from Glenfinnan in the north to Acharacle; its centre line is the boundary between Moidart and Ardgour. Until 1967 there was a ferry service between these two centres because the shores of the loch were roadless until the Forestry Commission constructed a track in 1966, down the Ardgour bank. The provision of the road ended a 70-year-old motor-boat service which lost much custom in favour of the road. To sail down this loch was to become immersed in history and the particular area of the Forty-five. It was down Loch Shiel that the Prince and his followers were rowed from Kinlochmoidart to Glenfinnan, where the standard was raised in

August 1745. This ceremony was performed by the ailing Marquis of Tullibardine. The old vessel *Clan Ranald* was the Loch Shiel ferry until 1955, when she gave way to a modern motor-driven craft which was able to do the return trip in one day. The sailings were run by David MacBrayne Ltd. The boat, the *Lochshiel*, was built in 1953 for the mail service on the loch which MacBraynes took over in that year. She was in 1962 transferred to Iona to handle cargo crossing the Sound of Iona and as a ferrying facility between the shore and Iona jetty and excursion steamers. Her place on Loch Shiel was taken by the *Lochailort*, built in 1954, which carried out her duties until 1967. The potential of Loch Shiel as a centre of boating and sailing activities has not gone unnoticed, and there are hopes that this might become a reality in the not too distant future.

Ardnamurchan is a peninsula which runs some 17 miles out from the Highland mainland to jut into the Atlantic. The name means, in Gaelic, 'Point of the Great Ocean'. Because it is quite exposed, high winds blow inland from its shell-sand beaches, giving the land a sufficient and regular dressing of lime to make a calcareous soil on its coastal strip. On a small scale, grass and livestock thrive to offer the population the only industry: agriculture, organized by an equal number of farms and crofts. A prosperous fishing industry was once prosecuted here but it failed, first, from a decline in manpower as a result of clearances; this was then followed by an unexpected change in course by the herring shoals; and the final blow came when continuous poaching by trawlers within the 3-mile limit ruined the fishing banks for line fishing. Salmon fishing round the coast offers some employment to a few men in the summer. Employment is also available from the Forestry Commission at Sunart. A handful of men work at collecting seaweed.

Typical of the social history of this district is Swordle, which was the scene of a notorious eviction in 1853 when the sixteen tenants were forcibly cleared by the landowner immediately after they had been forced to build themselves new houses at their own expense. No compensation whatsoever was allowed them. Forty years later, the sheep-farm which followed itself failed.

To the north, on a small peninsula of its own, clasping Kentra Bay, is Ardtoe. This is a typical clachan, a huddle of crofts in a green hollow between rocky knolls. A few hundred yards to the north a long sandy creek called the Sailean Dubh has been used since 1965 by the White Fish Authority for an experiment in fish-farming. Five acres at the head of the creek were enclosed and 200,000 inch-long plaice were released into it in an attempt to grow the fish to a marketable size. The Sailean Dubh was chosen because it had the right depth, clean sand, and good shelter from storm. But most of the original plaice were unfortunately killed off by crabs and eels—and by too much fresh water flowing into the creek from the burn at its head. Counter-measures were taken and the scheme is still being carried on. The population of Ardnamurchan realize that this venture represents a major industrial potential; it was, therefore, with much dismay that they learned recently that the White Fish Authority had made noises that it was considering moving its main effort in this field from Ardnamurchan. The district's Council of Social Service acted quickly to obtain an undertaking from the authority that the Ardtoe experiment would continue, and expand. This kind of research is inevitably a lengthy operation and fishery experts in the country do not expect that salt-water fish-farming in the British Isles will become an economic proposition for perhaps a decade yet. The elements of success are seen at Ardtoe particularly in the survival rate of more than 70 per cent of original stock. The stock of plaice is hatched at a small unit attached to Hunterston (Ayrshire) atomic power station, where they are reared to postage-stamp size in the warm-water effluent before transfer to Ardtoe to be fed and supervised in tanks until they are big enough to go to sea. Recent events emphasize the value of the authority's work in this field.

Quality fish stocks are under constant pressure in the North Sea and North Atlantic from an ever-increasing international fleet of frightening technical efficiency. It was the threat of over-exploitation which made Iceland go all out to establish a 50-mile limit. Against this background, it may well be that the unpolluted waters of the West Highlands will become an important food source and so create valuable employment opportunities in remote areas. The Highlands and Islands Development Board have assisted the Ardtoe project in the hope that its example will set off a string of commercial fish-farms in the Highlands, with Ardtoe continuing as an advisory unit and supplier of young fish. The work at Ardtoe has been concentrated on plaice, but there seems to be no reason why the experiment cannot be extended to sole, halibut and turbot, and even to the cheaper grades of white fish such as haddock and cod. If nothing else, fish-farming is an undoubted tourist asset.

The Morvern peninsula is diamond-shaped, with its boundaries comprising Loch Linnhe, the Sound of Mull, Loch Sunart and the neck of land between Strontian and Inversanda. One road straddles its centre to link up Glen Tarbert with Claggan and Lochaline; secondary roads go to Drimnin and Kingairloch. The name of the district is derived from the Gaelic for 'sea gap'. Lochaline is a village with sheltered anchorage on the southern coast with a population of some 150 people. There is a car ferry from here to Oban via Craignure on Mull across the sound. The village was once one of the delightful places in the Highlands, set in forested hills and in a land-locked bay, whose rocky shores are traversed by an old road through natural woods. The village is now greatly spoiled by sand-mining and timber-felling.

Glen Coe

(*top*) Glencoe village. (*bottom*) Fort William, Inverness-shire

In 1925 the Geological Survey reported that Lochaline had a bed of white cretaceous sandstone, about 18 feet thick. When hostilities broke out in 1939, this sand became Britain's only source of optical glass, a material which had hitherto come from Europe. When mining operations were begun, the sand was exceptionally pure and free of iron. At the present time, some 70,000 tons of sand are extracted from 27 miles of tunnel. The rock is drilled, blasted, screened, washed, stored in bunkers and then loaded on to steamers by conveyor belt. One third of the product is suitable for optical glass after purification; the remainder is used for a variety of glassware products including bottles. The industry, while offering much-needed employment, has made Lochaline a hideous place. Appalling scars hit the eye like a blast of hot wind. Waste is being spilled into the loch and the washing plant beside the original pier is slowly but surely silting up at the entrance to Loch Aline (once a favourite anchorage for yachts). The problems of the present day stem from the hasty opening of the mine at the beginning of the last war, when production figures were more important than amenity considerations, with the result that what was started has been allowed to continue unchecked. A local attempt has been made to impress on the mine owners (the mine was recently taken over by an English mining interest) that much of the works could be screened, at least, and the problem of the silting waste could be looked into.

Mining for minerals was attempted early in the eighteenth century at Lurga (where the lead mines were operated in association with the Strontian mines in the 1730s by the Morvern Mining Company) and near Loch Tearnait, where copper mines had been working since around 1750. Both these enterprises failed and were abandoned after only a few years' working; the Lurga mine was re-opened in 1803, but again without lasting success.

Lochaline today is crowded with lorries loaded with timber from the Forestry Commission plantations. The employment in this field is about thirty jobs, again a figure of social significance, since the population of all Morvern stands at present around the 500 mark. The Department of Agriculture lets four farms and near Drimnin, 11 miles along the coast, there are four crofts. The Ardtornish Estate, from whose land the sand is being mined, has a herd of dairy cattle which supplies the village of Lochaline with milk. Cattle and sheep are shipped from Lochaline to Oban for auction.

The lack of communications by land in Morvern today is a reflection of the lack of similar provisions in the past. Indeed, most of the communication links were by sea. In 1794 it was reported that there were "no fewer than 100 small boats . . . kept for the purpose of fishing, and carrying seaware as well as manure to their lands &c, as well as 12 or 14 barges of a larger size, well rigged, the property of the gentlemen tacksmen, for transporting themselves occasionally to the neighbouring islands, and for other purposes of usefulness and convenience.... Though a vessel called a packet runs at times between the Clyde and the Sound of Mull, it has only been set agoing and continued by private adventurers for their own interest, and is subject to no rules calculated for the public good." At about this time there were two regular ferries to other districts: one from Fernish at Rhemore across the narrowest part of the Sound of Mull, and the other from Doirlinn to Glen Borrowdale, Ardnamurchan. In 1822 the paddle-steamer, *Highlander*, began a regular passenger and freight service between Glasgow and the Sound of Mull, with Lochaline as a port of call. This event brought to public attention the isolation which the communities of Morvern had previously accepted as a normal part of daily life. Previously, if there was a calm spell of weather, travellers had to be rowed 15 miles from Oban to Lochaline.

7

The Central Highlands

THE whole of the area which lies to the north of the Highland Boundary Fault (running from Helensburgh to Stonehaven) falls into certain well-defined divisions which have combined similarities in respect of relief, structure, climate and historical development. The sub-region known as the Central Highlands includes the area of the Monadhliath mountains, the Cairngorms and the Perthshire Highlands. South and east of the Great Glen, this part of the Scottish Highlands has many features which have influenced the demographic patterns which largely exist today. It is accessible to the populous lowlands of the north-east, east and south. The development of the numerous valley systems has accelerated communications; and even though much of the sub-region consists of peaks, ridges and high-plateau moorlands, there are glens and straths which have proved eminently amenable to human settlement. Yet, as it has generally been in the past, it is an area of depopulation, with no large urban centres to act as social sheet-anchors. Despite this seeming disadvantage, however, it displays more vitality than does the western Highlands.

The Monadhliath mountains lie to the east of the Great Glen, rising to altitudes of over 3,000 feet. They have the same stepped plateau characteristics as are displayed by the Cairngorms farther to the south-east. Because they are lower, they display less evidence of local glacial erosion. The peaks lie along the watershed between the Findhorn and the Spey rivers, and consist, for the most part, of broad level surfaces with a dominant level of about 1,000 feet. Erosion has produced a smooth relief on both granite and metamorphic rocks. Occasionally, as seen in Cromdale parish, there is a great area of roughness which is in strong contrast to the smooth plateau surface of Dava Moor, which is quite monotonous. There are vast dumps of glacial material, with remarkable overflow channels cutting deep into the basic rock; an example can be seen in the Slochd, north-west of Carr Bridge. Grouse moors form the most common method of land use, crossed by main road systems between the south and Inverness, and by the railways. The valley systems are extensive and have brought into the heart of the plateau many lowland influences. Indeed, many of the larger straths have lowland characteristics, although temperatures in winter tend to be lower because of increasing distance from the sea. There are three groups of straths: those leading to the Moray Firth, the eastern straths which lead to the North Sea, and the southern glens which lead into Strathmore and the central lowlands area of Scotland.

Of the northern group, the most extensive and important is Strathspey, which is much like a broad well-planned Parisian avenue running from the Moray Firth to the Great Glen by its continuation in the Spean valley. It is the principal settled valley of the Highlands. To the north-west, there is good exposure; the slopes are gentle and give way to the moorland in benches which themselves can be used for agricultural purposes up to the 600-foot level. The principal attraction, however, is the valley floor. It is one of the few Highland valleys to possess a string of large villages, in Newtonmore, Kingussie, Aviemore, Nethybridge and Grantown on Spey. Today, these form important tourist centres because of the access they afford to the Cairngorms. There is a long and continuous history of settlement which will undoubtedly continue with the now-established attractions created for the tourist in recent years. North of Newtonmore, the valley is used for farms with arable land producing winter feed for sheep which graze in the summer months on the slopes of Cairn Liath and the Corrieyarrick Forest. There are numerous shooting lodges which feed well on deer and grouse. The section between the Truim and the Feshie rivers is notable for the flat floor of the valley in which Loch Insch is a surviving indication of the former lake floor in ancient times. Flooding is a handicap here, as elsewhere in the valley, with the result that the main arable land is confined to the lower valley slopes where centres like Newtonmore and Kingussie are also situated.

Land use changes as forests cover the floor of the valley and extend into the Cairngorm and Monadhliath mountains. The pine forests of Rothiemurchus, once the source of valuable timber floated down the River Spey in the eighteenth century, are today a dominant feature of the scene. Large farms use the areas of better soil on the slopes; crofts are found higher up the valley sides. Both these base their economy on raising cattle and sheep. Farther to the north-east are the extensively forested areas which spread up the slopes of the hills of Cromdale. This region is famous for the breeding of Aberdeen-Angus cattle; many pedigree farms use the arable land of the terraces to provide rotation grasses and root crops. In this section, are also found the principal Highland distilleries, either on the floor of the valley or in its tributory glens. Barley is an important consequential crop. Settlements are numerous and situated mainly in the south bank of the River Spey. The largest town, Grantown on Spey, an important tourist centre, is situated on the sunnier northern slopes. The presence of numerous deserted townships, indicating a greater population in the past, is a feature of the area around Tomatin, where there is a large distillery. The latter, with shooting lodges, provides employment as a supplement to the jobs provided by afforestation schemes.

Of the eastern straths, those of the Dee and the Don represent the proto-drainage direction of the Highland block. Deeply incised within the mass of the Cairngorms, they begin in culs-de-sac from which only trackways lead through to Speyside. There are only two roads, both of which are invariably closed in winter and spring by snow: from Strathdon, via Tomintoul to Ballindalloch; and that by Glen Clunie and the Devil's Elbow to Glen Shee and Blairgowrie. Similar straths originate to the south. For the most part they are of restricted importance at the present time, though in Glen Esk there is much evidence of higher population in the eighteenth and nineteenth centuries, as is Glen Clova. There are more ruins now than inhabited farms. Increasingly, land has been amalgamated as farms and townships are deserted, so that one farm now may possess several miles of the arable section on the alluvium and terraces of the valley floor. The valley slopes support birch scrub, grouse and sheep. The main strip of improved land in this area is along the River Tay and its tributary the Garry. It is also used for the main route of road and rail between the Central Lowlands and the Moray Firth. Developments of afforestation and hydro-electric schemes enhance the economic importance of the area.

The Cairngorms demonstrate to a high degree of perfection the nature of the ancient Highland tableland. Although the highest summits north of the Dee rise to over 4,000 feet above sea level, they are less imposing because they rise in steps from a 3,000-foot plateau. While in the past the area has been denied any history of permanent settlement, today they have been opened up to an appreciative public for climbing, ski-ing, hill-walking. To what extent these new activities will generate small nuclei of settlements is open to question, as indeed is the long-term effect on the provisions of nature being exposed to vast numbers of people and being destroyed, particularly in areas of high ground where natural life hangs on by a thread. Conservationists are of course aware of this problem and have recently made suggestions which, if carried out and while they mean restriction of access, will preserve the high mountain flora for future generations. It is only necessary to see how quickly a brown-earth track can be produced over a grassy sward to realize the real danger which lies in the new-found access to this area.

The south-western area of the central Highlands sub-region opens out from the broad, high plateaux of the Cairngorms into heavily dissected surfaces with sharp peaks, pronounced ridges and deep valleys with numerous lochs. Because of their proximity to the great Glasgow conurbation, the Highlands of Perthshire and Stirlingshire have been less remote than most other Highland regions. The great scenic beauty of the area makes it a main attraction for city holidaymakers. The lochs are used as reservoirs for water supplies to the western central lowlands and are the bases of the hydro-electric schemes. Though a great deal of the land area is unsuited for agriculture, it enters into the life pattern of the central lowlands to a greater degree than its relief would suggest. Great plantations of the Forestry Commission also make a substantial contribution to the economic viability of the area. Although depopulation of the upper glens still continues, as elsewhere, there is much more stability of population and less of the 'Highland problem'. The two main centres are Crieff and Perth, the latter known as the Gateway to the Highlands. The former is linked to the ports in the Great Glen by Wade roads.

The road link between Inverness and the south and south-east twists and turns as though trying to escape from the strictures imposed on it by a hostile topography. This very characteristic, however, provides the traveller with all kinds of vistas, and numerous opportunities to appreciate in full the extreme variations which make the A9 road almost a road back into history. All along its route, history is held in safe-keeping, either in the silent witness of roofless, deserted croft houses and derelict lands, or in the still-surviving communities which, in many cases, are now experiencing the exciting touch of the tourist—which often spells the difference between stagnation and a slump into limbo, and a hope of survival into the future.

The little village of Tomatin, some miles south of Inverness, owes its existence largely to Tomatin Distillers Ltd, a public company. Their product is a light yet peaty malt whisky, well-matured and comes from a still which is claimed to be the largest of all, with an output of more than a million proof gallons a year. Malt whisky is made from a watery extract of malted barley, fermented by the addition of yeast and then twice distilled in the characteristic onion-shaped pot-stills from which the flavoured alcohol is driven off by heat. The still has to be re-charged after each distillation. Malt whisky takes from ten to fifteen years in oak casks to mature properly. Although the greater quantity of malt whisky produced in the Highlands goes for blending, in recent years there has been a growing appreciation of single or unblended malts, now specially bottled to meet the demand.

South of Tomatin lies Carr Bridge, an attractive village and one which was a pioneering focus of the now-popular inclusive ski-ing holidays. It nestles cosily on both banks of the brawling River Dulnain, straddled at one point by the ruinous Old Bridge. The arch of this structure still survives, its roots being firmly bedded in the living rock on both sides of the river. It was built *c.* 1776 for the purpose of carrying funerals over the Dulnain to the churchyard at Duthil, after two local men were lost trying to cross the river in flood. Popularly attributed to General Wade, the bridge in fact is not one of his creations. In the summer months the village is chock-full with visitors who lend a bewildering multi-national character to the place; this is in striking contrast to the more leisurely atmosphere which greets one in winter, though the ubiquitous skier is ever to be seen making for the slopes or getting back to home base after a day on the Cairngorms. The village supports an industrial enterprise which specializes in hand-knitted sweaters, cardigans, hats and tammies.

To the east of Carr Bridge lies Grantown on Spey, a village first laid out in 1765. A note written in 1792 mentions Grantown as a village "erected under the influence of the Grant family, it being little more than twenty years since the place where it stands was a poor rugged piece of heath. It now contains from 300 to 400 inhabitants, some of whom are as good tradesmen as any in the kingdom." It is the largest township in the Spey valley and is an important market centre. In some ways it tends to be badly placed to take full advantage of the development of winter sports which has occurred farther south and centred on Aviemore. Even so, it has a genuine mellowed atmosphere which is enjoyed by the present population of some 1,600 inhabitants. It is a well-planned town, which has a spacious high street with an avenue of trees. The town's founder, Sir Ludovic Grant, produced a prospectus which proposed that it should develop into a centre of wool and linen manufactures, as well as of the timber trade and carpentry. The vision was not fulfilled. However, by the 1780s it did become a prosperous centre of the Highland linen industry and the market town for a large part of the Spey valley. Various kinds of cloth were also made, some of which found their way as exports to West Africa. The textile industry fell into decline about the end of the century. Grantown continued to grow and by the middle of last century became the second largest town in Inverness-shire.

In 1860 Queen Victoria paid a visit to the town: "... very amusing and never to be forgotten". Three years later the arrival of the railway enabled many of her subjects to sample what had delighted the monarch. Grantown Square is a planning delight and contains some of the oldest buildings in the town, for instance the charming eighteenth-century house with its double windows, near the north-west corner. On the south side, the clean granite lines of Speyside House, built in 1824 to replace an eighteenth-century orphanage, are more than pleasing to the eye. The clock under its neat cupola was paid for out of funds collected for soldiers in the Napoleonic Wars; but by the time the fund had reached its target, the wars had ended and the clock was installed as an aide-mémoire for the townsfolk. There are two ski schools in Grantown; between them they provide a mixture of British and Norwegian ski instructors who, as members of the Association of Ski Schools in Great Britain, are eligible to award proficiency badges in the sport.

South of Carr Bridge lies Boat of Garten, and to the east Loch Garten, the latter well known for the bird reserve created for the fish-eating ospreys which have nested in the area since 1959. The birds are safeguarded from disturbance, not always with complete success, by members of the Royal Society for the Protection of Birds. Facilities are provided by the society for the public to view the birds at their eyrie from an observation post equipped with high-powered binoculars. Boat of Garten itself is a small village with no history of significance except that it owes its existence to the advent of the railway in 1863. The population is about 300.

In contrast to Boat of Garten, the village of Nethybridge has a history of settlement going back many centuries and includes the era of the Lairds of Grant with their 'tails' of Highlanders, who disposed justice through baron bailies who tried local transgressors and administered an arbitrary justice in accordance with a rather liberal interpretation of the law. The main feature of Nethybridge is a fine hotel building catering for angling interests. Near the village, a mile or so on the Grantown road, is Abernethy Church, dedicated to St George and possessed of an old stone font. Nearby is the ruin of Castle Roy, an ancient and massive piece of work standing on a small mound and said to be the oldest castle in Scotland, dating from the twelfth century. The population of the village is about 450; all are aware of the fact that the settlement can point to at least 500 years of continuous habitation, from 1461, the date of a document containing the name 'Abirneithi'. The village itself, however, is comparatively young. It did not exist as such until the nineteenth century, when it came into being as Ceanndrochaid ('Bridge End'). It quickly grew as it established itself as a community focal point for activity, and took on itself the historical accretions of the surrounding countryside. Typical of the historic associations of Nethybridge is Coulnakyle House, built in 1770 to replace an even older manor. "Here", wrote Dr William Forsyth, "Edward of England may have flaunted his banners, here the trumpets of Claverhouse have sounded, and here Montrose and MacKay have pitched their tents. Here the Chiefs of Grant have dwelt; here Baron Bailies have held their courts; here the managers of the York Buildings Company have resided. . . . Coulnakyle has been the centre of life and interest for six hundred years." The mention of the York Buildings Company refers to that commercial enterprise which denuded much of the forest areas of the Spey valley. From 1730 to 1737 they felled the Forest of Abernethy and floated timber down the River Spey to Kingston and Garmouth on the Moray Firth coast. They were, Forsyth declared, ". . . the most profane and profligate set. . . . Their extravagances of every sort ruined themselves and corrupted others." The company, however, did build roads and sawmills and invented the raft, which greatly improved the technique of floating logs down the river. Coulnakyle is now a farmhouse.

The focal point of the Spey valley is Aviemore. It is truly unique. It is the most comprehensive holiday and conference complex ever planned in this country, and the first and major phase of development has enjoyed a tremendous popularity and success, though the economics do not present such a pleasing picture. The idea behind the creation of Aviemore as a holiday centre was that of Lord Fraser of Allander, who in his day was one of Scotland's most spectacular businessmen. He formed a consortium to obtain the £3 million necessary for the project. The realization of the Aviemore potential was slow at first. Then, in 1965, the Rank Organization opened a new hotel in nearby Coylumbridge. This was followed by the Aviemore Centre, erected to include an entertainment and sports complex comprising a heated swimming pool (25 metres), a seven-lane international-size curling and skating rink, a plastic brush-matting ski slope for learners, a nine-pin bowling alley, a Highland Wildlife exhibition, a cinema/theatre and a multi-purpose hall suitable for conferences. The result, at the present time, is the centre's provision of some 500 jobs for employees, of whom about 65 per cent have their homes in the Spey valley. The centre is operated by Highland Tourist (Cairngorm Development) Ltd.

The feasibility of the Aviemore Centre, some seven years after its inauguration, is still a matter of debate. A private investment of some £3½ million in 1965 was still unable to offer the investors a reasonable capital return. What the investment had done was doubled the local population figure in the time of its existence, contributed about £250,000 of additional spending power to the area, boosted the area's tourist industry with a strong international appeal and provided many leisure facilities which had previously been lacking. Apart from the commercial interests, the Highlands and Islands Development Board invested a large sum of money to help realize the obvious potential of the area, which, though centred on Aviemore, takes in the whole of the Spey Valley from Grantown on Spey to Dalwhinnie and Laggan. While this development has undoubtedly provided a much-needed shift of gravity from the south of Scotland into the Highlands, and provided employment, either full-time or part-time, during the summer months, it has been argued that the amount of cash generated by the various entrepreneurial interests in the area is not used for the further development of the valley; rather it is passed to the purses of the controlling interests of the entertainment facilities provided, which are based in London. A further objection to the development has been that the dominant emphasis on tourism has changed certain essential characteristics of the affected communities, brought in new blood, sometimes of an alien kind, and has not been so good for the local people.

Aviemore has little history to claim for itself. About a century ago nothing marked the site of the place save a grim building, like a tolbooth, which was built as a barracks in 1726. It was later used as an inn and change-house. In 1964 it was demolished to make way for new developments. As with other communities, it was the advent of the Highland Railway which created the basis of the village as it is now known. The original settlement provided no fewer than 140 employees for work on the railway, a situation which continued until the gradual decline in rail traffic; with a reduced staff of twenty soon after the Second World War, Aviemore joined the growing list of Highland areas with two serious problems: depopulation and unemployment.

Notwithstanding the dominance of the tourist industry, attempts have been made to create an industrial element in the economic structure of the area. In Aviemore a small site has been earmarked to serve as an industrial base on which an advance factory has been built by the Highlands and Islands Development Board. Its extent is 6,000 square feet and it is let at about 19p. per square foot. The effects of North Sea oil have spread to Aviemore in the form of a small industrial unit employing about fourteen people in the production of components and special-purpose machines for the sea-based side of the industry; these components are now being produced in the advance factory. Another commercial interest, dealing in clan crests and tartan souvenirs, is interested in establishing a branch factory in Aviemore.

Close by Aviemore, to the east, are Queen's Forest, Glenmore National Forest Park and Rothiemurchus Forest, all of which rest at the feet of four spectacular heights: Cairngorm (4,084 feet), Ben Macdui (4,300 feet), Braeriach (4,248 feet) and Sgoran Dubh Mor (3,635 feet). The Queen's Forest bears its name in commemoration of the Silver Jubilee of King George V and Queen Mary in 1935. The land was purchased from the Duke of Gordon by the Forestry Commission in 1923 and the creation of these woodlands has been a continuous process since that date. Within the forest are many remnants of the old Caledonian Scots pine which at one time covered much of Scotland with dense forest. These may now be seen as groups of old trees interspersed with the younger woods which have been planted in recent years. A number of forest walks, provided by the Forestry Commission, have been selected to give the walker excellent views of the Cairngorms, Loch Morlich and the Rothiemurchus area.

The Cairngorms National Nature Reserve is over 64,000 acres in extent and is the largest of its kind in Britain, and one of the largest in Europe. When it was first declared in July 1954, it comprised about 40,000 acres, but was extended to include a further 20,000 acres in Glenfeshie Forest and a further 5,000 acres or so at the head of Glen Avon. Apart from an area of a little over 5,000 acres owned by the Nature Conservancy on Invershie, the reserve is established under nature reserve agreements with the proprietors of Rothiemurchus, Inschriach, Glenfeshie, Mar Forest and Glen Avon. The reserve is quite unique among reserves in the British Isles because it includes the most extensive area of land over 4,000 feet in the Highlands. The reserve includes a series of great corries, in four of which are found lochs at elevations of over 3,000 feet. Furthermore the reserve contains some of the largest and finest surviving woods of native Scots pine and high-mountain plant and animal communities of particular interest. The area of the reserve ranges in altitude from about 840 feet, at Loch an Eilean, to 4,300 feet at the summit of Ben Macdhui, and thus offers great scope for scientific observations and research relating to meteorology, physical features, vegetation and animal life.

The main aim behind the reserve is the conservation of its native woodlands and mountain habitats, with their characteristic flora and fauna, so that these may persist and develop naturally, with the minimum of interference from man's activities, though controlled to some degree by scientific management. Over 200 species of flowering plants are to be found within the reserve area, some of these being among the rarest and most beautiful members of the British mountain flora. Of the mammals, regularly present are red deer, roe deer, wild cat, otter and badger. Some of the bird species include the golden eagle, peregrine, merlin, ptarmigan, black grouse, snow bunting, siskin, crossbill, crested tit, capercaillie and greenshank.

Craigellachie National Nature Reserve is a smaller but no less significant area of 642 acres; it was established in 1960. It lies immediately west of Aviemore and has as its dominant feature the birch-clad hill of Craigellachie itself, from which birch woodland, embracing Loch Pulladern and a disused reservoir, stretches north to the east-facing slopes of Creag-nan-Gabhar in the north-west corner of the reserve. The reserve was set up to conserve the exceptionally good and pure birch woods, with their naturally associated flora and fauna. The reserve forms a valuable supplement to the Cairngorms Reserve, where there are no pure birch woods. Of particular interest are the rare and local moths of the area. Both these reserves, like others in the Highlands, are under the general supervision of wardens of the Nature Conservancy, one of the constituent bodies of the Natural Environment Research Council, with the purpose of carrying out biological research and offering advice on the management of natural resources.

Glenmore Lodge is located in a superb setting in the Glenmore National Forest Park, which provides up-to-date facilities for those who wish to take up ski-ing, sailing, hill-climbing, walking, nature study and the general lore of the high hills. The lodge is sponsored by the Scottish Sports Council. The courses are intended to introduce, or further develop, skills in adults on a direct tuition basis in a number of outdoor pursuits, which vary according to the season. Children, from 14 to 17 years, are also introduced to these activities, either on a specialist basis, when they know their objectives, or on a sample basis, where during the course of a week they are exposed to all the possibilities and thus enabled to make a more educated choice of their leisure pursuits. The lodge runs a mountain leadership certificate on two levels: basic and, when more advanced, assessment. These two levels are divided between summer and winter. The courses are designed to lead to mountain instructors' certificates for those who wish to teach this activity on a professional basis. Mountain rescue and survival courses are run several times each year in conjunction with the mountain Leadership Training Board and the Mountain Rescue Committee of Scotland. The centre is one of the mountain rescue posts in the Highland region, and the staff form the team.

To the north of Loch Morlich, which lies at an altitude of 1,046 feet, is Reindeer House, the home of Mr Mikel Utsi and the representatives of the Reindeer Company, the focal point of administration for a herd of reindeer introduced from Lapland in 1946.

The village of Inverdruie has for some centuries been a centre of population. Originally, the village was part of an old drove road used for driving cattle to the Falkirk Trysts. Loch an Eilean is justly famed as a beauty spot, enhanced by its castle built on a small island. The building was begun by a chief of Clan Chattan in the fifteenth century, and added to over the centuries. In 1688 it was successfully defended by the laird's wife, Grizel Mor, against a band of adherents of James II after the Battle of Cromdale. The castle was last used in 1745 when the Laird of Rothiemurchus imprisoned some of his tenants in order to prevent them from taking up arms in the rising of that year. A nature trail, established by the Nature Conservancy, follows a well-defined track round the shores of the loch, a thieves' road in former times. These trails enable the public in general to gain a better and more significant appreciation of the countryside by guiding them through the area and explaining features of interest. In 1972, Sir Frank Fraser Darling, a vice-president of the Conservation Foundation, opened a visitor centre at Loch an Eilean. The centre, constructed from an older building, is leased by the Nature Conservancy from the Rothiemurchus Estate. The centre is open daily during the summer months and displays the story of one aspect of the Cairngorm National Nature Reserve, of which Loch an Eilean and the surrounding pine woods are a part. The display traces the development of the region from the end of the last Ice Age to the present. The Countryside Commission for Scotland co-operated in the venture.

At Kincraig, a beautiful little place situated on the face of a brae overlooking the waters of Loch Insch, there is a landing strip for small planes. Of particular interest are the gliding facilities which the Cairngorm Gliding Group offers to its members and visiting pilots.

The parish of Kingussie and Insch is one of the largest in Scotland, and is also one of the most beautiful. Standing 750 feet above sea level, Kingussie commands a sweeping view of the Cairngorms and the Grampians. Some 10 miles to the west, along the Monadhliath flank, a tiny loch gives birth to Scotland's fastest river. The Spey was once used for floating timber to the Moray Firth coast. Much of this timber was discharged through the Spey by the 'Spey floaters'. These were a hardy breed of men akin to the lumberjacks of only a few decades ago, before mechanization reared its head in the world's forests. The pines were felled in Glenmore and Rothiemurchus and dragged by ponies to the banks of the main streams going through the forests. Then, when all was ready, sluice gates on Loch Morlich, or Loch Eanaich, were opened and the logs thrown into the flood waters. They were guided on their downward journey by men of the district, each armed with a long pole with a sharp hook at the thin end. When the logs reached the Spey, their course was arrested and they were placed in the charge of the Spey floaters, who fashioned them into rafts equipped with oars. The floaters manœuvred these through the rapids of the river and across its broad pools. A Hull merchant, William Osbourne, in 1785 purchased from the Duke of Gordon the forest of Glenmore, which he then began to fell, clearing the area within twenty-two years. The timber obtained was used to build some forty-seven ships at Kingston on Spey at the river mouth. The largest of these vessels was 1,050 tons, built for service with the East India Company.

The Kingussie area has a very long history of human settlement. Close to Kingussie lie two mounds, one on each side of the River Spey. The mound on the south bank was for long surmounted by the Castle of Ruthven, about the gates of which were clustered the houses of the small hamlet of Ruthven. In 1863 the controversial James Macpherson was born here and, after a course at Aberdeen University, returned to teach in his native village. Later, through his Ossian writings, he brought world fame to Kingussie. In its day, this settlement boasted of some considerable import and formed what was known as the 'Castle-town'. The mound on the north bank of the river marked the proximity of the church, with its own satellite hamlet known as Kirktown. Until the end of the eighteenth century, Ruthven was the predominant settlement until it disappeared. The present village of Kingussie occupies the site of the former Kirktown. It is suggested by historians that Kingussie's history of settlement goes back for some 2,000 years. It held, by virtue of its location, some important place in the ancient Pictish kingdom. It lay close to the frontier, the Grampian Mountains, and was only 40 miles from the capital and seat of government in Inverness. One of the multilithic structures in the area is on a site known as Tom a' Mhoid, the 'Court Mound', a place where justice was dispensed. In A.D. 210 the Roman emperor Severus penetrated the north of Scotland and it is thought that his army returned through the Kingussie area. A mile or so from the village were found an urn containing ashes and a Roman tripod.

St Columba, on his pilgrimage from Iona to Inverness, passed through Kingussie and established a church in A.D. 565. Part of the walls of this chapel can be seen at the end of the graveyard which is still known as St Columba's Churchyard. When Caledonia was absorbed into the Kingdom of Scotland, Kingussie was included in the Province of Moray. Thus, from the earliest times Kingussie has had ecclesiastical connections. In the middle of the twelfth century the curé of Kingussie was one Muriach, the younger son of a local family. On the death of his brother he became head of the family and chief of Clan Chattan. He received a dispensation from the Pope and married a daughter of the Thane of Calder. His son, Ewen, succeeded him in the leadership of the family and his descendants became known as 'sons of the parson' or Macpherson. This is still the predominating clan in Kingussie today. In the year 1200 Kingussie was created a parish and was further established in the following centuries. In 1451 James II granted charters erecting the crofts and acres of the church of Kingussie and other church lands into a barony, to be held by John, Bishop of Moray, and his successors in the bishopric. A priory was founded in 1490 by George, second Earl of Huntly, the monks being of the Order of Carmelites. In 1563 Mary, Queen of Scots, stayed at Ruthven Castle in the course of a hunting expedition in the nearby forests. The first Protestant minister appeared in 1567 to take over a strange situation in which the church was so divided that Catholics used one end and the Protestants the other.

In the century which followed the north of Scotland was kept in a state of ferment by local feuds and risings, and by the warlike invasions of Montrose, Cromwell and Dundee. Ruthven Castle was a natural centre of hostilities during this period. Many men from Kingussie rallied to the Standard of the Chevalier when it was raised on 3rd September 1715 on the Braes of Mar. Again, in 1745, many local men were 'out'. After the Forty-five, and the abolition of heritable jurisdictions in 1747, the castletown of Ruthven lost much of its importance and the inhabitants of Badenoch devoted themselves to agriculture and the cultivation of flax. In order to develop the manufacture of lint, the Duke of Gordon had the idea of erecting mills in Kingussie. Towards the end of the eighteenth century, a lint mill was set up, with two others, on the banks of the Gynack Burn. A meal mill was also built and enjoyed a long and useful existence in comparison with the short life of the lint mills. About the same time two important institutions were transferred from Ruthven to Kingussie. One was the Baron Bailie Court of the Lordship of Badenoch, for the accommodation of which the Duke erected a new tolbooth. The other was the parish school. It was the removal of these central activities which caused Ruthven to fall into decline until, in the passing years, all traces have virtually disappeared.

Before the advent of the Highland Railway, Kingussie was on the route between Edinburgh and Inverness and was an important stopping place for coaches. In 1863 the Highland Railway was opened between Perth and Inverness and from this date the town began to increase in its significance as a holiday resort; steps were thus taken to improve the amenities offered to visitors. Application was made to the sheriff of the county to have the provisions of the General Police and Improvements Act of 1862 made relevant to Kingussie. The Act under which police commissioners exercised their powers, enabled these officials to control drainage and water supplies. In a short time the old system of taking water from the mill race and wells gave place to an up-to-date water supply from the Gynack Burn. Pumps were erected among the streets to accommodate those householders who could not afford the cost of having the water laid on in their houses. At the same time, a complete drainage scheme was carried out. The popularity of the town increased rapidly and its areas were extended so much so that the commissioners found it necessary, in 1890, to introduce a much larger water supply system and to displace the street pumps.

Industrial development was also tried in Kingussie. In the year 1896 the Speyside Distillery was erected on the west bank of the Gynack. However, this venture proved a failure and a few years later the buildings, erected at a cost of some £20,000, were sold at a public auction in Edinburgh for the bargain price of £750. The present economic base of Kingussie's population of 1,000 is tourism, which has been instrumental in opening up much of the area of the surrounding region which had hitherto been in the exclusive and private hands of individuals for the pleasure of the few. This particular point was the subject of an observation made about sixty years ago in the *Scottish Geographical Magazine*, in an article based on a survey of the Kingussie area:

> Midway between East and West and within the Highland Line, Kingussie is surrounded by a vast area, belonging to the Highland complex, all of which may be said in general terms to be a region of great natural poverty. . . . The predominating rocks are such as to give rise to poor soil. . . . Switzerland is the great rival of the Highlands as a playground—the country which above all has learned how to utilise its natural economic disadvantages as a means of attracting tourists. . . . In Switzerland, no visitor can fail to be struck by the evidence of a vigorous peasant life behind the waxing and waving stream of tourists: the ubiquitous cow, the little patches of hay, so carefully husbanded, the numerous chalets, many with marked signs of prosperity about them, are obvious to the casual visitor. Such a vigorous peasantry is at least not conspicuous in most parts of the Highlands, though in the Kingussie district, for example, the visitor will find many a trace of a former more extensive population. . . . The Highlands are markedly deficient in roads, yet every valley in the higher parts of Switzerland has not only its main road, but has radiating out from its tourist centres, a number of side roads which lead, perhaps by passes, into the neighbouring valley, but as often as not lead only to the 'alps' or upper pastures or to famous viewpoints. If we take the Kingussie district as a typical Highland district, we find that not only are the roads few in number, but traffic is what is called 'discouraged' by the owners or leasees of the shooting lodges. . . . While in earlier days the absence of definite tracks was probably of little importance, its effect in recent years has been to cut off from the use of the public vast areas of the country now used as grouse moors and deer forests.

The writer of that observation would most likely approve of the development of the area to meet the requirements of the tourist industry. The roads requirement is still an area for further development, though this is a point debated particularly by conservationists who see the dangers to natural life in the opening up of new areas to the press of thousands of insentient boots. One of the prime examples is the proposed Glen Feshie road, first mentioned by General Wade in the first half of the eighteenth century. At one time before the Second World War, this area in Glen Feshie had an element of beauty in its remoteness. Then came the war, with its customary disregard for all those slender and delicate values which distinguish the sensitive from the uncompromising requirements of hostilities. Many of the old pines which had stood for centuries, making their own particular and unique contribution to the environment and the scenery, were felled; lumber camps were established, roads were driven up the hillsides and the salmon were dynamited in the river. Towards the end of 1972 the proposal for a road through Glen Feshie to link the counties of Aberdeenshire and Inverness-shire was again aired. Officials from both sides of the glen decided that the project was definitely 'on', provided the finance, some £2½ million, was available. The general view was that the Glen Feshie road was a most desirable project and that it should

Glenfinnan monument commemorating the Forty-five

Pulp mill at Corpach, Inverness-shire

River Spey and Speybridge

Summer visitors to Cairngorm ski-slopes

Aviemore Centre, Inverness-shire

Rotary Precision Ltd., Kingussie

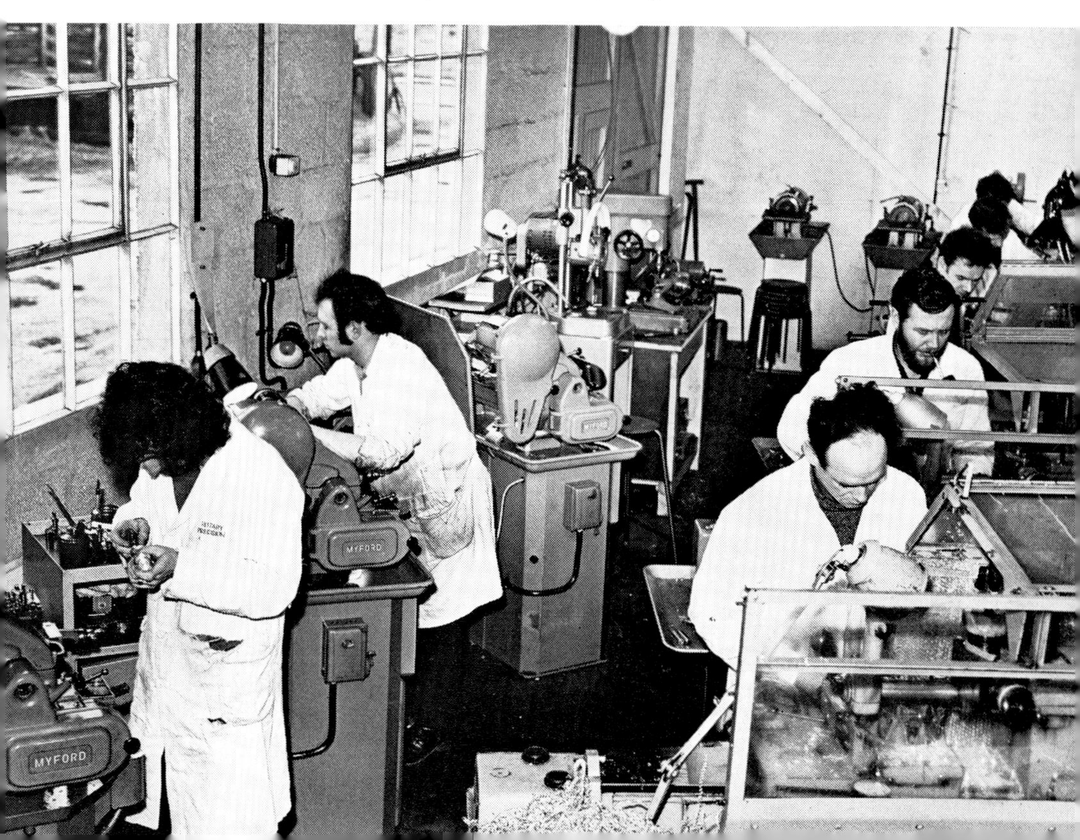

Loch an Eilean and the Wolf of Badenoch

Morar, Inverness-shire

proceed as quickly as possible, in view of the increasing tourist traffic and expanding industrial development—a feature which was accentuated by oil developments off the east coast of Scotland. The road would also offer a convenient link between the winter sports area in the Cairngorms at Glenshee and Beinn a' Bhuird. At the time of writing the project is still in the air, and one tends to side with the conservationists in their plea to make the area accessible only to those who wish to make the physical effort of getting out of their car-seats and walking some strenuous miles to appreciate what the glen undoubtedly has to offer.

The link, however, would connect the northern route from Blairgowrie to Braemar to the main Perth–Inverness road and thus bring into the Highland region proper the glens of Clunie and Shee, making more accessible from the western approach the definite scenic delights of the area around Braemar, the Deeside Highlands. This area has long since been popularized, some would say 'Balmoralized', by its association, first with Queen Victoria, Prince Albert and the adhesive John Brown, and subsequently by successive generations of the Royal Family. It is Highland in its topography, character and its Gaelic-derived placenames, yet always tends to be placed outside the pale of the region normally called 'Highlands'. The Pass of Ballater, to the east was, to Thomas Pennant in 1765, the "eastern entrance into the Highlands", as it was to other writers and more practical men such as the Roundhead Colonel Morgan who found it a useful gateway. The three great estates here—Mar, Braemar, and Invercauld—are under intensive afforestation, an activity which is adding to the interest of the hill contours. The dominant peak is that of Lochnagar, the "dark" massif, of Byron's poem, eroded out of a coarse pink granite. Parts of this mountain are easily accessible while, in the sharpest contrast, many of the gullies of the eastern corrie have never yet been scaled and continue to provide a first-order challenge to the experienced climber.

Braemar has a peculiar Highland character, yet belongs to the same county of Aberdeenshire which claims the flat, windswept plain of Buchan. The settlement was once an old and important castletoun, guarding the route to the south; it is now an important tourist centre. The normal population of Braemar, about 400, swells to up to 5,000 during the tourist season and to no less than a computed 20,000 on the day of the Braemar Gathering. Physical and mental recreation is not, however, confined to one day in each year. The Braemar Festival, started in 1952, offers annually a continuous feast of drama, music, ballet, film shows and art exhibitions. Local craftsmen have been encouraged to immerse themselves in the uniqueness that is Braemar and to work out the product of their assimilation in many excellent creations.

Six miles west of Braemar is the township of Inverey; small, but set as firm in its past history as it is in its more accessible scenic beauty. South of Braemar runs Glen Clunie, which carries with it the road to Blairgowrie, through Glen Shee—but not before it negotiates the Cairnwell Pass and the Devil's Elbow. This latter is a corkscrew road, now thankfully being straightened out, and has always been one of the first spots in Scotland to be blocked by snow and ice, both in winter and spring.

Glen Shee has, since ancient times, been a main communicating link between Atholl and Mar. The area redounds with antiquarian and historical interest, one instance of which is seen in the remains of a hut settlement of the late Bronze Age period. The glen also figures in early Celtic legend, associated with the Fingalian hero Diarmad Mac O' Duine who chased boar on nearby Ben Gulabin. The attractive town of Blairgowrie, settled at the edge of the Highland mountain edge, stands to the south of Glen Shee. Supporting a population of over 5,000, it is the centre of raspberry growing in Scotland, with canning and textile industries combining to form a sound economic base.

The writer of the above-quoted observation on Kingussie would no doubt have approved of the Highland Wildlife Park at Kincraig, which was opened in 1972 to display the past and present fauna of the region in superb natural conditions. The park uses about 200 acres of the Dunachton Estate. In time, it is hoped to build up a living collection of extant Highland wild life, with imported examples of species which, though they now exist only in other parts of the world, once roamed the Highlands. With its proposed full complement, visitors can see red deer stags, hinds and calves; a sika deer stag, roe deer buck and roe, the Przewalski wild horses, black and red Highland cattle, wild goat, St Kilda sheep, brown hares and rabbits. The bird life will be no less interesting with oystercatchers, black-headed gulls, siskins, pied and grey wagtails, grouse, partridges and black game, buzzards, curlews and smaller birds like meadow pipits and wheatears. In restricted areas are wild boar and Arctic fox, and a wolf pack. In enclosures are European brown bears, reindeer, lynx, wild cat, pine marten and so on. The venture, which involved an investment sum of £125,000, was assisted by the Highlands and Islands Development Board. It provides eight full-time jobs and twenty seasonal vacancies each year to cope with an eventual anticipated 40,000 vehicle visitations each year.

Kingussie is well known for its Highland Folk Museum, Am Fasgadh (Gaelic: 'The Shelter'), which has trebled in scope since the Pilgrim Trust bought the 'Old Lodge' in 1962 and gave it to the four main Scottish universities. The museum consists of a white-harled early Victorian residence and a number of modern annexes made necessary as the result of recent acquisitions. The idea of the museum was that of Miss I. F. Grant who, after seeing the methods used by the peoples of Scandinavia to preserve their living past, decided to organize a similar institution in the Highlands of Scotland. She had a disheartening start in a disused church on the island of Iona, off the coast of Mull, and her growing collection of exhibits was eventually moved to Laggan. By 1944 the exhibition was opened to the public in its present premises. The exact replicas of some of the old dwellings are extremely interesting. To ensure exactitude, one of the houses on view, a Lewis 'black house', was erected under the supervision of an old man who made the journey from Lewis for the purpose. It is a squat dwelling, ideally suited, with its design evolved over the centuries, for existing in the environment which obtains in Lewis. A rather more recent mason-built 'but and ben', of a type once common on the Scottish mainland, has also been erected in the museum grounds.

In the museum itself there are many items of interest for the naturalist, the sportsman and the social historian. One wing of the house contains examples of locally-produced textiles and linens. Primitive looms, spinning wheels, wool combs, spindles, cords and implements for scutching flax are shown. There is a display of plant dyes used in the colouring of tartan and other cloths. A large part of the museum house contains domestic articles which display the harmony with which man in the Highlands lived with natural things. Brooms and brushes are made from heather twigs, rushes, bent-grass and moss. Ropes were woven from horsehair, rushes and heather fronds as well as the roots of trees and shrubs. There are many beautiful examples of homemade wooden vessels made from birch and fir. The sides of cupboards, cabinets and chairs are constructed from oven oak scrub. Bent-grass appears in the form of pleated saddle-pads, chair seats and horse collars. There is a complete set of the pearl-fisher's implements, including the clap-stick and flat-bottomed flask which tinkers used when searching the bed of the River Spey for its pearls. The great dependence of the Highland population on the wild life of the countryside around them with the necessities of life is well demonstrated by this museum, which holds the key to the way of life and culture of the Gael. Behind the black house is a small 'clack' mill and a collection of dairy equipment. Crofting and farming implements are displayed in a large new building and in the house, being the donation of the MacRoberts Douneside Trust.

All is not, however, tourism and reflections of the Highland past in Kingussie. The town has a small industrial estate. Of particular interest is the firm of Rotary Precision Ltd, which is unique in the Highlands and rare in the context of the United Kingdom. It started operations in 1968 as a light-industry enterprise with a handful of people. It now employs about seventeen people, all local men and boys. The firm provides training in precision engineering work in a number of fields, based on the products which include computer components and ultra-precision parts for aircraft, instruments and satellites. Craft work, aimed at the tourist market and involving ram and stag horn goods and pottery, is made in Kingussie.

Much of the life in Kingussie centres around the school, which acts as the educational centre for Badenoch, drawing, as it does, secondary pupils from Aviemore and other villages. A new school building, erected in 1970, has made this facility an important aspect of the area. The history of the school dates to before 1642. The school of the parish, during the period of the school board, had such an excellent reputation that it attracted pupils from the Western Isles, Argyll, Sutherland and elsewhere in the Highlands. The present school has a good academic record, over 70 per cent of the eligible age group taking education certificate courses. Being in an area where the landscape dominates the theme of life and living, the school accepts its role of educating on a very broad basis and offers many outdoor subjects, so that pupils increase their appreciation of what it means to live in Badenoch.

South of Kingussie lies Newtonmore, an outpost of Speyside. Much of the charm of this village is in the variety of its scenic beauty. In common with other centres in the Spey valley, Newtonmore offers accommodation and interests for the tourist. History is both preserved and brought to life in the village. The Clan Macpherson Museum has brought the clan relics of centuries together in a building which has had to extend its area, with the financial help of the Highlands and Islands Development Board and other interests, including commercial patronage. One among a large number of items of interest is a prized Macpherson antiquity: the famous black chanter which, tradition has it, fell from the skies at the Battle of the North Inch (Perth) in 1346 and to which Sir Walter Scott made reference in his *Fair Maid of Perth*. Another clan relic is the Bratach Uaine, the equally famous green banner under which the Macphersons never knew defeat. A set of centennial coins in silver and bronze was gifted to the clan association and the museum by American friends in McPherson County, Kansas, U.S.A., to commemorate that county's centenary. History is vitalized in the village with the Clan Macpherson Rally and Newtonmore Games, held on the first Saturday of August of each year. The games constitute one of the biggest and more important events of their kind in the Highlands. Sheep dog trials are also held from time to time in the district. Shinty playing by the Newtonmore Camanachd Club provides exciting sport; this ancient game is a Gaelic-based activity which has a small but specialized following in the central Highlands and Argyll.

South of Newtonmore the artery of tarmacadam enters into Drumochter (Druim Uachdar 'Ridge of the Upper Ground'). This pass is almost 1,500 feet above sea level. Dalwhinnie is a tiny settlement at the head of the 20-mile-long Loch Ericht, which provides excellent free fishing for the large Ferox Trout. For many generations a tale was told about Loch Ericht. This concerned the west end of the loch, which was once a fertile strath but which, after a subterranean upheaval, was inundated by the loch submerging the houses. In the late 1940s, when hydro-electric work was being carried out in the area, an old gravestone was dredged from the loch, some 20 feet below the present level of the waters. A malt whisky distillery, owned by Distillers Company Ltd, is sited at Dalwhinnie, providing an excellent economic base for this remote village—remote, even though it is on the through route from Perth to Inverness. In Drumochter both road and railway climb steadily together until they reach the summit of the pass, at 1,484 feet, the highest point on any railroad in the British Isles. An inscribed stone on the road, below the summit, marks the point where the two parties of Wade's road-making troops, one working from Inverness and the other from Dunkeld, met on Drumochter, their great task completed. Two summits nearby towards the west, the Sow of Atholl and the Boar of Badenoch, define the two great territorial divisions of olden times which meet at this famous pass.

The Forest of Atholl, across the march between Inverness-shire and Perthshire, is an immense tract of land, largely unpopulated and reserved for deer; it is, therefore, virtually treeless. Yet, areas of this part of the central Highlands were the subject of afforestation experiments, particularly in the eighteenth century. For many centuries the natural pine forests of Rannoch to the west supplied the needs of the Atholl Estate. At first, the early tree-planting interest was merely to improve the look of the estate rather than to provide commercial timber. James, the second Duke of Atholl, developed his 'Wilderness of Diana' by planting about thirty varieties of trees, some of which were quite unsuited to both soil and climate. The larch, however, did rather well, being more suited to the higher altitudes, and from the original three seedlings planted at Dunkeld in 1737 were derived the larch woods which eventually formed an important part of the estate. These trees were, however, subjected to the depredations of the Government's soldiery, who were garrisoned at Blair Atholl in 1746. The third Duke, in 1764, realized that the larch had value as a forest tree and set about planting according to a formal programme of development; he first worked on the hill slopes in the vicinity of Blair Atholl. It was left to his son, the 'Planting Duke', to further develop the Atholl Forests and to use them for commercial purposes, which included ship-building.

By 1818, sufficient timber had been accumulated to commence the construction at Perth of the brig *Larch*, with a burden of 170 tons. The success of this ship was followed by an order from the Admiralty for a twenty-eight-gun frigate to be constructed entirely of larch. The decline in the supply of oak for ship-building was the most likely reason for the change from 'hearts of oak'; some thought, however, that larch was superior to oak for this purpose. The launching of the frigate *Atholl* from Woolwich Dockyard in 1820 was a tribute to the energies of the fourth Duke of Atholl. The *Atholl* remained afloat for forty-five years which proved the durability of larch timber. But by then the use of iron in ship-building prevented the real potential of the Atholl forests being exploited. In the decades between 1830 and 1850 large quantities of the timber were sold for sheep hurdles and for railway sleepers. When the fourth Duke died in 1830 it was estimated that over 14 million larch trees had been planted during his lifetime. So great was the potential that 100 years later the sale of the larches assisted the finances of the Atholl estate after the First World War. However, a serious problem began to show itself and to assume such proportions that it could have had disastrous consequences had the seventh Duke not had the fortune to have knowledge of the Japanese larch. The European larch, planted in the eighteenth and nineteenth centuries, had become infected by disease and planting activities were halted. In 1883 the seventh Duke introduced Japanese larch, the seeds of which he had brought back with him after a world tour. Hybridization between the two varieties resulted in a tree which is resistant to disease and is now the only variety planted on the estate.

Blair Atholl is a small feudal village which has grown under the protection and patronage of the successive owners of Blair Castle, the ancestral seat of the Dukes of Atholl. This place has had an inevitable stormy history. A fortalice is known to have been built here in 1290 by John Comyn, Lord of Badenoch. Part of this early structure is thought to be incorporated in the north-eastern tower of the present mansion. In 1653 the castle was blown up by the Roundheads, but was restored again in 1689, in which year it was occupied by Claverhouse before the Battle of Killicrankie. For about a week it successfully resisted a siege by King William's Government, represented by John, Lord Murray, brother of the castle's owner, the Marquis of Atholl. To relieve the castle, General MacKay undertook the famous march which brought him to disaster at Killicrankie. After the battle, the castle was dismantled in order to prevent it falling into Jacobite hands again. But it was restored, and in its later time gave lodging to Prince Charles Edward on his march south in 1745—and when he dragged himself northwards a year later. In 1746 the castle was besieged (the last siege laid on British soil) and was bombarded with red-hot shot. After a suitable lapse of time the building was once more restored by successive dukes, with the present result which is imposing and features many aspects of architectural interest. The contents of Blair Castle, open to the public, are a visual display of Highland history: military, economic and social. The old interest of the Dukes of Atholl in deer hunting are reflected in the magnificent display of stags' heads, the finest collection in Scotland if not elsewhere. One of these, dated 31st July 1781, is believed to be the most ancient trophy of its kind in Scotland.

The area known as the Perthshire Highlands has a pattern consisting of ridges and valleys, basically aligned on the proto-drainage east–west direction, with some guidance offered by fault-lines and rocks of varying resistance. There is a large intrusion of granite in Rannoch Moor. The effect of structure on relief is prominent. There are the resistant quartzites which form such marked ridges or summits as in Shiehallion (3,547 feet); and there are the grits which form the mountains of Ben Ledi (2,875 feet), Ben Lomond (3,192 feet) and Ben Vorlich (3,224 feet), a group which overlooks the lowlands to the south. These peaks, together with Ben Alder (3,757 feet) and Ben Lawers (3,984 feet) and interconnecting ridges, offer little but heath and rough grassland of the wetter western variety. However, a great deal of planting has been carried out by the Forestry Commission with some stock and grouse moors on the upper levels.

The inhabited parts consist mainly of the lower slopes and floors of the valleys where there are considerable stretches of alluvial material, often separated by wooded sands and gravels or rocky gorges. The lower part of Glen Lyon is one such alluvial basin, as is the eastern end of Loch Tay, above Aberfeldy, where there is a great stretch of arable land, liable to inundation at the lowest levels but capable of supporting a number of large arable farms. These contrast sharply with the crofting settlements which, in the past, carried cultivation higher up the glens and which now show many familiar signs of depopulation. The basic husbandry includes rotation grasses, oats, turnips and swedes for cattle and sheep. The great expanse of the Moor of Rannoch, with the deep cleft occupied by Loch Laidon, is a boggy basin which offers no particular incentive to either agriculture or settlement. The Pitlochry basin, which is mainly the valley of the combined Tummel-Garry river, extends at a higher level into the small basin of Moulin. The alluvial deposits hereabouts are generally ploughed for oats, rotation grasses and turnips, while the settlements are situated on the margins of the coarser fluvio-glacial sands and gravels or boulder-clay above. The value of this area lies primarily in the exploitation of the natural water resources for hydro-electricity.

The valley network is of particular interest because it saw the beginnings of public hydro-electricity development in the Highlands when, in 1930, the station at Rannoch near Killichonan was put into operation by the Grampian Electricity Company. This scheme used Loch Ericht, in its long fault-guided trough, as the main reservoir. In 1933 this generating project was co-ordinated with another station built at Tummel Bridge, at the eastern end of Loch Rannoch, which was supplied with water from Loch Rannoch and Loch Laidon. At the present time the River Tummel and its tributaries are harnessed in nine power stations with a total capacity of about 250 million watts, and an average output of about 650 million units of electricity; all this forms a great concentration of power near the geographical centre of Scotland. The post-war stations were built by the North of Scotland Hydro-electricity Board. Much of the interest of the board's work is not only in the civil and engineering achievements, but in the manner in which the various inter-connected schemes have merged, with reasonable success, into the scenic countryside. Loch Faskally was created by the dam at Pitlochry. The catchment area of the Pitlochry power station is over 700 square miles. The developments have been carried out with a special consideration for the preservation of scenery and fisheries. The Pitlochry dam fish-pass is a premier tourist attraction.

Section 9(1) of the Hydro-electric Development (Scotland) Act of 1943 requires that the board "... shall have regard to the desirability of avoiding as far as possible injury to fisheries and to the stock of fish in any waters". A necessary corollary is the provision of a regulated flow of water below the board's work to enable, as appropriate, adult salmon and sea trout to ascend the rivers and spawn, the eggs subsequently developing into young fish which then feed and grow in suitable conditions. Apart from providing the regulated flows (called compensation water), the board have concentrated mainly on the need to conserve the stock of salmon because of the importance of the Scottish salmon-fishing industry.

Among the measures taken have been the provision of fish passes to allow salmon to surmount dams, traps to enable adult salmon to be taken so that they can be stripped of their eggs, hatcheries in which the fertilized eggs are incubated, and facilities such as the easing of obstacles to enable salmon to reach previously unused spawning grounds. Fish passes, to enable spawning fish to ascend and, in due course, smolts and kelts to descend, have been provided only at dams where adequate spawning ground remains in the river system above them. The first of these passes were of the conventional pool type, with submerged orifices between the pools. Later the board used a new form of pass known as the Borland fish pass. This has several advantages and operates in principle in much the same way as does a lock on a canal or waterway. The fish are taken over the obstruction without effort and the design fits readily into the general design of a dam. Besides being cheaper than a pool pass, it is more economical of water. The board have about eighteen Borland passes in operation: at one dam, where there can be a variation in reservoir level of over 80 feet, four passes, each catering for a different portion of this variation in level, have been provided. After the fish eggs have been incubated in the hatcheries, the fry are planted in suitable waters where they develop naturally. Some fry are retained for feeding up to the yearling parr and smolt stages. These are then planted out and checks made to see that progress is favourable.

Tummel is well known for its forest, which is in an area designated officially as being one of outstanding beauty. The forest area covers over 20,000 acres, of which 12,000 acres are planted with trees. The Forestry Commission has been associated with Tummel since 1944; considerable attention has been paid to the retention of the area's famous birch woods. The forest lies between Strathtay and Glenerrochty, following the Tummel valley and, though the area is not wholly owned by the commission, the neighbouring private estates are all well forested. The main species planted by the commission are spruce and Scots pine. The area is immortalized in the song "Road to the Isles"; the actual road can be seen on the far side of Loch Tummel from the equally famous Queen's View. In 1972 the commission opened an information centre at Queen's View, housed in a converted byre, stable and coachhouse. The centre has been designed to tell the story of the whole of the Tummel valley, not only in the context of forestry, but including the history, archaeology and industry of the area.

One of the interesting features of Rannoch is the Black Wood of Rannoch, which is the most significant surviving part of the old Caledonian Forest which used to cover most of the Highlands until it was gradually cleared to make way for farmland, to provide fuel—or to remove the dangerous haunts of wolves. Although now it makes up a part of the State Forest of Rannoch, the Forestry Commission has not planted it with the ubiquitous spruce or fir, but has preserved the old Scots pines and birches as living relics of older times. It also serves a useful purpose as a forestry study centre. Thomas Hunter, in his book *Woods, Forests and Estates of Perthshire* (1883) gives a fair amount of space to the Black Wood. At that time it was part of the Dall Estate, which was fortunate enough to be owned by T. V. Wentworth, "an enthusiastic aboriculturalist". After a forest fire a few years before, Mr Wentworth ensured that the devastated areas were replanted with more of the same kinds of trees. The area never seems to have attracted any significant settlements. In old time the wood was dense and almost trackless, though there are mentions of its being a good spot for illicit whisky stills. Before paraffin lamps came into general use, the Black Wood at one time supplied resin and turpentine for northern Perthshire.

That there is anything of the old wood left is fortunate. In the early years of the last century, an English timber company bought part of it and set about chopping it down. Their section of the forest was high up on the hillsides above Dall and chutes were built alongside the burns to get the timber down to the lochside. The longest chute was a mile in length—a distance over which logs built up a fantastic speed as they careered on their way. Hunter mentions that "many went into the loch with such tremendous precipitation that they stuck as fast as stakes in deep water, while the sheer weight of not a few caused them to sink to the bottom never to rise again". The surviving logs were floated over Loch Rannoch, down the Tummel and into the Tay at Ballinluig.

The theory was that the logs would be stopped somewhere about Perth and handed over to a local sawmill. In practice, many of the logs were not intercepted but found their way into the waters of the North Sea, where they caused hazards to small coastal and fishing vessels. The company gave up after they had felled only a small part of the available timber. During its heyday it offered much-needed work and wages to the local men who, at the time, were at starvation level. In the area is a small cottage which was rented out to a junior secondary school in a mining town in Fife; the pupils used the cottage as a base for studies in an environment rather different from their own, and to work for the Duke of Edinburgh Awards. The story of how this idea progressed and developed, and how an extension of it was opposed tooth and nail by the forces of the educational establishment is well told by the school's former headmaster, R. F. MacKenzie, in his book *Escape from the Classroom.*

Pitlochry was originally established as a commercial centre and once boasted woollen textile mills. Nowadays it is a focal point for the tourist industry. It has about 2,500 inhabitants and is a well-appointed town, clean and most attractive. It houses the well-known Pitlochry Festival, a venture which began literally in a tent and which is now an essential and lively element in the artistic life of Scotland. Being at the geographical heart of Scotland, Pitlochry attracts many thousands of visitors. As a holiday resort it is, perhaps, unsurpassed for the facilities it offers for recreation and relaxation. Snug in the sheltered vale of Atholl, it is a useful base from which to explore the rest of Scotland.

Dunkeld is an ancient settlement with a long history. A town of just under 1,000 inhabitants, it has a certain dignity—as befits a cathedral city—and has a justified consciousness of its ancient fame as the former capital of the vast medieval dioceses of the central Highlands. It is a beautiful place and is probably the smallest of all the cathedral cities in the British Isles. It lies on the north bank of the Tay, across which strides a fine stone bridge of seven arches, erected by Telford between 1805 and 1809. The antique character of Dunkeld was, some years ago, confronted with a modern cancer: the insensitive developer who proposed to pull down the 'Little Houses', dwellings of ancient lineage in the precinct of the cathedral—which, admittedly, has fallen into decrepitude—a state of affairs which neatly fell into the hands of those who said that the only remedy was for the houses to be razed to the ground. But opposition was rallied and the National Trust for Scotland, with the co-operation of Perthshire County Council, restored the majority of the group and replaced those which had either disappeared or were beyond restoration. The restoration of the Little Houses earned public recognition from the Saltire Society and the Civic Trust. In their original state, these houses date from the rebuilding of Dunkeld after its destruction in 1689. The most famous Bishop of Dunkeld was

Gavin Douglas (1516–22), who was a statesman, scholar and poet and whose translation of the *Aeneid* into the Scots vernacular was "the first version of a great classic poet in any English dialect". A native of Dunkeld, Professor J. J. R. MacLeod, discovered insulin.

Just south of Dunkeld lies the Highland edge, coinciding with the major fault line which lies between Stonehaven on the Aberdeenshire coast and Helensburgh on the Firth of Clyde and is known as the Highland Boundary Fault. This has a distinct topographical expression for most of the way, as a result of the different erosion of rocks of contrasting resistance on either side of the fault line. Along this fault line, earthquake activity has occurred and has been on occasions sufficiently strong to cause considerable material damage. In 1839 an unusual earthquake was experienced in the Comrie district, where fissures appeared in the ground. This was the strongest earthquake ever recorded along the fault line and caused damage to local houses. The largest fissure produced was 200 yards long. Another major series of shocks occurred in 1841. It caused walls to crack and disturbed the balance of stone dykes. Reckoned to be the result of minor slips along the fault planes, they had no recognizable permanent effect on the landscape; their main effect was to frighten people in the district.

The town of Crieff was once an important tryst or centre for the great cattle-trading activities of the Highlands. Along the old drove roads vast herds of livestock were driven through passes to the south, to Crieff and Falkirk. In the early decades of the eighteenth century, the trade in driving cattle from the Highlands and Islands experienced a rapid expansion. The recently introduced system of cash credits was a boon to the drovers—many of them men of little substance—who were thus able to obtain from the banks in the lowlands sufficient cash to enable them to offer to the farmers and breeders in the north the strong temptation of a small cash payment for their cattle, the balance being met by means of bills payable after the sale of the beasts at Crieff. These bills passed from hand to hand, often for long periods, many of them ultimately finding their way into the hands of the merchant bankers or banking firms, who, if all went well, would get them cashed at Crieff or Falkirk where many of the bills had been made payable. The system of cash credits was begun in 1728 by the new Royal Bank and the old Bank of Scotland, and credit up to agreed limits was given against promissory notes signed by reputable applicants supported by two guarantors, without security other than the personal obligation of the borrower and his backers. Twenty years later the British Linen Company did much to develop the system through agencies in many of the Scottish towns.

The droving trade was derived from the fact that cattle had, from the earliest of times, been a major product of the Highlands. While a close estimate of numbers is impossible, it is certain that the cattle population of the Highland glens has for many centuries been considerable; a combination of cultivated land in the glens and large areas of hill ground for summer grazing was not unfavourable to the maintenance of large herds. For a long time the unsettled state of the Highlands made the transport of these beasts virtually impossible outside the territory of their owners. While the meat was for domestic consumption, the exports were mainly hides which could be more readily exported from the region. By the start of the eighteenth century, however, more peaceful conditions made it possible for cattle to be taken on the hoof to the lowlands for sale, albeit by long and perilous droving operations. When the Highlands were subjugated after the Forty-five, the droving trade expanded. Its growth and prosperity at this time were greatly stimulated by the growth of London and of the industrial towns in the English Midlands, and the increase in the population of central Scotland. The demands of the armed forces further increased the demand for Highland beef. The droving trade was hard for both men and beasts. It was also highly speculative. Money was often quickly made and as quickly lost. A few of the larger dealers made fortunes; but for each one who prospered there were many others who failed, bringing down in their fall those who were inextricably involved with them in the peculiar complexities of drover finance. It was to meet the needs of this droving traffic that Thomas Telford, mindful of the injurious effect of hard roads on the hooves of far-driven cattle, insisted on the use of plenty of gravel as a surfacing on roads.

Crieff acted as the gathering area for the cattle from no fewer than twenty-five points of origin, ranging from the Western Isles, the north-west and Caithness, the Great Glen, the Inner Hebrides, Islay, Mull of Kintyre and Aberdeenshire. After the bulk of the livestock had been collected at Crieff, the droves went south to Falkirk for the sales. Adam Smith regarded the expansion of the cattle trade as being one of the main advantages of the Treaty of Union in 1707. Until the mid-eighteenth century Crieff, which had acquired statutory market rights in 1672, was the main tryst; but then, owing to an increase in the number of English buyers, the natural node of Crieff was displaced by Falkirk, which developed to become the greatest Scottish cattle mart of all time. For 150 years the Falkirk Tryst occupied a unique place in the economic development and social life of Scotland. The export trade was worth about £250,000 in the closing decade of the eighteenth century. The end of the Falkirk Tryst came in 1901. The advent of the railway in the latter decades of the nineteenth century saw the finish of the drovers' craft, and with the railways a new phenomenon arose in Scotland's country towns: the auctioneer and the auction sale.

The city of Perth deserves a brief mention in this chapter, if only because of its long-standing reputation as a gateway to the Highlands. At least 1,000 years old, Perth was once Scotland's capital. At the heart of its history stands the ancient burgh kirk of St John the Baptist. Of early foundation, its record begins in 1126 when David I, son of Malcolm Canmore and Queen Margaret, granted it, with its tithes and parsonage, to the Abbey of Dunfermline, the burial place of his parents. The complete fabric was consecrated in 1242. In 1928 the fabric was completely restored by Sir Robert Lorimer, with a carillon being placed in the Gothic tower in 1938. Perth was confirmed a burgh in 1210 by King William the Lion. The vicinity of the mercat cross has revealed evidence of prehistoric habitation. Between the foot of High Street and the sadly decayed and neglected Watergate, an excavation in 1958 revealed the remains of a wattle hut on a rough timber platform, the whole with its adjacent kitchen refuse of shellfish apparently of date *c.* 4000 B.C., the earliest evidence of man in the area. The city today contains good measures of the elements which go to make up a well-balanced settlement: industry, theatre, recreational facilities, with good hotel and boarding-house accommodation for the tourist. The Bell Sports Centre offers all-year-round facilities for many activities. Commercially, most of Perth's activities are those connected with agriculture. The annual pedigree sales are world famous. Other elements in the economy are transport, insurance, dyeing, whisky-blending and bottling. It is also noted for the manufacture of glassware. At Perth there is the largest civil aviation school in the world.

8

Kintyre, Lorn and Cowal

THE Mull of Kintyre is at the southernmost tip of the Highlands, some 12 miles from the coast of northern Ireland and due west of Rathlin Island. It is about 250 miles south of Cape Wrath, along one of the most serrated coastlines in Europe. Kintyre, the longest peninsula in Scotland, is not crossed by a road for some 30 miles of its length, from between a few miles south of Tarbert, situated in the wrist-thin isthmus between Kintyre and Knapdale, and Campbeltown: it is 8 to 9 miles across. The height of the land on Kintyre reaches about 1,500 feet. The climate along the coast is extremely mild and, indeed, on the eastern side is particularly amenable to the growing of tropical plants. The peninsula is mostly composed of quartzose micaschist. Areas of limestone are found both north and south of Campbeltown and, as a consequence, the pasture provided is excellent. The arable agriculture of Kintyre is based on Old Red Sandstone and on the Carboniferous strata to the west of Campbeltown through to the west coast. This latter feature includes some typical fossiliferous limestone and both barren and productive coal measures. Some dozen miles north of Campbeltown, on the west side of Kintyre, is the alluvial strath of Caradale (population 600). Half a mile wide, it extends for about 5 miles and is exceptionally well sheltered by moderately-wooded hills.

From an historical standpoint, Kintyre is today much less 'Highland' than other parts of the region and displays little of the traditional

Highland way of life. It has had successive plantations of lowlanders—arranged by the House of Argyll, as these incomers would not have considered Kintyre unless there was the promise of good land to farm. The province of Kintyre was originally MacDonald country, this family being descended from the Lords of the Isles. But gradually the great Campbell family extended its grip on much of Argyll and by the seventeenth century conditions were set fair for the final blow: a quasi-religious war, the MacDonalds being Catholics or Episcopalian and the Campbells being strongly Protestant along with the Covenanting forces of the time. In 1647 the MacDonald forces found themselves retreating down the Kintyre peninsula followed by General Leslie, who was later to defeat Montrose. The Irish section of the MacDonald forces took ship back to Ireland and the Scottish remainder embattled themselves in the old fortress of Dunaverty. This was besieged, the water supply captured and, after parleys, taken over. The 300 MacDonalds surrendered, expecting quarter, but in fact were massacred, with only one boy, John MacDougall of Dunolly, being spared. The slaughter was carried out at the behest of a Presbyterian minister called John Neave. Leslie's army brought with it some biblical plague from which there was a great loss of life in 1647–8. Archibald Campbell, the Marquis of Argyll, found himself master of Kintyre, an unpopulated land which he immediately arranged to have planted over a period of two decades. There were further troubles in the latter years of the seventeenth century, but in time the new peninsula people settled down to intermarry with the remaining indigenous Highland population. There came some three centuries of settled conditions, with Kintyre playing little or no part in Highland affairs, or even in the 'Highland problem' as it exists in other parts of the region. Even so, there are elements in the peninsula which bear witness to its Highland past. The peninsula is not a crofting area; rather it is a district of small and medium-sized farms concentrating on the production of grass, potatoes, turnips, the arable component of livestock husbandry. Dairying is the principal occupation stimulated by the western industrial area of the central lowlands of Scotland, with some barley for distillation.

Macrihanish beach is the longest strand in the Argyll mainland. It stretches for some 4 miles north to south. There is an airport here, revealing all the horrors of an R.A.F. presence, both past and present. The airport has been called the "ugliest in Scotland". In 1965 the R.A.F. published a development plan for the place, costing some £2 million.

The village of Macrihanish (population 300) is approached by way of the Argyll colliery. The latter employed some 250 men before it was closed down in 1967. The coalfield, with that at Brora, in Sutherland, is one of the two commercial coal deposits in the Highland region. It is about 2 square miles in area. A maximum aggregate thickness of about 46 feet of coal is made up from eight seams. Historical records indicate that the field was worked in the Macrihanish district during the fifteenth century. A period of intensive exploitation was latterly brought to an end by a fire in the 15-foot main coal seam in 1925. The colliery closed in 1928 and became derelict but was re-opened in 1946. An underground fire again interfered with production, but working was continued until the mine was finally closed on economic grounds in 1967.

Campbeltown is the centre for the famous Loch Fyne herring fishing and a popular site for distilleries. Its present population is over 7,000, but because the town serves a catchment area the population is nearer the 9,000 mark. It is situated on the eastern, and therefore sheltered, side of the peninsula, lying at the head of Campbeltown Loch, which is protected at its mouth by Davaar Island. Though it looks rather isolated on the map, the burgh in fact is in good communication with the rest of the world. There is a daily air service (twice daily in the summer months) which puts Campbeltown within forty minutes of Glasgow. By sea there is a daily steamer throughout the year from Gourock to Tarbert, and thence by bus down the west coast; in summer there is a sea link direct between the town and Fairlie on the Ayrshire coast. It has industries, acts as an important service centre and is an essential element in the Scottish fishing industry. A sea link is maintained with northern Ireland by a daily vehicle ferry.

Campbeltown, despite its air of well-being, has been described as "a classic example of urban decline resulting from the failure of primary industries". By the 1960s, ship-building, herring fishing and coal-mining had slumped to the point where there was a real crisis of confidence in the future viability of the town. However, the revival of the shipyard, and the switch from herring to the more reliable nephrops (a kind of prawn) and white fishing, both made with the support of the Highlands and Islands Development Board, brought some degree of stabilization by the early years of the 1970s. The population of the town had been dropping—from 7,172 in 1951 to 5,961 in 1971—and the failure of the Macrihanish coalfield (affecting 250 workers) in 1967 aggravated an already serious unemployment situation: the past seven years saw an annual average of 9·7 per cent of the insured population. The jobs situation was further worsened by the inability of the town to absorb school-leavers in suitable employment, mainly because certain types of employing facilities (able to take on apprentices) did not exist. The main growth industry at present is the food, drink and tobacco group. In a situation such as this, the investment in the fishing industry by the Development Board has been significant. There are over twenty vessels in the Campbeltown fleet at present, half of these being under 40 feet in length. The fishing activity (nephrops and scallops amount to £550,000 out of a total catch value of £855,000 in 1969) reflects the size pattern of the fleet and also the swing away from herring fishing

Wildcat at the Highland Wildlife Park, Kincraig

Stag in the snow at the Wildlife Park

(*top*) Rannoch Moor. (*bottom*) Carrbridge, Inverness-shire

(in contrast with the herring fishing at Tarbert and Carradale). The herring slump in the 1950s affected Campbeltown fishermen, both financially and in morale. But there is a new air of confidence, stemming from the nine vessels provided by the Development Board, the fish-processing facility (using mainly shellfish, depending on the supplies of the home fleet and employing upwards of 200 in the season) and the shipyard, employing some forty persons at present but having a full employment potential of about eighty. The Development Board's financial intervention has enhanced the social, economic and general well-being of the community.

The present shipyard in Campbeltown was built on the site of a former once-thriving yard which turned out vessels of up to 10,000 tons. The first yard was hit by the Depression and lay derelict for more than thirty years until 1968, when excavating work was commenced for the new yard. The minority shareholders, Lithgow's Limited, Glasgow, became the controlling interest in 1971. The first vessel built by the yard was a ship commissioned by a local man. Steel-built craft are now coming from the yard in increasing numbers: stern-trawlers and a survey vessel. Of particular interest was the *Halcyon*, a fishery research vessel now operating on the inland 'sea' of Lake Rudolph in Kenya. The ship was bought by the Overseas Development Administration, Britain's premier foreign fisheries aid organization. The ship incorporated every conceivable type of fishing machinery, an electronics room used by scientists and a large wheelhouse crammed with modern navigational aids. After an 800-mile overland journey from Mombasa, the *Halcyon* was reconstructed on the shores of the lake. The yard also offers slip and repair facilities. The ultimate aim of the yard is to produce a rugged, stable fishing platform with powerful towing capabilities. It is generally accepted that a 53-foot Campbeltown boat in steel is equivalent in area to a conventional 65-foot wooden seinenetter.

A creamery in the town processes about 4½ million gallons of milk per annum, the output of over 160 farms. There are two distilleries, compared with the thirty-four once based on Campbeltown in the nineteenth century. It was alleged at that time that ships could find their way into Campbeltown harbour in thick fog by the pungent bouquet. The Springbank Distillery, built by the Mitchell family in 1823, is still operating, as are the family interests; the family is reckoned to be the oldest distilling and malting family still trading as such in Scotland. The product is mellow, light and rich, yet not at all heavy. Along with Glen Scotia Distillery, the Campbeltown whiskies are grouped with the West Highland malts, though in the trade there is a tendency to make a generic distinction between Campbeltown and Islay malts.

Davaar Island is a tidal piece of land which acts as a wind-break for Campbeltown harbour; it was once inhabited and is now only used for grazing. Its north point carries a lighthouse. On its southern side are a number of caves, the best known of which being that with the wall painting of Christ crucified. This was executed, in secret, in 1887 by the artist Alexander MacKinnon, when he was aged 33 years. Its discovery caused something of a sensation and Davaar has since been visited by many thousands of tourists. In 1934 MacKinnon returned to the island to retouch the painting when he was aged 80. Since his death the necessary retouching has been carried out by a local artist.

Contrary to expectations, Campbeltown has not yet developed its tourist potential. Many would prefer it that way; but others, conscious of the 'slumps' which have occurred in various native industries in the past, want some small foothold in the industry so that the community can fall back on the ubiquitous tourist for, at worst, a subsistence economy. Certainly, the peninsula hinterland offers an amenable climate and there are a number of places of interest to the visitor. There are many attractive facilities, including the championship golf course at Macrihanish. The town supports a sailing club and features a swimming pool.

Caradale, north of Campbeltown, is a small fishing village and holiday resort supporting a population of about 600, whose dwellings cluster together on a hillside overlooking a bay. The harbour faces north with a quay comprising a semi-circular breakwater of concrete and iron which gives shelter to the fishing fleet of some fourteen modern boats. The main fishing grounds are in the Kilbrannan Sound, for herring and mackerel, and off Ailsa Craig for whitefish. The herring industry is the most important activity in Caradale. However, the hinterland contains a score of farms devoted to raising beef cattle and sheep; the milk from the numerous dairy herds goes to the creamery in Campbeltown. The biggest landowner hereabouts is the Forestry Commission, which employs a workforce of about sixty men. The plantation is extensive—some 12,000 acres, of which about half is under trees.

The town of Tarbert (population 1,500) lies on the isthmus between East and West Loch Tarbert. Lying in its own bay of East Loch Tarbert, it looks out over Loch Fyne. It is a popular stopping place for ships *en route* through the Crinan canal; it also acts as a staging point on land routes between Glasgow and Islay, or between Kintyre and the Clyde. Its main reputation is as the centre of the Loch Fyne herring fishing industry. Its busy harbour, however, is only a fractional reflection of the activity which could be seen in former years. Last century the Tarbert fleet numbered seventy luggers and 300 men. Great brown sails filled the harbour and the quaysides were thronged with curers and gutting women. By the year 1949 the fleet was down to thirty boats, employing about 200 men, though the value of the landings was £200,000. There are at present twelve boats and 100 men. The boats at present are modern, equipped with echo-sounders to locate shoals of fish, are fast and have a total catching power which is far greater than that of the original home fleet. Herring, whitefish, prawns and scallops are included in the annual catch. The Loch Fyne herring, known as Glasgow Magistrates, are excellent. They are big, plump, full of oil and have a delicious melting taste when eaten fresh-cooked; when kippered in the slow smoke of oak chips, they are a sheer delight.

The small but famous yacht-yard of Dickie of Tarbert employed a score or so of men until it closed down in 1967. Boat-building, however, is continued in a new yard which had its first launching in 1972. The product is initially a new class of cabin cruiser, based on a basic fibreglass hull which can be used for a motor or sailing cruiser. It can also be modified to a fishing boat. The yard was set up with the help of the Highlands and Islands Development Board.

Another project recently established in Tarbert, and providing six new jobs, is the factory which kippers herring and mackerel and smoked salmon. This new venture is complementary to Lochfyne Seafoods, which processes scallops and employs some thirty local people. As well as supplying a home market, this factory exports to the U.S.A. and the Continent. It is something of a success story: a partnership between two local entrepreneurs who realized that there existed a Transatlantic demand for seafood. The factory received a building grant from the Highlands and Islands Development Board. Within a year of starting production the firm found it necessary to extend to provide room for a second blast freezer and more working space as export demands for scallops increased. The bulk of the production of frozen queen scallops is exported to Canada and America through a subsidiary of Associated Fisheries. Most of the employees are women, some of whom work full-time. As many as thirty extra employees are taken on when heavy catches of scallops are landed by local fishermen. The firm process about a ton of seafood per day.

During the summer months the harbour is chock-full with Clyde yachts, and the town itself is as full with tourists. Tarbert is attractive and offers many amenities for holiday-makers. One of the spectacular sights, particularly in early summer, is the garden of Stonefield Castle Hotel, which was built in the middle of last century. The owner, Sir Joseph Dalton Hooker, decided to introduce to west Scotland numerous large-leaved rhododendrons from the Himalayas, and specimens of these original plants survive today to add their colour to the younger bushes at Stonefield. The gardens contain some of the most wonderfully coloured of the genus to be seen in Scotland and probably rival their counterparts on Gigha Island. In 1328 King Robert Bruce created Tarbert a burgh with sheriffdom (the first in Argyll and forty-eight years before Inveraray), to grow around the centre of Tarbert Castle, which occupies a site dating back to at least A.D. 712 (when Selbach, King of Lorn, burnt it down). But the burgh failed to grow and the creation lapsed.

Looking at the map and noting the position of Tarbert, one wonders why the Crinan Canal was not built at Tarbert rather than at its present location farther north. There are many records of ships being drawn across the Tarbert isthmus. The Norsemen did this regularly, rather than face the dangers of sailing round the Mull of Kintyre. Robert Bruce also used this tactic when he 'sailed' in his galley across the isthmus, the craft being dragged along on tree trunks used as rollers. Pennant, in his *Tour of Scotland* (1771–5), records that vessels of 9 or 10 tons were drawn by horses across the isthmus. This custom was regular practice until the Crinan Canal was cut in 1801. The cut for a canal was not made at Tarbert even though James Watt had surveyed the ground in that locality in 1770 and pronounced that a canal cutting was feasible. In 1830 Henry Bell estimated that the cost of a straight cut through rock without the need for locks would be £90,000. Parliament considered and approved. A company was formed. But this whole process took fifteen years, by which time a money crisis gripped the nation. Costs doubled and the Crinan cutting was chosen instead.

Loch Fyne is a long narrow arm of the sea which reaches up from the Kilbrannan Sound. It has always had an important place in the history of the Scottish herring industry. Its recognition as a habitat for herring is on records dating back many centuries. In 1555 a question regarding the natural wealth in Loch Fyne engaged the attention of the Scottish Parliament and the western burghs "sic as Irwin, Air, Dumbertane and Glasgow", who had raised the matter of the "fisching of Loch Fyne and uthers Lochis in the North Illis for making of hering and uthers fischeis". The industry was developed and by the seventeenth century large-scale fishing for herring became important to the economy of the people living on the shores of the loch; in particular, it was a special source of cash. In the eighteenth century the development of the industry was affected by changes in methods of pastoralism and agriculture. At Inveraray, about 1744, and at Glassary in 1865, arable and rough grazing land was enclosed within dykes for better agriculture. This enclosing of land, taking place at a time when the population figures were rising rapidly, resulted in a large-scale emigration from inland areas to the lochside, and fishing became a primary occupation, particularly for the younger generation.

Fishing villages were established, in which industrial fishermen were given lets of land, sufficient to build a house and to establish a garden, and a certain amount of arable land suitable for a few cows. Typical fishing villages were Crarae, Inverae, Dryenlea and Goatfield. The early years of the nineteenth century saw good catches of herring and the growth of the market, particularly in the industrial Clyde valley where the daily food of the poorer classes of labouring people consisted of potatoes and herring, which they could afford out of their average weekly incomes of about 8s. But, as the demand for the herrings grew, and came from farther afield, so did the problems concerned with getting the fish to the market in an edible condition. No longer did the contemporary transport system—from Loch Fyne to the Clyde shore by creel or on horseback—apply. So it came about that curing stations were set up along the shores of the loch, though these also created further problems in ensuring a sufficient supply of salt and casks in an area where the lack of roads was much in evidence. The industry encouraged other service activities. Flax was grown for lint to be made into nets. Women found employment in gutting and cleaning fish to be later packed and repacked in salt. Coopers, barkers (for nets) and sail-makers all found a new prosperity.

But the years were not always golden ones. The herring, then as now, is a capricious fish, appearing and disappearing in a manner which brought some lean years to Loch Fyne as elsewhere. About 1803 there were no fewer than 500 large boats in the loch. "In December 1835, Loch Fyne was visited by a most extraordinary shoal of herrings. They made their appearance in some of the bays in such prodigious numbers that the usual method of fishing was departed from, and nets of every description were stretched across the bays and enclosed all the fish until the receding tide, when they were left high and dry upon the beach." In 1857 and 1858 the fishing was bad, while the fishing of 1862 was again unusually successful. In 1848 an outbreak of cholera occurred, a plague which was introduced by French traders who bartered French goods for Loch Fyne herring; the effects were felt in reducing the numbers capable of working at the fishing. The average income from drift-net fishing in reasonable years was from £50 to £60 per annum.

In 1838 the seine-net method of fishing was introduced into Loch Fyne, to become a recognized system by 1846. It was declared illegal in 1851, by an Act which permitted the use of the drift-net only for catching herring. But the Act was not recognized by many who preferred the seine or trawl method, despite its known property of destroying the potential of the industry, in that herring, mature, immature, half-grown and barely the size of sprats, were taken up daily and sold for a pittance (9d. per 1,000 as compared with 40s. per 1,000 had they been mature fish). Spawn was also destroyed by this method. The persistence of the trawlers led to much ill-feeling, which often broke out into direct violence with the threat of the use of firearms. So strong was the opposition to them that the trawling interests eventually left Loch Fyne to the more sensible drift-netters. In 1861 officers of the Fishery Board were empowered to seize boats, fish and nets when there was reason to believe that the boats had been engaged in trawling, and by this Act trawling was all but suppressed in Loch Fyne. But the following year saw a royal commission set up to investigate the operations of the various fishing Acts and Thomas Huxley, a scientist, visited Loch Fyne to seek out facts for himself. In 1866 a Bill was prepared which allowed fishing for herring with any kind of net, and so trawl-net fishing for herring became legal. This resulted in a decline in the social patterns around the loch shores, a situation which became aggravated by the fact that ships were engaged to carry away fresh herring from the loch to Glasgow; the curing industry suffered badly after this.

The vagaries of the herring shoals were a continual source of uncertainty in the years leading up to the turn of the present century, though the industry was prosecuted on a satisfactory level even in relatively poor years. Steamers were kept fully employed in taking fresh herring direct from the catching vessels to the market, where some were sold fresh, and some made into red herring, which are heavily smoked and highly salted. After 1883 the catches declined and by 1890 earnings were very small. The number of boats in Loch Fyne was also reduced; boats from the fishing villages of Sandhole, Minard, Furnace and Crarae, were numbered in handfuls, and had even disappeared from other villages. In 1910 there was unprecedented scarcity of herring in Loch Fyne, to be followed by many lean years. The result of the First World War and the Russian Revolution lost markets. Many a skipper, able to clear only £35 for fishing a whole year, worked in the woods for £1 per week, while the boats lay idle on the shore. By 1930 it was almost impossible to catch a herring in the loch. The fish returned to the loch in 1938, but the crews which netted them came from as far away as Fife and Ayrshire, with little participation by local men. Indeed, for the communities along the shores of Loch Fyne, almost living museums of social and industrial archaeology, the herring became a ghost word in their vocabulary.

The area north and west of Tarbert is known as Knapdale and connects Kintyre with the main body of Argyll. The eastern side borders on the shores of Loch Fyne; the western coast is indented by Loch Caolisport and Loch Sween. The name Knapdale is derived from 'hill and dale', a characteristic which is seen in the protuberant, sharp-sided hills which fall into dales like a choppy sea. The main line of communication is by road between Tarbert and Ardrishaig to Lochgilphead. The area is composed of poor rock, Dalriadian quartzite, with striations of hornblende and mica schist. A portion of Knapdale has been 'drowned' in Loch Sween by the sea, to make one of the most interesting natural features to be found in the Highland region. The entrance from the open sea is narrow, within its length are other narrow sea arms. It was one of these arms of this unusual loch which was chosen for experiments in fertilizing sea water to note the effects on the size of flat fish. There is much derelict and low-quality farming in Knapdale and the once-numerous crofts had virtually disappeared. Much of the area is owned by the Forestry Commission: some 20,000 acres of which about half is planted and the remainder included about 8,000 acres of agricultural and other land. There are also private foresters who are putting this land to good use. The population of Knapdale is strung out like beads along the shoreland. The southern part of Knapdale supports a much larger population (*c.* 2,000, which compares with the 3,162 maximum which occurred in 1871); North Knapdale has a population of some 300, which can be compared with the year of 1821, which returned a figure of 2,654.

The peninsular finger which lies along the Sound of Jura is possibly the most interesting part of Knapdale. Tayvallich (population 120) is the main village, set in a bay of this greatly shattered peninsula. There is an admirable shelter here for yachts and dinghies; perhaps inevitably the area is being developed for tourism, though one hopes that it will remain one of those places, off the beaten track, where those who genuinely have a desire for peace among beautiful surroundings can come for many years without the accompaniment of the worst elements which are now so apparent in other erstwhile 'off-track' resorts.

The whole area is a delight to the eye. Loch Taynish is a freshwater loch on woodland which harbours roe deer. Farther south, there lies the lagoon of Linnhe Mhuirich, 3 miles long with a narrow opening to Loch Sween. Oysters were once found in abundance on Loch Sween and in this lagoon in particular; a profitable fishery was prosecuted here at the turn of the century. It was here in recent years the Scottish Marine Biological Association proved that oysters planted above the mud-level would flourish; the setting up of a new commercial oyster fishery has since followed. The end product is the new and unusual delicacy of mussels smoked in oak chips. The owner, Mr Tom Stevenson, who is keenly interested in marine biology, first set out to experiment in rearing oysters. His method of cultivation involves mooring steel rafts on the loch with large numbers of ropes suspended beneath them. His early experiences with oysters showed that those which gathered on the ropes were largely outnumbered by mussels. Rather than fight off the mussel growth, he decided to exploit it. The young mussels, spawned in the spring, congregate on the ropes in large clusters and, suspended away from the muddy seabed and from their natural enemies, are able to fatten more rapidly. From spawning, the shells are mature for harvesting in about twelve to fourteen months. Research is still continuing to find a formula to provide a seasonal working year, with an envisaged output of anything up to 1,000 tons of mussels per annum. There is a large potential market for the product on the Continent.

The road ends at Keills Chapel, a roofless eleventh-century structure which has its gables and walls still in good order. Within the walls are recumbent slabs, dating from the fourteenth and fifteenth centuries, and carved with wild cats, wolves, otters, hounds, a griffin and a winged horse. This is reckoned to be one of the finest collections of its kind in Argyll, if not in Scotland. Yet, it has not received the attention of the

Department of the Environment, and is now exposed to the defacing effects of the weather. At Keillbeg there stands an old neglected jetty now overgrown with vegetation. Its construction is unusual in that no cement has been used; its long, narrow stones have been exactly cut and laid with care and attention, and have withstood a century's storms. The jetty was once used by ferry boats plying to and from Jura with cattle.

On the eastern shore of Loch Sween lie Achnamara, a small community comprising about twenty wooden houses, making up a forestry village with a population of about 200, Kilbride and Kilmory. Close by Kilbride is Castle Sween, maintained by the Department of the Environment as the earliest stone castle in Scotland. A twelfth-century structure, it was one of the first of square Norman build to appear in Celtic Scotland. It was the scene of many battles until besieged in 1644 by Alasdair MacDonald, known as Young Colkitto, a lieutenant to the Marquis of Montrose who burnt out its Campbell occupants. The tiny village of Kilmory is perhaps better known for the chapel of St Maelrubha and the fourteenth-century MacMillan's Cross. The engraved stones in this chapel are protected from the weather by a roof of glass. The MacMillan Cross is an impressive creation in which the Christ has been rather roughly carved but with an attempt to portray some ideal. Celtic interlacing appears on a long loin-cloth.

A mile or so south of Kilmory is Balimore, beyond which lies a glen which once contained a little village called Stronefield. Last century the landowner evicted its crofting occupants, not without some difficulty, however, for the crofters turned their faces to their oppressor and gave battle to both police and gamekeepers, to eventually win the day. Their victory was short-lived, for the police returned with reinforcements and set fire to the crofters' houses. These ruins can still be seen, standing as mute reminders, in association with thousands of others in the region, of the savage and inhuman acts which took place, with the blessing of the law of the land and its enforcers, all with the purpose of denuding a region and a land of the very essential element which makes a nation: people.

At the head of Loch Caolisport is Cove, where there is a cave supposed to have been used by St Columba. Whether this is true or not, the area is certainly reeking with evidence of a former holy use. The road to it winds through a private estate wooded with deciduous trees which stand out in sharp contrast to the Forestry Commission's obsession with other limited species cultivated for commercial gain with scant respect for people or land. The cave is high-roofed and about 6 feet deep. Inside a round bowl has been cut into the wall to the right. Within the cave is a rock platform with a drystone altar in good repair. A Latin cross has been cut into the wall about 3 feet above the mensa. Earlier this century the floor of the cave was excavated to about 3 feet, but the soil was not replaced—which tends to diminish one's appreciation of the place. Even so, the cave exudes a certain atmosphere of specific purpose and holy mystery. A basin in the floor of the rock platform was used for washing the feet before the holy service of mass was celebrated. Outside the cave stands a chapel in a quite ruinous condition, dating from the twelfth century.

South Knapdale tends to open farmland. There are many antiquities to be seen in the area. Near Kilberry Castle, to the north of Loch Stornoway, there is a collection of sculptured stones on public view, though the castle is not usually open to the public. The stones have been collected by the Campbell of Kilberry family for the last 150 years; they were recovered from ruined houses, stiles, bridges and the like. The castle is a private house incorporating some pre-seventeenth-century work in a Victorian façade. An excellent little guide to the antiquities of mid-Argyll was published by the occupant of the castle, Miss Marion Campbell, in 1970. Its value lies in the 'guided' tours which enable one to become quite immersed in Argyll as it was in pre-Christian times and in the centuries of recorded history.

As mentioned already, Loch Fyne is, with Loch Linnhe, one of the longest of the Scottish sea lochs: some 40 miles from the head to the open sea. Along the eastern shore of Loch Fyne lie some townships, the most important of which is Inveraray, following on which, in a southerly direction, are Furnace, Crarae, Minard and Lochgilphead. The latter lies at the head of Loch Gilp, and at the eastern side of the isthmus which is cut by the Crinan Canal. It is the main administrative centre in the county of Argyll and has a population of about 1,200. With the catchment area, the town serves a population of about 6,000 and acts as a market place and holiday resort. It is a tidy town, with well-maintained buildings and wide streets. One of the interesting industries in Lochgilphead is that started about five years ago: an embroidery factory. Though this industry is mechanized, with needles flashing about at the order of a computer, it provides work for about a dozen people.

Minard was formerly a fishing village, established when Loch Fyne was accruing its reputation for its stocks of herrings of excellent quality. The main areas of employment for its 160 inhabitants nowadays are forestry and quarrying. Nearby are the magnificent Crarae Gardens, which contain many species of exotic plants and trees, many of which were grown from seed by the creator of the gardens, the late Sir George Campbell, and his son. When Sir George succeeded to the estate in 1920, he greatly developed the existing garden. Some 30 acres in Glen Crarae were planted with many unusual conifers. In 1955 this forest garden was gifted to the nation and is now maintained by the research branch of the Forestry Commission. It is open to view throughout the year and is much visited by students of horticulture from all parts of the world. A full day is needed to take in all that the gardens have to offer in sight and scent.

Crarae has its place in the industrial history of Scotland, being the site of a quarry which is still in operation after a century, and proving to be a great economic asset to the district. The quarry was established in 1852, in an attempt to supply an improved system of street paving which had good and lasting qualities. During the 1830s a small portion of Jamaica Street in Glasgow was paved with dressed causeway stones from the vicinity of Crarae and its nearby village of Furnace. The stones proved to have a durability which resulted in a contractor, James Sim, obtaining permission from the Duke of Argyll to open up a quarry. The rock quarried was commonly called granite, but was in fact porphyrite. The stone presented difficulties: it was hard and required much effort to blast it out of the ground. Eventually a technique was evolved of large blasting, derived from experiments undertaken at the chalk cliffs near Dover on the works of the South Eastern Railway Company and afterwards by the contractors for the government breakwater at Holyhead. The first large blast in Argyll took place in 1852 with successful results, using between 1,500 and 6,000 pounds of gunpowder. Some explosions were so considerable that parts of the cottages in the vicinity of the quarry used to be blown into the loch.

These large explosions became something of a tourist attraction. In June 1883 it was advertised that a "Monster Blast" (of about 4 tons of gunpowder) would take place on Saturday, the 9th of the month, timed to herald the arrival of the *Lord of the Isles*, a paddle steamer, at Crarae pier. Three years later, another "monster blast" was advertised. Again the *Lord of the Isles* was pressed into service to bring almost 1,000 people to witness the shedding of thousands of tons of rock from the hill face. The event was to become something of an historic occasion, for it was the anniversary of the founding of the Police and Statute Labour Committee of Glasgow Town Council, under whose direction it was that Glasgow's streets were paved with Crarae and Furnace setts. Thus, there was a gala feeling in the air, added to by the presence on the steamer of many of Glasgow's town councillors and municipal officials, and their wives and daughters. This particular 'monster blast' (the similar present-day technique is called heading blasts) took some weeks to prepare.

To lay the huge quantity of gunpowder, a tunnel had to be driven nearly 60 feet long into the hill. The tunnel was in the shape of a Y, at the end of each arm a chamber being constructed to contain the explosive charges. Driving this tunnel was an extremely difficult task, for it was only about 3 feet wide and less than that high. In that confined space one man had to lie prone, drilling shot holes with an air drill, charging the holes with dynamite and then crawling back down the tunnel to fresh air and light. After the shots were fired, the miner went in again to clear away the rubble. The tunnel advanced a few feet each day and the deeper it became the more unpleasant did the job become. In each chamber over 6,000 pounds of gunpowder were stacked to the roof. Electric wires for exploding the charges were laid before the tunnels were closed in with walls, and sealed with cement. The tunnel was then filled up again to roof height right to its entrance. The reason for this was to ensure that the power of the blast was confined and used efficiently to heave the burden of rock forward and on to the floor of the quarry.

About 1.15 p.m. on the big day the *Lord of the Isles* arrived opposite Crarae and stopped midway between the two shores. The steamer's siren was sounded, and at the signal the manager of the quarry fired the blast. He did this from a rock shelter about 100 yards from the face. Wisely keeping under cover, he connected the firing current. A watcher on the road half a mile away felt the tremor of the round and saw the back of the quarry slightly heave before the sound was heard. It was a perfect blast. The watchers on board the ship felt somewhat cheated, expecting masses of cloud, smoke and fire. Instead there was a "dull and rumbling like distant thunder" and a movement of the rock face as some 700,000 cubic feet of virgin rock fell into the quarry. The manager, in a small party, went to the entrance of the quarry to inspect the results of the blast. They noticed, as they chatted, a "sulphurous smell", to which they paid little attention. Some twenty minutes later the first of the visitors off the steamer arrived to stand in the gorge which acted as the entrance to the quarry and then to move forward to inspect the new hill of rock rubble. A full half hour after the blast, some people in different parts of the quarry were seen to fall to the ground unconscious. When the manager saw this he realized what was happening and shouted warnings to clear the quarry. This only caused some panic and a crush of people jammed the gorge entrance. Confusion reigned for some minutes until rescue workers came along to help. The injured were carried or dragged across the roadside. Some of those who were unconscious recovered in the fresh air; others revived slowly. Some forty people were affected, of whom six died. It was a sad and subdued crowd on the steamer on the return journey. Though this disaster was not the direct result of the blast, one of Her Majesty's Inspectors of Explosives was commissioned to investigate the matter. But before he had his report ready, the cause was known: the suffocating nature of the blast fumes and gases. The blast had produced vast quantities of gases which are killers at low concentrations in the air. Added to this the fact that the gorge—which in normal circumstances acted as a vent—was full of people prevented the poisonous gases from dispersing quickly as they seeped up through the newly-fallen rock. It had also been a windless day, which meant that the gases remained in the vicinity of the quarry for a long time, even more than thirty minutes after the explosion. As the inspector put it: "the dullness of the day, coupled with the rain which began to fall when the steamer came alongside, was a merciful provision to dissuade a large number of passengers from landing, and this mitigated the calamity . . .".

After this event, the quarries continued in operation, attracting many men from many parts of the world, who were employed on the different tasks associated with quarry work. In 1922 there were no less than 180 men working at one time. By 1930, however, the demand for setts had diminished, because of the increasing use of tarmacadam. The quarry product became road metal, and the works were developed by the introduction of machinery. During the years of the last war, the quarries of Furnace and Crarae, by this time under one ownership, supplied crushed stone for the military and naval camps in the vicinity of Inveraray. At the present time about two dozen men are employed. In 1969 a ship from Hamburg took away a load of 750 tons of granite chippings for roadworks in Germany; this export order was followed by others, which led to a new pier being built at Furnace.

The village of Furnace, though associated by the quarry with Crarae, has its own place in the industrial history of Scotland, this time for the 'furnace' and the powder-mills, the former being connected with the iron-smelting activity established in 1754. It was an extremely important event in the history of the district and a development which so affected the neighbourhood that the former community's name was changed from Inverleacainn to Furnace. The introduction of smelting to the shores of Loch Fyne was evidence of a much larger movement which was affecting other parts of the United Kingdom. Until the beginning of the eighteenth century, English woodlands were being depleted at an increasing rate to provide charcoal for smelting processes; this was in addition to wood being required to construct ships for the navy. Various Acts of Parliament were passed for the protection of the forests, but the demand for iron overrode any statutory restriction. Eventually it became accepted policy for English iron smelters to ship their ore to Scotland, and particularly to the Highlands, where there were at the time extensive woods of oak, birch, holly, ash, elm and beech, all excellent for producing charcoal. Furnaces were thus erected at Taynuilt on Loch Etive and at Inverleacainn in Argyllshire. Under the name of the Argyll Furnace Company, a smelting interest from Lancashire constructed a blast furnace. The site was admirable and eminently suited for the short-term purpose. The long-term effect of this activity, as of others in the Highlands, is still seen today in scarred and denuded hillsides. The slopes of Beinn Ghlas and Dun Leacainn provided wood; a good supply of water could be taken from the river; there was access from the sea, via Loch Fyne; and there was a ready supply of labour in Auchindrain: all these summed up the advantage of Furnace. A large waterwheel provided the power for the forge hammer. The furnace itself was large, and capable of turning out 700 tons of pig per annum. The company imported ore and ironstone in vessels sailing from the west of England. Local ore from the district was also used: haematite or kidney ore, which may be still found at the mouth of the River Leacainn. This ore had a high percentage of iron (70 per cent) and produced pig iron which was of superior quality. The furnace required 1,400 tons of charcoal or 3,500 tons of wood every year. This not only raised the price of wood but gave employment to a considerable number of people, both male and female, who worked at cutting and peeling the wood and making charcoal. There may still be seen the small semi-circular built-up terraces used by the charcoal burners when they turned the local scrub oak and birch into charcoal. One of the social benefits which the company provided was a school, introduced into the village about 1790.

The smelting operations were carried on for many years. When the Seven Years' War started in 1756 the breach between Sweden and Russia, countries which had supplied Britain with iron, caused a scarcity. This, along with a big demand for cannon and shot, because of other hostilities, created full employment at the Furnace works. However, progress in the technology of iron-making began to overtake this west Highland industry. At the Carron ironworks in Falkirk coal was being used to smelt iron. Steam began to replace water-power for driving machinery, and iron-works tended to be located nearer coal-fields. By 1813 work at Furnace had ceased and the place was dismantled. To indicate the extent of the damage which these industries caused in the Highlands (furnaces were also built at Bonawe in 1711, Invergarry in 1730, and Abernethy) one must consider that to make 1 ton of charcoal, 2½ tons of wood were required, and 2 tons of charcoal for each ton of pig; so that for a ton of pig iron, using good quality haematite, 5 tons of wood were needed. A furnace could burn about 170 tons of wood each week. And it took a copsewood sixteen years to grow to sufficient maturity.

The licence to "erect mills and other engines for making gunpowder" at Furnace was given at Inveraray Quarter Sessions in 1841. The 'powder-mills' as they were known produced gunpowder in considerable quantities. The material, which is made from saltpetre, sulphur and charcoal was in the course of its manufacture passed through a series of operations, each of which was carried on in a separate building. The ingredients were first roughly mixed in the correct proportions in the mixing house, and then incorporated in the incorporating mills (the remains of which are still seen in Furnace immediately below the dam). The 'millcake' thus produced was broken up and then, by hydraulic pressure, converted into 'presscake' in the press house. This, in turn, was 'corned' or made into grains of required size in the corning house. The grains were then freed from dust and glazed with blacklead to give an external polish in the glazing house. They were dried or 'stoved' in the stove, which was heated from the boiler house. Finally, they received a dusting in the dusting house. After manufacture, the gunpowder was stored in the expense magazines, of which there were two, and in the Faraday magazine, before being packed in the heading house into barrels or kegs. In addition to these process buildings, there was a watch house, a non-danger building located at the entrance to the mill area, in which the workmen were searched for matches when they changed their normal clothes for factory clothing which had no pockets.

In 1875 the Explosives Act was passed containing regulations drawn up by the Home Office for the control of the processes involved in the manufacture of explosives, and of the conditions of storage and handling the manufactured products. It was found that the Loch Fyne Powder Mills did not conform to the requirements of the Act. The stove was too near the dusting house; the heading-up house was too near one of the expense magazines; and other buildings were found in close and dangerous proximity to each other. What was more serious was the fact that one of the expense magazines was sited near to some cottages; and the factory magazine, which was certificated to contain 80 tons of gunpowder, was within 100 yards of the post office and the school, instead of being over 3 miles away as was required by law. However, since the factory had been erected some thirty years before the passing of the Act, the owners were allowed to continue operations. The day of reckoning was to come.

The day of what in local tradition is known as the 'Furnace Explosion' occurred on 29th September 1883. It was a Saturday afternoon, when the factory was closed for ordinary work. Only a small skeleton shift was on the premises, and no one was in the vicinity of the stove. A shinty match, scheduled to take place in the park of Goatfield, next to the factory, was interrupted by the grace of God. During play a horse bolted on the road nearby and a cart overturned. Shinty players and spectators went immediately to the scene of the accident to render assistance. The factory manager was at the roadside watching for the boat which was due to appear on Loch Fyne to on-load barrels of gunpowder. The explosion occurred just after 3 p.m. The manager was struck by a large stone which took off one of his legs; he sustained other serious injuries from which he died a couple of hours later. The men working on the skeleton shift were luckily protected from the blast. But the outer and inner doors of the factory magazine were burst open. Yet another chance of fate had decided that the wind should be in the north-east. Had it been in the prevailing direction about 23 tons of gunpowder would have exploded within 100 yards of the post office and school, setting off other explosions which could have wiped out most of the houses in the village and caused an untold number of deaths. No less than six cartloads of stones and boulders were lifted from the playing field, deserted by both players and spectators. The cause of the accident originated in the stove: a spark set the chimney on fire, which led to burning soot falling on the roof of the building, to be followed by a rapid conflagration and the resultant explosion. Both the stove and the boiler house, with its 40-foot chimney, were entirely destroyed. After this occurrence, the Furnace inhabitants, not unnaturally, presented an iron-bound case for the cessation of the factory—which is now in ruins, though the cottages are still standing.

North of Furnace lies the Auchindrain Farming Township, a museum of country life. The place is a huddle of old croft houses dating from about 1770. A trust has been formed with the purpose of restoration, and to furnish with faithful accuracy three of the houses: one in the style of the eighteenth century, a second in the style of the nineteenth century and a third in the style of the early twentieth century. The venture has the support of the National Museum of Antiquities and the universities of Edinburgh and Glasgow. Part of the new museum was opened in 1967, since when it has been an attraction to an increasing number of visitors. A complete tour takes about an hour and it is well worth a visit to see the farm tools and household equipment used in days now gone, which have been collected locally and from the site itself, and to see how life was lived out on a multiple-tenancy farm. The exhibits include a 250-year-old tweed loom.

The Burgh of Inveraray, though its population is only about 500, is the acknowledged capital of Argyll, and includes the seat of the Duke of Argyll, Inveraray Castle. A continuing programme of restoration will eventually make Inverary a centre for living and functioning examples of eighteenth-century Scots architecture. The burgh was established on its present site in a grand scheme of rebuilding and town planning which took place in the second half of the eighteenth century, a scheme which included the razing of an older castle and the erection of the present most attractive edifice. From about 1457, when Colin, second Lord Campbell, was created first Earl of Argyll, the old castle had been the Campbell seat, but was by 1743 beginning to show its age. In 1744 the third Duke of Argyll began rebuilding, taking advantage of the architect, Roger Morris, to establish Inveraray anew. Morris was probably the most renowned member of his profession at this time and it was indeed a wise duke who let him loose on the scheme, for he had, as clerk of works, one no less than William Adam, builder of Hopetoun, and the father of the better known Robert Adam, who, in fact, followed his father on the Inveraray project.

The plan drawn up for the new Inveraray was a grand scheme, which plotted the new site on Gallows Foreland Point. But little work was carried out before the third Duke died in 1761; only the old courthouse, the inn, the gaol and a few cottages appear to have been completed. The construction of the new castle went on well, however, though it was to fall to the fifth Duke to carry out the major part of the building, under the care now of Robert Mylne. The work of this architect was mainly confined to the interior of the castle; but he was also responsible for the major part of the new town, after Adam's plans. The rather beautiful Aray Bridge, taking the main road over the River Aray, is the work of John Adam. The castle was finished about fifty years after it was commissioned. Its exterior, while ornate, gives little indication of the magnificent settings of the interior, provided by rich Georgian decorations.

Mylne, the last of the master masons to the kings of Scotland, did an excellent job of Inveraray, with its formal layout. If the burgh is approached from the south, or Glasgow road, one obtains a good view of the framework of six tall arches, the Great Inn, which is now an hotel, and the imposing custom house, now serving duty as the municipal offices. From the old Cross of Inveraray (which is earlier than the fifteenth century) the broad Main Street runs straight up to divide like a river flowing on both sides of the solid square church which Mylne clearly intended to act as a focal point. It was 1794 before the last workman had tidied up the builders' rubble and called it a day to leave Inveraray as a 'quaint' town—until 1957 when the Historic Buildings Council drew the attention of the then Ministry of Works to the need for its preservation and, in some cases, restoration. The tenth Duke relinquished possession of the town in favour of the ministry, and the work of renovation and restoration, begun in that same year, was put in hand, and is still going on. The church lacks a steeple at the present time. This is not the result of Mylne, its designer, forgetting to provide the building with this mark of distinction. Indeed, he provided the church with an elegant and graceful steeple which set the building off to perfection. But, in the early years of the last war, the weight of military traffic thundering through the small town threatened to bring the steeple down, and it was dismantled for safety. The kirk session is still trying to raise enough money to put it back up again. The interior of the church is unusual in that it is divided into two equal sections by a solid wall which goes across the middle of it and right to the roof. When it was being built, a strict lingual segregation was observed, the 'English' half being used by the castle family and staff, while the 'Gaelic' half was used by the native population. Only the English half is used nowadays, the other, erstwhile Gaelic portion, serving duty as a church hall. The Historic Buildings Council declared that Inveraray was "an entirety designed to delight the eye from every angle of approach, both by land and water". Nearly 100 houses have been renovated so far.

The present population of about 450 indicates the decline of Inveraray from its peak of 1,233, which occurred in 1841. Much of the decline was the result of the disappearance of the Loch Fyne herring fishing

The dam at Loch Faskally, Perthshire

Kenmore, Perthshire

Fishing boats at Campbeltown, Argyll

and the amalgamation of crofts into larger farm units in the immediate countryside. There has also been a steady migration from the town to industrial areas in search of higher incomes. The burgh's motto—"May you always have a catch of herring"—is sadly anachronistic. The pier at Inveraray is still used in the summer months by passenger steamers from the Clyde coast.

Ardrishaig (population 1,200) is a former fishing village which owes much to its existence at the entrance from Loch Fyne to the Crinan Canal to allow the passage of Clyde shipping to reach the Western Isles and the western coast of Scotland without having to make the 80-mile voyage round the stormy Mull of Kintyre. Controlled by the British Waterways Board, it operates with a working loss of some £10,000 per annum. The annual passages include about 600 fishing boats, 600 small coasters, including the 'puffers', and about 1,000 yachts. The canal is reckoned to be of greater economic importance than the Caledonian Canal in that the route serves as an essential link between the west of Scotland and the larger conurbations of the country.

The Crinan Canal was first conceived by the magistrates of Glasgow, who petitioned the Commissioners of the Forfeited Estates in Scotland with the suggestion that a cutting, either at Ardrishaig or at Tarbert, would be of great benefit to the fishing busses, and that such a canal would open "easy and short communication between the Clyde and the west coast as far north as Cape Wrath and with all the Western Isles, so that timber, bark, kelp, grain and fish might be brought to market cheaper and with less danger than by doubling the Mull". The two routes suggested were surveyed by James Watt. That at Tarbert, with a length of 1 mile, would save a 55-mile voyage and cost £23,000 for a 10-foot cutting. That at Crinan, with an estimated length of 4¾ miles would save 75 miles at a cost of £48,000. In the end, in 1793, an Act authorizing the canal from Loch Gilp to Loch Crinan was obtained. The promoting company appointed John Rennie as chief engineer at a salary of 200 guineas and Captain Joseph Huddart, one of the best-known marine surveyors of his day, was asked to make a survey of the two lochs and to report on the best situations for harbours. Work was started in 1794 but the company found itself in many difficulties, financial problems being only one of the worries. The completion of the work was scheduled for 1796 but was delayed by the "unfortunate situation of public affairs" which made money scarce. The year 1798 was then suggested as a new completion date, but money came in so slowly that by 1799 efforts had to be made to raise some £22,000 needed to complete the canal. The cutting was opened in an unfinished state on 18th July 1801.

The canal was filled with water by slow stages, because it was thought that until the banks had settled and consolidated the full depth might impose too much strain on them. By April 1802 the canal had 8 feet of water throughout its length. But its unfinished state did not attract vessel-owners, who rather preferred to be cautious than sorry. Even so, the tonnage dues for the canal's first twenty months, despite a setback to the western fisheries, amounted to over £1,300, which was a satisfactory state of affairs. The waterway was still incomplete in 1804 when it was proposed to apply for government aid to enable the canal company to complete the work. It was claimed that over £140,000 had been expended on the canal, of which sum about £108,000 was raised by private subscription. Eventually an Act was passed which authorized the Treasury to issue £25,000, and further work was put in hand. But the canal was far from being free of trouble. Repair work and maintenance claimed more money and in 1812 a state of affairs was reached when the Government decided to call in Thomas Telford to make a survey of the canal and to estimate a once-for-all figure for completion of the canal. His estimate was £18,000, coupled with the observation that the canal was of extreme importance and of great use, considering that the "intercourse of that part of the kingdom would be materially injured if this communication was now abandoned". The subsequent history of the canal is one of widely fluctuating dues, complaints about the suitability of the canal for large ships, the further provisions of facilities such as coal stores for steam ships, and the increasing debt on the works.

One highlight occurred in August 1847, when Queen Victoria passed through the canal in the track-boat *Sunbeam*. The Queen recorded: "We and our people drove through the little village [Ardrishaig] to the Crinan Canal, where we entered a most magnificently decorated barge, drawn by three horses riden by postillions in scarlet. We glided along very smoothly, and the views of the hills—the range of Cruachan —were very fine indeed; but the eleven locks we had to go through were tedious, and instead of the passage lasting one hour and a half, it lasted upwards of two hours and a half." The return journey was speedier. Later the canal became a tourist attraction, which also brought a welcome increase in dues. By the 1850s the passenger traffic from Glasgow had increased significantly. Excursions to Staffa and Iona were advertised on cheap rates "in order to afford the operative classes an opportunity of viewing the islands". Steamers such as the *Cygnet*, the *Lapwing* and *Duntroon Castle* became familiar sights. Almost 45,000 passengers were being handled annually. By the end of the century, after years of frustration for those interested in seeing the waterway playing its full role in the economic welfare of the area, the annual income was £6,000, virtually insignificant when seen against the accumulated expenditure which a century had demanded of the Treasury. In 1919 an Act of Parliament caused the Caledonian and Crinan canals to be transferred to the Ministry of Transport. In 1930, a £100,000 renovation scheme was begun, included in which were new sea-locks accessible at all states of the tide, a new reservoir to supplement the eight locks which had so far served the canal, and a 15-foot increase in the depth of Ardrishaig Harbour. The shortage of water, however, remained a problem, even when the British Transport Commission took charge of the waterway in 1948. In 1953 the loss on the canal per annum was given as £12,000. In 1958 an inquiry reported that the canal, though unprofitable, was of greater economic importance than was the Caledonian, since it was used by more than twice as many vessels, carried 50,000 tons of goods annually, and formed an important link in the communications between the Clyde and the Hebrides. The canal's restricted capacity, however, was detrimental to the economic working of cargo vessels. There was also a recommendation that the canal be used more extensively by the Forestry Commission for the shipping of timber from the north-west. In 1962 the canal was transferred to the charge of the British Waterways Board.

Inland from Loch Fyne, to the west, lies Loch Awe. In earlier geological times this loch drained south to the Sound of Jura, carving out Kilmartin Glen. When the last glacier disappeared some 12,000 years ago, it left deposits of gravel and glacial drift which made the glen fertile and offered the first human settlements well-drained ground to cultivate. The loch has two heads, at Ford in the south and Dalmally some 23 miles north, where it is fed by the River Orchy. The area south of the loch holds an extremely large mass of archaeological wealth, and it is little wonder that it has been described as the cradle of Scotland. There are old churches, castles, carved stones, Celtic crosses, sun-circles, standing stones, duns, vitrified forts, chambered cairns, all of which have yet to be given their full and acknowledged recognition by professional archaeologists—particularly the Scottish species, who tend to display a particularly and peculiarly marked inclination to ignore the archaeological wealth on their own native land, and especially on the western seaboard of Scotland and in the Hebrides. On low farmland south of Kilmartin there are prehistoric relics which are strong rivals to Avebury and Stonehenge. There is a sun-circle at Templewood. This stands in a field surrounded by scrub oak. It dates from the Bronze Age, around 1700 B.C. The main group is a central monolith ringed by eight other standing stones.

But perhaps the main point of interest in this area is Dunadd. This is a tall rocky hillock which rises about 180 feet above the Great Moss. Even without the man-made fortifications on it, it is a natural fort; its strategic importance was recognized at a very early date and it eventually became the capital of Dalriada. From all cardinal points, Dunadd was to the west of Scotland what Rome was: a focal point of great political and military importance. All approaches to Dunadd are safeguarded by no less than seventy forts within a 10-mile radius. Kilmartin Glen, to the north, offered a good pass to Loch Awe and thence to central and north-east Scotland, and to the west coast to Inverness through the Great Glen; the isthmus at Crinan offered a fast eastern route to Loch Fyne and the Clyde. Sheltered waterways and hill passes encouraged all kinds of traffic. It was to Dunadd that Fergus came with the stone supposedly used by Jacob as a pillow at Bethel. The stone had long been held at Cashel Cathedral in Ireland, where it became known as the Lia Fail (Stone of Destiny) and was used in the coronation of Irish kings. Fergus used the stone in Scotland for the crowning of Scottish kings until it was removed by the English in 1296. The stone, which now rests in Westminster Abbey, is claimed to be an expert fake and the real stone is at present lying in security in Scotland, on a remote hillside awaiting the day when Scotland regains her independence from the 1707 union which bound her with England. Dunadd was besieged in the seventh and eighth centuries by both Britons and Picts, taken twice and then retaken, and it remained the seat of Scottish power until the reign of Kenneth Macalpin. When he conquered the Picts in 843, he removed his capital to Forteviot and Scone in Perthshire. Dalriada, before then a separate kingdom for almost three and a half centuries, became a 'remote' region and even had its name replaced by Argyll.

Loch Awe forms the south-east frontier of Lorn. Throughout its great length of 23 miles it is ranked with Loch Maree and Loch Lomond as one of Scotland's most beautiful lochs. Good roads run down both sides of the loch, which are heavily wooded. The area on the west side is Forestry Commission land with coniferous plantations. The commission's Inverliever Forest was bought in 1907 and is the oldest state forest in Scotland. The loch is also the scene of one of the North of Scotland Hydro-electric Board's most ambitious projects: the first large-scale pumped-storage hydro-electric development in Scotland. The project uses the water flow from 324 square miles, consisting largely of the catchment area of Loch Awe. The three separate sections of the scheme have a total capacity of 440 megawatts. The Cruachan section is a 400-megawatt pumped-storage development in which energy from the South of Scotland Electricity Board system is used to pump water from Loch Awe to a high-level reservoir on Ben Cruachan, the pumping being done at nights and at weekends when the demand for electricity is light. This water, supplemented by water diverted into the reservoir from 6½ square miles by some 10 miles of tunnel and piped aqueducts, is used to generate electricity at times of peak demand. The machine hall is a vast excavation inside Ben Cruachan, a cavern of 300 feet in length and almost 80 feet high. It involved the removal of some 200,000 tons of rock.

At Ford, a small village at the south end of Loch Awe with a population of about 100, there is a rainbow trout farm. In the space of a handful of years, this enterprise has reached an annual output of more than 200 dollar-earning tons, which represents a vast quantity of half-pound trout. Visitors are made welcome here, to view at any time about half a million trout in idealized conditions. All the fish are from three to nine months old, with replacements under the three-month stage at the hatchery and nursery pools some 3 miles away. Trout farming is an all-year-round task, and demands full-time attention all round the clock. In winter the eggs for the hatchery come from Denmark and North America; in summer the eggs arrive from Australia and Tasmania. From the moment these are hatched, feeding, though little in quantity, has to be continuous: for the tiny fish, every half hour; in the first 'nursery pool', every hour; and so on, graduating by way of two-hourly and three-hourly feeding at three months, by which time the young fish are ready for transferring to the lochside farm. There the fish grow quickly in raceways fed by Loch Awe water circulating at the rate of 35,000 gallons per minute. There are about forty-two raceways at the time of writing, which number will be trebled in the future. After nine months at the farm, the trout attain a weight from 7 to 9 ounces, the ideal size for table use all over the world. Each week, refrigerated lorries carry their loads of several tons of trout, frozen and packed in the farm's special 'Scotrout' cartons, on the first single-track road stage of a journey which takes the product to the most expensive boards of Canada and the United States. As at conventional farms, the product is available for purchase at the 'farm gate'.

The area known as Lorn lies to the west of Loch Awe and borders on the firth of Lorn. Loch Leven forms a northern boundary, and the Bealach Mor, the Great Pass at the head of Loch Craignish, the southern marches. Between these two boundaries stretch about 40 miles of wild land. Nether Lorn, the southern part, is a hilly plateau land which is split inland by glens, rivers and lochs. Along its periphery to seaward there are points, peninsulae and an archipelago of about thirty islands and countless skerries. The principal islands are Seil, Luing, Scarba and the aptly named Isles of the Sea. In their narrow straits run tide-races of which the Corrievreckan is probably the most famous.

Both Seil and Luing are based on metamorphic slate. Seil is a first-class grazing subject, while Luing provides a large proportion of good farming ground. The subsidiary industry of slate-quarrying was once of importance, but not now. The islands were once known as the Slate Islands. One by one the quarries closed down, at first through a catastrophic flooding by the sea at Easdale, on Seil, when no less than 240 men lost their lives; then through loss of markets, mainly through rising freight charges and the competition of cheaper and lighter roofing materials; finally there arose a growing shortage of skilled men. In 1965 the only quarry remaining active was at Balvicar on Seil, but that too has now closed down. The present population on Seil, numbering about 500, live by farming, lobster-fishing and tool-making at

Easdale. In 1950 Brittany oysters were laid experimentally in Seil Sound; those sewn in Balvicar Bay produced the second largest of all the west Highland layings. But the potential has yet to be explored. Luing, with a population of about 200, was at one time an important centre for dairy cattle. Some 90 gallons a day were once exported to a creamery at Oban. The island was eventually bought over by farmers who have closed down the dairy farms and are now running a cattle ranch for stock raising. The main village on Luing is Cullipool, where the slate quarry was first opened in the late nineteenth century. It became the most important of its kind in the west Highlands and employed about 150 men producing about 15,000 slates each week. It too was closed down in 1965 and the resultant deadness of Cullipool is still felt to some extent.

Upper Lorn is bounded to the north and west by Lochs Leven and Linnhe and includes the long and narrow sea loch, Loch Etive. To the east it extends across the country to Glencoe, to the Rannoch Moor and the Perthshire border. Much of the area is high and often dangerous; many peaks are over 3,000 feet. The area includes some of the finest scenery in Scotland, but much of it is deer forest, with a few big farms and some interest in cattle. The presence of the Forestry Commission has been described by the ecologist, Sir Frank Fraser Darling, as "an undoubted blessing" in view of the state of dereliction and the disintegration of communities which was much in evidence twenty years ago and even more so now.

As might well be expected in an area which has seen so many centuries of continuous community formation, change and socio-economic upheaval, there are many points of interest. Almost every small community has some story to tell of its part in the formation of Argyll. In Taynuilt village and neighbouring Bonawe there are the remains of the Lorne Furnace, now the subject of restoration work, firstly being carried out by the Department of the Environment, who hope to see the site as the first industrial archaeological monument of its kind in Scotland. Some of the furnace-workers' houses are being modernized privately in another project.

The Lorne Furnace was originally started by an Irish company in 1730. They worked with imported ore and for fuel they bought the woods of Glenkinglass. They also experimented with peat made into charcoal, but without much success. Their initial venture ended in tragedy. The partners, while engaged in a drinking bout one night at Dalmally Inn, quarrelled, with matters becoming so serious that a fight ensued in which one of the men was fatally stabbed. The works were then taken over by another consortium which obtained a lease of 110 years for all the woods in the neighbourhood from the local lairds, who were all Campbells with little cash in their sporrans and so were glad for the chance to realize some of their natural-resource assets. The lease began in 1750 and the business was carried on successfully for a number of years. The ore was brought from Ulverstone in Cumberland and the charcoal made locally. The sites and pits where the charcoal makers worked can still be seen here and there, particularly on Loch Etive side. To facilitate loading and unloading, the company built a jetty on Loch Etive, still known locally as Kelly's Pier, from the name of the man who was foreman of the construction. The pier is now almost a complete wreck. About 7,000 to 9,000 tons of iron were turned out annually and shipped to Ulverstone.

The company did not confine itself to smelting iron, but entered into other speculations. At that time Glen Etive and other glens were well clothed in pines and oak trees. Their timber was considered far too valuable to be made into charcoal and so the company felled these and shipped the logs for export. Oak was felled in late spring, when the sap was rising, and bark peelers set to work stripping the bark which was then sent to tanneries in England. Up to the last decade of the nineteenth century, good quality oak bark fetched up to £16 to £18 per ton (equivalent to about £80 today). Bark peeling as an occupation in its own right continued down to the end of the last century, but latterly only in a small way; about 1880 a German chemist invented a chemical way to tan hides. Oak bark, however, is still used to make expensive leather. At the peak of the barking activity the number employed was about 600. The company's original lease ran out in 1860 and it was taken over by another commercial concern which also had connections with the iron mines in the Ulverstone district. This second lease was for twenty years, after which, in 1883, the furnace was closed down and the buildings left derelict. The quarry at Bonawe has been worked for over a century and at one time offered employment to more than 300 men. The present employment figure is about fifty.

About 7 miles west of Taynuilt, at Connel, Loch Etive displays the Falls of Lorn, perhaps a mile or so from the open sea. The falls are in fact impressive rapids caused by the outflow cascading across a rock-ledge at ebb-tide. The loch at this point is crossed by a road carried on a cantilever bridge under which ships may sail at high water, provided the mast height is less than 45 feet. At North Connel an airstrip, opened in 1967, is used by a once-daily flight service operated during the summer months by Benmore Flights Ltd, to reach Glasgow in thirty minutes. The railway line, which formerly crossed the Connel Bridge to serve the Lorn coast to Ballachulish, was closed in 1966.

The coast road to Oban passes Dunstaffnage, famous for its castle which rises in a grey mass out of a tree-covered hill. This gaunt building, aloof and justifying its place in Highland history, is an exceptionally well-preserved example of a thirteenth-century castle. Dunstaffnage is known for another 'sight': one of Europe's leading marine biological research centres. It attracts distinguished scientists from all over the world, either to study the work being carried out, or to take part in the research programmes. The laboratory is the headquarters of the Scottish Marine Biological Association. This organization was founded in 1914, but in reality originated from other bodies, the first of which was set up in 1884. The association exists to promote the study of marine science through research and education and is financed by the subscriptions of members, donations from universities and other sources; a government grant is now its main financial support. For a number of years the Marine Station at Millport, on the Isle of Cumbrae, was the association's research and teaching laboratory with, from 1950 to 1970, the Oceanographic Laboratory in Edinburgh. In 1967 the construction of a new laboratory was begun and by 1970 most of the research and other activities were transferred to Dunstaffnage. The site was chosen because it provided the right conditions necessary for a modern marine laboratory: unpolluted sea-water, shelter for vessels, the proximity of a sizeable town (Oban), good road and rail communications, and access to a variety of marine habitats ranging from enclosed sea-lochs to the open Atlantic.

There is a total staff of about ninety. Although the main research programmes are concerned with basic marine science rather than the practical problems of fisheries—which are the responsibility of the Government's fisheries laboratories—basic research of the kind carried out at Dunstaffnage is essential for the wise exploitation and conservation of the sea's resources. The work of the laboratory is concerned in particular with the ecology of the west-coast lochs, finding out what are the important factors in determining the kinds of organisms and fish and the amounts produced in different areas. The circulation of the waters in the lochs is important in determining the degree of exchange with the open sea. For instance, Loch Etive has a shallow sill at its mouth which restricts the tidal wave so that inside the loch spring tides have a range of only 5 to 6 feet, whereas outside in the Firth of Lorn the range is over 12 feet. Another somewhat deeper sill at Bonawe influences the replenishment of water in the inner basin and evidence shows that this may occur very irregularly and perhaps not every year. The drainage area of Loch Etive is about 500 square miles, so that there is a considerable in flow of fresh water at the surface, some 3,000 million tons per annum, which overlies the sea water which is sometimes found in a layer as deep as 30 feet.

This fresh water carries in it a vast quantity of dissolved organic material, the 'brown humic' products of peat bogs and fragments of grasses, leaves and the like, which probably makes a major contribution to the nourishment of the fauna of these lochs. At the same time, there is an extensive growth of annual seaweeds on their shores, which also supplies food for the animals in the water. Work on the fish populations of Loch Etive and Loch Creran, farther north, has shown that these are primarily nursery areas. Young whiting, for instance, move out to deeper waters off shore from January to March each year. There is a small resident population of whiting which may prove to be a separate stock. Haddock, poor cod and Norway trout seem to be almost absent from Loch Etive and a larval survey is being carried out at present to find out why this should be.

The sea-lochs also seem to be nursery grounds for herring and sprats, and attention is being paid to the feeding of these species, which depend very much on good supplies of plankton. Among shellfish of economic importance, mussels are being studied in a number of lochs, to discover which areas are favourable for settlement, growth and fattening, and to reveal the influence of salinity and other environmental factors on these stages. Observations and experiments at sea are carried out from research vessels and a number of in-shore craft. The new and specially-designed 1,400-ton ship *Challenger*, based on Dunstaffnage, has extended the laboratories' activities to the open sea off the western coasts.

Loch Creran, an inlet of the Lynn of Morvern and sheltered by the island of Lismore, is the location of yet another shellfish venture: a £100,000 oyster hatchery, which is the largest commercial undertaking of its kind in Europe. The buildings were leased in 1970 by the Highlands and Islands Development Board to Scottish Sea Farms Ltd, whose aim it is to satisfy a Continental demand for oysters. The conditions for almost making a kill in this market are due to circumstances abroad. In France, the oyster industry is only now beginning to recover from a very harsh winter in 1962–3, which cut the oyster-seed production by 90 per cent. And the industry in Holland is gradually being reduced as the Zuider Zee reclamation programmes make progress. The Loch Creran venture thus finds itself in an enviable position. The firm estimates that some 80 per cent of the seed-oyster production will go for export while the remainder will be retained in Loch Creran for rearing to maturity. The eventual production target is 10 million seeds per annum. It takes from three to four years for table oysters to mature in the selected beds in Loch Creran. In their natural environment the mortality rate among young oysters is very high, with about one in a million larvae managing to survive. Under controlled conditions, with many of the natural predators (crab and starfish) removed, the larvae are able to develop to the size of a 5p. piece before they are 'planted' in Loch Creran. The initial work force here is nine men, which number will be increased to between thirty and forty once the venture is in full commercial production.

The sea in Loch Creran yields yet another important resource—sodium alginate extracted from seaweed, the processing of which provides about 150 jobs at the Barcaldine plant of Alginate Industries (Scotland) Ltd. When the factory was set up in 1940 the weekly production was 3 tons. The present output is up to 45 tons per week. This quantity represents about 170 tons of air-dried seaweed, which in turn is equivalent to 500 to 600 tons of wet weed collected by an army of weed hunters in the Hebrides, Orkney, Shetland and west Ireland.

Lying in the mainstream of the waters of Loch Linnhe is the island of Lismore, which means in Gaelic 'great garden'. Though it tends to look a grey and dull island, in fact it is an island highlight; access is by means of a motor-launch ferry which plies between the north end of Lismore and a jetty at Airds Bay. The ferry is not continuous but sails on call. The ferryman's house is at Port Appin. The other access is by means of a converted fishing boat which plies twice each day from Oban to Achnacroish, a crossing of forty-five minutes. The island is about 10 miles long by a mile wide and is traversed lengthwise by one road. A particular feature of Lismore is that the land is heavily furrowed by shallow troughs running lengthwise to give many sheltered grazings and making for a good farming environment. The northern part of the island is quite heavily wooded. Both cattle and sheep graze off the grasslands which cover most of the island. Cattle are numerous and are bred more for sale than for dairying. The bulk of the population lives in the northern portion. Achnacroish in the south has the island's main pier and the post office, but only a few houses. The main 'centres' of population are found along the high road itself and Port Ramsay in the north-west bay. The larger part of Lismore is owned by the Duke of Argyll and the island farmers are his tenants.

The present agricultural situation is reckoned to be nowhere near its full potential. Rather, the island has always been under-used. Based on Dalradian limestone, the island's fertility is more than significant. For many years the island was poorly farmed; little ploughing took place and breeding of cattle was not pursued intelligently. Crofters let their land as grazing rather than creating what could have become an important cattle-rearing centre in the Highlands. Cattle, in fact, cannot avoid but become good specimens on Lismore and the potential for breeding the cream of both cattle and sheep is still a goal to be realized without too much difficulty.

Limestone was once quarried on Lismore and there is still to be seen the old stone quay at Sailean near the quarry; active work was abandoned about fifty years ago. In 1947 the Reverend Dr Ian Carmichael took up a ministry charge on the island and, from his experience in community work in Lewis, started an association whose purpose was to explore the potential of the island and then to realize the assessed resources. But the association was not able to achieve the degree of success which Dr Carmichael and others had achieved with the Lewis Association, though the need for a unifying social facility was real enough.

In 1861 the population of Lismore was 853, and there has been a steady decline ever since, with a tendency to level off in recent years.

In 1951 the figure was 191, with a slight excess of females, and the 1972 estimate was 180, showing the community to have reached stability, though whether this is a viable social numerator remains to be seen. As with other islands, the problem of efficient sea-links is ever a topic of conversation and controversy. As mentioned, Lismore has two mainland links: Port Ramsay and Achnacroish. The latter, however, being in the south is exposed to severe wind and seas. Often boats from Oban have had to return there, unable to land either cargo or passengers. The islanders in 1972 had the not so unique experience of being told by a delegation from Argyll County Council and the Scottish Transport Group that the longer, Oban, crossing was the better one for them. The Port Ramsay crossing, on the other hand, is only 1,400 yards from the Appin shore on the mainland, involving a travelling time of some ten minutes. This northern anchorage is first class, in that whatever the direction of the wind boats are always protected and always make a landing. The experience of the islanders is typical of the kind resulting from decision-making of a type abundant in the Highlands—where solutions to problems are imposed on those who, apart from never being consulted or only superficially so, are often provided with *faits accompli* which are more often than not detrimental to the lifestyle of the communities who have to suffer the new conditions.

With its bustling population of 7,000 people, the burgh of Oban is a focal point in Argyll, and serves as the link between the Scottish mainland and many of the islands in the Inner Hebrides and the southern isles of the Outer Hebrides. The harbour is one of the best on the west Highland seaboard. The setting of Oban is more than just functional; it is almost an environment, and as such has proved to be a strong attraction to both the tourist and to those who wish to spend their retirement days in an invigorating climate. The Oban hinterland is criss-crossed by the roads which fertilize the communities in Lorn; to seaward the 'roads' are channelled isleways which take one to communities of another kind: island-based, yet mindful of the part which Oban plays in their survival and normal routine. The town is surrounded by low wooded hills whose upper slopes are vantage points for large houses. Oban Bay is almost landlocked by the island of Kerrera, whose 4-mile length offers the bay a landscape of green hills above which rise the higher peaks of Mull. The plan of Oban suggests a far-from-formal approach. Few of the town's streets run towards each other in that monotonous grid system which unimaginative and failed planners have too often accepted as the easiest way out of providing a town with walkways and roads. Rather, Oban displays an almost off-hand preference for the changing vista. Roads curve, dive round bends, run back on each other, short-circuit fine sweeps and present the traveller on foot with a continuous feast for the eye. As it is today, Oban can be described as a well-preserved, clean and proud-looking Victorian town. It is more than this, however, for the site of the burgh has had an estimated period of continuous occupation amounting to some 8,000 years. Towards the latter part of last century, when the new town was expanding, workmen uncovered seven caves in a stretch of low cliff where the present George Street runs north to south. There were remains of Azilian Man (6000 B.C.), a Stone Age people who had migrated from Europe after Britain had become an island. Among the finds were human skulls, flints, stone hammers, harpoons of deer horn and various other implements of horn and bone.

Oban started to grow in the early years of the nineteenth century, doubling its population from 600 to 1,500 as shipbuilding took root and as farming developed. The town was created a burgh in 1801, when town planning was undertaken, piers built and the centre began the point for sailings to the Western Isles and the Lorn coast. The town was finally established when steamboats arrived from the Clyde coast *c.* 1850, and then enhanced its status in 1880 with the arrival of the railway. Since then the population has grown steadily to the present 7,000. Oban draws most of its wealth from the tourist trade, but relies significantly on the fishing fleet (about seventy boats), whisky and other industrial activities.

The fishing industry based on Oban was represented in 1971 by landings worth some £1 million. This figure, however, though significant, was less than in previous years and it is possible that Oban is now declining as a fishing port, as boats tend to favour Mallaig, Uig in Skye, Ullapool and Lochinver. These latter ports, being nearer to the fishing grounds, naturally attract a bigger fleet. In 1971, the lack of adequate pier facilities was a factor mentioned as the contributory element in the Minch fishing fleet preferring these northern ports. However, Oban was much nearer the markets and the decision in that same year of Oban Town Council, to shelve a £250,000 development scheme for the town's South Pier, came in for much criticism. One firm of exporters based on Oban had managed to capture Spanish markets by sending catches of fish landed at Oban to Spain in special container lorries. The decrease in the number of boats landing their catches has now led to a reduction in this side of the firm's business. The observation that the town is more interested in tourism than in consolidating established industries seems to be well founded.

One industry of particular interest is glass-making, producing hand-made modern glassware with distinctive colourings. The firm is a subsidiary of Caithness Glass Ltd, founded in Wick in 1969. The Oban Glass part of the set-up was established in 1970 with four glass-blowers being transferred from the parent Wick works to start production. At first the Oban prospects were good, until technical problems loomed large and the factory was closed down with the loss of eleven jobs. But, after a soaring increase in the demand for glassware, it was decided to restart the Oban factory and, at the same time, instal new plant. The product, Oban Glass, is now showing sales figures which are comparable with those of the parent factory and has placed the Oban side on a sure footing, offering good prospects for the fifteen full-time employees and the half-dozen extra staff called in during the tourist season to cope with orders. The parent firm employs over 100 people and the extension to another part of the Highlands is being seen as a good case of cross-fertilization.

In 1947 a mill was erected in Oban for the production of tweed cloth. At the time this was a much-needed employment facility and, at the peak of production in 1951–2, took some 150 men and women out of the unemployment queues. In 1959 the original firm was bought out by a larger holding company with a similar cloth-making factory in Keith, in Aberdeenshire. In 1971 the firm gave notice of closure, throwing forty-five people out of work. The main reason was that the plant required modernization and that the cost of this could not be justified in view of a £100,000 modernization programme carried out at the Keith works. The closure of the Oban factory came at a time when the order book was full. But centralization, necessary it seemed for the greater viability of the parent operation, was the overriding consideration and the outpost had to be sacrificed.

The island of Kerrera lying in Oban Bay is a green fertile island covered with good pasture grazed by livestock. The island has a slight industrial diversification in the Lorn Lobster Industry, which takes the form of a packing station at Horse Shoe Bay. Here, rafts floating on the sea's surface may hold as many as a thousand lobsters, brought here from the storage pond at Cullipool to be sent to market. In former times, Kerrera was important as a stage on the route from Mull, and the islands beyond, to the mainland. There was a ferry from Auchnacraig, at the south-east of Mull, to Kerrera, and thence from Kerrera to Oban. At the end of the eighteenth century some 2,000 head of cattle were conveyed annually to the trysts, as well as a considerable number of horses. The population in 1861 was 105; at present it is less than fifty.

Cowal is a long peninsula lying between Lochs Fyne and Long; part of its coastline lies in the Firth of Clyde. The geology of Cowal is a continuation of that of Kintyre proper: mostly quartzose mica schist with narrow bands of metamorphic limestone. Old Red Sandstone appears at Toward Point and at Ardlamont, at the southernmost tip of the province on the west side. In this area crofting as such has now disappeared and much of the land is under Forestry Commission plantations. The area from Strachur to the Holy Loch, where the hills rise very steeply and shadow the narrow Loch Eck, is extremely good for forestry, the rainfall being very high. On the south coast lie Dunoon, Inellan, Tighnabruaich and other towns which have developed from being obscure communities to popular Clyde holiday resorts. Most of these communities and their associated hinterlands saw their maximum population almost two centuries ago, and then a gradual decline, due to migration to the industrial magnets of Glasgow and Clydeside. Though the population of the area has declined, however, this really applies at the present time to the rural parts. Dunoon, the main town, supports a population of 10,000, compared with Inellan (1,200) and Lochgoilhead (400).

A large part of the peninsula forms the Argyll National Forest Park. Though it lies close to the industrial zone of mid-Scotland, it is a region of quite different character and scenery. Rugged bens soar from sea-lochs and foothills are clad in green woods of spruce and pine. The park extends to some 60,000 acres in the five forests of Ardgartan, Glenbranter, Loch Eck, Glenfinart, Benmore and Ardgoil. It is so broken up by mountain peaks that it can only be approached by one of two routes; these are linked by a good road but not by through public transport. The main camping site is at Ardgartan, well placed on a promontory jutting out into the sea. Above it rise the well-known climbing grounds of the Cobbler and the peaks of Beinn Narnairn and Beinn Ime. On the east side of the Holy Loch, close to Kilmun Church, stands a forest garden containing many plots of unusual trees. The park was the result of a committee set up in 1935 by the Forestry Commissioners to advise, among other things, on recreation. The park was, in fact, the very first of its kind to be created and was in existence for ten years before the Dower Report advocated the setting up of National Parks in England and Wales.

Dunoon, the chief town of Cowal, derives its income from the many thousands of tourists who make their annual way out of their stressed and overcrowded environments to sample the mind-stretching spatial facilities provided by Cowal. The town has an ancient lineage going back to the eleventh century and has loomed large in subsequent centuries in both political and economic history. The first official ferry service began in 1658, operated by the Campbells of Ballochmyle under a charter from the Marquis of Argyll. But the importance of this link between the urban area of Glasgow and the rugged Highlands was diminished when the first overland route was opened up round the head of Loch Long. It was the advent of the steamship on the waters of the Clyde which began to change Dunoon from a collection of thatched cottages, huddling round the church on the hill where the castle chapel once stood. The first recorded account of Dunoon as a holiday resort dates from 1779. In that year a Glasgow family named Reid embarked at the Broomielaw in a hired wherry and set out for Dunoon. It was a potentially dangerous journey: the trip took most of the day because their boat stuck on a sandbank and the family had to wait until an incoming tide floated her off. The family was in no doubt as to the 'safari' character of their trip, for they took with them provisions to last them out the summer because they could put "no dependence on getting provisions, not even fish, in such an out-of-the-way place". After their arrival in Dunoon, they found the only person who could speak English was the minister. Things have changed since; though Gaelic was spoken quite freely in Dunoon until a century ago, it is not spoken at all now. The first Clyde steamer, Henry Bell's *Comet*, made its maiden voyage down the Clyde in 1812, to open up an era which, while not displaying its former glory, is still significant to the economy of Dunoon and the rest of Cowal. Everything in the town is geared to ensuring that the holiday-maker goes back home with the memory of a good time and two weeks' glorious refreshment—even if the sun does not shine all the time. When one considers that Dunoon's population trebles in the summer months, it takes little imagination to realize that Dunoon is the holiday capital of Glasgow folk, a veritable New Delhi.

9

The Inner Hebrides

IN common with the islands of the Outer Hebrides, the islands of the Inner Hebrides have a sad history of depopulation stemming from long periods of socio-economic depression. That they have tended to suffer more is due to the fact that they lie close to the Scottish mainland and therefore are in positions which have brought them under the more direct influence of 'civilizing' agencies. In addition, and this applies particularly to the islands in the South Minch (Coll, Tiree and Colonsay), they have appeared as attractive, self-contained estates and as such have frequently come on the market to be sold, with their human residents, like goods and chattels at a second-hand auction mart. Some of the islands are now social tragedies, witnesses to the failure of their owners to fully appreciate the social responsibilities which come with land possession, with the inevitable result that their resident populations have been, sometimes slowly, at other times rapidly, replaced by a non-indigenous resident population. While this in itself may be satisfactory—in that it would be a greater tragedy if an island were to become wholly deserted of population—it is a thought that only recorded history will remain as evidence of an island's former character and the role it played for an indigenous population which was for centuries Gaelic-speaking and so able to make a significant contribution to the corpus of Gaelic traditional culture. One island, Rum, is today devoid of any socially-significant population whatsoever except for

Oban from McCaig's Tower

Castle Stalker, Loch Laich

Inverary Castle, Argyll

resident and visiting scientists and tourists. Maintained now as an experiment in conservation, it supported a population of over 400 less than two centuries ago. Perhaps it is their accessibility to external influences, their smaller populations (in the case of small islands in particular), their tenuous grip on a fragile economy, and the real events in their history which have caused these smaller islands to succumb to the factors which have contributed to their present state and status in the rather peculiar and particular realm of Scottish islands.

On the other hand, there are islands which seem determined to maintain themselves into the years of the near future at least. Islands such as Canna are fortunate in having sympathetic owners who, fully immersed in the ethos of island-living and in Gaelic-based lifestyles, are able to offer to an indigenous population standards of living which, in the context of certain closely-defined sociological terms, both satisfy and offer rewards of a special kind. These communities are rare, however, and as yet their only important function is to act as bright stars in an otherwise darkened firmament, and to underline the simple fact that perhaps it requires special people to accept that there is more to living than obeying the call of a factory hooter, an office clock and the doubtful attractions of urbanized jungles.

Inevitably islands have formed the most difficult nuts to crack in the programme of regeneration, repopulation and development of the Highlands and Islands Development Board. For a number of years after the board was established, islands, except those which already had some kind of viable and realistic economic base, had to stand aside until the board had managed to close its credibility gap and move the location of the economic centre of gravity in Scotland from the central belt of the country to a little farther north, using Invergordon as a magnetic growth point. The main problem, from the board's viewpoint, has been that island-based communities are special in that they have rather peculiar and stylized ways of living which differ from island to island, and tend to contain themselves within definite social and economic parameters. On many islands it is essential for the maintenance of the community to ensure that a viable relationship is established and nurtured between the population and the available natural resources, whether these be land-based or in the surrounding seas. This, in fact, is the extreme end of the Highlands and Islands population problem: the matching of population to existing resources—and it matters little in general whether it is an island or remote mainland community which is being considered.

Part of the problem with islands is the hard and sad fact that communities are often too small to support even a minimal provision of the range of social services which urban communities find on their doorstep and thus take for granted. In former times, even when the populations of individual islands were larger, the communities tended to be self-sufficient and satisfied with both occasional and irregular facilities of access to larger communities usually on the nearby mainland. Nowadays, daily access is required for educational and medical facilities, and unless a community is self-perpetuating, with a potential for socio-economic viability, the political administrator will endeavour to run down services, mainly by hastening the process of centralization. It is, of course, a paradox, in terms of per capita expenditure on services, that the smaller the community the greater the costs in granting access to these services.

The tragedy of our society today is that it has created contemporary social and economic standards which dictate the minimal conditions for survival. If a community falls below a certain numerical level, the process of depopulation, leading to desertion, follows rapidly and the decision to withdraw minimum provisions becomes as much a political as an economic decision. However, it can be argued that island communities, from a social point of view, are but part of the larger national community and as such, irrespective of the numbers involved, are entitled to the same range of services as are provided for those who live in conurbations. The outstanding fact of the Highlands and Islands of Scotland is that the region still supports a significant population of island-dwellers. The influx of new blood into island communities could be justified on economic grounds; but whether this has been followed by a true social integration with the indigenous population has depended on many factors, not the least being that the incoming population has often little or no common ground with the resident population from which to begin tentative negotiations for the future of the island. In particular, a cultural gap often exists between the new and old residents of an island, a gap which often is based on a language difference; each group will thus try to assess the other's values in a context which is obviously prejudiced. Cultural and often linguistic differences, different lifestyles, different ceilings and character of ambition over a life-span: all these can contribute to the widening of any gap which might initially exist between incomer and resident. When the old residents are inferior, either socially or numerically, the island generally tends to lose its place in the old Hebridean order of things—though, of course, it maintains its geographical location as an island in the Inner Hebrides, and, often, is significant in the overall picture of land use. The islands of the Inner Hebrides prove a picture of extremes. Many are in a parlous social state and one can thus appreciate the plea for time on the part of the Highlands and Islands Development Board to take a look, first at the more immediate and short-term soluble problems of the Highland region and then to look at the islands to see what can be done, both for the islands themselves, as part of the pattern of land use, and for the island communities.

One of the very real problems of all the Scottish islands is the high cost of shipping and ferry charges. In 1971 Professor Maxwell Gaskin of Aberdeen University was commissioned by the Highlands and Islands Development Board to survey the cost of freight and to enquire into whether this was a factor which militated against economic and social development in the islands. The board was convinced that increased shipping charges were impeding development and so initiated the survey which, it was hoped, would produce the confirming evidence. It was much to the board's surprise that Professor Gaskin claimed in his report that freight charges alone are not a deterrent to island development: "I have formed the view that in no areas of economic activity, existing or potential, are freight charges in themselves a significant deterrent to desirable change." Some developments, he pointed out, such as the manufacture of heavy and bulky objects, were inevitably excluded by the transport factor. "But such extreme cases aside, it appears to me far easier to exaggerate than to underestimate the significance of freight charges, particularly when one considers the whole range of factors which determine location decisions." Among these, labour supply, both in quantity and in skill qualities, appeared to him to be far more decisively adverse to development in many of the islands than the freight factors. Other relevant factors were the physical nearness to suppliers or customers, or possibly to parent plants, ready availability of factory premises, provision of houses for key workers, and amenity.

Communications at times might be an adverse factor in island development. "As a problem, its dimensions have been vastly reduced by air transport, but the full significance of this may not be widely appreciated." The most general conclusion reached was that the burden which high freight costs laid upon the islands took the form principally of an income-reducing effect. "This operates most pervasively by raising consumers' prices in the islands above the level ruling in many mainland areas. Freight charges are by no means the sole cause of higher prices in the islands; but to the extent that they contribute to this they are responsible for reductions, of varying proportions, in the real incomes of the islanders." He estimated that these reductions might possibly fall within the range of 2–6 per cent.

Inevitably, the board was embarrassed by the report's findings, for it knocked down their main argument, as presented to the Secretary of State for Scotland, for proposing a new system of freight charges, based on the assumption that the high cost of shipping and ferry charges were impeding island development. But they issued in response to the report, a point-by-point statement which was derived from within their own experience. One example was a 20-ton lorry which normally costs about £5 to run 25 miles on the mainland, but which costs £80 at contemporary prices to travel the same distance across the Minch. The board's thinking on the matter was based on the simple proposition that water crossings should be regarded as extensions to the mainland roads, so that the charge for providing the 'flexible' or sea-borne 'road' should be related to the same base as was used for charging the building and maintenance of the national road network. The board agreed with Professor Gaskin's conclusion on the cost of living on the islands, but felt that the income-reducing percentages were on the low side. Even taking them as they stood, they were significant evidence from the board's standpoint, and tended to strengthen their arguments for special considerations to be given to islands. If the middle figure of 4 per cent were taken, this was a 'transport tax' equivalent to an increase of over 50 per cent in the income tax of a married man with two children earning £1,200 per annum.

The island of Raasay extends for some 13 miles along the eastern coast of Skye. It has a diverse character which presents much of interest to the botanist, the geologist and the archaeologist. The sociologist, too, will find much which will entertain him, surprise him, but also give him food for thought. The northern end of the island is composed of Archaean gneiss. Then occurs an area of Torridonian sandstone which, being in no place very high or much pocketed, is well drained. There are two considerable areas of granite and a cap of Tertiary basalt, the distinctive landmark of Dun Caan (1,458 feet). Oolite and lias are strongly represented, forming a long stretch of the island's east coast and crossing over the centre of the island before coming through to the west coast. The vegetation on this belt is good grassland. The part known as the Glen of Raasay is quite unique in the Highlands: it shows a good depth of strong loam at a height of between 600 feet and 900 feet. It is in fact one of the very few places in the Highlands where the techniques of deep ploughing and direct re-seeding of hill land can be applied. Bedded ironstone occurs at the south-eastern end of the island in sufficient quantities to have been worked earlier in the present century, around the time of the First World War. Inverarish, the main community on the island, consists of two inward-looking rows of houses which were built for workers in the mine. Prisoners of war were billeted here and worked in the mines to boost Britain's war effort—and, so it is said, sabotaged it at times by shovelling dirt out along with the ore. The mine was abandoned in 1920. In recent years several proposals to reopen the mine have come to nothing, mainly because the ore has only about 25 per cent iron content. Even so, the ore, which is self-fluxing, would normally contain after calcination more than 30 per cent iron, a figure which compares favourably with the English Jurassic ironstones. But the Raasay deposit is remote from established furnaces and the probable reason for its non-development is that there would be excessively high transport and handling costs involved in its exploitation, making the deposit uneconomic.

As mentioned, the rich vegetational cloak covering the basic Raasay rocks distinguishes the island from other Hebridean islands. There are well-tended crofts and fine livestock. A herd of Guernsey cows on Raasay Home Farm tends to raise eyebrows, but they do well on this green island. The Guernseys are probably at about a record latitude for the breed in this country and, because of this environment, are tending to develop a thicker winter coat. Their milk is of a high quality. Sheep-rearing is important on the island and is an activity in which many local folk are involved as an added source of income to supplement that received from crofting. The sheep are pastured on the rougher ground. Most of the shepherds participate continually in either of the two stock clubs. About 700 acres are planted with conifers, as part of the Forestry Commission's interest in Raasay. The commission has a small staff which is mainly engaged on maintenance work.

A sizeable community once lived at Arnish, at the north end of Raasay. The drift of population to the south end of the island has been accompanied by an overall drift to the mainland and to Skye. There is no fishing activity to speak of, no new forestry development, and no outside interest in the iron deposits. Crofting, an intensive activity in itself, is not sufficient to maintain a good standard of living. Tourism, however, does offer possibilities, though the island's present roads could never cope with any real influx of car-bound visitors. A useful number of tourists could, however, be accommodated. The income and stability which the tourist trade could offer would be important socially, in that the population could benefit from the 'extras': in better communications and increased social facilities, the former always laid on by the civic authorities for the tourist and rarely with the resident population initially in mind, though it stands to benefit.

In 1861 the population of Raasay was 388, a figure which rose to 478 by 1881. By 1951 the population figure had fallen to 290 and in the past twenty years or so has decreased further by over 40 per cent; at present the figure is under 160, with nearly half the population over 60 years of age. The Raasay people tend to be tied by place and origin to their home, more so than other island communities. In the middle of the last century, when the MacLeods sold the island to a sheep farmer, some ninety families were cleared to the neighbouring satellite islands of Fladday and Rona. It is only necessary to place a casual foot on Rona, now uninhabited except for lighthousemen, to realize that farming here can be carried out only against impossible odds. A few years before the last war, some of the descendants of the clearance victims returned to Raasay and laid claim to what they considered was their rightful land. The claim was inevitably contested and taken to court, but the crofters won their case. For reasons which are now historical, Raasay is owned for the most part by the Department of Agriculture, which acquired the island at the end of the First World War. Raasay House, the traditional residence of the MacLeods since

Dr Johnson's day, became a hotel and was sold by the department to a wealthy doctor, backed by a syndicate, both originating in the south of England. An attempt was made by the doctor to renovate Raasay House and re-open it as an hotel, which was one of the conditions of the sale. But work came to a halt for some reason and the building is now deteriorating rapidly. The doctor owns a small part of the land on which it was recently proposed to build a ferry terminal, for a new car ferry to Skye. The doctor, however, refused to sell the land for the purpose of creating this essential link between the island and Skye. The affair caused national headlines and reached the heady heights of television; these underlined the doctor as representing the worst kind of absentee landlordism which, seen at its most extreme in the context of the Highlands and Islands, is a cancer and also commonplace manifestation of land ownership while shirking the inherent social responsibilities which go along with the land.

Matters came to a head when high-level officials tried to make personal contact with the doctor, popularly known as 'Dr No'. At the time of the flare-up it transpired that he had not even been on Raasay to see his property for a period of some ten years and thus had no first-hand information about the island and the needs of its people. The Highlands and Islands Development Board was drawn into the controversy and said that it would be willing to inject capital into the island for the development of tourism, but required the establishment of a vehicle ferry as a condition for its involvement. The board was strongly castigated for its refusal to meet a deputation of Raasay people led by the local Member of Parliament, which led to its being accused of favouring the landlord system rather than the indigenous population whose needs were of far greater importance. Apart from one guest-house and the youth hostel, there is no formal tourist accommodation on the island. At least three properties which are empty and derelict could be made into hotels. The board's offer thus could be of significance to Raasay in the fullness of time.

Meanwhile . . . the island economy and social patterns are slowly crumbling away. If nothing else, the public enquiry resulting from Dr No's refusal to sell the small part of land for a ferry terminal, produced essential information about the state of the island and underlined just how serious was the whole problem of Raasay's future. It was claimed that the island was nearing a point of no return. The ferry service as proposed would bring to the island cheaper food, transport of livestock, road maintenance and easy passage for islanders, vets and ambulances. The continual drainage of young men of working age was a particular problem. In 1972 some 40 per cent of the population were of working age; if this dropped to 30 per cent life could not be supported on the island. The lack of the ferry service created exceptional difficulties in times of emergency and it was claimed that if a person fell ill at the wrong time, death could possibly result because of the lack of proper medical facilities.

The island of Skye is a large mass dominating the west coast of Scotland and lying athwart the Minch, to offer shelter to much of the gashed and deeply-indented coastal areas of Ross and Cromarty. The island extends to about 430,000 acres and contains several small parishes. The proportion of inbye land to the total area is small: about 20,000 acres, of which about a fifth is in tillage. Skye is cut by long sea-lochs, so much so that no place on the island is more than 5 miles from the sea. Indeed, the extreme peninsulation of the island has had great social and economic significance. The narrow ratio of tillage and inbye land to the total acreage tends to reflect the different types of ground involved and the geology of the island, though the tillage and inbye ratio used as a social index shows an unsatisfactory state of affairs. The rocks of Skye are principally Tertiary basalt, gabbro, granite, Jurassic lias, Dolomite limestone, Torridonian sandstone and Archaean gneiss.

The northern two-thirds of Skye are typical basalt country. It is a porous rock which breaks down easily to form a brown loam. As a consequence, the smooth western glens of Trotternish, Haultin, Romesdal, Hinnisdal and Uig are good feeding grounds for cattle and sheep. Crofting lands appear on raised beaches. This basaltic area is the island's great pastoral wealth and has yet to be developed in full. The Cuillins are among the most spectacular rises in the British Isles. Composed of gabbro, a hard igneous rock, the peaks rise to over 3,000 feet. From a pastoral viewpoint, this area is useless, but it has a great tourist potential and as such is an amenity and asset of economic importance. The red granite area to the east of the Cuillin Hills is poor and covered with scree, though sheep graze successfully on the northerly hill of Glamaig. The south-eastern peninsula of Sleat is poor; peat covers the flatter parts and bogland is common. The crofts are small and are not able to compete agriculturally with those on other parts of the island. At the south-eastern part of Sleat, however, there is a coastal strip of about 3 miles wide. Though composed of Archaean gneiss, there is comparatively little peat and, as a consequence, the green hills, crofts and farms facing the Sound of Sleat are generally prosperous. At Tarskavaig there is good grazing with an expanse of well-drained arable land of light loam.

Skye is largely in the hands of small farmers and crofters. Since the schemes of land redistribution were undertaken by the Congested Districts Board at the turn of the century, and later by the Department of Agriculture for Scotland, there has been a progressive decline in the number of large owners and occupiers. The history of crofting tenure is well written up elsewhere (see Bibliography), but in Glendale an unusual situation exists.

To summarize crofting activity: a croft is first and foremost a holding or piece of land, varying in size from 1 or 2 acres to 50 or more acres (the larger holdings are usually called small-holdings). The crofters pay rent to the estate proprietor for the land, but the house on the croft is the crofter's own property, erected by himself or his predecessors. He may assign or bequeath his croft to someone else (subject to certain conditions), and normally the eldest son succeeds his father. If a crofter resigns his tenancy, the incoming tenant or landlord pays him a sum of money (as assessed by the Scottish Land Court) in compensation for the house and other 'permanent improvements' on the land. The crofting system and its history is an integral part of the socio-economic history of the Highlands and Islands. Towards the end of the eighteenth century, communities of small tenants occupied a farm or township (Gaelic: *baile*) on the run-rig system. They occupied the hill pasture in common. The arable land they divided into portions, which were re-allocated at regular intervals, usually annually, so that each man got his turn of good and bad land. For the land they owed the laird rent (in money or kind) and services (helping the superior at spring and harvest work, peat-cutting, and the like). Towards the end of the eighteenth century, the practice began of allowing each tenant to hold his arable land indefinitely (without periodical redistribution) while the hill grazings were still occupied in common. These permanent holds were called crofts. In its heyday, the crofting system required a great deal of co-operation. Neighbourliness (*nabachd*) was the principle of joint action. In addition to regulations fixed by the estate management and carried out by the factor's local agent (the *maor*), each crofting township, meeting in council or *mod*, made decisions as to what was to be done, how and when, and by whom. While this system was better than the older run-rig system, there was still no security of tenure, nor was there any protection from rack-renting and burdensome services. During the nineteenth century, the increase in large-scale sheep-farming and over-population operated against the system and led to its breakdown.

With more and more land being let as sheep pasturage to farmers from the south, which frequently meant depriving townships of their hill grazings, whole communities began to disappear to provide low sheltered ground for wintering sheep. By the 1880s the situation had become really intolerable and there began a vigorous and widespread agitation for the reform of the land laws. Gunboats were sent by the Government, at the behest of landowners, to Skye and other parts of the region to overawe the unarmed crofters who protested against flagrant injustice. The Reverend Donald MacCallum, a Skye minister, was jailed for "inciting the lieges to class hatred". One stirring episode, among many that could be mentioned in the fight for justice, was the Battle of the Braes in Skye when, on 17th April 1882, a contingent of the Glasgow police was sent to deal with the crofters there who had deforced a sheriff officer. The police marched from Portree to Braes and, in a narrow define, were met by the local folk. Sticks were used and there was some stone-throwing: "No life was lost, but much blood was shed. The servants of the law won the fight, but the people reaped the fruits of the battle." The fruits were, first, a royal commission, under Lord Napier, which made a thorough investigation of the condition of the Highland crofters; this was followed by the Crofters Act of 1886. This Act, known as the Crofters' Magna Carta, gave them three valuable rights: security of tenure, a fair rent and compensation for improvements.

In 1904 the Glendale estate was taken over by the Congested Districts Board, and in the following year the crofters were given the opportunity of becoming owners of their own crofts by paying annuities which were not any higher than their previous rental. The period set before them for payment was fifty years and during that period each crofter paid a sum equivalent to his former rent. But along with this, each crofter also had to pay higher rates than ordinary crofters, because they placed themselves in the position which required them to pay demands for owners' and occupiers' rates. In 1954 the Glendale crofters completed their fifty-year period of payments and became owner-occupiers in the full sense. In addition to their croft land, they owned the former Glendale farm lands with the lodge and fishing and shooting rights. The decision taken in 1904 by the Glendale crofters to ultimately become their own masters was regarded as being something of a gamble. But the feeling in 1954, when the last of the payments had been made, was that they had strong advantages over the ordinary crofter, and that the 1904 decision had been the right one in the long term.

Land use in Skye today involves livestock (worth an annual £200,000), farming and crofting, with pockets of afforestation operated by the Forestry Commission. The average livestock holding on a croft is about four cows and fifty ewes. The potential of Skye is, however, in cattle rearing. In the old days, some 40,000 head of cattle per annum were exported from Skye. At present all cattle sales in Skye are fully accredited under the brucellosis eradication scheme. Cattle are mainly kept for beef, with the exception of one or two dairy farms (much of Skye's milk is imported). In the last forty years or so the predominant breed has changed from Highland to Shorthorn crosses and to Aberdeen Angus. About 4,500 beasts are exported each year, perhaps half of this figure being weaned calves. The sheep bred on Skye are almost all either the Blackface or Cheviot breed, the former being the more numerous. About 12,000 sheep, including lambs, cast ewes and wethers, are sent off the island each year.

An interesting development was announced in 1972. This was the setting up on a commercial basis of the first intensive deer-farming unit in Scotland. The location is Scalpay, an island off Skye. An area of 4,000 acres of hill land on the north-west side of the island was fenced off for the initial herd of 150 red deer and thirty suckler cows. Previously, ninety hill ewes used this ground, but were removed to make way for the deer. The cost of the project was £27,000, and the venture received the support of the Highlands and Islands Development Board. The plan is to slaughter culled deer—stags only for the first few years—at fifteen months and ship them to Skye. Refrigerated lorries will take the carcases to the Continent where there is a huge demand for venison. The initial responses are good and the operators hope to have a herd of 600 to 700 animals within seven years, by retaining female stock for breeding, with an eventual annual cull of about ninety-five animals of each gender. The aim is for an annual income of £4,000 per annum, augmented by the same of beef from the suckler herd. The sheep were removed initially because they compete with the same grazings as deer, while the cattle complement the enterprise by removing the rougher grazing. The operators, the Walford brothers, took a lease on the island from the Walford Trust, to prove that similar enterprises could add significant elements to the Highland economy. As part of the programme, some existing cottages on Scalpay are being renovated for tourists.

There is often controversy about the presence of the Forestry Commission on Skye, revolving around whether the land used for trees would be better used as grazing for livestock. There are some thirty forestry employees on the island. They work on the 1,000 or so acres being planted annually and in the thinning of older plantations. Sitka spruce, much in demand for pulping, is well suited to Skye climatic conditions, but so are hill sheep and cattle. It has been suggested that more co-operation between farming and forestry interests would create a better environment and programme of land use. Forestry could provide, in belts of trees, shelter for stock, something which most of Skye lacks; too often an area is planted without regard to the possible use of certain of the better parts for animals or even cultivation. When one observes the drainage operations of the Forestry Commission on wet hillslopes, one wonders whether some of the capital and equipment might also be employed on some of the better hills to improve them for grazing cattle and sheep, and for the former in particular.

It is only in recent years that Skye has participated seriously in the Minch fishing activity, for the island has been long dominated by the importance of Castlebay, Stornoway, Lochboisdale and Lochmaddy in the Outer Hebrides, and Mallaig farther south on the mainland coast. The focal point in Skye at present is Uig. Here, despite setbacks and active opposition from official quarters, Captain Kenneth Stewart has established facilities which are of the greatest importance to the Skye economy and with consequent valuable social overtones. Captain

Stewart returned to his native island in 1968 to set up a fish-buying and selling agency at Uig, as well as a ships' chandlering business. He was a prime mover in a scheme which included massive in-season klondyking* and road-transportation of herring catches brought into Uig by the Minch fleet. The use of the facilities now at Uig is seen in the employment of up to forty men on a daily basis in an area of Skye which has always had the highest registered number of unemployed (20 per cent). The enterprise of Captain Stewart and his associates has not been without its setbacks. In 1970 both Norwegian and Faroese interests expressed the desire to start up a fish-processing facility at Uig and plans were prepared for the factory. But the Highlands and Islands Development Board advised them to opt for Mallaig rather than Uig. This was done in the context of the board's knowledge that Uig required a considerable injection of capital to make the whole operation viable: for breakwaters, dredging and pier improvements. Progress along the originally envisaged lines has, however, been made by the entrepreneurial venture. A fish-processing plant is in operation and the products are flown out of Skye to Glasgow and London. Blast-frozen prawns are in London within a period of five hours. The firm has a payroll of just under twenty persons and is being supported by local fishermen. In 1973 another problem loomed large. The pier owners, the Department of Agriculture and Fisheries, announced its intention to sell it to the Scottish Transport Group, on the grounds that the pier was primarily used for transport. But the pier was handling up to 2,000 crans of herring each day during 1972 and though the local fishermen thought this was more than significant, the department thought otherwise. In addition, the record of the Scottish Transport Group has not indicated that it is primarily concerned with community interests. A petition was drawn up with fishermen signatories from Broadford, Buckie, Castlebay, Fraserburgh, Peterhead and Stornoway. The boats at present using the pier represented a capital outlay in excess of £250,000 and in fact were paying pier dues and landing charges for facilities which were non-existent. The withdrawal of the pier from Uig for the use of fishermen would virtually create a dead area in Skye, for the replacement would in fact be a provision of a through facility represented by a Skye–Uist–Harris car ferry, with roll-on/roll-off facilities, hardly conducive to development and of benefit to the local community.

The problems of Skye have presented a considerable challenge to the facilities and expertise of the Highlands and Islands Development Board. It is an island community with a rapidly declining population, beset by uncertainties, tensions and fears for the future; there are,

* A term commonly used in the fishing trade for those large cargo vessels that buy catches of herring for processing abroad—derived from the Klondyke gold-rush during which dealers bought gold dug up by others.

within the community itself, many conflicting attitudes to traditional and new practices and developments. There is a certain kind of prosperity, derived in particular from the tourist sector of the economy, but a chronic emigration problem, an unbalanced age structure and high unemployment levels all contribute to the picture of an island with a clouded future. The Highlands and Islands Development Board has provided considerable assistance for economic and social development: by 1972 no less than £35 per head of population had been spent, spread over about sixty projects employing about three persons per project. The criticism that the board's interest in Skye is preoccupied with tourism may well be justified, considering that nineteen of the projects mentioned attracted about 45 per cent of the finance. On the fishing side, under a dozen boats have been assisted financially. At present there are about thirty boats fishing around Skye, giving employment to about sixty men who are mainly full-time. The main centres are at Portree and Uig. At one time there was criticism of the local authority that the fishermen using Portree pier were being sacrificed in the interest of the tourist trade in that proper facilities were not being provided for them.

One important facet of the Skye fishing industry is shellfish—and its problems resulting from intensive poaching and illegal trawling by non-island boats. This problem is now a serious threat to the livelihood of inshore fishermen on Skye, as indeed it is elsewhere on the Highland west coast. In many respects the 'cod war' between Britain and Iceland in 1972–3 was similar, except that the local fishermen were being hounded by trawlers who have made a systematic and planned destruction of the Minch fishing grounds. In 1972 a local boat set out from Skye to set its baited long-lines. No sooner had its crew done so than two trawlers appeared with their trawl in operation close to the shore-line, within the 3-mile limit. The men in the local boat asked the trawlers to steer clear of their set lines, which they did. As soon as the trawl had been completed, the trawls were lifted on to the trawlers' decks and the local men saw something like a ton of fish being discharged: huge cod and a preponderance of small immature bottom-frequenting fish (haddock, whiting and plaice). The small fish were shovelled overboard and the trawl set again and let into the water. The technique used was 'pair-trawling', in which a heavy hawser between each trawler is connected, and attached to it along its length is fixed a great trawl, to which weights and buoys are attached, to keep it in a fishing position. Heavy chains are fastened to the bag end of the trawl to take it right down to the sea bottom and keep it there. This contraption is dragged between the two trawlers along the sea bed to catch anything and everything in its path, and to leave behind it a trail of destruction, having crushed all kinds of small fish and shellfish. This was only one of many instances of illegal trawling at the present time.

Although appeals are made regularly to fishery protection ships, seldom, if ever, are any arrests made.

Late in 1972 the Skye fishermen proposed a scheme of dumping old cars and lorries into the sea in the island's sea lochs and bays. This would have two results: first, and most important, trawls would be badly damaged by the mass of metal; and, secondly, based on a suggestion by a Stornoway seaman, William Crockett, the dumping areas would act as new breeding grounds for shellfish. This technique has, in fact, been used off the coasts of New England, in the United States. When a fishery protection cruiser was stationed at Dunvegan the amount of illegal trawling was minimal; but the ship was withdrawn. The Skye fishermen in that year rightly asked for the same kind of protection against English-based trawlers as these same trawlers asked of the Royal Navy in connection with Iceland's unilateral declaration of a 50-mile limit. After hearing the complaints of the Skye fishermen, the chairman of the Herring Industry Board agreed that airborne control of fishing using helicopters would be the best method of protection. But, being based in far-off Edinburgh, the chairman tried to minimize the problem by saying that he did not think poaching within the 3-mile limit was as widespread as it was made out to be. The statement was made at the same time as one of the Skye deputation to the Herring Industry Board told of incidents in Loch Dunvegan, which is recognized as being one of the finest spawning grounds on the west coast of Scotland. These included skin divers going to the bottom of the loch bed after trawlers had used chain gear on it. They found large quantities of freshly broken scallops and a seriously disturbed sea bed. The problem has still not been solved by firm government action, despite threats by some fishermen to go to sea armed with rifles—which, in their view, is sadly the only way open to them to rouse a complacent Government which seems to have the vested interests of English-based trawler organizations more at heart than the poorer, yet socially more significant inshore fishermen of Skye and elsewhere. This indifference is in fact at least ninety years old and was the main reason why the Sea League of Barra was founded in 1930 (described in Chapter 10).

The economic picture of Skye contains some interesting elements. The distillery at Carbost produces a high-quality malt whisky; the plant is owned by Scottish Malt Distillers Ltd. The product is a malt which belongs to the West Highland group: a fine, subtly flavoured whisky. The distillery was established in 1830. The year 1972 saw 140 years of traditional whisky-making come to an end when the plant was changed to include a central mechanized process which produces the qualities of malted barley required at a more economical cost. The change marked the last of the forty-three distilleries operated by the group, which previously had traditional maltings. The whisky is now made by a steam-distillation process which has replaced the original exterior coal fires beneath the copper stills. The result is that the sole Skye constituent in Talisker Whisky is Skye water, the malt now being imported from mainland maltings. The capacity of the distillery was not increased at the time of the process changeover, and indeed the permanent work force was reduced from thirty-two to eighteen.

One of the natural resources on Skye is diatomite. This is a mineral formed from the fossil remains of microscopic one-celled water plants. It is a finely-textured substance; diatoms resemble chalk in appearance and are so minute that one cubic inch contains 40 to 70 million cells. It has a great absorbent capacity: one unit of diatomite is capable of absorbing three times its own weight of water. This simplest of plants derives its name from the Greek (*diatemno*: 'I cut through'). This in fact explains how the cell divides and constructs the missing half of its cell wall to remake two complete cells. The tiny cell walls are composed of almost pure silica, dissolved by rains, springs and rivers into the lochs and seas in which the diatoms exist. This silica is deposited at the bottom of the water when the plant dies. When diatomite was first discovered, Loch Cuithir was drained and the material extracted in three distinct operations, the first nearly eighty years ago, the second at the turn of the century, and the third, the most unimaginative, after the last war. Previously diatomite was dug out of holes, which were flooded overnight, while a pump had to be used to maintain constant level at the workings. Crude material was dumped beside the main road, risking further soaking by quick changes in weather conditions. Later, reloaded in lorries, the material was conveyed to Uig, where it had to be dried and partially refined. The consistency of the diatomite resembled diluted porridge, while ooze dribbled on to the Skye roads like gruel. During an earlier venture, the product was taken direct to a small jetty at Invertote, via bogies and a chute at the gorge nearby, and thence direct to Glasgow by puffer. The installations used in the last scheme were of foreign origin. Breakdowns were frequent and spare parts difficult to obtain. It seemed strange to the operators that while conveyor-belts for potash exports could be supplied to the Gilbert and Ellice Islands—12,000 miles away—no suitable equipment was available for the efficient and economic working of this deposit. Diatomite has a variety of uses which depend as much on its physical as its chemical properties. Its main use is as a filtering medium, but it is also used as a liquid absorbent, an abrasive in cleaners and metal polishes, as an insulator against both sound and heat, as a filler, an ingredient of paints and as a carrier for catalysts and insecticides. The chief occurrence of the material is at Trotternish, with the deposit at Loch Cuithir being some 22 acres in extent and up to a depth of 45 feet. This is a very large deposit by any British standard. A deposit at Sartil was worked from 1908 to 1913. More recently, the Loch Cuithir deposit was worked for ten years until 1959, when it was abandoned largely because of high transport costs. The Highlands and Islands Development Board has investigated the possibility of re-opening the deposit workings, using mechanized gear, to achieve an annual production of about 7,000 tons per annum.

At Dunvegan stands the nursery, an enterprise which Donald Tinker brought with him to Skye in 1965. In his first year of production (1966) the nursery produced over a ton of tomatoes and cucumbers. The latest figure is over 4 tons of produce, with an expansion of the venture to produce plants and forced flowers. Mr Tinker's enterprise has been recognized by the Highlands and Islands Development Board, which was worthy of support in that the nursery is yet another instance which proves that a largely hostile natural environment need not deter entrepreneurs from setting up small pockets of economic stability in communities which are in need of such injections to give them a purpose for living.

In 1967 Skye saw the first of its light industries brought to the island by the Highlands and Islands Development Board. The factory was opened at Bernisdale School, which had been previously gutted by fire. Because there was no ready supply of skilled labour, local applicants had to be trained to learn an intricate engraving skill. Some 15-year-old school-leavers were taken on as apprentices, but not all lasted the pace. Some became disillusioned at the intense initial work and effort involved in becoming a skilled operative; others were tempted away by bigger wages offered by construction schemes. These teething troubles were overcome eventually and the factory now has a small permanent work force and a resident manager. The products range from fancy clan crests to door-name plates, all of which involve engraving with precision machinery.

At the present time it is the ubiquitous tourist who is providing a significant cash supplement for many Skye families. Recent estimates indicate 700,000 tourists and some 200,000 vehicles arrive in Skye during the holiday months. This influx comes by way of Kyleakin ferry, from Kyle of Lochalsh on the mainland, the private ferry between Kylerhea and Glenelg, and from Mallaig to Armadale. The rapid increase in visitors has brought home the need for a Skye bridge. In 1970 a committee was set up to investigate the possibility of linking Skye at Kyleakin with Kyle of Lochalsh. Two years previously, the Scottish Council (Development and Industry) produced a detailed report in favour of a bridge, which was costed in the region of £3 million. The project is still being pressed for. The opening of an airstrip at Ashaig provided Skye in 1972 with a much-needed air link. This facility was constructed by the army under its O.P.M.A.C. scheme, which allows military personnel to be used for community needs.

Despite Skye's proximity to the mainland, remoteness is still a factor to be considered in many of the island's communities. An example is

Kylerhea. This community has at present a permanent resident population of six, compared with 150 in 1851 and 127 in 1881. There is no public water supply. Those houses which have piped water—which include buildings now occupied during the summer by people who have bought them as 'holiday' homes—have had to make their own small water reservoirs and cesspools for sanitation. There is no public electricity supply either. The old township road has a one-in-six gradient and takes only a little snow and ice to close it to vehicles from the village motoring to Broadford for essential supplies. Often the road, the only access by land the community has to the outside world, is blocked for periods up to six weeks at a time. The sea route is the Kylerhea–Glenelg ferry which was started in 1935 and in 1971 was threatened with closure because the link was uneconomic. The Scottish Transport Users' Consultative Council made no recommendation for its retention when a public enquiry was instituted to investigate whether hardship would occur to the community if the ferry was withdrawn. The composition of the council would indicate a general disinterest in the communication problems of remote mainland and island communities. The local authority, Inverness County Council, decided not to subsidize the ferry, although it was in its power to do so. The plight of Kylerhea highlights the plight of many communities which, because of railway closures, the withdrawal of bus services and the like, have made otherwise acceptable places as remote as points in the Sahara Desert, and has often placed these communities quite outside the normal provisions of social and other services which are taken for granted elsewhere. In places like Kylerhea, however, there is often found a determination by those isolated that the new situation will not force them away from their homes. Sometimes Christmas does appear. In 1972 the north Skye township of Bay, after many years of fruitless negotiations and applications, received a piped-water supply. The six-house community was given this service at a cost of £3,000, which ensures now that the crofters no longer have to go downhill, as they did previously, to their only source of supply, a well, and then trudge uphill with all the water required for both man and beast. The Bay success, however, only serves to underline the problem: the present-day costs of providing non-viable communities with services which, had they been provided with these even a decade ago, would, firstly, have cost much less, and secondly, have been provided for a greater number of people. There is a widespread feeling in the Highlands that there is an active policy of alienation being pursued to discourage people from living in remote areas. Even when the people of the affected communities offer help, in both cash and free labour, the authorities drag their feet. Often in one's travels in the region, one comes across a rough road, built by a crofter over a period of years by the labour of his own hands. This is determination indeed on the part of an individual or

Looking down Loch Sunart towards Strontian

(*top*) Uig Bay, Isle of Skye. (*bottom*) Portree, Isle of Skye

a family to keep hold of what is recognized to be valuable, not in some remote economic sense, but in a rather intense personal context. It does seem strange to foist on society a welfare situation which tends to diminish the will of the individual to strike out for himself, while those who could be termed real individuals are loaded with more difficulties to cope with than seem justified.

One problem which has grown out of all proportions in Skye, as elsewhere in the region, is the withdrawal from the community market of houses suitable for local people by their purchase by people from the more affluent parts of the British Isles for use as 'holiday homes'. Many newly-weds find themselves unable to compete with the inflationary prices now being paid for croft houses which are occupied for only a small part of each year. Ruined buildings have actually been advertised for sale in the *Inverness Courier*, with the purpose of attracting purchasers from outside the region. The prospect of young families having to live in caravans until local authorities build houses is a daunting one. This, in conjunction with a high unemployment rate, inevitably leads to thoughts of migration to other parts of the region, or outside it, which offer better prospects for living. The clearances of the Highlands is a continuing process and has not finished by a long chalk.

For a mainland community, the prospect of the future is a dark one at the present time; for an island community the prospect of the future is even darker and also contains an element of tragedy. The population decline in Skye has been rapid. In 1841 the island's population was 23,082. By 1951 it had fallen to 8,267 persons; it was 7,478 in 1961. The present figure is just under 7,200, representing a loss per annum of about 100 persons in the past two decades. The feature of this migration is that it is mainly composed of young people, married and single, which leaves Skye with a seriously imbalanced population-age structure. Some parishes are worse off than others. That of Kilmuir has lost more than half its population in four decades.

In 1949 a submarine cable was laid across the narrows at Kyle of Lochalsh and the southern end of Skye up to Broadford, to provide the island with its first public electricity supply. A small hydro-electric station had been completed at Nostie Bridge, about 6 miles from Kyle, the previous year to be augmented by a diesel plant at Kyle. These two stations supplied Skye. Until 1949 the only supply was at Portree: a small diesel plant belonging to Portree Hotel which was used to supply street lighting and a number of houses in the village. In 1952 the Hydro-electric Board commissioned the station at Storr Lochs and Skye was then provided with its own independent supply. In 1956 Raasay was included in the Skye electrification scheme, being supplied by a submarine cable laid across the Sound of Raasay. About 99 per cent of consumers on Skye, about 4,000, are connected to public electricity cables. The board employs a small staff on the island—in connection with the station, electricians, linesmen and commercial staff.

There is an adequate distribution of general medical practitioners and district nurses throughout the island. The early years of this century saw the building of the hospital in Broadford and the fever hospital in Portree. At the same time the geriatric hospital, a much-needed facility for old people, was opened in Edinbane. In later years the John Martin Maternity Hospital was built at Uig. At the present time the services of visiting specialists are available to the islanders. Serious cases are taken to the central hospital complex at Inverness.

Portree is the island capital with a population of about 1,000. It is a straggling town with a magnificent square as a saving grace. This accommodates a handsome war memorial designed after the style of an old Scottish market cross. There is an excellent secondary school, county buildings and a hostel for boys. There is a moderately flourishing export trade, mainly in fish, cattle, sheep and wool. The only industry is a small tweed mill. The town is at the centre of the island's road system. Broadford has a pier and the usual social services. Kilmuir has Skye's first museum, opened in 1965. It comprises an old croft house renovated and re-thatched, with many interesting exhibits reflecting Gaelic life in Skye, including a communion cup used at Trumpan Church in 1579. Perhaps one of the most interesting places to see in Skye is the restored water mill in Glendale. This building was subjected to restoration work in 1971. When work began only the walls of the mill and part of the waterwheel remained. This building is part of a project designed to bring vitality back to Glendale. The project received the support of local men and others who saw in the venture the seeds of regeneration of a kind so much needed elsewhere in the Highlands. The owner, Peter Macaskill, won through a vast amount of initial inertia and disinterest. The complex contains an old 'black house' and the replica of an old illicit whisky still.

The island of Soay lies on the western side of the entrance to Loch Scavaig in Skye, and not far from the famous Loch Coruisg. The island rises to a height of 455 feet and has some respectable sea cliffs. The rocks are of Torridonian sandstone; between them are some good patches of cultivable ground. Towards the end of the sixteenth century Soay was described as a very rough island "where deer used to be and hunting game". Before 1823 Soay was inhabited by only one family, that of a herder employed to look after the stock on the island. Soon after that date the island began to fill up with families evicted from the districts on the nearby island mass of Skye. Because it was largely an infertile island, efforts were made to establish an industry. According to the reports of the Highland Destitution Relief Society, in 1849 there were on the island two east-coast fishing boats which employed eight east-coast fishermen and six natives, one east-coast fisherwoman and four native women, and a fishcurer. Six native boats were supplied with fishing lines, each with a crew of four. In the following year, there were four east-coast boats and six native boats, altogether giving employment to forty-four men. The industry failed to get off the ground, however, and the economy of Soay tended to stagnate. In 1861 the population was 129. By 1951 it was thirty. Early in 1953, when the population had dropped further to nine families totalling twenty-five people, the islanders were evacuated at their own request and settled on Mull.

The island was later re-settled by incomers, and the 1961 census recorded a population of eleven persons. In 1945 the proprietor of Soay established a slip and a small factory for handling the carcasses of basking sharks, which fish are numerous in the waters of the Minch during the summer months. This activity had waned by 1950. The story of the sharking has been recorded by both Tex Geddes and Gavin Maxwell. The island was once a port of call for MacBraynes vessels, and a launch owned by the proprietor was used for general passengers and goods from the island to Glenbrittle or Loch Scavaig on Skye.

To the south-west of Soay, across the Cuillin Sound, lies a string of islands: Canna, the farthest west, Rum, Eigg and the satellite Muck. This is the parish of small isles. The island of Canna, and its neighbouring Sanda, are in some respects more akin to the Outer Hebrides rather than to the Inner Hebrides. Because they are sheltered from both north and north-east winds, winter leaves the islands early and daffodils can be in bloom by the end of January. Canna is not such a mountainous island as is the larger Rum to the east. Its ground slopes gently from the south. On the north side, however, are sea cliffs which rise to some 600 feet above the water and offer a habitat to large populations of sea fowl. The peak of Canna is Carn a' Ghaill (690 feet). Another hill, Compass Hill (458 feet), is conspicuous from Canna's harbour. This hill is noted for its effect on ships' compasses, derived from the basaltic rock from which it is composed. Pennant, in his *Voyage to the Hebrides* (1776) wrote: "On the top [of this hill] the needle in the mariner's compass was observed to vary a whole quarter; the North point standing due West: an irregularity probably owing to the nature of the rock, highly impregnated with iron." Martin Martin (1703) also mentions the hill in his *Western Islands of Scotland.*

Although Canna is remoter in distance from Rum, Eigg and Muck, the other islands in this parish, it has a firmer hold on a maintained and continuous dynamic social and agricultural existence. It is fortunate in having an excellent sheltered harbour, of which the island of Sanda forms one side. It is also fortunate in its basic rock of terraced Tertiary basalt, covered with good green grass. The Cheviot sheep on the island are thus of high quality as is the high cattle stock maintained on the island. A careful watch is being kept on the cattle–sheep ratio, essential if the problem of bracken is to be kept to manageable proportions. At the eastern end of Canna the arable ground is based on Tertiary tuff, which is even more fertile than the basaltic soil. A very high standard is thus maintained of land use with these incentives. Excellent crops are grown and, sheltered from the direct blast of wind and sea by Sanda, it is reckoned to be among the earliest ground in the whole of the West Highlands. Early potatoes can be produced for market by the end of May. Fishing boats find the island's shell-sand beach of the harbour more than useful and a freight steamer can come in alongside the pier at all times except during the low spring tides.

In Thomas Tennant's time (1776) the population of Canna and Sanda combined was 220. In common with other island communities, depopulation has been a feature of the social pattern. By 1881 the population had fallen to a drastic sixty-two. However the 1931 census returned a figure of sixty, indicating a reasonably stable environment. But by 1951 it had again fallen to twenty-two, which number is maintained at the present time. The island is owned and farmed by Dr John Lorne Campbell, a man who has made an inestimable contribution to the corpus of Gaelic tradition and literature. He has published a number of books ranging from Gaelic glossaries to analyses of traditional song and story, and has contributed many papers and articles on all aspects of Highland history. His wife, Margaret Fay Shaw, published in her own right an excellent book dealing with South Uist traditions, recognized for its musical content as being among the most relevant and important collections of the present century. Dr Campbell has not always concerned himself only with locked-up and living Gaelic traditions. From 1933 to 1938 he lived on Barra and, with the late Sir Compton Mackenzie, promoted the local inshore fishermen's protective association, known as the Sea League, of which Dr Campbell was secretary and Sir Compton president. The league, described in Chapter 10, existed to promote the interests of Hebridean inshore fishermen who were then suffering—as indeed they still do—from the piratical activities of English-based trawlers in the Minch fishing grounds. In 1938 Dr Campbell made the first-ever electrical recordings of Gaelic folk songs in the Outer Hebrides, which were published by the Linguaphone Institute in 1938.

In olden times Canna was much frequented by Baltic traders, attracted by the island's sheltered anchorage. It was also used as a staging point on the long sea journey from the Uists and Barra to the Scottish mainland. Until the middle of last century, Uist seafarers used to row large open boats all the way to Glasgow, their craft laden with hides and other produce, to return with essential stores. Tobermory, on Mull, was another important staging point on this route. The constant plying back and forth between the islands was a unifying factor which linked, albeit tenuously, all the islands of both the Inner and Outer Hebridean archipelago, and gave the island communities a real sense of identification with their common socio-economic bases.

The island of Eigg (Gaelic: 'a hollow') lies nearest to the Scottish mainland, the 'urban' link between Arisaig and Mallaig. This basalt island has a high potential fertility which has, sadly, been allowed to go into a derelict state. Over 5,000 acres in extent, Eigg has a great deal of low ground, which makes the highest peak, the Scuir of Eigg, 1,289 feet, an outstanding landmark. This eminence stands sheer from the 1,000-foot contour and is a residual block of pitchstone lava resting in an Eocene river bed containing fossil driftwood, itself above the Tertiary basalt. The river bed is now on the top of the hill, except for the gigantic Scuir.

Eigg's township, Cleadale, lies on the north side of the Bay of Laig. For a number of decades, Eigg has seen its population–age pyramid gradually becoming distorted. When a survey was carried out of the west Highland area in the 1950s, the surveyors commented that the future of the island as a crofting unit was precarious. The population in 1795 was 399; 309 in 1861; 138 in 1931; and 115 in 1951. At present the figure is less than seventy. The island, apart from Cleadale and its grazings, is used for grazing both sheep and cattle, with a welcome increase in recent years in cattle stock, to create a better use of the land. Bracken, however, is still a problem on Eigg. Because it lacks a good harbour or safe anchorage, Eigg has ever had to rely on a ferry service between calling steamers and the shore. This lack has prevented the island's agricultural potential from being fully developed.

For many years the island was the property of joint owners, one of whom was Sir Steven Runciman, the historian, along with his ship-owning brother. The estate is a small paradise of lush woods, rare birds and wild flowers, with three modern farms, and a lodge set in a tropical garden. The woodlands extend to some 50 acres and are predominantly larch and pine. When the Runcimans bought Eigg in the 1920s, they took both a benevolent and practical attitude to their new role as owners of an island, and to those of the resident population who found their fate in the hands of strangers. Evictions, characteristic of the eras of previous owners, were brought to a halt. Whatever profits were made from the farms were ploughed back to strengthen the community and, in general, good living conditions were created. Facilities were provided, the result of the appointment by the owners of a first-class factor who set about erecting a foundry workshop and sawmill. The 7,000-acre home farm is entirely self-sufficient. One of the most modern hay-drying plants was erected on Eigg a few years ago. But the problem of depopulation, stemming from the lack of a real programme of community development, was aggravated by increased mechanization. The times of squads of six and eight men scything grass, cutting swaths 12 feet wide and 18 inches deep, are now all gone. In 1966 Eigg was put up for sale at a figure of £100,000. The prospectus said: "Today it is one of the few places left in the world where over almost half a century one family has transformed a rugged, beautiful island into a peaceful retreat. Woodland has been planted, a delightful country house built, safe from the inroads of civilization, with attractive modernized cottages and a productive hill and stock farm. The natural harbour and pier provide a base for cruising to the innumerable islands and beautiful sea lochs of Western Scotland, and on the island itself there is shooting and fishing, broad sandy beaches and seclusion unaffected by the modern world."

In the Bay of Laig are 'musical sands', which emit sounds under the traveller's feet, resembling the strains of an Aeolian harp. This sound occurs at times of change of temperature, such as at sunset.

Muck is the smallest island in the small isles parish, extending to under 1,600 acres. It has one hill which rises sharply to 451 feet; otherwise the greater part of the island is low with a high proportion of the arable ground on the north and east sides. Being based on Tertiary basalt, the island is extremely fertile, especially on the north side where there has been a contributory element from wind-blown shell sand. Less fortunate than Eigg, apart from a small but insufficient anchorage on the south-east corner of the island, there is no safe anchorage on Muck and, despite its high degree of fertility and that in such a small area, the future of Muck as part of a continued pattern of occupied islands is held in great doubt. Only through the tenacity and benevolence of private ownership has the community held together. In 1795 the population was 193. In 1828 there was a mass emigration from the island, reflected in the 1861 census return of fifty-eight people. Since that time the population has held steady. In 1921 it was forty-two; in 1931, forty-eight; and in 1951 about thirty. If Muck is ever deserted by its resident population it will be the result of the reduction of communications by sea rather than a hostile environment providing only subsistence living, for the island is eminently viable and an excellent environment for any community.

The island of Rum is the largest in the small isles group. It is about 20 miles in circumference and extends to about 30,000 acres. It is different from its neighbours in that it is particularly mountainous. Several of the peaks on the south side of the island are over 2,000 feet; the highest is Askival at 2,652 feet, which terminates in a sharp, pointed and almost inaccessible pinnacle. One remarkable geological feature on Rum is the vein of blood-stone at the north-west corner of the island which is, however, not considered suitable for commercial working. The coasts of the island are generally steep. The main access to Rum is at Loch Scresort on the eastern side, facing Sleat in Skye.

For many years Rum has been known as the 'forbidden island'. MacBraynes steamer does not touch the pier in Loch Scresort, but merely anchors in the open loch; passengers are then transferred to the island's motor launch—but only if permission has been obtained from the proprietors, the Nature Conservancy.

In 1595 Rum was described as a "forest of high mountains with an abundance of little deer". In 1795 the population was 433. Then, in 1826, by enforced eviction and emigration, about 400 of the inhabitants left for America, leaving a residue of about 130 people behind. The island was then turned over to the ravages of 8,000 sheep. In 1861 the population was seventy-three and fifty-three thirty years later. In 1951 the figure was twenty-five and the present resident population is about forty, including ten children who attend the school which also serves as a church. The population is in fact the staff of the Nature Conservancy, which body bought the island in 1957 from Lady Bullogh. The Conservancy staff are engaged in farming, forestry, deer and scientific work relating to the various unique aspects provided by an open-air laboratory, which Rum now is.

The island itself consists of a square platform of reddish Torridonian sandstone, between 500 feet and 1,000 feet high, with fine sea cliffs in places around the coastline. The northern peaks of Allival, Askival and Trallaval consist of rocks allied to gabbro. The scenery of Rum is quite unlike that of any other neighbouring island. The Cuillin of Rum are as bare as their namesakes in Skye, although Alpine plants abound, partly because of the absence of sheep. The only trees on the island are in the extensive plantations at Kinloch and a mixed wood at Papadil. A large area of granite exists west of the road to Harris, and extends to the western tip of the island at Steamer Point. The island's wild goats are seen in this area.

At the turn of the century, Sir George Bullogh, owner of Rum, built the imposing Kinloch Castle at the head of Loch Scresort, and endowed it with landscaped gardens, conservatories and a heated turtle pool. The lavishly furnished red-sandstone building had a relatively short hey-day, for the onset of the First World War put an end to the use of the splendid Edwardian edifice, reducing it to its present status: an impressive memento of a former era. After the Second World War, the island's grazings were leased to Walter Mundell, who built up a stock of fifty cows and their calves, 1,200 ewes and their lambs, and some 500 blackface wethers. But the venture was fraught with difficulties: staffing problems due to isolation, heavy freight charges, louping ill with lambs, and red water in the cattle, coupled with limited capital—all these militated against the whole operation being placed on a viable basis. In 1957 the Nature Conservancy took over the island because of its intrinsic value. At the same time the tenant withdrew his sheep and cattle and thereupon ensued a legal battle still remembered in the Highlands. The opponents to the Conservancy were the Northern Pastoral Club. The club contended that the incoming tenants should continue to stock Rum, which had been the subject of heavy government agricultural subsidies, and argued that the production of mutton was vital for the country at that particular time. Opposing this view, the Conservancy held that they should be allowed to go forward with their plan of solely maintaining the stock of red deer on the island. In the end the Nature Conservancy won, and since then the island has had a herd of about 1,500 red deer.

In 1959, the Conservancy began a ten-year survey to investigate the optimum culling rate and to study the behaviour, movements and feeding habits of the red deer. This has yielded valuable information. But there have been side effects. One professional stalker returned to Rum a few years ago after an interval of about twelve years' absence and was taken aback at the deterioration in the condition of the native red deer. There was little doubt that the loss of cattle and sheep over a period of ten years with a consequent lack of manuring and a coarsening of the grass had had a detrimental effect on the island's grazing.

Apart from the herd of about 200 wild goats, there are the distinctive wild Rum ponies which are supposed to have originated from horses which swam ashore from wrecked ships of the Spanish Armada. More likely these animals are related to the Eriskay pony. One aspect of the Conservancy's research has been an investigation into the methods needed to restore vegetation after over-grazing and over-burning. It has been suggested that the Conservancy should evolve a policy which would show other estate owners in the west Highlands the best way to achieve integrated management involving not only wild life but also domestic stock, forestry, fishing and tourism. There is an extreme shortage of ploughable ground on Rum, there being only a few acres at Harris on the west coast, in Kilmory Glen to the north and some more of indifferent quality in Kinloch Glen on the eastern side. There is remarkably little coastal grazing, the general nature of the coast being high cliff. The Old Statistical Account of 1793 complained of Rum's remoteness and the difficulties of living on the island, and it is thus perhaps not so surprising that by the middle of the nineteenth century, the island had become a self-contained deer forest. At the present time it is possible to visit Rum on day trips only. Visitors are welcome in that they offer the introduction of an essential ecological element which, were it lacking, would create a false environment for research. There are efforts to ensure that man as an element in Rum is not a destructive one. Longer visits are thus allowed by the Conservancy but usually only to scientists, naturalists and qualified mountaineers.

The social history of the small isles parish is one of a serious decline in population. Being small islands, they offer a special kind of environment; their usefulness to man, resulting from their characteristic climates, soils and minerals, is inevitably modified by the isolation imposed by the surrounding waters and by the degree of access available to the communities. Thus, Muck is in the worst position, being, as it were, more of an oceanic island, unlike Canna, which is rather an offshore or outlier. In general, the greater the difficulty of access, the more is the reduction in the effective value of intrinsic resources. The highest population for the parish was recorded in 1821, with a total of 1,620 persons, an increase of about 700 persons over the previous seventy years. After a sudden decrease to just over 1,000 persons in 1831, the population figure was reasonably stable for three decades until another sharp decrease brought the figure down to 567 in 1861. From then on the decline has been gradual and at present totals some 140 persons, representing less than 10 per cent of the maximum 1821 figure. The clearance of the island of Rum had a profound effect on the overall pattern of population. The present density is hardly acceptable in terms of a viable community; the tendency now towards an ageing population means the inevitable process of desertion within the next two decades or so. When the Highland Transport Board reported in 1967 about the state of the transport services in the Highlands and Islands, it was pointed out that it was essential to have the sea services to the small isles considered as part of an integrated system served from Mallaig, the nearest mainland port, and further suggested that one vessel, of the fleet of David MacBrayne Ltd, the *Loch Arkaig*, be devoted to servicing the islands. However this vessel is not adequately fitted for the carriage of goods and livestock, an essential provision if these islands are to continue their existence and justify this by the undoubted contribution they can make to the national economy.

Lying athwart the eastern side of Mull is the island of Coll, about 13 miles long and of average width 3 miles, with a slender taper towards the south. The island extends to just over 18,000 acres. The main port is Arinagour, on the east side, situated at a small indentation made by a sea-loch; it is, in fact, the only possible place where a port could develop. A pier was constructed in 1933, a provision made after thirty-three years of agitation. Coll is composed of Archaean gneiss, an extremely old rock formation which does not of itself break down into good soil. It is characteristic of the gneiss to form low rocky hills with numerous lochans, and this is the nature of Coll: low-lying with the highest point reached in Beinn Hogh (340 feet). The south-western end of the island is mostly overlaid with deep shell sand, a feature which at one place between Breacacha and Caolis results in several hundred acres of sand dunes, some 100 feet high. This area is of limited value for agriculture as it is waterless and subject to drought. Truer machair land occurs at Caolis and Crossapol. These areas provide excellent grazing and are of immense importance to the economy of Coll. There are many fine sand beaches, though in general the coast is rocky. An archipelago of skerries and small islands lies to the north-east of the island and offers good breeding grounds for lobsters.

The roads on the island, about 20 miles or so, are mainly laterals; suggestions made over the past two decades for a circular road to the north have been ignored by the authorities. Yet, such a provision would open up other areas and indeed provide a useful social function in that 'visiting' could be more agreeably and incidentally carried out, an essential facility in any small community. A deep-water pier has for long been another issue. Not so many years ago it was necessary to manhandle livestock on and off the island. Cattle had to be slung aboard the launch and then on to a waiting steamer. The inevitable repercussions on the state of the animals was seen later at market. In 1944 it was made compulsory by law for pregnant animals to be slung in a horse-box to and from the vessel. Again, however, pregnant animals were often late for market because the weather conditions prevented on-loading. Good facilities, as an essential for animal husbandry on the island, are thus important for the sustenance of the economy.

In 1840 the island supported about 1,400 people, representing problems of congestion. One-third of the population had to be supported directly by the Laird of Coll, because the island could not raise the sustenance necessary for the whole population; this drain on the laird's resources prevented him from developing the existing farms. The contemporary cattle stock was about 1,300 beasts, with an export of about 220 head per annum. A further eighty to ninety head were slaughtered each autumn. There was also an unproductive stock of about 500 horses, ponies of the Barra type, which were a severe drain on grazing.

As a first step in solving the problem, the laird reduced the sheep stock to 500 animals, for, with some remarkable foresight, he realized that the presence of the sheep jeopardized the stability of the machair by their digging up the stems of the marram grass and breaking up the sward so that the sand was exposed to blowing by winds. The second step was a drastic one. In 1852 a clearance was organized in which the bulk of Coll was cleared of crofters, though the township of Arinagour was established as a measure of mercy. Two years later the land, now distributed into farms with new houses and steadings, was offered to incoming farmers from Ayrshire. The result was a period of increased prosperity. The present population is thus derived largely from the Ayrshire-Kintyre pioneers of 1854 with a minority of true Highlanders of crofter-fisher stock. The general outlook is therefore that of a farming community rather than crofting.

The present population structure has deteriorated considerably, particularly in the younger age groups. In 1861 the population was 779; 210 in 1951 and at present is about 150. The population of Arinagour is high compared with the services which the township returns to the community as a whole. Arinagour has a post office, hotel, two churches, a school, with private and local authority housing. The hotel is the only licensed premises on the island. Enjoying such an amenable climate (an average of 1,300 hours of bright sunshine annually), Coll has proved popular with holiday-makers, though accommodation has often proved inadequate for the numbers who visit the island each year. An airstrip on the island has proved a valuable communications asset.

At the turn of the century 'Coll Cheese' was renowned, and indeed reached 'connoisseur' degrees of perfection. It was said that specialists could name the farm that had produced a cheese by detecting its particular flavour. During the last war, cheese-making was centralized by a creamery at Breacacha, but the factory was closed down, mainly as the result of the prohibitive cost of replacing old equipment. The annual exports from Coll include sheep and cattle, some 600 head annually, with wool, bulbs, potatoes and whelks.

An interesting development is taking place at Breacacha (Gaelic: 'speckled field') Castle. The island home of the original MacLeans of Coll, it was probably erected early in the fourteenth century, about the time when there was a considerable redistribution of territory in the Highlands and Islands, in which Angus Og of Islay was granted the island of Coll among other extensive Highland districts. The castle is small, sited with easy access to the sea, and is considered to be the most perfect and least altered example of a medieval stronghold in the Hebrides. The main part of the castle is the rectangular towerhouse or keep, with additions of outer buildings to the south and east, including a round tower. The keep itself was four storeys with a garret. The castle was bought in recent years by Colonel MacLean Bristol, a descendant of a branch of the original Coll family, who is developing the castle to become the headquarters and training centre of an overseas voluntary aid organization which hopes to send up to 300 young workers to under-developed countries in the next few years. The organization, the Projects Trust, is designed to encourage, select and train young candidates up to the age of 21 for voluntary work in many countries. The only cost to the candidates is that of getting themselves to Coll. There they remain the responsibility of the trust until they return to their homes waiting overseas posts. Colonel MacLean Bristol has said: "Islands like Coll produced an enormous amount of manpower in the past which went all over the world, and they were empire-builders. This was because they had a certain toughness, having been brought up in a place like Coll. Such a place has a lot to offer those living in urban surroundings, even if it's only for a few weeks. The majority of candidates, in the 18–19 age range, have a year or so to spare before going to University or to full-time jobs." The trust's training scheme has already produced over 100 trained volunteers.

Close by the castle is the 'new' castle, a mansion built about 1750 by

Hector MacLean, who was chieftain at the time of the Forty-five. He was the uncle of Donald, 'Young Coll', the lively figure of Dr Johnson's book. It was in this house that he and Boswell stayed for some time when they visited Coll in 1773.

Cornaig Bay, to the north of the island, was once a busy spot for the fishing industry, but has been deserted for decades. This decay was the direct result of the depletion of the fishing grounds round Coll shores by trawlers. Ling fishing, salting and drying was once an important island activity, exceeding 120 tons per annum at the turn of the century. Today, to catch a ling in Coll waters is rare. Lobster fishing is prosecuted but not to its full potential.

The island of Tiree, lying to the south of Coll, provides a unique environment, which is partially reflected in the air of prosperity which one meets on landing on the island. It is a low-lying mass, set in the sea with only four rises above 100 feet. Although officially belonging to the Inner Hebrides, it is in fact farther west than Lewis and much of Harris in the Outer Hebrides. The island is about 34 square miles in extent; it is about 12 miles long with a width which varies between 1 and 6 miles. Being almost flat, with a consequent lack of rivers (save one: An Fhaddil), the Atlantic winds race across the ground. The average rainfall is quite low (50 inches) and the island has the highest number of sunshine hours recorded in the British Isles. In summer, the green of the sand-based machair, the blue of the surrounding sea and the silver of its many beaches make the place one of subtle charm and quiet beauty. The island lies on a base of Archaean gneiss in which there are a few dykes of hornblende. There is a moss in the interior and an area of good-bodied loam above Balephuil; but the island is largely influenced by shell sand, so that its Archaean character is seldom seen and has thus become a freely draining calcareous terrain of wide expanse which is readily ploughable. At one time Tiree was known as the granary of the isles. Because of its calcareous nature, Tiree is essentially a stock-raising island and the concentration in fact is quite remarkable. There are about 12,000 sheep and about 4,000 head of cattle, about a tenth of which is exported each year. Dairy farming tends to be restricted to local use. The cultivation of crops is largely confined to providing fodder for winter feeding, although the mild climate permits most cattle to remain outside during the winter months. Farming is the main occupation. Fat cattle lie contentedly at the water's edge. Often the wind whips up the sand of the pulverized seashells and carries it to the meadows, spreading over them more efficiently and regularly than any machine a layer of natural fertilizer. Its constant moisture makes pastures abundant with clover. The crofters raise beef cattle for which, each year, dealers pay top price. At one time bulb-growing seemed to offer good potential for development and a boost to the economy; but the venture failed. Tiree-grown bulbs, however, were of very high quality, rivalling Dutch bulbs; but they required too much labour at an inconvenient time of the year. Tomato and lettuce growing in the northern part of the island has had a reasonable success and has laid the foundations for further development to become an activity in its own right.

The present structure of society in the island, and its land-use pattern featuring co-operative action, was not achieved without a struggle against the evictions of the nineteenth century, enforced emigration and the amalgamation of the land into big tenanted farms. This regime, in neighbouring and comparable Coll, resulted in the total clearance of its indigenous population, and today it is probably approaching a crisis of under-population. By the year 1845 the Tiree crofters had lost all security of tenure and were in the main found to be working at a wage of £6 the half year, with £3 for women, on the big farms newly created. Hundreds emigrated temporarily and annually to supplement these wages by working at the harvests in lowland Scotland. It was at this time that many of the people built houses on the foreshores, which they could not be prevented from doing, or in the townships, with only the permission of the controlling committees; this has resulted in many of their present-day titles being only 'squatter' or 'cottar' titles. The matter, however, is of little contemporary consequence. In 1884 the tenant of a big farm, Greenhill, gave up his tenancy to emigrate to Australia. He had promised the people that the land would be broken up again into crofts, but the lease of the whole farm was granted instead to his brother. The would-be crofters invaded the farm, tore down fences and uprooted a hen roost to provide themselves with staves with which to fight the force of police summoned to quell them. There was no battle, but a surreptitious arrest of the ringleaders was later made and they were imprisoned. In the summer of 1885, H.M.S. *Ajax*, with a force of thirty soldiers, was sent in to deal with fresh agitation. Again there was no fighting. The soldiers stayed to help with the harvest and then left. The Crofters Act of 1886 then appeared to give such crofters as remained on Tiree security of tenure. The final break-up of the big Tiree farms which has produced an admirable pattern of land use, was not begun until 1910 and then took until 1921 to complete.

Fishing is an important element in the Tiree economy. At one time great quantities of cod and ling were caught, to be salted by the ton to serve as food during the winter. This activity has now disappeared as the result of over-fishing by trawlers. Whiting can still be caught but, though excellent for eating, they are too soft for salting. Lobster fishing, however, has remained a profitable sideline to crofting. In 1972 the industry was given a boost by the construction of a new jetty and access road at Caolis, on the north-east of the island. The facility was provided with aid from the Highlands and Islands Development Board. The value of the catch in 1971 was in excess of £16,000; more than double the 1970 figure. About fifteen boats fish mainly during the summer months. Most of the craft are small, with one large boat recently introduced with a keel of 36 feet. The new jetty is in a natural harbour and the access road now allows fishermen to transfer lobsters to Scarinish where they are picked up by the steamer for sale in Oban. Scarinish itself is the old harbour of Tiree, used for long by the Tiree luggers which carried coals, peat and other goods, and brought in essential items to the island. The harbour is tidal and small, but has a pier constructed in 1914. The main pier for Tiree is in Gott Bay, which allows the steamer to make fast in almost all conditions. The bay itself, however, provides good anchorage. In 1973 the *Loch Seaforth*, of the MacBrayne fleet, went aground at Scarinish pier to block access to other shipping. For some weeks after the ship, holed below the water-line, caused great concern because the island became slowly strangled by lack of goods into and out of the island and fears were expressed that the economy would be damaged. Indeed, until this ship was raised Oban markets were lost to cattle-breeders and relief ships had to anchor off-shore and be served by a ship-to-shore tender. Bulk essentials such as feeding stuffs were almost rationed. The situation in fact underlined the total dependence of the island on good sea links with the mainland.

Tiree has a daily air service which uses an airfield established during the last war. The roads are good, the result of the R.A.F. requirements. Glasgow is less than an hour away from Tiree and an increasing number of tourists make for the island annually. The tourist industry has in recent years become an important element in the island's economy, with many private houses catering for guests. Interesting developments, associated with the tourist, include crafts (making jewellery from the high-quality marble found encrusted in Tiree rocks) and a bakery, set up with the aid of the Highlands and Islands Development Board, for local consumption and the tourist trade. Until 1972 all bread in Tiree was imported from Glasgow, which made it at least two days old before it reached the island's counters. The new bakery produces fresh bread and assorted baking items for hotels and boarding houses; it employs young people and is acting as an incentive to the improvement of catering standards. The Old United Free Church at Gott Bay has been converted into a factory containing knitting machines.

The island society is a close-bound community, but not without problems. Depopulation is no stranger. The maximum population in Tiree occurred in 1831—some 4,450 persons. Thirty years later the figure had dropped to 3,200. In 1931 a figure of 1,448 was returned and by 1951 a further drop to 1,206 was experienced. The present figure is about 1,000, of whom 300 are over 65 years of age. The two most populous areas on the island are Scarinish and Balemartine. Many young people now prefer to leave the island, and this drain has tended further to distort the population age pyramid. Another rather peculiar problem is the high incidence of blood pressure and other factors which contribute to heart disease, an ailment which is appreciably greater in Tiree than on the mainland. Scotland itself has one of the highest incidences of coronary disease in the world, and the population of Tiree has been found to have an unusually high proportion of the factors which contribute to cardio-vascular disorders. The cause of the island's difference from the mainland incidence rate has not yet been isolated.

Many of the houses on Tiree are the product of the island's windy situation. Basically of the 'black house' type, there is a built-in chimney in the gable end (an advancement from the design of earlier times which had a hearth in the middle of the floor); they are square-cornered and plastered outside, thereafter being whitewashed. The gable extends above the roof timbers and heavily-tarred felt takes the place of the original thatch. The house walls on the Tiree houses are especially thick (up to 9 feet) and the wall to windward is thicker than that to leeward. The roof still comes to the inner edge of the walls, but as the old dry-stone principle of a house that 'breathes' has now been abandoned by plastering and lime-washing the exterior, the top of the wall is usually cemented over and a channel made in the cement to take away rain-water. These houses are cosy and comfortable and are provided with all modern amenities. In addition they are entirely in keeping with the landscape and are eminently products of the Tiree environment. There are at present about twenty houses of the old black house design with thatched roofs surviving; they have low 5-feet-thick cavity walls.

The island of Colonsay lies in the Firth of Lorne, 10 miles to the south of Mull. It is about 8 miles long and about 3½ miles at its widest part. Extending to some 10,000 acres, the island, like its southern satellite of Oronsay, is composed of the lower mudstone strata of Torridonian sandstone, intersected with a few dikes of basalt. The highest hill is only 470 feet. The surface of the island is quite broken to provide a wide range of scenic views; and there are sharp escarpments above the shore at the north-west part of the island. The general vegetation complex is that of heather-sedge-bent fescue moorland of the sweeter kind. There are small areas of natural scrub consisting of birch and oak, with occasional appearances of roan, hazel, willow and aspen. Shell-sand dunes and incipient machair are found at Kiloran Bay in the north-west and at Ardskenish to the south-west. There are several good beaches and strands on the west coast. A large number of raised beaches on the island have produced a light, gravelly but calcareous arable soil. The most interesting physiographic feature of Colonsay is the valley of Kiloran, in which the proprietor's house, Colonsay House, is situated. The west-coast escarpment is 400 feet high and slopes very gradually eastwards into the valley about a mile and a half away. The east-coast heights of around 300 feet also slope gradually westwards so that the valley is unusually well sheltered from the Atlantic blasts and has the advantage of extreme maritime mildness. There is, in fact, no comparable situation in the whole of the west Highland region as Kiloran. Successive proprietors of the island have taken advantage of the opportunities to create policies, plantations and an excellent farm. The tropical gardens are an unusual attraction, rivalling the gardens at Inverewe in Wester Ross. The species here include rhododendrons, azaleas, magnolias and embothrium; bamboos and palm trees grow in the open. The village of Scalasaig on the eastern side of the island acts as the island capital. It lies on the edge of a shallow bay on the east side and has a pier, built in 1965 at a cost of £159,000, for steamers. Before the pier was constructed, the visiting ship had to anchor offshore and be serviced by a ferry boat.

The present population of Colonsay, just under 140 persons, is well stratified: farmers, fishermen and crofters, to those who provide professional services, and tradesmen. It is, as might be expected in a close-knit community which maintains an intense interest in its identity, more than concerned with its present as it affects the future and in the hard business of survival. This latter aspect of Colonsay life is much dependent on an appropriate shipping link with the mainland for services, supplies and markets which it does not have itself and without which it could not exist as a viable entity. In particular, Colonsay's problems echo those of other islands in both the Inner and Outer Hebrides and in the northern archipelagoes of Orkney and Shetland.

Quite unlike, say, the Norwegian Government which recognizes that all parts of that country, including islands and remote mainland areas, must contribute to the national whole and be integrated as fully as possible to enable them to make that contribution, the British Government, through its agency in Edinburgh, seems to be blind to the fact that while England and Wales have no serious 'island' problems, Scotland has a significant population, amounting to approximately 120,000, still living on islands. Thus, an appropriate shipping link must, in the context of Colonsay, mean that which most nearly reconciles economic viability with users' needs. For many years Colonsay has been served by the ships of David MacBrayne Ltd, now part of the larger and state-operated Scottish Transport Group, which serviced the islands of the Inner Hebrides with multi-purpose ships and an all-round transport system. MacBrayne's operations in the four islands in this area (Colonsay, Jura, Islay and Gigha) have cost the Government astronomical sums in subsidies. Yet a private company, Western Ferries Ltd, has been able for some years now to operate a successful ferry service, carry their own risks and that with a notable degree of success. However, the suggestions made by representatives from Colonsay that the company could include Colonsay in their routes would mean the

Loch Scavaig and the Cuillins from Elgol

Stacking peat on Skye with the Storr in the background

Loch Leathan and the Storr

reconstruction of the pier at Scalasaig at a further cost of £60,000, to cater for the bow-loading roll-on/roll-off ferries.

At present the island is served from Tarbert, Loch Fyne, a distance of 50 miles, and is part of the runs which also serves Jura and Islay. The suggestion of a new route, originating from Oban 40 miles away, seems to offer a solution which would match economic viability with the needs of the islands in that, in summer months, tourists based on Oban would welcome a circular tour (Oban–the islands–Tarbert and back to Oban by road). When the Secretary of State for Scotland announced in 1971 that he was proposing to withdraw the subsidies from MacBraynes, who then operated the islands' sea services, and apply it to Western Ferries Ltd, the reaction was dismay in Colonsay, for the proposed service (being a vehicular service only) hardly suited the requirements of the island. Efforts were made by local representatives to meet their counterparts of the Scottish Office in Edinburgh, the Scottish Transport Group, the Member of Parliament, the county council, and the Highlands and Islands Development Board. But no one in any official capacity wished to discuss the matter of Colonsay's communications; only the Development Board came to listen and advise, but little else. It is not surprising that the islanders were ready to fall into a state of despondency, and were at a loss to understand why the Government was prepared to spend £159,000 on a pier which was outdated within five years of its completion. Nor were they able to understand why an automatic telephone exchange costing £68,000 was installed on the island and put the local exchange operator out of a job. The island still lacks mains water and electricity. There is the widespread feeling on Colonsay that officialdom is playing games in its usual inimical fashion with only one ending: inconvenience to the Colonsay community. In 1973 it was announced that Colonsay was to be given its much-wanted link with Oban, three times weekly, and it is now to be considered what will be the effect of the new service in the long term.

There have also been internal problems on the island which have more than concerned the community. In 1970 there was a dismissal of workers from the estate of the island's owner, Lord Strathcona, which resulted in some emigration. The reasons given by the estate were that there had been a loss of several thousand pounds which meant an inevitable cut-back in staff numbers. The reaction of the community was to establish a committee to consider the simple, and at times complex, issue of survival. One of the community's contemporary problems stems from the fact that the proprietor's family has been for some fifty years a benevolent interest, almost cocooning the island and creating a social condition which, while it was stabilizing, was also stagnating, in that during the period the population had hardly decreased. While this in fact spoke well for the management of the island, the modern age, with its demands for the continual re-assessment of values and responsibilities in land ownership, set up its own conditions which the proprietors finally were forced to meet. The highest population occurred in 1841 with 979 persons, a figure which also included the satellite island of Oronsay. In 1901 the population had fallen to 213 and was still healthy at 227 in 1951, representing a net loss of only 86 people in half a century.

Oronsay, lying at the southern tip of Colonsay, is important for the ruins of Oronsay Priory, a magnificent structure built about 1380. These monastic ruins are said to be the finest in the Highlands. The island itself is joined to Colonsay by a tidal stretch of muddy sand. Both islands have produced evidence of habitation stretching over a period of some 7,000 years; the earliest remains found have been dated as being of the Azilian culture (7000–5000 B.C.). Neolithic, Bronze Age and Norse relics have been found in plenty. The many monoliths indicate that the islands have had a continuous history of some importance for at least two millennia. The priory ruins are impressive, both in their size and in their situation, and are second only to Iona in importance. The cloisters are still beautiful, though many of the arches of the arcading are broken; the medieval high altar is still in position, which is extremely rare. A dignified free-standing cross, with a crucifix dating from *c.* 1500 is perhaps the most beautiful stone cross in Scotland and is an excellent example of the art of the medieval church, so soon afterwards to be obliterated by the iconoclasm of the Reformation.

The island of Jura lies off the northern coast of the Mull of Kintyre. It is 28 miles long and about 8 miles across at its widest part. It lies in the southernmost group of the Inner Hebrides and is well protected on the south-east and west by Kintyre and Knapdale, and on the south-west and north by Islay and Mull. Craighouse is the main village and accommodates the usual social and commercial services. The island is about 94,000 acres in extent and is the largest expanse in the Highland region of that very poor rock, metamorphic quartzite. Only on an extremely narrow strip, on the eastern side, are different rocks to be found. The entire western side of the island is trackless and holds virtually no human habitation. The surface of the island is very broken and difficult to cross. In the southern half of the island are the fine conical hills known as the Paps of Jura, rising to 2,571 feet, with their lower slopes to the sea clothed in blanket bog. The northern part of the island contains rises which do not exceed 1,500 feet. The Paps themselves are composed of fine-grained quartzite, which weathers into angular fragments and covers the steep sides of the mountains with greyish-white scree. The prospect from the Paps may, on a clear day, include the north coast of Ireland, the Atlantic Ocean and most of the Inner Hebrides from the Skye Cuillins down as far as the Isle of Man.

The name of the island means in Gaelic 'deer island', reflecting its long history as a hunting ground rather than an island with any other purpose. The main activity on Jura is crofting, with supplementary employment in stalking. The present deer population is estimated to be in the region of 5,000, though this is regarded as being too high for the effective and healthy continuity of the deer population. More realistic figures suggest a population in the region of 1,500 with an annual cull of 250 per annum for marketing as venison.

A new modern and architect-designed malt distillery at Craighouse has yet to market its product, for whisky, if it is to be good, takes its time to mature. This takes the place of an older distillery which was closed down in 1912. The original works covered some 3 acres of ground and were established in 1810, built on a site where the smuggling founder of the distillery carried on his operations for many years without discovery. In 1875 the old distillery was modernized and designed for an output of 180,000 gallons of pure Highland malt. But the actual production was never much above 60,000 gallons.

The island is served by one main road which links the eastern and southern parts and Craighouse with Feolin Ferry, which looks across the Sound of Islay to Port Askaig on Islay. The northern limit of the road is Ardlussa. The maximum population on Jura occurred in 1841 with 1,320 persons, a figure which was halved by 1901 and has steadily decreased since then, though at a less dramatic rate. The present population is about 250.

To the north of Jura is Scarba Island, separated from Jura by the Strait of Corriebhreacan. This is the most formidable tidal race in the British Isles and has been officially deemed as unnavigable by the Royal Navy; its speed is about 8 knots. The direction of the flood is westwards towards the open sea, as a continuation of the tide running up the Sound of Jura, and eastwards on the ebb. It is at its worst when the flood tide is opposed by a westerly wind, when its roar can be heard many miles away. It contains dangerous overfalls—or patches of breaking water caused by irregularities, often very deep, in the sea bed—which are capable of overwhelming small vessels; and numerous whirlpools which, though they would not suck down a vessel, present difficulties in steering. There is only fifteen minutes of slack water time.

Islay is the largest island of the Inner Hebrides. Extending to over 150,000 acres, its geology is a mosaic of various rock types. The southern part of the Rhinns is of Archaean gneiss with characteristic topography. The northern part of the Rhinns, at Bridgene and at Bowmore, has calcareous Torridonian sandstone which is low in elevation. The north-east of the island is Cambrian quartzite with belts of limestone. Towards the south-east a belt of Dalriadian quartzite runs from Port Askaig district to the south coast of the Oa. This part is the most barren to be found on the island and is a sporting reserve. While much of Islay is green, with some good arable land, a quarter of the area is peat, used in the preparation of malt, which in its turn plays an important part in the making of the various distinctive Islay whiskies. The peat is still used as a domestic fuel.

The three main population centres on Islay are Bowmore, Port Ellen and Port Charlotte. Bowmore is the administrative centre with a population of some 900 which is increasing slowly (in 1931 it was 600). The township has many contrasts. Substantially-built traditional dwellings stand cheek by jowl with modern postwar effusions. The secondary school, hospital, council offices and fire station are located in Bowmore. Perhaps the most outstanding feature is the white-walled round church of Kilarrow. It dates from 1769; the legend is that it was built round so that there could be no corners in the structure in which the devil could hide. As with the rest of Islay, there is good accommodation for the tourist in the form of hotels and boarding houses. The road north from Bowmore passes the hydro-electric station, skirts Loch Indaal and takes one up to a junction beyond which, on a hill, is the memorial to John F. Campbell of Islay, who spent a lifetime collecting and preserving much of the lore and traditions of the Gaelic west Highlands.

Port Ellen is the largest township on Islay and is the island's chief port, airport and centre of activity. Accommodating several whisky distilleries, the port was built about a century ago and lies in a gently sweeping bay, protected by off-shore reefs and the headland of the Ard to the immediate south, and by the peninsula of Oa to the south-west. The Oa area has many cliffs and caves and was once the main location of illicit whisky stills and smugglers' hideouts. At the hill of Oa there stands the first landmark visible when entering Scottish waters: a monument erected by the American Red Cross in remembrance of those who lost their lives in the troopships *Tuscania* and *Otranto* wrecked in nearby waters during the First World War.

Port Charlotte is the main centre of the area called the Rhinns of Islay. A large creamery takes the island's entire milk production and converts it to cheese, which product has a considerable home and export market. Port Askaig, facing across to Jura, is a ferry terminal and more of a hamlet than a village. The pier handles the sea links with the mainland and the passenger traffic to Scalasaig on Colonsay. There is also a vehicular ferry which plies across the narrow Sound of Jura to that island. At Ballygrant there is a large limestone quarry which yields some 12,000 tons of ground limestone annually to meet the island's agricultural requirements and those of the adjoining islands. The quarry also supplies the island's roadstone and the needs of building contractors in the way of crushed stone and chippings.

Connoisseurs of malt whisky will be more than familiar with the products of the various distilleries on the island which grew out of the 'illicit' and 'home' distilling activities of about 150 years ago. Even at the time of the Old Statistical Account (1793) whisky distilling was a big industry in Islay and used, then as now, the extensive peat flats as a source of fuel. The *gearraidh*, or skimmed land, created by the continuous removal of the peat has, however, never been reclaimed for agricultural purposes as it has in other parts of the Highlands; perhaps this is because on Islay there was plenty of good land otherwise available. Even at the time of the highest population, in 1841, there was little effort made to bring this unproductive land into use to support the population. The presence of the extensive and easily-worked peat deposits made whisky distilling a natural activity for Islay, as did the excellent barley which the islanders grew in huge quantities on the lime-based lands. For some reason, Islay's whisky was not liable to excise duty on the island itself, and this led to some rather undesirable side effects. Ministers continually complained about the high incidence of drunkenness on the island; indeed, small tenants would sell their barley to the distilleries rather than using it for feeding their families. Many of the distilleries operated the offensive and pernicious truck system, whereby small advances were made on the barley crops and a man was tied to the stage where he was forced to take a price for his crop which was fixed by the distiller, even though it was below the general level. It could be said that even today the presence of the Islay distilleries on Islay tends to make a considerable imbalance in the existing uses of land and its potential, and it is surprising that a feasible and much-needed cash crop is not grown alongside the very industry which could use and absorb the total production on the island.

When Alfred Barnard made his remarkable tour of the distilleries in Scotland, and published his book on them in 1887, he recorded nine distilleries on Islay, some of which, like Lagavulin, claimed descent from smuggler origins. The present Islay whiskies produced by the seven distilleries share with those produced in Campbeltown the same feature that distinguishes Highland from Lowland malts: the malted barley is dried over peat. They tend to be powerful in flavour and bear some traces of their seaside cradle, although they are less heavy than old Campbeltown. Lagavulin has a strong peaty flavour, which could be called aggressive, but once the taste is cultivated it forms a fast and firm friendship with the drinker and almost insists on being his exclusive drink. Laphraoig has been said to be the most distinctive of all whiskies. Some there are who say that they can taste the sea vegetation of the Islay peat in it.

The distilleries of Caol Ila, Lagavulin and Port Ellen are in the Distillers Company group. The Highland Distilleries Company, a firm which dates back to 1887, has Bunnabhain. The Bruichladdich distillery, situated on the shores of Loch Indaal, is owned by A. B. Grant Ltd. The Ardbeg distillery is independently owned; it was established in 1815, on a site which was previously noted for its being a haunt of smugglers. For many years supervisors had difficulty in tracing this particular nest of Islay traffickers; most of the band were known by sight and many were the escapades involving sea chases when the excise caught a whiff of a still. At length the spot was discovered and destroyed with the seizure of a large amount of illicit spirit. Later the site was occupied by the founders of Ardbeg distillery, who chose it on account of the water, whose chief characteristics are its softness and purity. The chief characteristic of the peat in the Ardbeg vicinity is the absence of sulphur and other offensive minerals. Lagavulin is said to be one of the oldest distilleries, going back to 1742, again to the concentration of about ten small and separate smuggling bothys which were subsequently merged into one 'establishment'. Smugglers in their time could clear at least 10s. per day and afford to keep a horse and cow.

Despite the potential of Islay, the island today supports only a quarter of the maximum population of 14,992, which occurred in 1831. Decline has been continuous since that date, and in particular the 'hubs' on the island have tended to attract the population from the remoter areas. The population in 1951 was 4,267. In the decade 1861–71, for instance, the rate of natural increase on the island was 4·9 compared with an emigration rate which at one time was as high as 28·9 per cent. In general there has been, since 1931 (population 4,790), a large natural decrease. Part of Islay's problem is its proximity to Glasgow, which offers a number of important incentives.

Internally, Islay is well supplied with 150 miles of roads which are tough and well-surfaced, though they are somewhat narrow in places. External communications include air, steamer and vehicular ferry. The air journey from Glasgow takes about one hour, via Campbeltown. B.E.A. operate a morning weekday service during the summer months, Mondays to Fridays. A comprehensive service is provided for passengers and freight by David MacBrayne Ltd, which also connects Gigha, Jura and Colonsay with Port Askaig and Port Ellen on Islay. The vehicular ferry is a roll-on/roll-off facility operating seven days a week (up to four times daily in summer) run by Western Ferries Ltd.

For many years now the problem of ferry services to and from both the Inner and Outer Hebrides and the mainland has been a baffling one. On the one hand there is the need of island communities to have easy, convenient and regular contact with important mainland centres; on the other, there is the desire, on the part of private and state-owned transport and shipping facilities, to provide the communications services at least cost and preferably at a profit, or with state subsidy. The controversial Islay run has generated heat for many years; yet it was easy to forget that the alleged culprit, David MacBrayne Ltd, carried a heavy responsibility over a century, usually against considerable odds, acting as the lifeline for many islands, running passengers, tourists, residents, freight, livestock and mails. Indeed, the inability of MacBraynes to run profitable services in later years was directly due to the massive depopulation of the region's western seaboard and meant an increasing difficulty in servicing communities with dwindling populations. In addition, when one is dealing with sea services, adequate provisions have always to be made even for a small number of people. On a bus route, it is merely the changeover from a large bus to a mini-bus to maintain a service at cheaper cost.

In 1965 a delegation from MacBraynes, Argyll County Council and the Department of Agriculture and Fisheries presented a plan to the islanders for a new service by large car ferry between West Loch Tarbert and Port Askaig, on Islay, also running to Colonsay. Jura would be serviced by a Port Askaig–Feolin ferry link; and Gigha would have a separate service. The plan met with immediate opposition. Instead, the now familiar 'overland' route (from Keills on Islay to Lagg on Jura and thence, more briefly from Feolin to Port Askaig) was presented as a more viable alternative and was argued for both fiercely and cogently by the Islay Transport Users' Committee and Islay District Council. The Secretary of State for Scotland favoured the MacBrayne plan, mainly on the grounds of cost and time. Nothing, however, was decided. In March 1967 the Highland Transport Board came out in favour of the 'overland' route, which also received the support of the Highlands and Islands Development Board. Despite these big guns, however, the Secretary of State decided on the original plan. Then, almost without warning, a new operator came on the scene. Western Ferries Ltd, who made a rather dramatic appearance. The story of this company begins in November 1966 when the landing barge *Isle of Gigha*, then owned by Eilean Sea Services, overturned at sea. Before this tragic mishap, she had given some good idea of the goods demand service that existed on the Islay run, and also what could be achieved with careful planning. From this grew a clear concept that the primary function of a ferry was to serve the whole community without exception, and that a purpose-built vehicle ferry running to schedule and carrying anything that uses a road—not merely a car ferry—was the desirable answer. Islay, with its thriving community, and with a steamer service which left much to be desired, was clearly a proving ground. In July 1967 the new company was formed and in April 1968 the ferry boat *Sound of Islay* started operations. It was modelled on a Norwegian-built ship which had plied in the waters of the Faroe Islands for years without losing a single day. A jetty was leased at Port Askaig and renovated at a cost of £18,000; a virgin island at Kennacraig in West Loch Tarbert was leased, a causeway built to it and a terminal from it out into the loch was also constructed at a cost of £22,000.

This was a startling new concept: the provision of a ferry service at a fraction of the cost had state-run or state-supported enterprise been involved. Economical and very competitive rates for passengers, vehicles, livestock and journey times were offered. In the summer of 1968 the ferry ran to about 85 per cent capacity. Thus, Islay found itself with two services. In 1972 a public enquiry was held into the proposal of MacBraynes to withdraw their services to the islands following a government decision to end their subsidy in respect of their routes to Islay, Jura, Colonsay and Gigha. Despite decades of grumbling about the services provided by MacBraynes, there was in fact a whole-hearted support for the older company; this was because Western Ferries were unable to give an assurance that they could provide all the services which MacBraynes offered. The objections to Western Ferries included: the company could not cope single-handed with the expanding tourist industry; its vessels were lacking in comfort and unsuitable for the elderly and invalid; the small crew carried by the ferries would be unable to cope with an emergency at sea; and the terminals used by the company were in a state of unreadiness. Though the bulk of the objectors were from Islay, cases of hardship were presented on behalf of Jura, Colonsay, Gigha and Tarbert. In the event, MacBraynes continued their existing services. All the evidence at present available indicates a state which is not unusual in the region: a continued imperfect facility resulting from the often diametrically-opposed ideas of private enterprise providing suitable facilities and bent on making a profit, and government-run concerns—such as the Scottish Transport Group of which MacBraynes form a part—always mindful of getting the maximum social benefit out of the minimum cost, while presenting a face of bland unconcern to the real needs of the islanders.

Late in 1972 the Highlands and Islands Development Board announced that the mineral potential of Islay was to be the subject of a survey using geological, geochemical and geophysical techniques. Lead, with silver, was mined in Islay during the nineteenth century and earlier; occurrences of copper and manganese on the island have been recorded. The deposits of quartzite, limestone and ultra basic rocks had some economic potential. Veins rich in manganite (hydrated manganese oxide) form a network cutting quartzite at the southern end of the Oa peninsula. The locality is at the foot of a cliff; previous exploitation ceased because of the problems of access. There are numerous abandoned lead mines in Islay in the area to the south-west of Port Askaig. Some of them are very old, having been worked, according to legend, by the Danes and Norsemen. Authenticated records date back to the sixteenth century and mining was carried on from time to time until the abandonment of the most recent venture in 1880. Production in the final working period reached a maximum output of 291 tons of ore (218 tons of lead and 2,570 ounces of silver) in 1867. Trial pits were dug during the 1939–45 War and indicated that further investigation was not considered worthwhile. At least one mining group considered the prospects of central Islay in the late 1950s; although no developments resulted it was indicated that the area remained of interest.

The island of Gigha lies athwart the western coast of the Mull of Kintyre. It is a small island, 6 miles by 2, with an uninhabited satellite island of Cara to the south; it constitutes an area of over 3,600 acres of green and pleasant land with attendant unproductive areas of hummocky, heathery and bracken-infested ground rising to a peak of 331 feet in Creag Bhan. This latter is a good example of ice-ground rock and affords an excellent view of the neighbouring islands and Kintyre. Gigha has always been a fertile place; in 1955 there were thirteen productive farms (eleven now) and ten small crofts on the island. The island holds a good stock of tuberculin-tested Ayrshire cattle which represents a valuable export trade in both beasts and milk. The concentration on dairy farming and the production of cheese has led to an increase in the population of Gigha. A rule that every tenant farmer of Sir James Horlick's estate of Gigha island must run a dairy herd and produce milk for the island's creamery has bolstered a declining population figure and has provided an incentive to young people to remain on the island. Beef and sheep farming is allowed on the farms in addition to dairying, but, on an island where the Gulf Stream ensures grazing until December, dairying, with its higher returns and comparatively high labour requirement, has established itself as an ideal way of halting depopulation. The production at the creamery is a ton a day of the distinctive Gigha white cheese.

The proprietor of Gigha, Sir James Horlick, of malted-milk fame, is also a specialist in rhododendrons and has created extensive gardens which have not only led to the employment of many specialists, but added a very useful attraction to Gigha with a consequent effect on the island's economy in the tourist sector. The island tends to be regarded as being 'usefully remote': yet it is only 55 miles west of Glasgow as the crow flies. Sir James has proved himself to be an unusually responsible landlord, a rather bright light in an otherwise darkened Highland firmament. He has taken his estate to be more than a pleasure-ground for himself and his friends. He has encouraged development, provided water for houses and renovated farms and cottages. In 1955 a submarine cable was laid to bring electric power from the mainland. The island's consumption of electricity has soared from 186,000 units in the first year to the present figure of over 400,000, proof of a rising standard of living.

The population recorded for Gigha and Cara in 1755 was 514, a figure which remained steady until 1851, when it dropped to about 400, to remain steady again for another sixty years. Since 1911 (population 324) there has been a decline to 190 in 1951. The population today is still 190, with 60 of the inhabitants in the school-age range, surely the best sign for a good future. The 6 miles or so of roads on Gigha are sufficient for the few resident cars. The terminus for the Gigha ferry is at Ardminish.

In January 1973 the islanders found themselves faced with a crisis. The immediate cause was the withdrawal of the regular motor vessel *Arran* for a face-lift and transformation into a roll-on/roll-off ferry. The replacement link was a small launch from Tayinloan which could carry only thirteen passengers and half a ton of cargo at a time. It was stated by the owners of the *Arran*, the Scottish Transport Group, that there could be no guarantee that when the ship resumed normal service she would be a regular caller at Gigha. Maintaining a service to the island would require government assistance and this was to be seen against the regular sailings to Jura being abandoned because they were uneconomic. For an otherwise healthy and productive island community to be faced with the bland face of state-owned services, the problem became more of one of survival into the future. The previous regular service was of particular importance to the farming fraternity, who required something in the region of 2,000 tons of fertilizers and animal feeding stuffs to be imported into Gigha each year. With every farm supporting a dairy element a regular supply of cattle concentrates is essential; the problem of getting large quantities of cheese off the island was also of great concern. A hopeful sign came from the direction of Western Ferries Ltd who promised that if the island eventually found itself abandoned by the Government and the Scottish Transport Group, it would be serviced somehow by the private operator. At the time of writing the matter was unresolved.

On Gigha are the ruins of the ancient church of Kilchattan, Haakon's tumulus and the Ogham Stone, together with the remains of a Norse thing (meeting place for dispensing justice and making laws); this is a mound in a loch and is said to be the only structure of its kind in the Hebrides.

The famous island of Staffa lies 6 miles north of Iona. Less than a mile long and half a mile wide, it extends to little over 70 acres. The cave known as Fingal's Cave is the biggest of several on the island. The island is of Tertiary basalt surmounted by amorphous lava and is geologically associated with the smaller islets of the Treshnish group farther west, the southernmost islet of which is known as the Dutchman's Cap on account of its retained volcanic cone rising 284 feet from the sea. Staffa is perhaps the best-known tourist attraction in the whole of the Hebrides. As they were being rowed in a boat from Inchkenneth to Iona, Boswell and Dr Johnson passed the island but could not land on it because of the sea swell. Staffa had by then come to the notice of the public as the result of a visit made to it by Sir Joseph Banks, who brought the island's wonders into the itinerary of what was gradually replacing the 'Grand Tour' of Europe and which culminated in the late nineteenth century in visits to St Kilda at the "edge of the world". Sir Joseph's visit was made in 1772 and was an incident during a more serious journey to Iceland. The French geologist, St Fond, came to Scotland in 1784 to make a special visit to Staffa. Another visitor was the Welsh squire, Thomas Pennant.

The result of this attention was that Staffa became a 'must' and artists in particular flocked to the island. Staffa was inhabited in 1795 but not in 1837. St Fond says that in the year of his visit the population was two families, who lived apart in two huts, sixteen persons altogether with some livestock. Twelve years earlier, the island had only one inhabitant according to Banks who wrote: "There is only one hut, which is occupied by a peasant, who attends some cattle that pasture there. To testify his joy for our arrival, he sang all night long in the Erse language, which we did not understand. He regaled us with fish and milk." The famous Fingal's Cave is in fact an English translation of a misunderstanding of the Gaelic, An Uamh Binn, the melodious cave, so named on account of the strange music which the sea makes among the pillars of this natural cathedral. The highest point on Staffa (135 feet) is directly above the cave. The cave is about 200 feet long and 50 to 60 feet deep at its entrance. The island itself is grassy and featureless.

In 1972 Staffa was put up for sale at a price of £20,000, a vast increase in the price paid for it in 1968. The buyer was an 'unknown' person from the south of England. The previous owner had sought planning permission for a £1 million tourist development comprising an hotel, chalets and improved pier. This brought objections from the Nature Conservancy, the National Trust for Scotland and the Countryside Commission. The last owner's intention was to open up the island for tourists; the new owner is said to have bought the island largely for 'sentimental reasons'.

For its small size, the island of Iona occupies an inordinate place in the history of Scotland. This tiny island, lying off the south-west corner of Mull was, in its time, the source of Scotland's faith, its royal house and, indeed, her very name. To Iona in A.D. 563 came Colum Cille (St Columba) with a handful of followers to set up the small colony of Gaelic Celts, called Scots, who had moved from Ireland to carry light into a darkened country, as did the contemporary stream of Christian missionaries who brought their religion to England and Europe in a gathering tidal wave of humanity. By the seventh century, Iona was the unquestioned centre of Christian teaching in Europe, surpassing even the great Celtic foundations in Ireland. To Iona came men of religion; and from the island they went out to deliver their messages of peace and goodwill. They disseminated their knowledge to the daughter monasteries in Germany and Switzerland, and even to Italy: such was the sphere of Iona. The mortal remains of Scotland's kings were taken to Iona, and during the two centuries of the island's greatest fame and influence the bodies of royal personages, of chiefs and of noted men of the Church were interred in Reilig Orain, near where the cathedral now stands. According to a record dated 1549, some forty-eight kings of Scotland lie here, including Kenneth MacAlpin, the first king of a united Scotland; Duncan, the reputed victim of MacBeth; and MacBeth himself. Seven Norwegian kings and four kings of Eire also lie in this place.

The greater part of Iona is composed of Lewisian gneiss; on the eastern side of the island are clay beds of Torridonian age, minor igneous intrusions related to the Ross of Mull granite, glacial erratics and raised-beach deposits of late-glacial and post-glacial age. The 'Iona Marble', an altered gneiss of sedimentary origin, is found in bands in the gneiss, some 300 yards north-north-east of the summit of Dun Bhuirg and at the marble quarry on the coast. It is a pinkish-grey, mottled green by serpentine. Iona is not a mountainous island. The highest point is reached in Dun I (332 feet). The interior of the island is wet moor, much of it without paths. Yet Iona is extraordinarily green and fertile and blown shell sand at its northern end adds to make a pastoral excellence. The population of the island has always lived with the main attraction: the abbey, which draws many thousands of visitors each year. The population in 1861 was 264; 141 in 1931 and 173 in 1951.

Much of the history of Iona is confusing and uncertain. Even so, there is much visible evidence of the part which the island has played in Scotland's history. What is of even greater contemporary consequence is that Iona is still the centre of a movement which seeks for a better understanding between men and nations. In 1900 the abbey was in ruins, 700 years after its foundation as a Benedictine house. In 1938 the Iona Community was founded by the Very Reverend Dr George F. MacLeod, now Lord of Fiunary. The present leader is the Reverend Ian Reid. The community is made up of about 130 men and women, ministers and lay folk, the greater majority of whom are adherents of the Church of Scotland. The remainder represent the Anglican, Baptist, Congregationalist and Methodist Churches. In winter the members are found scattered at places of challenge on the Scottish mainland; about forty are in mission or are in teaching abroad. Some 600 ministers, women, laymen and youths are enrolled as associates of the community and the movement is supported by about 4,000 friends in all parts of the world. The community has done sterling work in restoring the abbey church, material for which has come from the four corners of the earth. But the community is also working at the heart of society, one aspect of this being seen in Community House in Glasgow.

In many respects, the large and peninsulated Isle of Mull, lying at the seaward end of the Firth of Lorne, reflects all the problems and ailments of the west of Scotland. Tourists visit the island in large numbers, often passing through it to get to Iona, and seldom have the time to see the real facts involved in life and living on this island of nearly a quarter of a million acres. A steady drift of population in the past still continues at a rate which is far from healthy. In 1961 the census return was over 2,300. Today the figure is just over 1,700. Yet Mull has a great potential, economically and socially and could be, with careful thought as to its development, the kingpin in any scheme of revitalization and regeneration of the west Highlands. Mull raises store cattle and sheep. About 4,000 head run on an island which it is estimated could easily support 20,000. Its climate brings timber to maturity up to twenty years before plantations on the mainland. The fishing grounds round the island and its satellites have yet to be fully exploited. Tourists pack the hotels and boarding-houses brimful and leave in the island an estimated £400,000 each year. Forestry provides 100 jobs out of the 500 to 600 jobs available for the adult male population. But the Forestry Commission's policy of planting only Japanese larch and Sitka spruce means that the wood is good only for pulp and builders' shuttering.

Mull is a volcanic island, largely composed of Tertiary basalt plateau lavas. Ben More, the highest peak, strikes out for 3,170 feet, with several other peaks reaching between 2,000 and 2,500 feet. At Carsaig, on the Ross of Mull, there is a chalk layer beneath which is an expanse of lias constantly washed by lime-laden water. It is reckoned by experts that there are few places in the British Isles so favoured as Carsaig. It is one of only two places in the west Highlands where watercress grows in a stream as it does in the chalk-streams of England. Forestry Commission plantations are found in Glen Aros. The plantings are not without their problems: rapidly-draining Tertiary basalt, with spring droughts coupled with dessicating winds from the east—this though the climate tends to be wet. The broad peninsula of Ardmeanach is high moor set above great cliffs and terraces. It is very fertile here, so much so in fact that grass scarcely stops growing throughout the year.

Tobermoray is the chief town on Mull, on a site where there has been a settlement of one kind or another for centuries. The present town was founded in 1788, with the intention of developing it into an important fishing port. In 1875 the local fishermen petitioned the Sheriff of Argyll to have the town made into a burgh and the charter was granted in that year. The town prospered for a few years until the railway reached Oban, when stagnation set in. Boats drifted away and the population dwindled at a rate which is still continuing. In 1843 the population was 1,500. By 1947 it had fallen to 900. The present figure is under 650 persons. Recently, however, there have been signs of a revival: fishing boats are beginning to use Tobermory and the setting up of a fish-processing plant is under consideration. The main ferry service between Mull and the mainland runs between Oban and Craignure, where a new sixty-bedroomed hotel was constructed and opened in 1971, the result of a literal concrete interest of the Highlands and Islands Development Board in Mull and its tourist potential. At Salen, an airstrip is used for a regular summer service between Mull, Oban and Glasgow. Another air service links Mull with Coll and Tiree, with return flights on the same days.

Mull is full of interest: historical, archaeological and wild-life. Other unusual attractions include the Mull Little Theatre; this venture deserves a mention because of the faith which its owners, Barrie and Marianne Hesketh, had when they decided to convert a barn at Dervaig into a theatre with a seating capacity of forty-five. The theatre, which is now coming up for its tenth season, generally mounts plays which are adapted for a cast of two, though there have been additions to the basic cast. The theatre won the Scottish Television Award in 1970 for services to the Scottish theatre and in 1972 it received support from the Scottish Arts Council to go on tour throughout Scotland. It is well supported on Mull, where during the summer months the theatre plays all week to packed houses. Another attraction on the island derives from the fact that Mull is remarkable for its fossil remains, notably at Ardmeanach, where the McCulloch Tree and other similar trees are lodged in the basalt columns. They are about 50 feet high and were engulfed in waves of culumnar basalt-lava which flowed from volcanic activities more than 35 million years ago. Certainly they are among the most spectacular geological phenomena in Scotland.

In 1972 Mull received a welcome addition to its economic structure: the re-opening of Ledaig Distillery after a lapse of nearly half a century. The original works were established in 1823, after which the pot-still distillery changed hands a number of times until it was purchased by the Distillers Company Ltd in 1916. Production ceased in 1924 solely because of the whisky recession then prevailing and the final closure of the plant coincided with the world depression of 1933. The new distillery will provide about fifteen much-needed jobs. All malt used is brought from Inverness and then peated to requirements. The water used is taken from a half-acre reservoir some 2 miles away. It emerges from natural quiet springs and some surface water, imparting to it just the right element of peatiness. To make for a perfect product, the air is damp, with just the right amount of humidity and clarity for maturing the product. The final output planned is 800,000 gallons per annum.

The distillery was one of a number of projects established with aid from the Highlands and Islands Development Board. Up to the present, about £100,000 in grants and loans has been invested in Mull, to create a better economic base and on which new grounds can be made for the future. On the social side, improvements have made Mull a better place: at Salen, for instance, the hospital now has beds to cater for geriatric cases which, before, had to be sent to the mainland for attention. While these may well be regarded as pinpricks, in the context of the overall Mull situation they are important and form the bases for other improvements and the introduction of other services. The Mull and Iona Council of Social Service is an active body which keeps a firm finger on the island's pulse, though occasionally the tactics of bodies such as the Scottish Transport Group wreak havoc with good intentions. In 1972 MacBraynes retimed their winter service at the weekends from Oban to Craignure, with the result that what was virtually a school boat, taking older pupils from Mull to Oban High School and back again at weekends, became more a service for a public which was virtually non-existent. The school's headmaster, concerned that some 250 children were due to miss out on their education, decided that the children should not be allowed their weekend trips home. The furore which that decision caused among Mull parents was only one of a long list of 'happenings' which are rarely designed to make life, difficult at the best of times, any easier. Lack of consultation between various bodies resulted in a serious threat directed at two important aspects of island life: the cultural side of Mull and the education of the children. The solution was the usual compromise which, as it does in other places in the region, merely acts against the indigenous population and is yet another of the many burdens islanders have to bear.

The island has a useful source of employment in the cloth factory at Tobermory. This enterprise specializes in weaving tweed and mohair. Begun in 1968, the owner advertised for apprentices with no success, despite the fact that young people are leaving Mull. However, the business was eventually established and has now grown to the extent that it provides local employment and has an export trade of impressive dimensions. The hand-weaving processes are on view to visitors. In 1972 the Highlands and Islands Development Board, which was interested in promoting the use of the high-quality Ross of Mull granite, announced that there was the possibility of re-opening the quarry at Fhionnphort in the south-west of the island. When cut into thin slabs and polished, the attractive pink and grey granite can be used as an external cladding for buildings. Virtually all granite used in this country is imported from Scandinavia, Italy and South Africa. The Ross of Mull quarries were closed about fifty years ago. The stone at that time was used for the construction of harbours, lighthouses, bridges and major buildings—for instance, Blackfriars and Westminster Bridges in London, the Holborn Viaduct and the foundations of the Albert Memorial.

10

The Outer Hebrides

IT IS, perhaps, only in the Outer Hebrides that island-living is becoming more of a duty to one's lifestyle than a pleasure. Twice in the last decade have these islands been placed at the mercy of external influences, the results of seamen's and dockers' strikes. These industrial actions, quite outside the sphere of influence and control of the islanders, threw into jeopardy vital lifelines across the Minch. It seems strange that while island-living in other parts of the world (one can quote the more human attitude of Norway's Government towards islanders living in a similar and generally inhospitable environment) can be made to work, with the help of a sympathetic central administration with a genuine social conscience and consciousness; yet, in the British state, the attitude of central government has been continually set against the continued occupation by citizens of remote, yet socially relevant, fringes of our land, to the extent that remote mainland communities are now as much at the mercy of the remote political administrator as are islanders. Of course it can be pointed out that in the Orkney and Shetland Islands the living is some degrees less precarious and the future is reasonably assured. But these northern islanders have ever maintained their difference, even to the point of disclaiming any relationship with the Scottish mainland. On the other hand, in the Hebridean islands the events of a millennium of recorded history has drawn a huge backcloth against which the present situation must be seen. To say that oppression,

Kyle-akin, Isle of Skye

Dunvegan Castle, Isle of Skye

(*top*) Distillery at Bonahaven, Islay. (*bottom*) Bowmore harbour, Islay

neglect, alienation and repression are all part and parcel of the history of the Outer Hebrides is to say that these tactics have been used, either by accident or design, in what some quarters regard as an unconscious policy of genocide. Rightly or wrongly, these quarters suggest that the nub of the whole socio-economic problem of the Western Isles today has been the distinct linguistic and cultural difference which has produced a gap of ever-increasing dimensions between that part of the Highland region known as the Gaidhealtachd (or Gaelic-speaking) and the rest of the Scottish mainland. While it is a fact that Gaelic in 1901 was spoken in half the land and island masses of Scotland, the 1971 census showed how rapid has been the recession of Gaelic, it having withdrawn itself into a corner from which there is no obvious escape. This 'difference' (though basically all Scotland is Celtic and therefore Gaelic-based in one way or another) has now become so prominent that many Scots react with considerable vehemence to the suggestion that there is an element in both their physical and mental make-up that is Gaelic-based. It has ever been the policy of colonialists to establish linguistic and cultural norms in the people they colonize, to bring in one or other of the many definitions of 'civilization', forgetting that the civilizing process should ideally be one of both liberation and refining, rather than one intent on the imposition of alien terms and values.

The process of change is most evident in the Uists of the Outer Hebrides since the introduction of a completely alien way of life in the military bases which were first set up in 1958. The distortion of the economic structure of the affected islands is all the more pitiful since it is now based on military expenditure and not on the efficient exploitation of land, sea and human resources. Much of the cultural conflict between David and Goliath has not been given the press which it merited, perhaps because, in our materially-oriented society, small items such as the erosion of inherent human values faithfully preserved over many centuries, are not headline material and require a kind of sympathetic interpretation—not associated with the more influential sections of the British press. Values such as are generated by a continued process of community living are deemed less important than the ability to purchase the products of technologically-oriented communities, made by people whose own lifestyles are influenced and shaped by exacting modes of existence and whose destinies are fundamentally just as vulnerable as those of the people who live in the islands.

All the main island masses of the Outer Hebrides are attended by small satellite islands. These latter range from the larger habitable islands to small grassy islets useful for fattening a few sheep. In their own time, these small islands fulfilled both social and economic functions. Now they are for the most part as much extensions of the common grazing areas of crofting townships on the main islands as the farms on the mainland of Scotland which are split in two by dual carriage-ways. Some islands are rented by tenants for grazing stock. By and large, the small off-shore islands which have retained their population are within good communicating distances of their associated larger islands. These former include Vatersay, separated by the Sound of Vatersay from Castlebay in Barra, and Eriskay, a mile distant from Ludac in South Uist. Farther north there is Berneray, in the Sound of Harris, within striking distance of North Uist; and Scalpay, which supports one of the liveliest communities in the whole of the Hebridean archipelago. The most recent small island to become deserted is Scarp, which was left by its native population in November 1971, and which perhaps underlines the fact that an island, even though within good striking distance from a mainland point, has no guarantee of continuity into the future.

Many factors are involved in the overall pattern of pressures which act against island-living. For many centuries both small and large islands have been part of an integrated pattern of living which finally disappeared only in the early years of the present century: the result of various stresses placed on the indigenous population from outside the Hebridean area. These stresses or pressures were mainly derived from the increased socio-economic standards (both numerative and qualitative) enjoyed by British society as a whole. Thus, a whole way of life and living in the Hebrides found itself at a disadvantage when it was placed in comparison with the quality of life to be found elsewhere outside the area. As if to aggravate the situation, the islands of the Hebridean chain were subjected to visits from people who were able to 'tune' themselves into the Hebridean wavelength and come out of their 'trip' with a fund of words to describe their discoveries. Through their rather narrow interests and vision the islands they wrote about were at once clothed in an air of romanticism which undoubtedly did much harm in that the real social and economic problems of these same islands were ignored. Had there been a realistic social writer, say at the turn of this century, with a zeal to perform a public service of propaganda for the people of the islands, the picture might well be different today, and island-living, even on the smaller Hebridean islands, would have been more readily accepted by society in general as a commonplace aspect of modern living.

Instead, the islanders were projected on to the outside world by well-meaning writers (the process is continuing today) as 'charming' because of their 'quaint' ways, because they had out-dated housing standards, because they were living anachronisms, and because their economic bases were limited in extent and scope and too deep-rooted in a ravaged history of depression and oppression. Inevitably, the result was a growing desire on the part of many islanders to disassociate from the imposed image. Added to this was the general neglect by successive governments of the nation in the simple matter of relatively inexpensive economic aid when it was needed most—and cheaper to provide—to develop the natural resources of the islands and the islanders. It took a decade of hard work on the part of the crofters of Lewis to win back some 18,000 acres of good grassland from the peat bogs of the island for new grazing, and that on a shoestring. Yet, in 1971 the Government announced the expenditure of some £22 million on extending the rocket range facilities in the Uists. One cannot but think that someone, somewhere, has the priorities wrong.

In the Hebridean chain an average of five islands have become deserted in each decade since 1841. This process of desertion continues. Only the very large islands remain populated, or else, in the cases of Eriskay, Berneray, Vatersay and Scalpay, the islands support dedicated communities who prefer to live a fuller, though more exacting life in a familiar and well-tried environment which offers them escape from the eroding influences which so beset urban societies today. An investigation into the reasons for island desertion reveals that the ultimate critical factor leading to desertion has been, in the main, social rather than economic. The need for social intercourse has increased during the past half century or so. Where and when it was not satisfied, desertion followed.

The Outer Hebrides, or Western Isles, form a chain of islands comprising Lewis, with Harris, North Uist, Benbecula, South Uist and Barra. These are the largest islands in the group. Four smaller islands which still maintain a vigorous population are Scalpay, off Harris; Berneray, off North Uist; Eriskay, off South Uist; and Vatersay, off Barra. Measured from Barra Head in the south to the Butt of Lewis in the north, the distance is roughly 130 miles, and contains an unexpected variety of scenic vistas, cultural domains, dialects, population patterns, historical backcloths, methods in land use, and lifestyles. In addition, there are numerous smaller islands, existing singly and in clusters, all now uninhabited, which add an extra dimension of interest to the seascape of the area, for the farther south one travels in the chain, the more the sea dominates the horizon and the sky to impress upon the visitor that one indeed is standing on an island mass. Only in Lewis does the island become too large for any particular feature to demonstrate that it is not connected to a larger land mass. One can look to the Lewis horizon from the centre of the island without being conscious of the fact that the distance just over the hills, the moors and the lochs, is significant, in that one eventually comes to the end of a road or a track; or that a river or stream runs itself out for ever into the anonymity of the sea. Indeed, the very size of Lewis has enabled the island to offer its population a cohesive element with which the island's communities can combine in a common interest. It is large enough to support a goodly number of people who, despite the ravages of emigration, have managed to stabilize their numbers and who are now making a concerted effort to give their future years a good solid foundation on which future generations of islanders can build.

The geological foundation of all the islands in the Outer Hebrides is Lewisian gneiss, with a pleasant and unexpected surprise in the outcrop of Torridonian sandstone around Stornoway, in Lewis. The basic rock of the islands is very old, among the oldest in the world. This age has resulted in the threadbare appearance of many of the islands' hills: denuded, barren, elongated domes and ridges which give a hummocky appearance to the landscape. All along the eastern coast of the island chain, fiord-like submerged valleys, over-deepened by glacial action, present their characteristic narrow and steep-walled heights to the eye. A little farther inland is the almost continuous ridge of high hills which reach their peak in the Clisham in Harris at over 2,600 feet. The lower ground is intensely ice-worn and presents the rounded, bossy, tarn-dotted type of scenery which is characteristic of western Sutherland.

Another geological surprise awaits the eye on the western coast of the island chain, though this is more prominent between Barra and Harris; Lewis tends to stand apart in its individuality except in coastal patches, say, at Uig and at the Butt. This is the large and beautiful stretches of sand and machair. Hundreds of acres of blown sand have produced a shore landscape of dunes, plains, sandhills and ridges. Textural and microscopic examinations have revealed that this sand is a highly variable mixture of silicious and calcareous fractions. The latter are derived from crushed marine shells and other marine organisms which either have arrived continuously in the islands' beaches over a long period of time or may represent the legacy of former marine conditions when organisms were more abundant on the basic rock platform. The silicious fraction appears to be derived from glacial drift formerly deposited on the rock platform. The outstanding characteristic of the machair is its low altitude and flatness, with sandhills rarely exceeding 30 feet in height. Centuries of rainfall, strong winds from all directions, soil creep and grazing and cultivation, have all acted to reduce the relief amplitude. Erosive factors, introduced by man and his animals, and the inevitable rabbit, have also contributed to the changing scene of this unique area. The existence of this type of land has played a vital role in the viability of the islands. The vegetation-covered coastal sand-plain has made the difference between healthy viable crofting communities and those whose continued existence hangs on the whims and caprices of an unstable land surface.

Though the natural history of the Western Isles reflects both the insulated and isolated nature of the area, it is full of interest and has thrown up many highlights which are peculiar to the islands. The seas around the islands are, of course, full of fish, a fact which has not escaped the piratical exploiters ever since the final years of last century (illegal trawling began around the year 1894). Ignorant of the meaning of conservation and careless of the dangers of over-fishing, they have virtually cleared the once-fertile Minch waters of fish. It was a sad man who met me in Stornoway harbour not so long ago and told the tale of having seen three generations of herring in a catch by a modern net, all destined for no other purpose than reduction to fish meal. Though protection was offered for in-shore fishers in the creation of the 3-mile limit, this has proved inadequate, and even today some of the violence which attended the early attempts by the islanders to clear the trawling scum from the sea continues as part and parcel of the island's sea-life.

The so-called island of Lewis is really the northern and predominant mass of a twin existence with the southern part called Harris. It is the largest island in Britain and the only one in the Hebrides which boasts a town of burgh status. It is a place of low, rolling hills, covered with a mass of fresh-water lochs and, to the south-west, higher rises which are truly desert areas. Both east and west coasts are deeply indented by fiord-like cuts which, like Loch Seaforth, drive with a positive intention far into the island. High cliffs, often dropping sheer to the sea, are a feature of the Lewis coast, the only relief being the occasional wide-mouthed sandy beach. The sand-based machair is found in Lewis, but less frequently than in the southern Hebrides. The island is one large and unrelenting mass of bog, with peat deposits varying in depth to some 15 feet. The peat is of a fairly high quality, and in some parts yields a fuel which compares favourably with coal in thermal energy output. The main attraction of peat in Lewis has been its possible reclamation; indeed, the crofters have converted some 18,000 acres into good grassland. The entrepreneur to exploit the peat deposits of Lewis and apply the processed product to the many applications to which foreign and Irish peat is being put in Britain today is still awaited; though now that the future of the island and its resources have been subjected to local scrutiny, one may yet see this particular resource being converted into hard cash and jobs for the indigenous population.

The Lewis community is to be found in the typical crofting townships which are virtually all coastal except Achmore and Cleascro. Most of the communities are involved in the triple and interrelated activities of crofting, weaving and fishing, with a tendency towards an increase in full-time fishing as opposed to the more ambivalent crofter-fishermen category of employment. The impact of the Highlands and Islands Development Board on the island's economy has been largely concerned with fishing; it has succeeded in performing something of a resuscitation exercise which will no doubt be of lasting benefit to the island as a whole. The board's interest in the fish-processing side of the industry is another indication of what the future could hold for Lewis if the island's economy is to be better structured than it has been in past years. The local Lewis fishing fleet comprises seventeen vessels at the time of writing; all these are operating successfully with no particular financial troubles. The obvious financial benefit to the community was confirmed in a report on the Highland fishing industry published by the board in 1972. The horizon of the future, however, is not at all clear. The average earnings of Stornoway fishermen are below those of Scottish east-coast fishermen who also operate in the Minch waters. In addition, Stornoway as a fishing port finds itself at a distinct disadvantage with ports on the mainland such as Lochinver, Mallaig, and the developing facilities at Uig, in Skye. Direct land routes are important, particularly if fish are destined to be sold as such and not to an anonymous market for ultimate conversion into fish meal and pet foods. There has been the suggestion that a facility for landing fish on the west side of Lewis would be of benefit; in 1972 a local man with experience in fish-marketing in Glasgow decided to take this idea up. The plant is located at Kirkibost, on the island of Great Bernera on the west of Lewis, an inset of Loch Roag. The economy of Bernera is almost wholly dependent on shellfish and the processing facility, with its employment potential, is significant to the community.

The importance of the Harris tweed industry in Lewis has often been stressed. Certainly in past years, while the fishing industry was in the doldrums and crofting offered only a subsistence-level economy, the opportunity given to crofters to become crofter-weavers was a significant factor in stabilizing the population. Without the tweed, the island would have seen a more rapid decline in its population than it did. Though the main processing and commercial activities associated with the industry have always been centred on Stornoway, the actual weaving is done by individuals on their own crofts; thus a semi-craft product is available to command a rich market. Recent streamlining and amalgamations have created new problems, as have the occasional recessions in world markets; these have caused the islanders to take a long, cool and hard look at their position, and to make an attempt to diversify the island's economic elements so that a cold wind blowing in one main sector will not result in a mass emigration, as has so often happened in the island's past.

Stornoway has been mentioned as the only town in the Outer Hebrides. With a population of over 5,000, about a quarter of the total island population, it provides a focal point for commerce, administration and entertainment. It combines the rhythms of a seaport, country town, island town and exudes an air of satisfaction which is somewhat belied by the dullness and lack of activity around its extensive pier and harbour system. Much of the town's original character has been uprooted by the town council in an effort to smarten the place up, to provide new housing facilities and services for the citizens. The green fields and pastures which were once the town's green belt (between concrete and asphalt and the bog of the hinterland) are now a mass of new private and municipal housing, the ration being about fifty-fifty. The town is large, but one feels that the new size, while a welcome addition to the rates, has been obtained at the expense of the depopulation of the country areas. Unfortunately, there is no foreseeable opportunity of any reversal of this process of migration from country to town, unless new development techniques, philosophies and projects establish small centres of entrepreneurial growth in the hinterland which will at once stabilize small communities where they exist already and also offer the chance of an increase in their numbers by offering young folk the opportunity to work and stay in one spot.

In 1972 the Lewis Development Fund was launched, with the intention of raising capital to support development projects in the island. This fund, seen in association with the simultaneous appointment of a development officer for Lewis, is a new element in the life of the island community, and perhaps a sign that, after years of neglect by outside interests, the community realizes that only self-help can provide the kind of salvation which will be truly characteristic of the island and satisfy its needs without introducing foreign factors which can so often, as they have done in the past, damage the socio-economic patterns of life and living.

While Lewis now seems intent on going forward into the future and is promised a reasonable measure of success, the situation in the southern part of the island, in Harris, is quite different. Although, again, one meets the desire to move on with confidence into the future, those who wish to make their community more stabilized and a better place in which to live, find that the resources are not available to them to exploit to the same degree and extent as exist on other Hebridean islands. Harris is a mountainous country, much of its area being virtually barren wastes. Yet, particularly on the west coast, the flat expanses of sand-based land, the machair, offer unique opportunities for development in an agricultural context. Indeed, up until about a century ago, this land was used by the Harris population, but clearances and social upheaval forced the Harris folk over to the more inhospitable and infertile land of the east coast, with its high cliffs, where, in many cases, soil had to be made, rather than it being there already, waiting for the touch of spade and rake. The living patterns and rhythms changed too. Instead of the more regular seasonal changes the life became more dependent on the mood of the sea, and years of hard work went into the creation of the crofting townships which now exist in a pleasant-looking string of communities down the coast between Tarbert, the urban centre of Harris, and Rodel, at Rudha Renish. The visitor today who winds his car round the twisting roads rarely realizes that his eyes are seeing the product of a century of untold toil in the conversion of thinly-slippered rock into patches of fertile earth for growing produce.

Indeed, the whole of the Harris scene tends to be depressing, though the place itself offers unrivalled opportunities for tourism, which, in any case, may well be of doubtful long-term benefit to the 2,900 people on Harris (the 1951 population figure was 4,000, representing a decrease of 1,100 persons). The lack of economic activity of any real significance, the dangerously unbalanced demographic structure (many communities have average ages bordering on the 50s and 60s), the relatively little benefit which Harris has had from the tourist industry, and continuing depopulation: all these offer little hope for the future. Yet, there is a spirit of defiance in the Harris community, which may well bring them into a sunnier economic atmosphere and one hopes that this will be realized.

Alkali feldspar is found in deposits at Northton and Roneval. This material is used in the manufacture of glass, in which it may constitute up to a few per cent of the composition for clear glass and up to 50 per cent for opaque varieties. The deposits in South Harris are of workable dimensions and were investigated for strategic purposes at the time of the Second World War; in 1956 a fresh evaluation was made by the Scottish Council's Mineral Resources Panel, when it was considered that the deposits were of no economic consequence. The deposits were worked for a short time during the last war, and after the 1956 survey a further interest was shown despite the report's view of the potential. South Harris also has small deposits of metallic ores such as uranium, but these are not significant. The exploitation of anorthosite, or white rock powder, occurs north of Rodel, though the workings there, begun in 1965, were eventually abandoned.

Harris has hardly touched the resources of the surrounding sea. This is in sharp contrast to the Harris off-shore island of Scalpay, lying at the mouth of East Loch Tarbert and which has an economy almost wholly dependent on fishing. Scalpay has one of the few communities in the region which has deliberately set its face against the wind of depopulation and won through. It is a lively community of about 450 residents, intent on creating for itself the best conditions available and, perhaps surprisingly, obtaining these, though not without difficulty and hard work in pressing claims.

The island fishermen have retained their interest in herring fishing and have successfully made the transition from drift-net to ring netting. This was done initially through private initiative and enterprise, though by 1970 half of the twelve-boat fleet carried some investment made by the Highlands and Islands Development Board. Over 60 per cent of the economically active males are in full-time fishing. The Scalpay tradition in fishing extends back well over a century, though all has not been well. There was in its history a period of very serious depression, but the community, by its own efforts, pulled itself out of it and went on to build its present successes. The community has been most fortunate in that it had reliable local leadership and that capital was available for investment. The late Captain Cunningham, a local businessman who operated a small fleet of coasters, willingly invested in herring (ring-net) fishing in 1948. Though there were initial difficulties, these were overcome while the fishing interests shifted across to prawn-trawling in the 1960s. Thus by the time the board was established there was an active base on which to build with further capital investment. The Scalpay community is probably a prime example of where investment in people, to offer a degree of confidence, pays off handsomely in that the confidence spreads to others and finally leads to a community where all members pull their weight to reach a common goal.

It is of interest to record that in Scalpay there has been a direct move from school to fishing; despite the arduous work conditions there is the attraction that each member of the crew, be he an experienced skipper or a young boy fresh out of school, gets an equal share of the boat's earnings. This democratic distribution scheme does not altogether occur on mainland-based boats. Thus, the Scalpay people do not merely possess a strong sense of community; they also possess something more basic to living: a strong sense of their community's rights which is now being expressed through their recently-formed Village Council. The homogeneity provided by the common professional interest of virtually all the islanders in fishing has provided a basic element of cohesion for the expression of effective political and administrative pressure. All this has taken time to achieve, but a study of Scalpay would be more than advantageous to any other community who finds its threads being loosened by the events of external and remote occurrences.

In the sharpest possible contrast there is the island of Scarp, which was deserted by its indigenous population in November 1971. This island lies off the west coast of Harris, separated from the Harris mainland by a short though difficult and treacherous channel of water. So near and yet so far: a condition which finally resulted in a decrease in population of 100 in 1942 to zero almost exactly thirty years later. Now Scarp is in the same category as those other deserted islands of North Rona, St Kilda and the Monach Isles off North Uist. The process of desertion continues and society in general accepts it with no particular pangs of feeling that it was itself, in the various conditions for living it has created, ultimately responsible for these islands losing their social significance and their place in the map of the British Isles.

Farther south, however, yet another small island is intent on staying the pace for as long as its community feels that it offers them the optimum environment for life and living. This is Berneray, in the close of Harris, and close to the North Uist shore. The community here has recently come to terms with itself and has determined to agitate for all things—social services, communications and the like—which have been denied it for many decades mainly through neglect by central administration. The island folk have prepared an excellent programme for the future and have established the right kind of contacts with officialdom to have it considered seriously at least, if not brought to some degree of fruition. The community of 140 people depend on crofting, lobster fishing and knitting for their livelihood and hope to add tourism, with a projected air strip as an incentive to visitors.

North Uist is, for the most part, a low-lying island, with some prominent hills to the east and north-east, and flat, sandy machair to the west. It has what has been described as the most complex pattern of fresh-water lochs to be found in the whole of the British Isles. As with most of the main islands in the Hebridean chain, it is attended by satellite islands, notably Grimsay, which is yet another small island intent on making a future for itself based on fishing activities, notably shellfish.

The bulk of the island's population is concentrated on the western coastal area. The island's capital, Lochmaddy, is content to act as a terminus on the east coast, linking, as it does, Harris and Skye. The population of Lochmaddy is just over 300, and compares with the island's total population of about 1,850. The introduction in recent years of the vehicle ferries has increased the importance of the village, and there are plans to consolidate development of the harbour facilities to integrate the port's function more closely with the needs of the community.

The economic structure of North Uist includes crofting, alginates (the reduction to milled form of dried seaweed for subsequent industrial processing), shellfish, calf-rearing and bulb-growing. This latter activity is concentrated at Balemore and has been the subject of a survey conducted with a view to the possible build-up to viable proportions. The survey revealed that it was technically feasible to reclaim an area of some 1,500 acres of tidal calcareous sands, known as the Valley Strand on the northern coast. The whole idea was put up by the Highlands and Islands Development Board to the Scottish Office in Edinburgh. The scheme, to cost about £2½ million, was turned down. A year later the Government authorized an expenditure of almost ten times that sum for the extension of the rocket-range facilities in South Uist and in Benbecula.

In the Balranald area is the 1,500-acre reserve established on the island by the Royal Society for the Protection of Birds. Breeding birds of special interest include the red-necked phalarope, whose only other British nesting site is in the Inner Hebrides, in Orkney and in Shetland. The reserve comprises a wide variety of typically Hebridean habitats, ranging from Atlantic beaches with sweeping white sands backed by dunes, large stretches of meadow land (machair) with an abundance of wild flowers, and a variety of lochs. Of particular interest and significance is the fact that the land use in the area, which includes the township of Hougharry, has changed little over the years; this has resulted in large numbers of corncrakes and corn buntings which frequent the reserve, in sharp contrast with other parts of the British Isles where changes in harvesting methods have driven these species away. The small off-shore island of Causamal forms part of the reserve; it acts as a breeding station for a small number of Atlantic seals and a natural refuge for a large part of the winter population of surface-feeding duck.

North Uist abounds with the evidence of its ancient past. The neolithic pottery kilns at Eilean-an-Tighe, in Loch nan Geireann, have been accepted as the oldest recorded example in Western Europe of a potter's workshop. The pottery found at this site is of a very high quality and is found in such quantity that nothing less than a pottery factory must have existed here to supply the needs of the island and its Hebridean neighbours.

From documentary evidence dating back to at least two centuries, North Uist has enjoyed a fairly well balanced economy, based on a wide range of produce, both raw and processed, derived from the island's natural resources. While there have been the expected, almost inevitable, changes in degrees of importance of certain elements in the economy, and while other items have appeared for short periods to be replaced by others, there is today the same broad base to the economic picture which undoubtedly assists the island to maintain an acceptable standard of living in an otherwise hostile environment, the latter not always the product of imposed physiographical factors. Over a century ago the produce exported from the island included livestock (horses, cows and sheep), salt beef, hides, grain, potatoes and hay—all the usual items associated with a reasonably intensive agricultural activity. The Old Statistical Account for Scotland mentions that the island supported some 2,000 cows, of which number about 300 were exported annually. Sheep were reared mainly for wool and mutton for domestic use.

The produce pattern varied, however, with good years and bad. Meal, for instance, had to be imported on not a few occasions. Potatoes, introduced into the Uists *c.* 1743, became so plentiful during the ensuing half-century that they formed the principal food for about five months in each year—when there was no blight such as that which occurred in 1846.

The passing of the Crofters Act in 1886 marked the end of an era of insecurity and the beginning of a new phase in which the crofters were given reasonable incentives to improve their land and stock. The island crofters have done exactly this. Today, there are about 460 crofts on North Uist, varying in extent and degree of fertility. Most crofts on the island are far larger than those found in many other areas of the crofting counties in the Highland region. When well-worked, the crofts are capable of producing a reasonable standard of living without resort to a full-time ancillary occupation. Land on the island tends to be used principally for the raising of store cattle and calves.

Fishing is an important element in the island's economy. The association of North Uist with this activity extends back for some three centuries to the fishery schemes of Charles I, when Lochmaddy was created a fishing centre. The interest, which was mainly fostered by external enterprise, died away and was not revived until the middle of the eighteenth century. Again, however, those who participated in the industry from the island tended to be employees rather than employers or entrepreneurs. Island-based fishermen tended to concentrate on inshore activities. The island's current interest in fishing is largely concentrated on lobsters and crabs. The lobster grounds off the west coast of the Outer Hebrides are considered to be among the best, if not the best, in the British Isles. In recent years, with the introduction of large diesel-engined boats, the areas fished have been extended to cover the whole of the western approaches of North and South Uist. Large boats regularly fish up to the 20-fathom mark. No fishing of any importance takes place off the eastern coasts of the islands because the sea bottom is generally mud and is not suitable for lobsters.

The development of the shellfish industry has been of recent vintage and is mainly due to the interest of Minch Shellfish Ltd (formerly Atlantic Seafoods) and the Highlands and Islands Development Board. In 1968 a lobster-storage facility was built on Grimsay Island, representing a total capital investment of some £20,000. The storage ponds hold lobsters alive and fresh to be released according to assessed market demands. Although boats from Barra, South Uist and Mallaig also participate in the fishing, about three-quarters of the landings are made by North Uist boats. Some £75,000 is derived annually from lobsters. The position of the industry at present, and indeed its future, is uncertain. The uncertainty, however, is not due to natural causes. The massive developments which have taken place on the military rocket base on South Uist, with an increased demand from the military authorities for more and more cleared and controlled sea areas for test firing, has placed this indigenous industry in an unenviable position. The military authorities have a 40-foot boat which patrols the lobster grounds to warn fishermen of the times of test firings. But the constant disruption of work is often a serious drawback to successful fishing. The lobster fleet requires to visit fishing areas twice in each day to set down pots, lift others, re-bait and generally to have continued and uninterrupted access to the grounds. Generally, if a lobster boat cannot reach its fleet of pots daily at any time during the hours of daylight, the area is said to be unfishable. At the present time, one is left with the impression that the potentially-obsolete defence missiles (the life of the testing range has been quoted as less than fifteen years) are considered to be of far greater importance than the more basic need of an island community to retain its identity and maintain its place in today's scheme of things without attracting the inevitable subsidy from the rest of British society.

Other economic activities in North Uist includes work at the factory at Sponish owned by Alginate Industries (Scotland) Ltd. This works was opened in 1957 to produce meal from milled and dried seaweed. About twenty-five local collectors of seaweed ('tangle' or laminaria and rockweed) keep the factory supplied with raw material. The tangle is collected after it has been washed ashore by the winter gales. It is then air-dried on the beaches and brought in this condition for further drying and milling. Rockweed is an all-year-round crop. It is cut from rocks at low tide and towed in large rafts by small boats to various bays and inlets from whence it is taken to Sponish, or the sister factory on South Uist.

Both knitting and cloth-making feature in the island's economic picture, the latter activity being of ancient lineage and traceable back to *c.* 1750 when the wife of the seventh Baronet of Sleat founded a 'linnen manufactory' on North Uist. The present-day interest is centred on one of the recognized types of Orb-marked Harris Tweed, the mark being given by the Harris Tweed Association to indicate authenticity in the product. Though the output is small, it is significant in that, despite the presence of a spinning mill at Loch Eport, it is a domestic product designed for the export market. The two primary weavers, Lachlan MacDonald of Grimsay and Mrs Peggy MacDonald of Locheport, are now far-famed for high-quality cloth made from their own designs. Mrs MacDonald performs all the processes herself, including the making of her own dyes from the wild flowers of North Uist. A new addition to the industrial scene on the island is the knitwear factory set up at Bayhead. The ultimate aim is for an employment of sixty persons. The factory is equipped with hand flat knitting machines to produce a range of specially-designed knitted sweaters of distinctive Hebridean design which could rival similar products from Shetland and the Aran Islands.

The cancer of North Uist, as with other islands, is depopulation. The maximum population figure was reached in 1821 with a record of 4,971 persons. Thereafter there was a steady decline to the present figure of about 1,800. Perhaps to those in cities and large conurbations, with populations of mere suburbs counted in tens and hundreds of thousands, the loss of some 3,000 souls in 150 years is not great. But when seen against the smaller, and perhaps more human, scale of island living, one must reflect that much strength, initiative and enterprise has been the real loss to the island. The record of depopulation is seen in the educational picture. Even in 1837 there were eleven schools; by 1864 the number had increased to sixteen. Now there are eight schools, three small schools having been closed in the past decade as a result of centralist policies of the education committee of the county council of Inverness. One of the latter schools to be closed was on Grimsay Island, which had a school population of seventy in 1903, reduced to nine in 1969 and then closed.

Despite its depressing history of clearances, social distortion and disruption, North Uist has a rich corpus of potential which has yet to be fully developed for the future. Considering the many pressures which have been placed on the island's population over the years to tempt them to pull out their roots and leave, the residual island folk feel a deep sense of belonging. Their resilience is a factor which enables the observer of North Uist to express the hope that the future holds no unsurmountable fears and blocks and that, while erosive processes may continually gnaw at the island's socio-economic structure, there will be a significant population at North Uist for many decades to come. And, though the ratio of old to young on the island is at present rather high, this is not so bad a sign as at first appears, because old people in the Hebrides generally tend to live independently and purposefully for longer than elsewhere. Young people are also returning to the island. At present, there are no less than six people waiting for each piece of land that falls vacant.

To the south of North Uist lies Benbecula, the Mountain of the Fords. Despite its name it is a flat island, a place of machair-land, green and fertile, with bogland on its eastern side. The interior of the island is full of small lochs which provide excellent trout fishing and, inevitably, are havens for many species of birds, both resident and migrant. The bulk of the island's population is centred on the western coastal plain. The island supports just under seventy crofts, which offer a lifestyle now under a continual barrage of scrutiny and pressures as the result of the provision of work and services generated by the presence of the rocket range on South Uist. While this additional element in the island's economy has undoubtedly represented an opportunity for locals to remain on the island to enjoy a raised standard of living (which would not be entirely available if the economy were solely dependent on crofting and fishing activities), there are doubts as to the morals involved implanting a large population with different values and lifestyles in a much smaller community. In the end, it really rests with the indigenous community on Benbecula to try and arrange matters so that they can enjoy the benefits of the military presence while retaining intact and even consolidating the more traditional facets of their island's economy and social patterns. Another aspect of the problem affects the island's Gaelic-based culture. This is involved with the increasing proportion of the island's present population which is wholly English-speaking. Even in 1961, out of a total population of 1,312 persons, thirty-four people were wholly Gaelic-speaking. The 1971 census figures revealed that the proportion of wholly-English monoglots on the island had risen to some 60 per cent, compared with about 48 per cent in 1961. Thus, in a decade an indigenous Gaelic-speaking community on an island in the Outer Hebrides has found itself in the minority.

The main feature in the history of the island has been its role as a literal stepping stone between North and South Uist. Benbecula ceased to be an island *per se* in 1943 when the bridge connecting the island to South Uist was opened. This bridge stretches across the South Ford: sand and shell beaches that once had to be crossed either on foot or by horse-drawn carriage. The bridge was not built entirely with the needs of the islanders in mind. Rather it was constructed to create a vital through land link between the port of Lochboisdale in South Uist and the R.A.F. aerodrome at Balivanich in Benbecula. The North Ford Causeway was opened in 1960, thus creating a through route of some 70 miles between Pollachar in South Uist and Berneray off the north of North Uist.

The township of Balivanich acts as host to the airport, a necessary link in the Hebridean air transport system. Developed from the Second World War aerodrome established by the R.A.F., air travel has now become commonplace and has proved to be of some economic significance in allowing such produce as live lobsters to be flown, within a few hours of being caught, to the markets of Billingsgate and the Continent. The airport facility has been of social significance too in that the island and its neighbours are less remote. It takes less time to get to London by air (two and a half hours) than it does by road to that city from many large towns and cities in southern England. Flights of lobster freight are thus sent direct to the Continent and are normal for Balivanich Airport. With the introduction of the Minch vehicle ferries, however, there has been a reduction in the number of terminal passengers at the airport. Even so, the facility will always remain the door which is always kept open, even though there may be no desire to take the road out of the island.

Perhaps the true character of Benbecula lies not so much in its topographical features nor in its interesting past history, but more in its indigenous population, which has demonstrated, in the context of its two religions (Catholic and Protestant), that harmony in human relations does not depend on a homogeneous belief, but in a single desire to work together to hold fast to the basic essentials necessary for the community to continue into its future as a visible and viable whole, with as many as possible of the values which have enabled it to live successfully through the centuries of its past existence. However, as an indication of the concern now being felt by a wide spectrum of public opinion, a letter to *The Scotsman* expressed horror at the violation of the island by the military presence:

> As I left the [airport] terminal, I was confronted with a massive concrete and metal complex already spreading out over a large area of the northern part of the island... learned that this was the start of a new R.A. rocket-testing range. The vast complex nearing completion was nothing to do with the actual technical side of things—that was to come later. This was merely the accommodation and hospital blocks. Travelling south I could see, stretching out in all directions, evidence of further excavating, digging and flattening out, generally ruining the ground. No doubt in the next few years nearly all of Benbecula will be covered in ominous concrete buildings, barbed-wire fences and notices telling people to stay away.

South Uist is the second largest island in the Outer Hebrides. It is a place of sharp physical contrasts. All along the western seaboard are flat sand-based machair lands of about a mile wide. These support most of the crofting townships and offer good soil for cultivation and for grazing. The eastern side of the island is wild, with boggy moorland that rises west to east to meet a long spine of high hills running the length of the island. Three long sea-lochs enter from the Minch: Skiport, Eynort, and Boisdale. These cut South Uist into three distinct parts. In addition, the island is threaded through and through with many fresh-water lochs well known in ornithological circles for their populations of wild duck. Anglers more than appreciate the brown trout that thrive in this natural environment. Loch Druidibeg, at Stilligarry, is a nature reserve of over 400 acres. Largely owned by the Nature Conservancy, it contains a wealth of topographical features ranging from lochs with miniature islands, peninsulae, indented shorelines, marches and machair. The highlight of the bird life in this area is the grey lag goose which breeds wild hereabouts, though some might prefer the golden eagle, the hen harrier, or the red-necked phalarope.

As with other Hebridean islands, South Uist has some wealth of evidence of its ancient past. In particular there are the wheelhouses, drystone-built structures with a most distinctive form. Some are free-standing, with a well-built outer wall of earth faced with stone, up to 8 feet thick. Others have a much less substantial wall, being built in pits dug in sand dunes. Both forms have an inner diameter of between 20 feet and 40 feet. In the centre of the house is a square or horseshoe-shaped hearth, made from large flat slabs, outlined by stones placed on end in the ground to make an enclosure for the fire. This type of house received its name from the thick stone piers, built radially like the spokes of a wheel, that divide the space near the wall into eight or more compartments. The piers end at some distance from the hearth which represents the 'hub'. There the family could sit and follow their various domestic occupations. The two prominent examples of the wheelhouse in South Uist are at Kilphedar and Drimore. The former example is not as yet classified as an ancient monument, though it is standing to a

Standing stones at Callanish, Isle of Lewis

Mending the nets at Stornoway, Lewis

(*top*) Tarbert, Harris. (*bottom*) Thatched house at Ardhasig, Harris

higher level than many others of its type. One wonders about this curious omission by the Department of the Environment, which has the responsibility, held on behalf of the nation, for all structures of this age.

Among the historical remains on South Uist is the castle on Calvay Island, at the mouth of Loch Boisdale, which dates from the thirteenth century. In this ruin, Prince Charles hid for some nights in June 1746. Farther north is Ormaclett Castle, the ruin of an unfortified house of the early eighteenth century. It was once the home of the MacDonalds of Clanranald. At Milton can be seen the remains of Flora MacDonald's house: tumble-down drystone walls of an *L*-shaped dwelling. A cairn in the centre of the present enclosure was raised to her memory by the Clan Donald. At Stilligarry can be seen the ruins of the house of the MacVurichs, now called Curries. This family were the hereditary bards and historians of the Clanranalds. They kept commonplace books in which items of clan history, anecdotes, geneological information, panegyrics and elegies for their own and other chiefs were entered. These records were written in Classical Gaelic which was the common literary language of Ireland and the Scottish Highlands and Islands until the beginning of the eighteenth century. The MacVurichs were in fact the last practitioners of Gaelic bardic verse anywhere. Their Red Book of Clanranald has been published, with a passable translation, in *Reliquae Celticae*.

The island of South Uist has always been a fertile place and has an old-established tradition of exports which includes potatoes, cereal crops, cattle, pigs, eggs, fish and kelp. Towards the middle of the nineteenth century the annual export of cattle amounted to some 1,500 head. The present-day crofting activity tends to be a more viable enterprise than it is in many other parts of the Highlands and Islands. The existence of the fertile machair strip on the western side of the island has provided a factor for stability and continuity which has not been undervalued, though at many times it has been subjected to such excessive demands that it has failed the community temporarily. The island is famous for its cattle. Sheep are also raised, but these are confined to the island's steep and hilly pasturage, with little arable land, which characterizes the area of South Uist towards the east. There are under 750 crofts on the island, a number which is declining at a rate of about 150 crofts every decade. The decrease, however, is accounted for mainly by the process of amalgamation of crofts to form larger and more economical units. The existence of the rocket range, which offers full- and part-time employment, fishing, particularly shellfish, seaweed collection, and general construction work, have all helped to stabilize the population with the result that few crofts are left vacant.

The number of cattle stock raised on the island justified local sales meetings to which come auctioneers from the Scottish mainland. A successful scheme in operation at the present time is one in which calves are sold and taken to mainland farms for intensive rearing. The scheme, known as the Uist Calf Scheme, has received a significant amount of capital, in economic and non-economic grants, from the Highlands and Islands Development Board. The idea behind the scheme is the improvement of the marketing and breeding of cattle in the Uists. Hebridean Calf Producers Ltd are the principals in the scheme. This company is a co-operative based on Lochboisdale and formed by the Scottish Agricultural Society Ltd to carry on a scheme of calf marketing which they themselves had been operating previously. The crofter gets paid for his beasts by Hebridean Calf Producers on the spot at the Lochmaddy Sales, in North Uist. The calves are then fattened on mainland farms through the winter months. This is a more economical proposition than wintering the beasts in the islands. After the animals have been sold, any profit made by the co-operative is distributed among the crofters who originally sold the calves. On the breeding side, research is being carried out to improve the calf strain.

Alongside crofting, fishing has been an important element in the island's economy. In the early years of the industry, last century, in common with other islands, the indigenous population, through lack of capital, were not able to become principals in the industry. Since the turn of the century, when both herring and white fishing were at their peak, there has been a decline which has been overshadowed by an increase in the importance of shell fishing. The interest in this activity is centred in the Loch Carnan area. Lobsters are the main harvest. Almost an echo of the boom years of the old kelp industry, seaweed collection and processing is carried on in South Uist, being an almost continuous association with this natural resource since *c.* 1746 when the manufacture of kelp was first started in North Uist. After the interest in kelp had waned or died off completely in other parts of the Highlands and Islands, the activity was maintained with a fluctuating intensity until after the 1914–18 War, during which the product was required for its iodine yield. Then it ceased, to be revived in 1943—by which time new properties of seaweed had been discovered and new market possibilities opened up. The present factory at Boisdale, at the south end of the island, had its beginnings in 1933. Ten years later the interests of the private company running the factory were taken over by Alginate Industries Ltd. The factory is supplied with raw weed collected by crofters on an incidental basis and offers full-time employment for up to twelve men.

Probably the biggest economic and social impact ever experienced by the island has been the rocket-testing range. In 1955 the Ministry of Defence proposed that the Iochdar site on South Uist be developed for weapon-testing purposes, which would be associated with another site on St Kilda to act as a monitoring facility. The proposal met with a great deal of opposition based on many relevant grounds. In particular, there were fears that the influx of a military population would destroy, or lead to the destruction of, the vulnerable thin-ice cultural base on which the whole of the Hebridean society was founded. The inevitable took place however: the area to the west of Loch Bee became a military base and this initiated a series of changes in the island's economy and social patterns. Private sources available to the author indicate that the site was a haphazard choice and quite arbitrary. In 1968 further plans for the extension of the Hebrides range facilities were announced. The plan was to provide permanent facilities at a time when other military sites in Britain were coming under critical fire; the Hebrides thus were regarded as being conveniently 'remote' and therefore represented a useful military dumping ground for the rejects from other parts of British society. In 1971 a further government announcement indicated that the final phase towards the completion of the range would cost an astronomical £22 million. While the 1955 objections were rather concentrated on the inevitable dilution of social and cultural values, with a forecast of the erosion of the position of Gaelic as a spoken language, the 1968 objections were founded on surer economic grounds: the real danger that the army's restrictive requirements of the fertile fishing grounds around the Monach Isles would seriously impair the lobster fishing, one of the main props in the economy of North Uist, Benbecula and South Uist.

The present uneasy peace between the military authorities and the local fishermen is a delicate one and it could take little to upset it to bring local interests into direct confrontation with the military presence and its purely functional requirements of these islands. One prominent advantage of the military presence has been the factor it has contributed to the stability of the population of South Uist. The maximum population in the island was reached in the decade 1836–46, following a steady increase during the previous century from about 2,200 to 7,300 in 1841. Thereafter, the general decline reached the figure of 2,400 in 1951. The 1961 census showed a similar figure and the latest estimate is better, being in the region of 2,500. The real and hard effect of the military population has not yet been established or interpreted, but it is significant perhaps that the population figure has remained the same for a decade, even though one might, with some justification for an all-Catholic community, expect an increase due to the birthrate alone.

Lochboisdale is the main port facility in South Uist. In its time it has seen the mass forced emigration of 'voluntary' candidates for Canada in 1851. And, in later years, it saw the days of the herring boom, when it was one of the main fishing centres in the Hebrides. Nowadays the port is quiet, the effect of the Skye–Lochmaddy vehicle ferry connection across the Minch having diminished considerably the commercial importance of the port.

The community on South Uist is a close-knit one, with the same social patterns and rhythms which characterize rural communities in other places in the region. The community enjoys all the intangible, and some of the physically accessible, advantages which such a social structure produces as spin-offs and which are denied to most urban societies. The full and long-term effect of the incomer 'alien' population associated with the army has never been subjected to a pre- and post-situation study by sociologists and anthropologists. But it would hardly need any great degree of insight or academic knowledge and training to realize that when a vigorous incoming population brings along with it its own set of values and social patterns, these are bound to impinge on the resident culture with varying degrees of damaging effect. The continual confrontation of imported values against the bulwark of a Gaelic-based community will inevitably result in a deterioration of what has been so faithfully preserved for many centuries. Even so, the values of island communities with their strength and experience of community welfare and concern for the individual within the close-knit framework, will serve as a main survival factor for a long time to come.

There seems to be a growing realization that the Hebrides are part of the outer and utter fringe of Europe, with the latter's growing economic, social and political integrations creating a hub that may well make already 'remote' areas, such as the Scottish island communities, remoter still in terms of socio-economic viability and political administration. It will remain with the islanders to assess just how much they value their inheritance to make it relevant in modern terms and in the simple context of people living together. There is a relevance of the Western Isles to our lives now, and particularly to our society, which is deteriorating rapidly, simply because it is ceasing to be a society of living creatures and becoming more a creation of technology with the Gross National Product as the be all and end all of human endeavour. Only in small societies such as exist in South Uist and elsewhere can a possible remedy be found for the salving of what remains of human values, and this is mainly because these values still exist on the island. Of course, the same can be said of many other small communities whose harshness of existence has made their populations appreciate the fact that moving must always have a sharp edge to it, to make it relevant and to obtain some degree of spiritual satisfaction. But as we are dealing with the Outer Hebrides, it is sufficient to put on record that there is much that we, as members of much larger societies and communities, should attempt, not merely to preserve for academic dissection, observation and dissertation, but to use—perhaps as a magic touchstone which could yield a new meaning and vista to those of us who desperately need to be loosened from the stranglehold of so many of the irrelevancies which create almost impossible conditions of living for us in these times.

Barra is the most westerly inhabited island in Great Britain and forms a predominating feature in the southern archipelago between Eriskay and high-cliffed Berneray Island, some twenty-two miles south. The island is largely covered with great stretches of peat moorland, though some relief is offered by areas of rich pasture and meadows which occur on lower levels of ground. The coastline of Barra varies from sheltered inlets and the fine harbours of Castlebay and Northbay, to great cliffs and wide sandy bays guarded by huge dunes. One sight on Barra which must be seen to be appreciated to its fullest extent is in springtime, when masses of wild primroses transform the otherwise green machair into a sea of pale-yellow scented flowers. The fragile beauty of this flower belies the steel-cored hardiness of everything that lives on the island.

The economy of Barra has always been based on the land, which provided a subsistence living, supplemented by what was obtained from the coastal waters. Only during the last century or so has maritime fishing been a significant economic activity. The crofts on Barra are small, usually under 10 acres on average in extent, with grazing rights on the hills. There is a dangerously high number of vacant croft houses on the island, witness to the considerable emigration process from which the island still suffers. Even so, the number of crofts on Barra (about 380) has remained fairly constant in recent years, perhaps indicating that they provide an acceptable basic income for their owners, whether or not this is augmented by income from other sources such as fishing, tourism (which is as yet in a very low key) and general public work. The arable crops grown on Barra are used mainly for feeding to stock, the crofters' cash income being derived from the sale of livestock, and store cattle in particular. The sandy soils of Barra provide good grazing land. In some parts of the island, stock can be wintered with little or no hand feeding. The sheep stock on Barra is significant: about 13,000 animals, which provide wool for the Harris Tweed industry, centred on Lewis.

Barra has little in the way of activity outside crofting and fishing. However, in recent years some attempts have been made to introduce other elements into the island's economic picture. In 1967 the Highlands and Islands Development Board announced, with some justified pride, that technology was going to Barra in the form of a new spectacle-frame factory. The initial intake of employees was twelve, with the hope that within the year the work force would be increased to thirty. This was a bright star in the island's economic firmament and hopes were pinned on its success, not just for itself but to convince other industrial and commercial interests that it was feasible to establish branch facilities on remote islands. But by 1969 the bubble burst with the announcement that the firm concerned had gone into liquidation. Not only Barra suffered from this; the associated factories at Campbeltown, Argyll, went to the wall. But the venture, however ill-fated, proved that the potential was there and was sufficient to act as an incentive for Barra-born men to return to their island from Glasgow and other cities.

Another venture, smaller in scale but no less significant, which is catering to supply the demands of an increasing market, is the Barra Perfume Company. The product is made in a tiny two-man factory at Tangusdale, near Halman Bay on the south-west side of the island. The perfume products are hand-made in small individual batches by half a dozen girls. The low overheads involved in operating the firm have resulted in the perfumes being marketed at really competitive prices. The names of the perfumes ring with the sights and sounds of the Hebrides: Tangle, Plaid, Dark Glen, Legend, Caluna, Love Lilt and so on. During 1969 a science-based industrial interest moved into Barra to engage in the manufacture of thermostat components and micro-switches. These components are light in weight as are the subsequent assemblies and this advantage makes it economic to ship items into and out of Barra by air. At Vaslain, behind Traigh Mhor, is an enterprise which concentrates on the manufacture of shell grit used for harling in the building industry. The shells in the vicinity have a high lime content and are extremely white, so that the rough-cast produced is at once durable and comely. The market for this harling material is growing and the whole interest adds yet another star of hope in the economic sky of the island. These industrial pockets were the result of combined interests and efforts represented by the Barra Council of Social Service and the Highlands and Islands Development Board. Whether these industries will continue to remain in existence or not, they have in concert proved that with careful management attention, they can be translated into real social terms and provide a sense of meaning and purpose to living on the island.

There are hopes that a shellfish processing plant might be established on Barra. Such a plant would fit well into the island's traditional pattern of life and offer the island fishermen and their dependants the opportunity to take a realistic and rewarding part in a steadily developing and profitable market. There is a ready market for crabs, for instance, of which there is an abundance around the Barra shores. Such a development would act as an incentive to increase the number of lobster boats from the present eight. The tourist industry, so much in evidence on the Highland mainland, has yet to be developed on Barra. There has, however, been a long-standing tradition of catering for visitors. The original inn at Northbay was known as Tiorbagh Inn. During the reign of King Charles I, a law was passed which decreed that inns separated by water, such as straits and channels, were to be built opposite each other. Pollachar Inn (at the southern end of South Uist) paired an inn called Keil Inn. Later, it was thought that a more convenient site would be at Tiorbagh and the structure was completed in the 1820s. The inn was very small at first and it was not until the end of that century that it was extended and heightened. There was a tap-room at one end and coachhouses at the other. Tiorbagh was always very busy. The expanding herring industry at the time brought fishermen and fish-curers from the east coast of Scotland. Nearby, on the Ardveanish side of the bay, the herring was poured on to the ground and women knelt on the grass to do the gutting. The stone 'stations' they used can still be traced. Markets were also held at nearby Loch-an-Duin, twice yearly, in July and September. These were important occasions, in both social and economic contexts. Drovers came from the mainland and adjacent islands to buy cattle and horses. Barra ponies in particular were in great demand. To supplement the resources of Tiorbagh Inn, innkeepers from Uist and Skye came to set up their marquees for the sale of whisky. And merchants came from the Scottish mainland to set up their tents and stalls to sell their merchandise. The inn was closed about the turn of the century on the grounds that too much drinking went on and caused domestic troubles.

In an effort to establish an initial base for tourism on Barra, the Highlands and Islands Development Board sponsored the construction of a large hotel, one of a chain of such buildings designed to expand the tourist industry in specific areas of the western Highlands. Research carried out by the board's tourism division, with advice from tourist consultants, suggested that Barra had a great tourist potential and that, to exploit it, and to ensure a reasonable financial return on capital, the hotel should be of reasonable size and operate on an all-year-round basis. The hotel, recently opened, will undoubtedly act as a catalyst and offer perhaps the necessary incentive for the islanders to derive some benefit from those who nowadays see a visit to the Hebrides as the equivalent of the eighteenth-century Grand Tour.

Barra's association with fishing did not begin until the end of the eighteenth century, when the commercial possibilities offered were slowly realized. An initial impetus to thinking in this direction was given by the MacNeil of Barra who proposed to local fishermen that they should cast lots for the fishing banks around the island. This scheme proved a success and had the advantage that it eliminated the previous disputes over fishing areas which beggared any attempt to prosecute fishing with any degree of success, whether the activity was for supplementing the domestic diet, for sale to the island community or for export. The scheme was further improved when the Barra waters were demarcated and chartered by the Marine Survey Service of the Royal Navy, and located by means of landmarks on adjacent hills and headlands on the island. The accurate location of the individual fishing banks by these landmarks was of great importance, since the fish population in species and in quantity is influenced by the nature of the ground and its water depth. Ling, cod, halibut and skate were the predominant species caught, the first two being favoured because they could be dried and cured easily on the shore-based curing stations. Thereafter, the produce was exported in bundles of stated numbers and shipped to the Clyde ports to be sold either to Scottish fish merchants or made ready for re-export particularly to Catholic countries such as Spain.

During the latter half of the nineteenth century, the herring overtook other fish species as king of the Scottish fishing scene, and was the cause of boom conditions in the Hebrides. Castlebay, among other island ports, experienced a painful stretching of its facilities when it became swollen with an influx of people following the herring round the British coasts. It is on record that there were occasions when Castlebay's spacious harbour could not hold all the boats which required berths. Some boats had to land their catches at Northbay and on the adjacent island of Vatersay. While the island population undoubtedly benefited from this activity, local participation was largely confined to the employee category. Little contribution was made to the total annual catches by Barra fishermen, this mainly because they lacked the necessary capital to buy larger boats than those they had, which were small and could not venture out to any useful distance from the shore. In any case, like most Hebridean fishermen, they found themselves continually in debt to the fish-curers who supplied them with boats and gear. At the end of the fishing season it was often the case that the books were either 'just balanced nicely', or came out with a debtor balance. In the 1880s, some 400 boats congregated in Castlebay from the beginning of May to the end of June in each year. And, during the height of each season, some 2,000 persons connected with the fishing were on the island, all in the employment of a small army of fish-curers who ran up temporary huts and bothies surrounded by piles of white-staved barrels destined for St Petersburg, Konigsburg, Danzig, Hamburg and Stettin.

After the First World War, the industry slowly fell away. Though there were years when Castlebay herring fetched top prices in German and Russian markets, there were many lean years. By 1931 the declining trend had set in and the industry became of less significance until it received the *coup de grâce* by the advent of the Second World War in 1939. After 1945, though a certain amount of fishing was prosecuted, it was obvious that the former years of glory would never return. Significantly, however, while herring ceased to play an important role, the catches of shellfish were increasing and in 1948 were valued at some £18,000, a figure ten times the value of the catch a decade previously. This was a pointer to the future and the present-day interest in this line of fishing.

Six vessels at present operate out of Barra, equipped for dual-purpose fishing: ring-net fishing during the normal herring season and nephrops trawling at other times. The potential for an increase in the island fleet exists and will be realized as the Fisheries Scheme of the Highlands and Islands Development Board are completed. The industry has not been without its troubles, however. In 1969 Castlebay lost its status as a recognized herring port, a blow administered by the Herring Industry Board. This meant that the sale of herring from Barra was prohibited. However, during the winter of the following year, the port received a welcome boost when a steady stream of klondyking ships arrived from the Continent and the Faroes to buy Minch-caught herring for shipment to foreign ports for subsequent processing. Castlebay, as a result, saw its busiest winter for many years. In one year, no less than £70,000 of herring had been klondyked.

During the 1930s Castlebay was the centre of an interesting and now forgotten activity on behalf of the Minch fishing. This was concentrated in the organization called the Sea League. The main reason behind the formation of the league was the serious illegal trawling which was taking place in Minch waters, and particularly within the statutory 3-mile limit. In 1893 an Act of Parliament provided for the formation of fishing districts all round Scotland, provided that a sufficient proportion of those connected in any way with fishing applied to their respective county councils to move in the action necessary for the formation of these districts. The Act also said that a 14-mile limit would also be imposed as soon as the then North Sea Convention met and approved such a limit (the convention members included Britain, Denmark, Holland, Belgium, France and Germany). Those who opposed the 14-mile limit were the trawler owners of Hull, Grimsby and Fleetwood, the very people who were fishing illegally, and they acted to such an extent that the convention was never summoned and the fishing districts were never formed.

It was in an attempt to bring publicity to the situation of illegal trawling in the Minch that the Sea League was formed in 1933 "... to demand the same protection for the livelihood of the crofting fisherman as is given to the sporting fishing of the landowners themselves". The objects of the Sea League were:

1. That the Minch between a line from Tarra Head to Tiree and a line from the Butt of Lewis to Cape Wrath, shall be closed to trawlers, and that the fishing in this area shall be regulated to the benefit of the fishermen who live round it.
2. That the penalties for illegal trawling shall be increased, and the policing of inshore waters be made more efficient.
3. That the fines for illegal trawling shall be used for financing fishermen who have lost their gear through illegal trawling, or who want to commence inshore fishing for the first time.

The two men behind the Sea League were Sir (then Mr) Compton Mackenzie, who died in 1972, and Dr John Lorne Campbell of Canna, who is happily with us and is a well-known figure in the Highlands and furth of the region for his output of scholarly books touching on many aspects of Gaelic and the Gael. The league managed to stimulate the Government into preparing proposed legislation to increase the penalties for illegal trawling. But it met with real opposition from the trawling interests. Indeed, it was not until 1964 that the Fishery Limits Act was passed, long after serious damage had been done to the Minch fishing grounds by illegal trawling on behalf of the vested trawling interests, and indiscriminate dredging of the sea bottom, destroying spawning beds and doing irreparable damage, the effects of which are only too evident today. The following petition of the fishermen of the Hebrides sums up the situation and the feeling of the times. I am indebted to the late Sir Compton Mackenzie for permission to quote the petition from his book *Octave Seven*:

> We, as members of the fishing communities of the Islands of Vatersay, Barra, Eriskay, South Uist, Benbecula, and North Uist, are unanimously of the opinion that the practice of ring-net fishing should be entirely prohibited in all the lochs and bays of our district, and in all that part of the Minch adjacent to our coasts. We therefore crave that the necessary steps be taken, without any delay in this connection.
>
> The main grounds on which this Petition is based are as follows:
>
> (1) The fact that all the local fishermen favour, and have always favoured the drift-net method of fishing.
>
> (2) Since the ring-net began to be used here by fishermen from across the Minch, the earnings of the local fishermen have fallen considerably, owing to the increasing scarcity of the herrings. The local fishermen are agreed that this deterioration, which began soon after the ring-net was first used, here, is due almost entirely to this method of fishing.
>
> (3) Fishermen from other districts commenced to come here after they had ruined the fishing in their own districts by using the ring-nets there. It is a fact well known to fishermen, which any fishery officer can verify, that no herrings worthwhile have been caught in the lochs of Skye since the ring-net boats began to frequent them immediately after the end of the war.
>
> (4) The ring-net fishermen, and indeed all who take an interest in the matter, know that the herrings round our shores are very much more difficult to catch in the ring-net than those of places such as Loch Fyne and the Firth of Clyde; where, of course, the ring-net is almost always used, to the great deterioration of the quality of the fish caught there. Since the herrings here are difficult to catch in the ring-nets, the use of ring-nets is bound to be ever so much more destructive in breaking up the herring shoals hereabouts.
>
> (5) It is impossible for ring-net fishing and drift-net fishing to be carried on at the same time and place, without great damage arising to the drift-nets, caused by the crossing of the ring-net boats when trying to locate shoals. The ring-net fishermen often thus cut off buoys, and have been known often to destroy the nets themselves.
>
> (6) The ring-net fishermen, and indeed all seine-net and otter-trawl

fishermen, by their methods of fishing, break up the herring shoals. They thus prejudice the drift-net fishermen's catches, and also destroy the spawning beds.

(7) The ring-net fishermen can only work in comparatively calm weather. Thus they cannot supply the market regularly, as the drift-net fishermen can, since the latter can operate in all but the most severe weather.

(8) As all the herring fishermen of these islands use the drift-net method, it is obviously very unfair if the fishing here is going to be ruined by ring-net boats; for then the drift-net fishermen will be entirely deprived of their means of lifelihood.

(9) The ring-net fishermen are so greedy to catch the herrings that they very often take within the net two or three times the amount of herrings their boats can carry. After they have taken aboard what they can manage, the rest is dumped and left to rot on the bottom, polluting the waters of the area in which the catch was made; other shoals will avoid the spot, and experience shows that the herring will not return there for many years.

The petition then went on to give some examples of dumping of excess catches:

There was good fishing in Loch Eynort, South Uist, inside the narrow channel known as South Beag in the winter season of 1926–1927. Again in the winter of 1927–1928 the same place was full of herrings, and there were many local boats and herring drifters from the East Coast there. But the ring-net boats were also there in force that winter, and dumped so many herrings that the whole place was polluted with putrid fish so that the people could not come out of their houses owing to the smell of decaying herrings. No herrings have been caught there since that time. The local people petitioned the Fishery Board twice, and were finally told that they could prohibit the use of the ring-net in that place altogether for reasons of sanitation.

Despite the petition—which finally asked that "immediate steps be taken to make ring-netting illegal . . . to protect the interests of the local drift-net fishermen and give them a reasonable chance of making a living"—the campaign never came to anything. The inevitable result was that the prospects for the drift-net fishermen were quite ruined. Another inevitable result was that the same fate stared the ring-netters in the face by the 1960s, when purse-net fishing techniques were used in the Minch. This is an even more destructive method of fishing than ring-netting. And, with history repeating itself, it became the turn of the ring-netters to petition for the banning of purse-net fishing; nothing has been done so far and is unlikely to be done.

The population of Barra has always been small, the present-day figure of about 1,100 being the same as that recorded for the year 1755. The maximum population occurred in 1911 with 2,620 persons. The prosperity brought by the herring industry most likely accounted for this high figure, which then began to fall away as the industry declined.

The decrease, however, is not quite as steep as one might expect. It was still possible, until the beginning of the Second World War, to live in the Hebrides on a very modest income, and while standards of living were not particularly high—nor were they even desired to be—many islanders probably found it more convenient to retain their modest levels of comfort than to become expatriates in large cities. That this seems to be the case is shown in the figures between 1921 and 1947, which indicate a decrease of only about 300 persons. By the time of the 1961 census, however, the rate of decline became more rapid to reach the estimated figure issued in 1971 by the Registrar General for Scotland: 1,159.

Living on Barra is a way of life which is at present rather fragile. Because it tends to be literally at the end of a chain of islands which are otherwise reasonably well provided for in the way of services and the like, the isolation of Barra tends to be more acute and felt in a number of almost personal ways. Communications, high freight charges for materials imported from the mainland, lack of opportunities for work for both unemployed males and for school-leavers, lack of advanced schooling facilities; these are a few aspects of island life which have created no small problems, both for the political administrator and for the islanders themselves. With the entry of Britain into the European Common Market, the centre of things has shifted from Westminster to Brussels—and so much farther away, despite the protests of politicians in this country that the E.E.C. is good for Britain. But Britain is not necessarily a small island of some 1,100 souls, faced with a distorted population pyramid and looking to a future which is by no means clear in the context of the survival of the island's community into the years of the twenty-first century. Certainly, the degree of tenacity which the Barra community has displayed in the past will serve them in good stead in the coming years and undoubtedly they will try to retain their grasp on their own characteristic interpretation of what life means to them. If survival depends on this factor then the future is reasonably assured. If it does not, it will only remain to calculate the lowest numerator for the island, on reaching which the island will be added to the growing list of deserted islands of the Hebrides. Perhaps the ultimate fate will be its acquisition by a holiday firm, helicoptering the workers from the industrialized conurbations of Europe for a regulation and rationed gulp of fresh Atlantic air and a few hours of peace and solitude among the fresh, pastel-coloured flowers of the Barra machair and the island's brilliant white sands resounding to the eternal beat of the sea.

At the moment the future of Barra seems to lie with fishing. The various developments which have taken place in the island, both failures and successes, fostered by private and Development Board interests, have tended to restore a failing confidence. Steps for social and economic improvement are being taken slowly, and in the advance fishing is taking its rightful place, as befits any island. Six boats have in recent years been provided with assistance from the Highlands and Islands Development Board. One of these underlined the element of risk and danger, when it was the subject of a tragedy in which five men and boys lost their lives. Even so, the increase in participation in fishing activities is encouraging and, adding to the broadening pattern of current development, augurs well for the community; and even if this only manages to halt its population decline for a decade or so, the point of island living, for Barra as for other island communities, will have been well made. Indeed, the future pattern of fishing round the north and west coasts of Scotland, and the development of industrial fishing, tends to confirm the opinion that Barra could well be strategically placed as a centre for fish-processing activities in the future.

While Barra may think it has problems, these are of no less significance to the satellite islands of Eriskay and Vatersay. The former island lies to the south of South Uist and is in ferry contact with its neighbour. The seventy crofts on Eriskay support a population of just over 200 people, who augment their incomes by fishing. This occupation pays rather well and has given an air of prosperity and hope for the future of the island. The average gross earnings of the Eriskay fleet of eight boats is in the region of £85,000 per annum, making a net income of some £45,000. The result of this is seen in a number of fields, for instance the desire of men to return to Eriskay from the Scottish mainland or the Merchant Navy, and the fact that younger women (who before went to the Scottish mainland to seek work) are now tending to remain on Eriskay. The main components of this island's remarkable economic and social development are a fishing tradition, strong and reliable leadership, convenient access to good fishing grounds, and the available means of expanding their fishing fleet, this latter particularly through the Fisheries Scheme of the Highlands and Islands Development Board. Considering that the island has only halved its population since 1861, it seems that the Eriskay community has found some kind of formula for success. Perhaps it is when the numerical factor becomes important to the maintenance of the community that a sense of identity and resolve to improve becomes dominant and initiative and leadership is generated within the group to result in a burst of effort which has the best of chances to succeed. There are not a few problems remaining to be solved, however, to provide the community with a thicker and warmer social weave so that they can feel part of the new socio-economic infrastructure which the Development Board is trying to create in the Highland region. These will no doubt be solved in time, though one would wish that, considering what the community has done for itself, the bureaucrat would accelerate the flow of paper to bring about more quickly the relatively simple needs of the community, such as the community hall recently constructed and which has already served to strengthen the community and its composite individuals.

It remains to mention only one of a number of interesting aspects of Eriskay—the Eriskay pony. This animal is small, docile and hardy and has been on the Eriskay scene for many years. The number of animals has been declining for quite some time, however, until recently when an association for the preservation of the animal was set up to save it from extinction. There are about twenty-seven animals of the breed now remaining, although only sixteen exist on Eriskay itself. Considering the success of the Shetland pony, breaking into existing and new markets, the thought here is to study the Eriskay animal to formulate a breeding policy which would lead initially to an increase in the numbers and then to a method of selection for the maintenance of the definite individual characteristics which the animals have. As a class, the Eriskay pony is of great antiquity, the nearest to the native race that peopled Scotland before the arrival of recorded man. The pony is about 12 to 13 hands high and has small ears. The foals are born black and grow up white or grey.

The island of Vatersay lies to the south of Barra. The community here numbers some seventy persons and comprises the most southerly inhabited island of the Outer Hebridean chain. There are no roads on Vatersay, although there is an efficient network of tracks in good condition totalling some 5 miles. The island community is closely tied to life and conditions on neighbouring Barra. The economy is more land-based than one might expect, though the intermittent prosecution of lobster-fishing provides a reasonable source of income and adds significantly to the island's economy. The island has a good export in cattle. The beasts swim across Vatersay Sound to Barra from where they are taken to Oban by boat. The cattle swim has been an annual event for more than half a century. It may be picturesque, but in fact results in the cattle reaching the Oban sales in poor condition, which affects the final price paid for them. The crossing to Barra is made by using a small motor boat towing a dinghy. The cattle are tied to a long painter fixed to the stern of the dinghy. The haltered animals are then towed, four at a time, across the channel. Men are positioned beside the cattle to ensure that their heads stay above water. Half a dozen crofters on Vatersay have built up between them a good herd stock of over 100 cattle of the Aberdeen Angus, Shorthorn and Hereford breeds. The annual value of exported cattle is in the region of £3,500.

The current problem for crofters on both Barra and Vatersay is the absence of adequate sea services to the mainland. Often the islands' cattle, numbering more than 200 head, have to be taken off Barra a week or so before they come under the auctioneer's hammer at Oban. Facilities are limited for beasts on MacBraynes' vessels. The crofters, forced to take advantage of the ships available in the shipping company's timetable, have to ship their cattle to Oban and then face charges incurred for a lengthy period of penning, feeding and other expenses. The autumn sales at Oban are of vital importance to the crofters. Suggestions for the re-routing of shipping facilities at this time have been presented to MacBraynes by the Barra Council of Social Service, but have not been taken up. Recently, representations have been made to the Scottish Transport Group, but even that body is forced to accept the reasons, or other statements, made by MacBraynes. The Secretary of the Council has said: "We look with incredulity at the apparent inexhaustible storehouse of excuses MacBraynes can draw upon to justify their inability to provide the basis of an adequate service!" The comment underlines the over-dependence of islands and islanders on external factors. Indeed, it could be said that should any of the present significant islands become deserted it will not be the fault of the islanders themselves, but of those who are incapable or careless to realize that these islands and their communities are a part of the society of the British Isles and not, as seems to be the case, far-flung outposts of an administrative empire.

Select Reading List

Barnard, A., *The Whisky Distilleries of the United Kingdom*, David and Charles, 1969 (first printed 1887).

Campbell, J. L. (Ed.), *Hebridean Folksongs*, Oxford University Press, 1969.

Colier, A., *The Crofting Problem*, Cambridge University Press, 1953.

Cooper, D., *Skye*, Routledge and Kegan Paul, 1970.

Crofters Commission annual reports (in progress).

Darling, F. Fraser, *The West Highland Survey*, Oxford University Press, 1955.

Darling, F. Fraser and Boyd, K. Morton, *The Highlands and Islands*, Collins, 1969.

Duckworth, C. L. D. and Langmuir, G. E., *West Highland Steamers*, David and Charles (Distributors), 1967.

Fresson, Capt E. E., *Air Road to the Isles*, David Rendal, London, 1967.

Gaskell, P., *Morvern Transformed*, Cambridge University Press, 1968.

Grant, I. F., *Highland Folk Ways*, Routledge and Kegan Paul, 1961.

Gray, M., *The Highland Economy*, Oliver and Boyd, 1957.

Haldane, A. R. B., *The Drove Roads of Scotland*, Edinburgh University Press, 1968.

Haldane, A. R. B., *New Roads Through the Glens*, David and Charles, 1973.

Highlands and Islands Development Board annual reports (in progress).

Lindsay, J., *The Canals of Scotland*, David and Charles, 1968.

MacCulloch, D. B., *Romantic Lochaber*, W. and R. Chambers, 3rd edn, 1971.

Mackenzie, A., *The History of the Highland Clearances*, Gairm Publications, Glasgow, 1946.

MacKenzie, W. C., *The Highlands and Isles of Scotland*, The Moray Press, Edinburgh, 1949.

MacKinnon, K., *The Lion's Tongue*, Club Leabhar, Inverness, 1974.

MacNab, P. A., *The Isle of Mull*, David and Charles, 1970.
Mitchell, J., *Reminiscences of My Life in the Highlands*, 2 vols, David and Charles reprints, 1971 and 1972.
Murray, W. H., *Companion Guide to the West Highlands*, Collins, 1970.
O'Dell, A. C. and Walton, K., *The Highlands and Islands of Scotland*, Nelson, 1962.
Prebble, J., *The Highland Clearances*, Secker and Warburg, 1963.
Ross, J., *Whisky*, Routledge and Kegan Paul, 1970.
Sillar, F. C. and Meyer, R., *Skye*, David and Charles, 1973.
Simpson, W. D., *Portrait of the Highlands*, Robert Hale, 1969.
Simpson, W. D., *Portrait of Skye and the Outer Hebrides*, Robert Hale, 1973.
Thomas, J., *Highland Railway* (1963), *West Highland Railway* (1965), *Callander and Oban Railway* (1966), David and Charles.
Thompson, F., *Harris and Lewis*, David and Charles, new edn 1973.
Thompson, F., *Harris Tweed—the Story of an Island Industry*, David and Charles, 1969.
Thompson, F., *St Kilda and Other Hebridean Outliers*, David and Charles, 1970.
Thompson, F., *The Uists and Barra*, David and Charles, 1974.
Thomson, D. and Grimble, I., *The Future of the Highlands*, Routledge and Kegan Paul, 1968.
Turnock, D., *Patterns of Highland Development*, Macmillan, 1970.
Wilson, R., *Scotch, its History and Romance*, David and Charles, 1973.
Youngson, A. J., *After the Forty-five*, Edinburgh University Press, 1973.

Index

Index